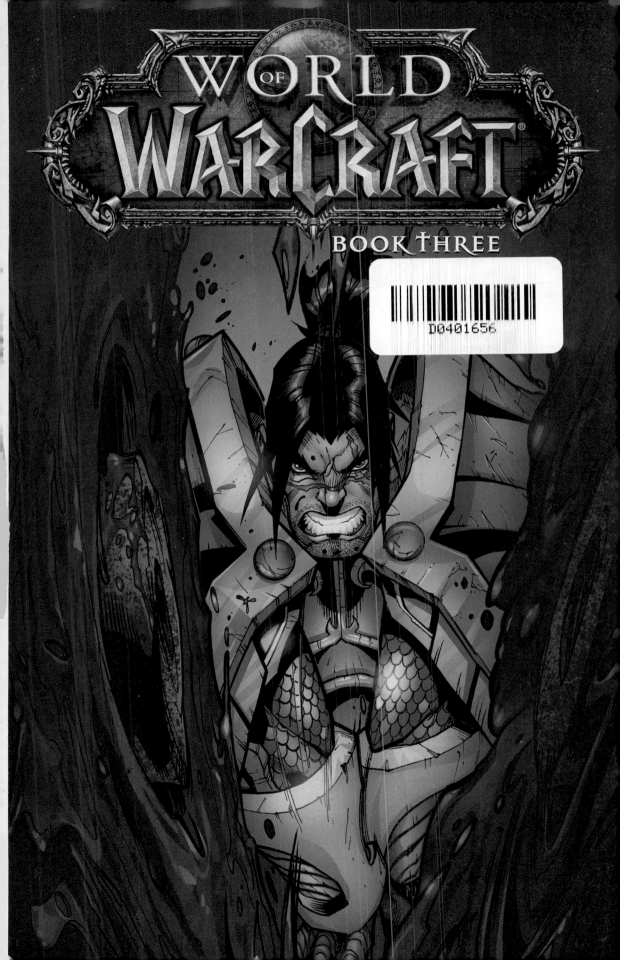

WORLD OF WARCRAFT

BOOK THREE

Writers: Walter & Louise Simonson

Pencils: Mike Bowden
with Jon Buran and Pop Mhan

Inks: Jerome Moore, Pop Mhan,
Tony Washington and Walden Wong
with Derek Fridolfs, Richard Friend,
Sandra Hope, John Livesay and Philip Moy

Colors: Randy Mayor, Gabe Eltaeb
and Tony Washington with Jonny Rench
Letters: Wes Abbott

Story Consultants: Chris Metzen, Micky Neilson and Alex Afrasiabi

Collected Edition Cover and Original Series Covers
#15-18 by Jon Buran and Tony Washington
Cover #19 by Pete Woods and Tony Washington
Cover #20 by Walter Simonson and Randy Mayor
Cover #21 by Mike Bowden and Tony Washington

For DC Comics:

Hank Kanalz	Editor, Original Series
Sarah Gaydos	Assistant Editor, Original Series
Kristy Quinn	Editor
Ed Roeder	Art Director
Diane Nelson	President
Dan DiDio and Jim Lee	Co-Publishers
Geoff Johns	Chief Creative Officer
John Rood	Executive Vice President–Sales, Marketing and Business Development
Patrick Caldon	Executive Vice President–Finance and Administration
Amy Genkins	Senior VP–Business and Legal Affairs
Steve Rotterdam	Senior VP–Sales and Marketing
John Cunningham	VP–Marketing
Terri Cunningham	VP–Managing Editor
Alison Gill	VP–Manufacturing
David Hyde	VP–Publicity
Hank Kanalz	VP–General Manager, WildStorm
Sue Pohja	VP–Book Trade Sales
Alysse Soll	VP–Advertising and Custom Publishing
Bob Wayne	VP–Sales
Mark Chiarello	Art Director

For Blizzard Entertainment:

Chris Metzen	Senior VP—Creative Development
Jeff Donias	Director—Creative Development
Micky Neilson	Story Consultation and Development
James Waugh	Story Consultation and Development
Glenn Rane	Art Director
Cory Jones	Director—Global Business Development and Licensing
Jason Bischoff	Associate Licensing Manager
Additional Development:	Samwise Didier, Evelyn Fredericksen, Cameron Dayton, Tommy Newcomer

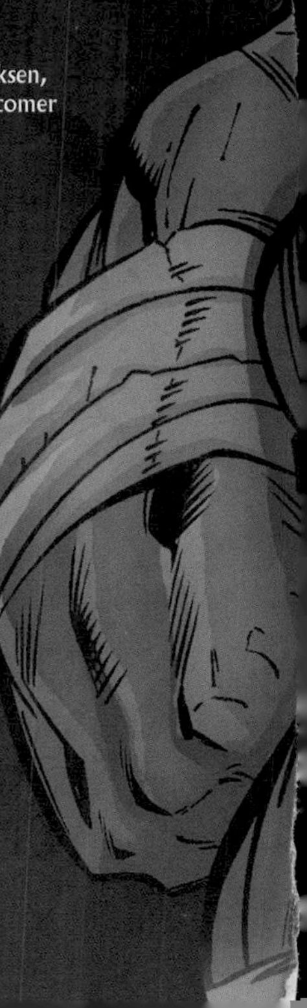

DC Comics, 1700 Broadway, New York, NY 10019
A Warner Bros. Entertainment Company
Printed by RR Donnelley, Roanoke, VA, USA 2/25/11
First printing.

ISBN: 978-1-4012-2811-8

LICENSED BLIZZARD ENTERTAINMENT PRODUCT

SUSTAINABLE FORESTRY INITIATIVE
Certified Chain of Custody
Promoting Sustainable Forest Management

Fiber used in this product line meets the sourcing requirements of the SFI program. www.sfiprogram.org SGS-SFI/COC-US10/81072

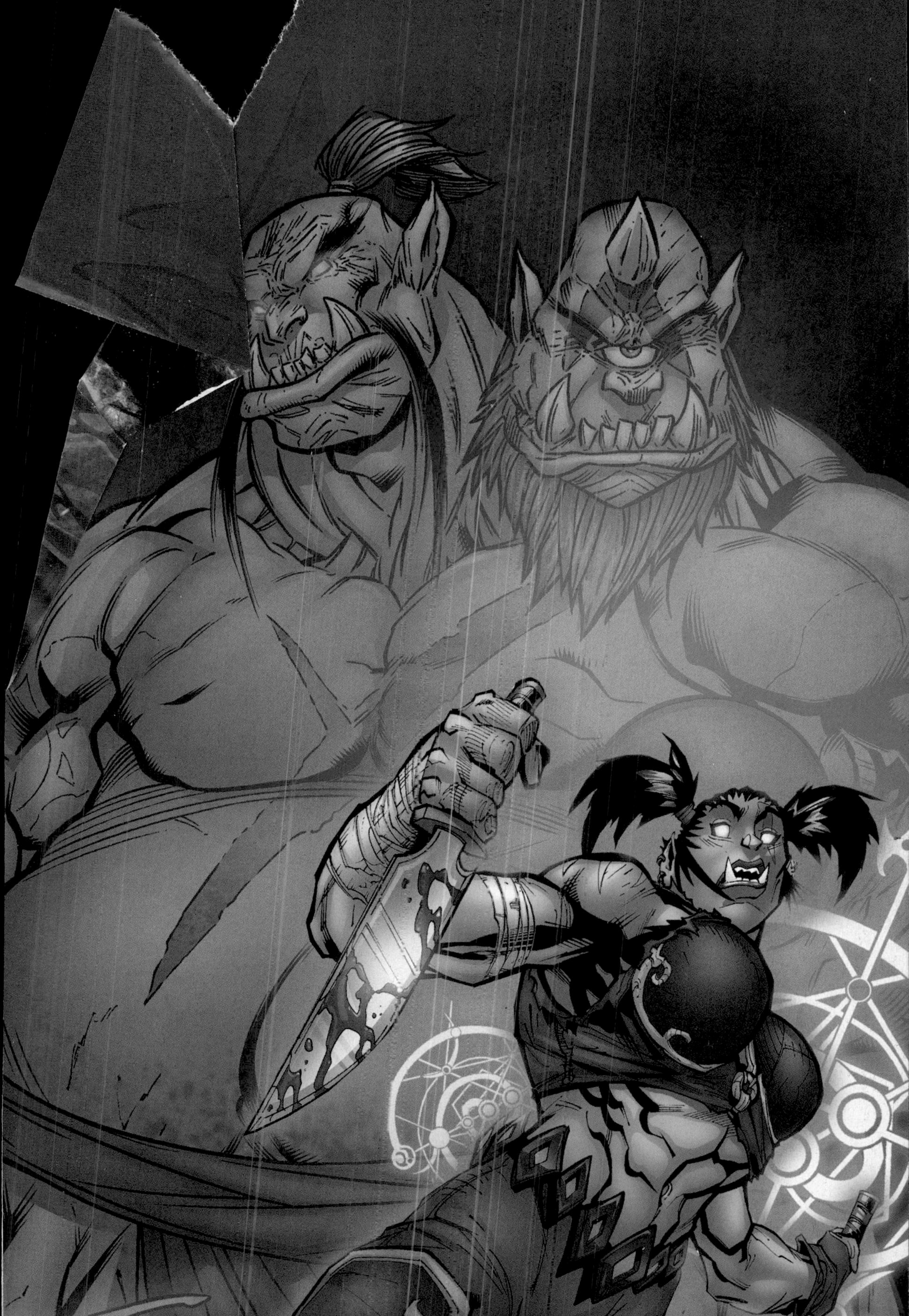

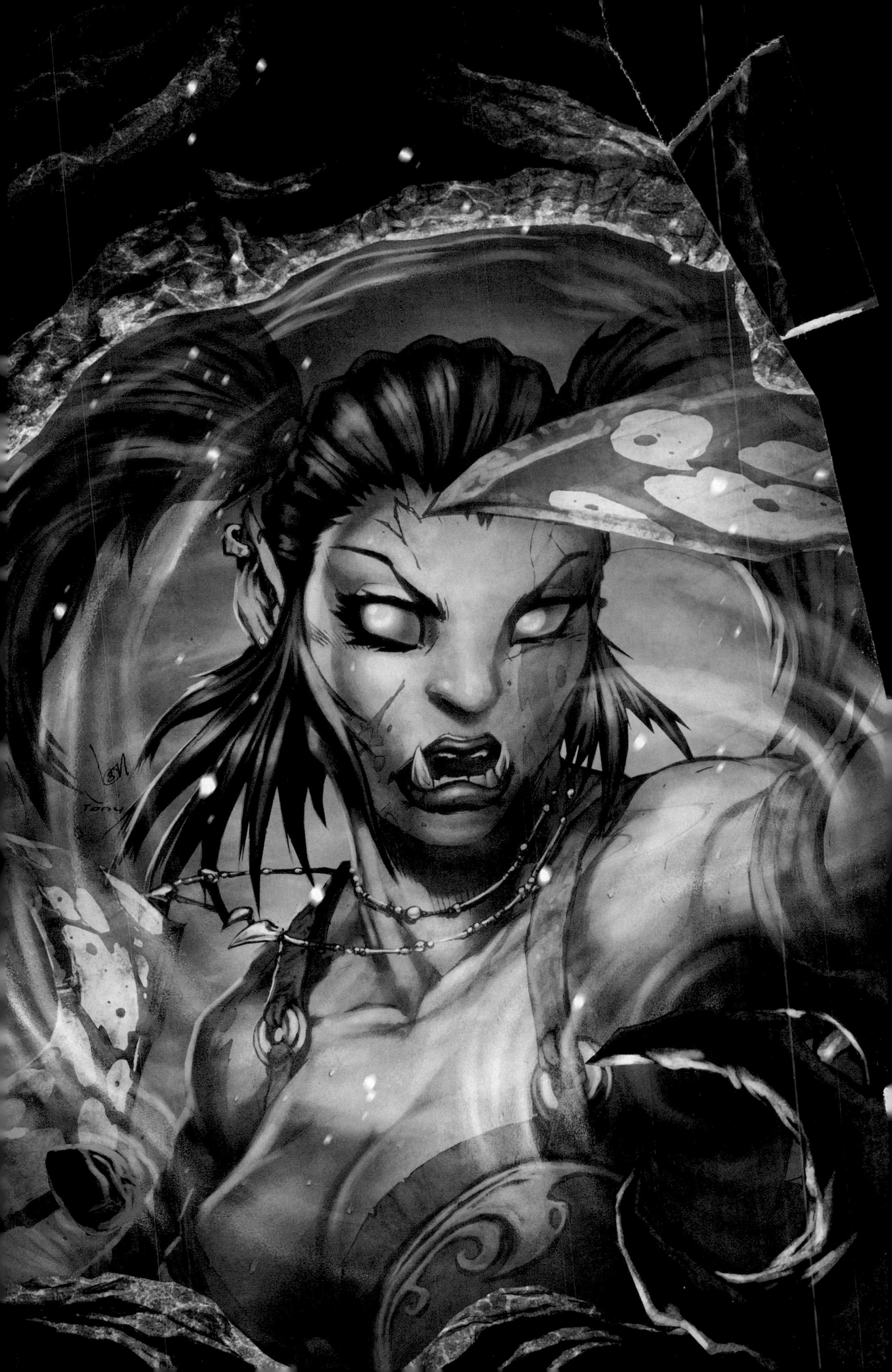

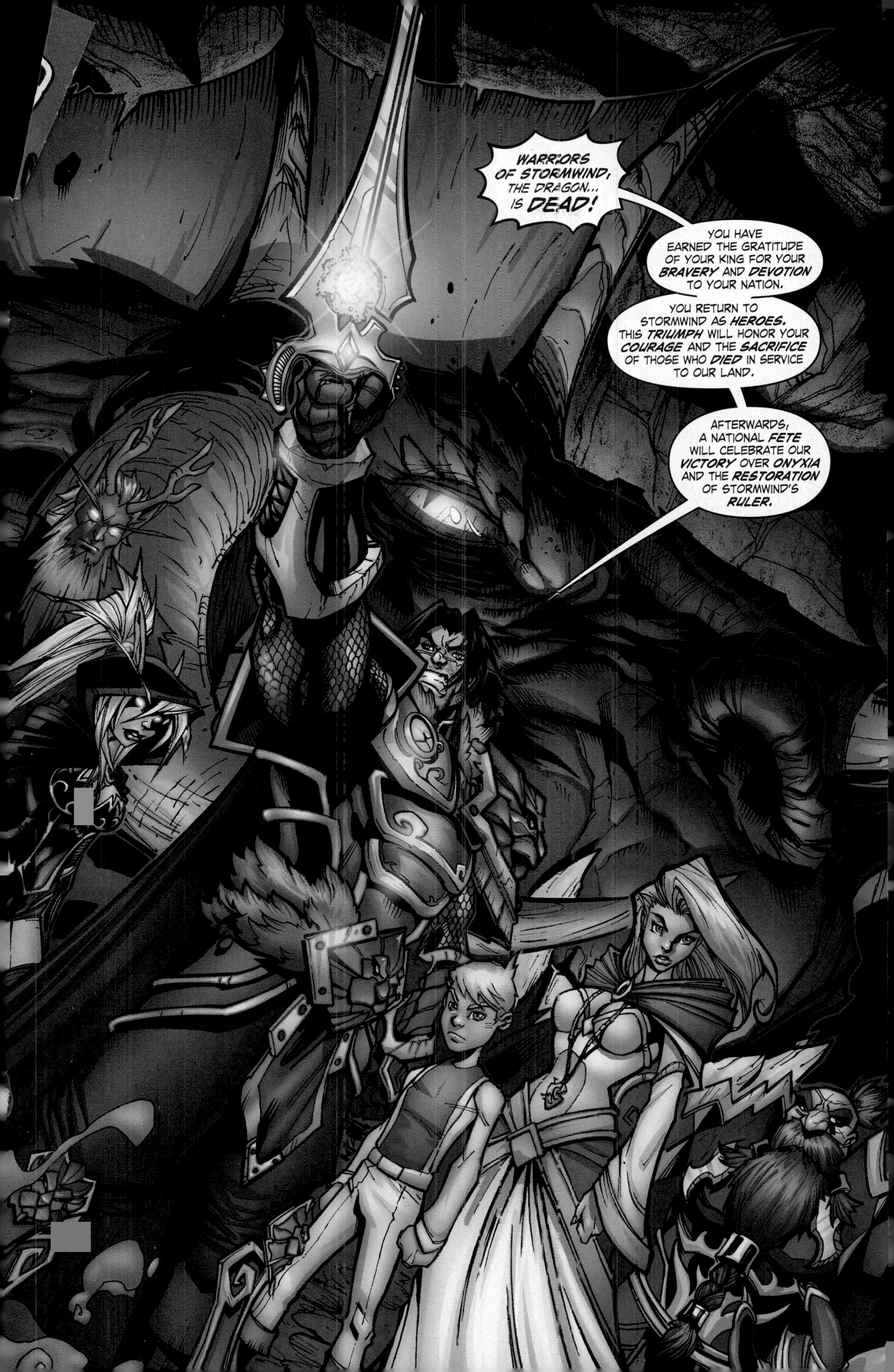
WARRIORS OF STORMWIND, THE DRAGON... IS DEAD!
YOU HAVE EARNED THE GRATITUDE OF YOUR KING FOR YOUR BRAVERY AND DEVOTION TO YOUR NATION.
YOU RETURN TO STORMWIND AS HEROES. THIS TRIUMPH WILL HONOR YOUR COURAGE AND THE SACRIFICE OF THOSE WHO DIED IN SERVICE TO OUR LAND.
AFTERWARDS, A NATIONAL FETE WILL CELEBRATE OUR VICTORY OVER ONYXIA AND THE RESTORATION OF STORMWIND'S RULER.

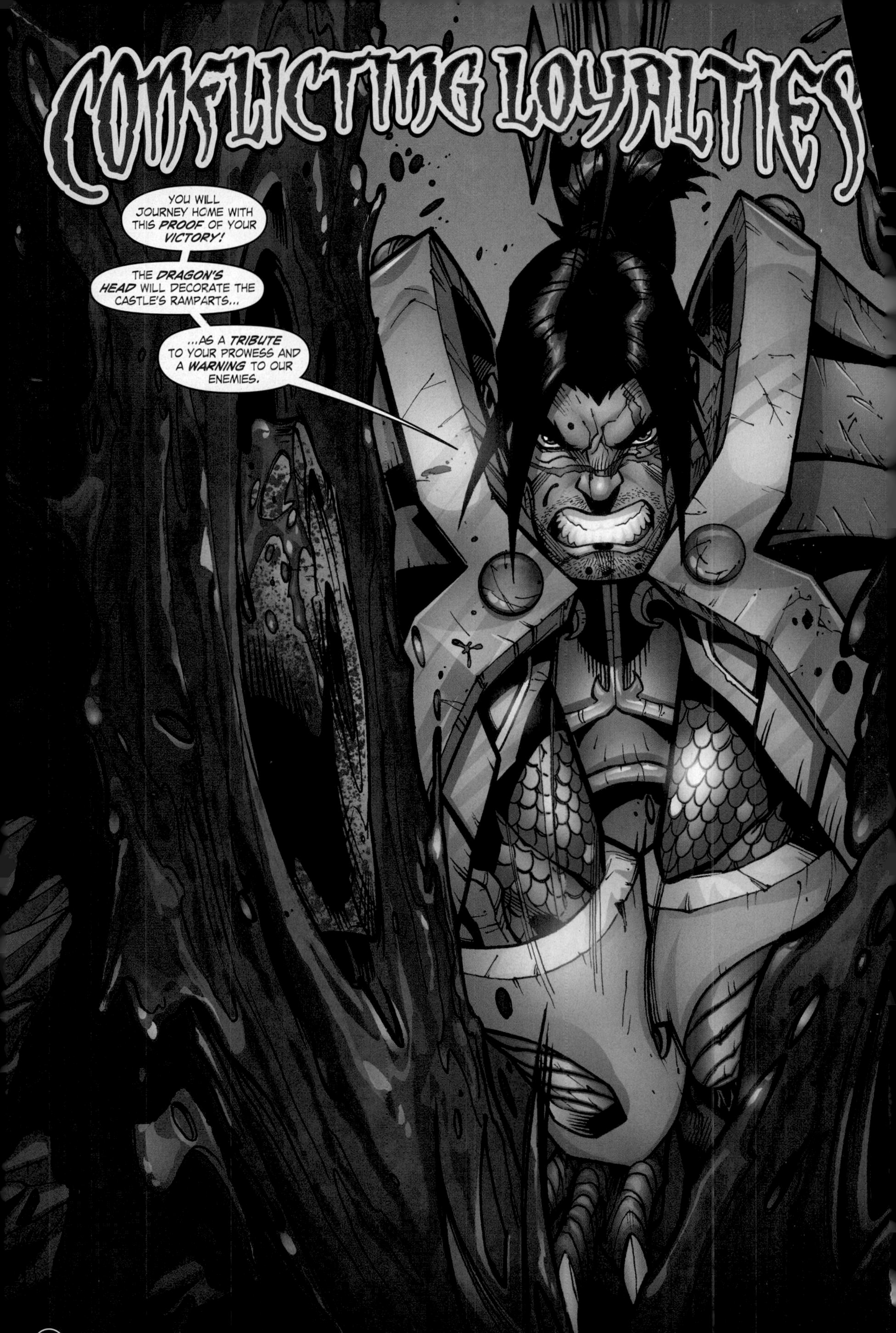
CONFLICTING LOYALTIES
YOU WILL JOURNEY HOME WITH THIS PROOF OF YOUR VICTORY!
THE DRAGON'S HEAD WILL DECORATE THE CASTLE'S RAMPARTS...
...AS A TRIBUTE TO YOUR PROWESS AND A WARNING TO OUR ENEMIES.

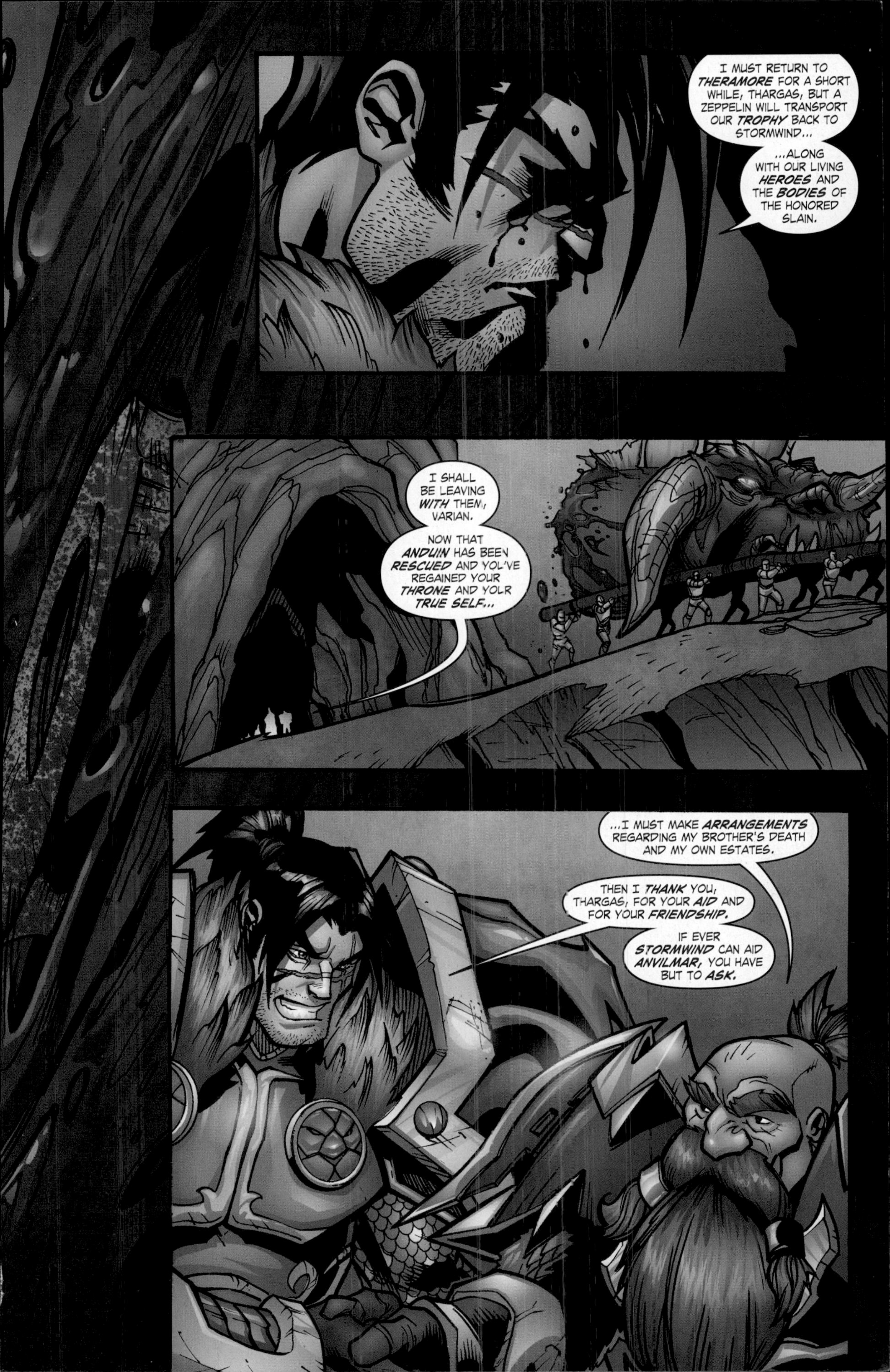
I MUST RETURN TO THERAMORE FOR A SHORT WHILE, THARGAS, BUT A ZEPPELIN WILL TRANSPORT OUR TROPHY BACK TO STORMWIND...
...ALONG WITH OUR LIVING HEROES AND THE BODIES OF THE HONORED SLAIN.
I SHALL BE LEAVING WITH THEM, VARIAN.
NOW THAT ANDUIN HAS BEEN RESCUED AND YOU'VE REGAINED YOUR THRONE AND YOUR TRUE SELF...
...I MUST MAKE ARRANGEMENTS REGARDING MY BROTHER'S DEATH AND MY OWN ESTATES.
THEN I THANK YOU, THARGAS, FOR YOUR AID AND FOR YOUR FRIENDSHIP.
IF EVER STORMWIND CAN AID ANVILMAR, YOU HAVE BUT TO ASK.

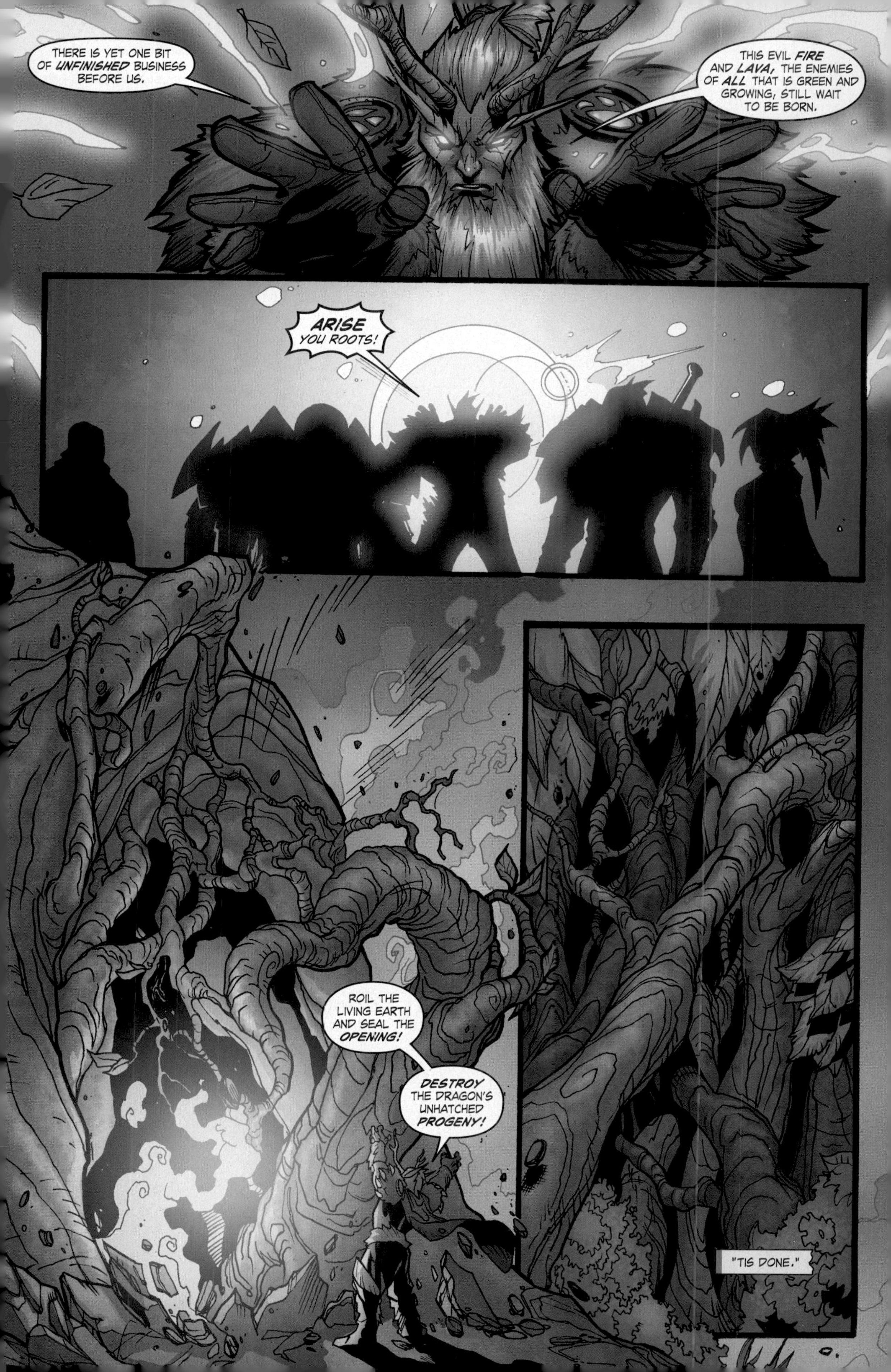

THERE IS YET ONE BIT OF UNFINISHED BUSINESS BEFORE US.
THIS EVIL FIRE AND LAVA, THE ENEMIES OF ALL THAT IS GREEN AND GROWING, STILL WAIT TO BE BORN.
ARISE YOU ROOTS!
ROIL THE LIVING EARTH AND SEAL THE OPENING!
DESTROY THE DRAGON'S UNHATCHED PROGENY!
"TIS DONE."

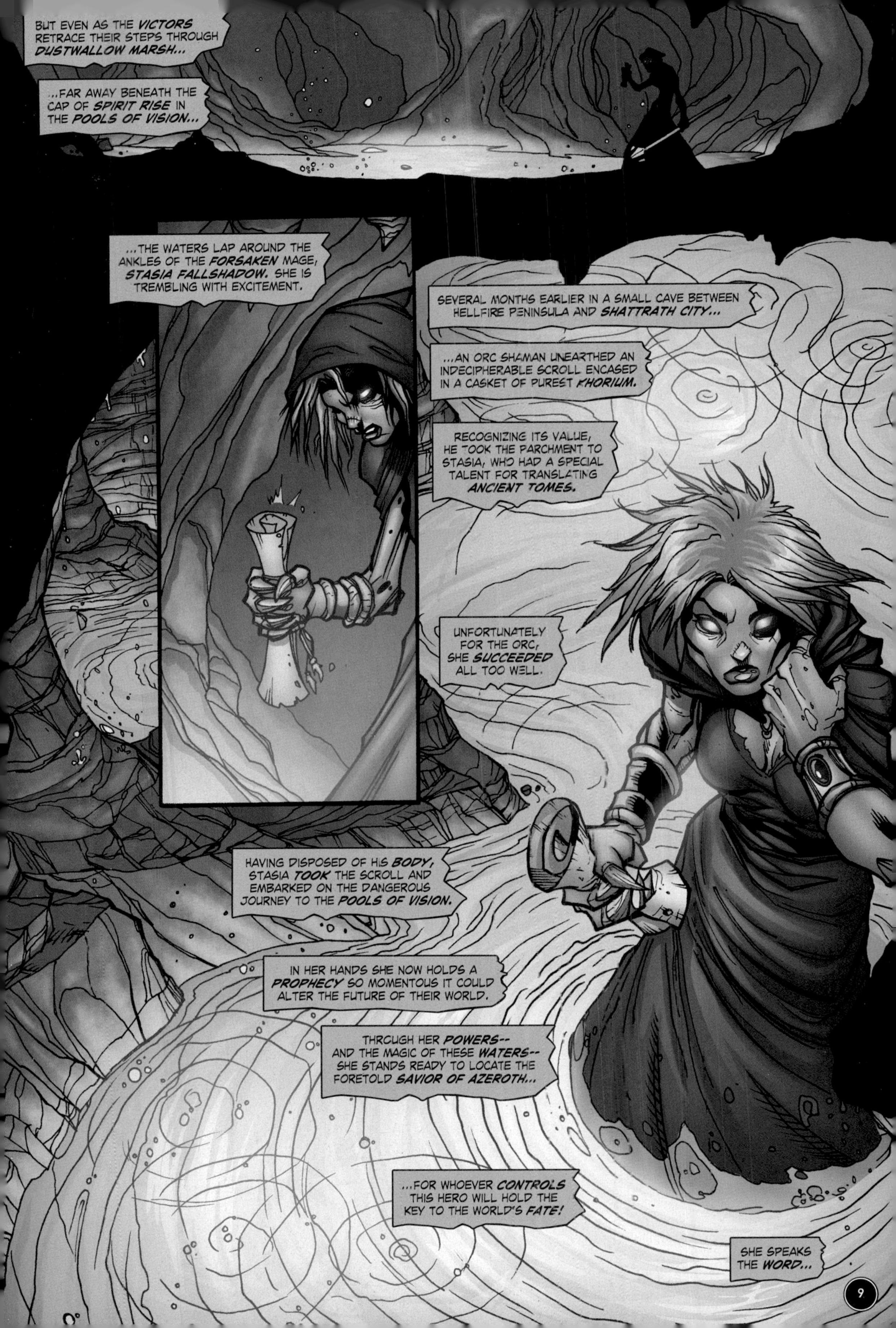
BUT EVEN AS THE VICTORS RETRACE THEIR STEPS THROUGH DUSTWALLOW MARSH...
...FAR AWAY BENEATH THE CAP OF SPIRIT RISE IN THE POOLS OF VISION...
...THE WATERS LAP AROUND THE ANKLES OF THE FORSAKEN MAGE, STASIA FALLSHADOW. SHE IS TREMBLING WITH EXCITEMENT.
SEVERAL MONTHS EARLIER IN A SMALL CAVE BETWEEN HELLFIRE PENINSULA AND SHATTRATH CITY...
...AN ORC SHAMAN UNEARTHED AN INDECIPHERABLE SCROLL ENCASED IN A CASKET OF PUREST KHORIUM.
RECOGNIZING ITS VALUE, HE TOOK THE PARCHMENT TO STASIA, WHO HAD A SPECIAL TALENT FOR TRANSLATING ANCIENT TOMES.
UNFORTUNATELY FOR THE ORC, SHE SUCCEEDED ALL TOO WELL.
HAVING DISPOSED OF HIS BODY, STASIA TOOK THE SCROLL AND EMBARKED ON THE DANGEROUS JOURNEY TO THE POOLS OF VISION.
IN HER HANDS SHE NOW HOLDS A PROPHECY SO MOMENTOUS IT COULD ALTER THE FUTURE OF THEIR WORLD.
THROUGH HER POWERS-- AND THE MAGIC OF THESE WATERS-- SHE STANDS READY TO LOCATE THE FORETOLD SAVIOR OF AZEROTH...
...FOR WHOEVER CONTROLS THIS HERO WILL HOLD THE KEY TO THE WORLD'S FATE!
SHE SPEAKS THE WORD...

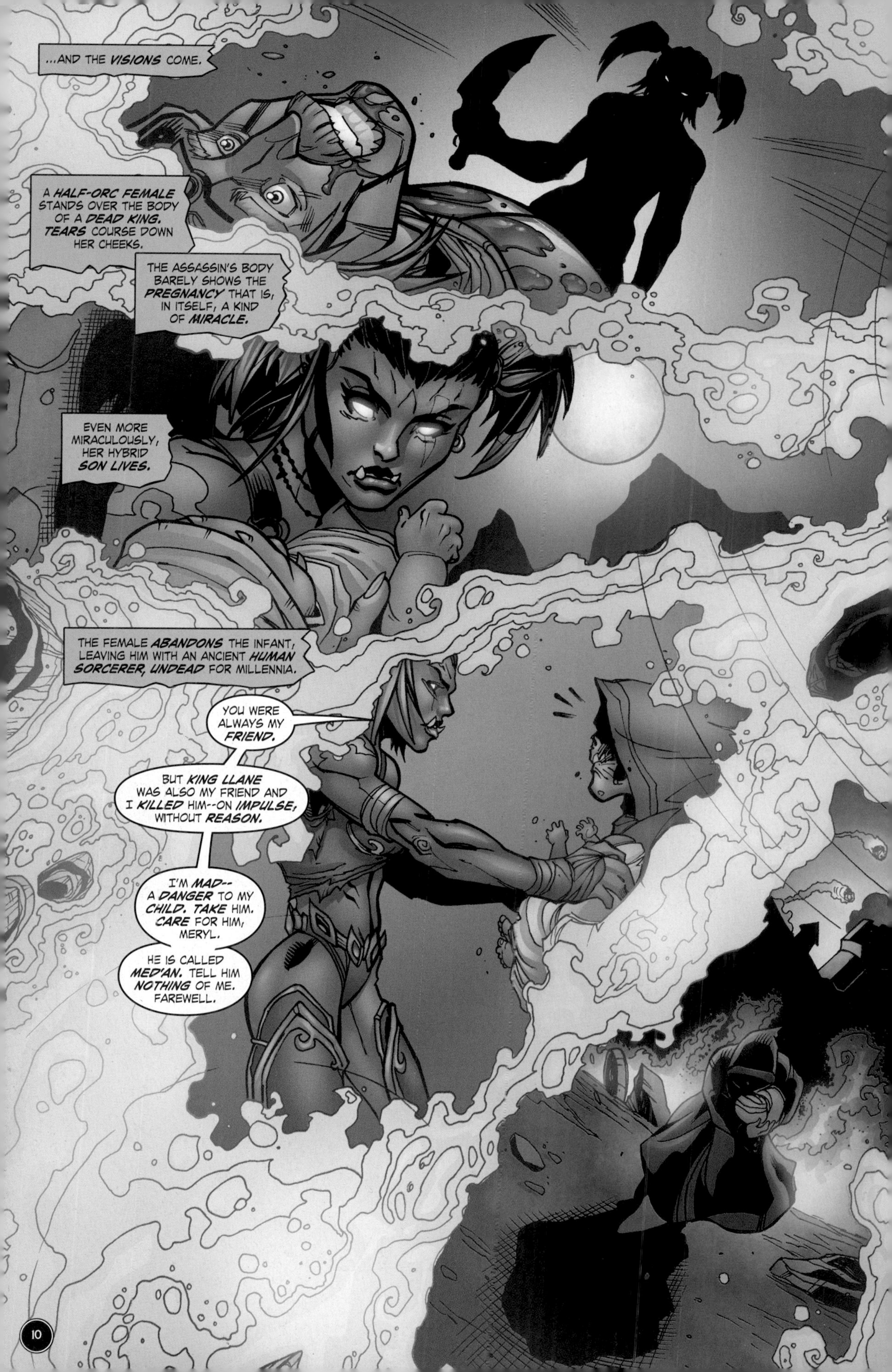
...AND THE VISIONS COME.
A HALF-ORC FEMALE STANDS OVER THE BODY OF A DEAD KING. TEARS COURSE DOWN HER CHEEKS.
THE ASSASSIN'S BODY BARELY SHOWS THE PREGNANCY THAT IS, IN ITSELF, A KIND OF MIRACLE.
EVEN MORE MIRACULOUSLY, HER HYBRID SON LIVES.
THE FEMALE ABANDONS THE INFANT, LEAVING HIM WITH AN ANCIENT HUMAN SORCERER, UNDEAD FOR MILLENNIA.
YOU WERE ALWAYS MY FRIEND.
BUT KING LLANE WAS ALSO MY FRIEND AND I KILLED HIM--ON IMPULSE, WITHOUT REASON.
I'M MAD-- A DANGER TO MY CHILD. TAKE HIM. CARE FOR HIM, MERYL.
HE IS CALLED MED'AN. TELL HIM NOTHING OF ME. FAREWELL.

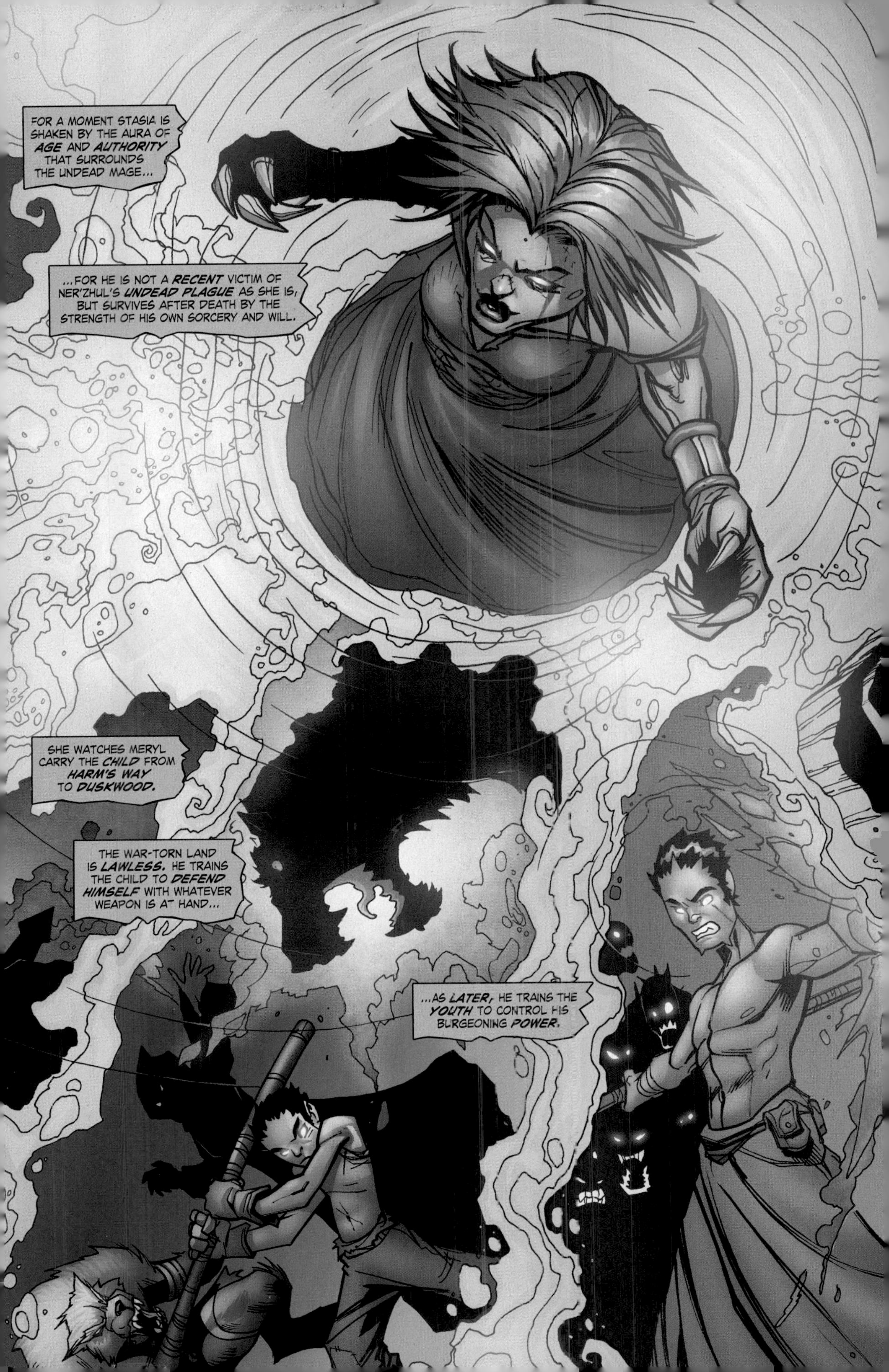
FOR A MOMENT STASIA IS SHAKEN BY THE AURA OF AGE AND AUTHORITY THAT SURROUNDS THE UNDEAD MAGE...
...FOR HE IS NOT A RECENT VICTIM OF NER'ZHUL'S UNDEAD PLAGUE AS SHE IS, BUT SURVIVES AFTER DEATH BY THE STRENGTH OF HIS OWN SORCERY AND WILL.
SHE WATCHES MERYL CARRY THE CHILD FROM HARM'S WAY TO DUSKWOOD.
THE WAR-TORN LAND IS LAWLESS. HE TRAINS THE CHILD TO DEFEND HIMSELF WITH WHATEVER WEAPON IS AT HAND...
...AS LATER, HE TRAINS THE YOUTH TO CONTROL HIS BURGEONING POWER.

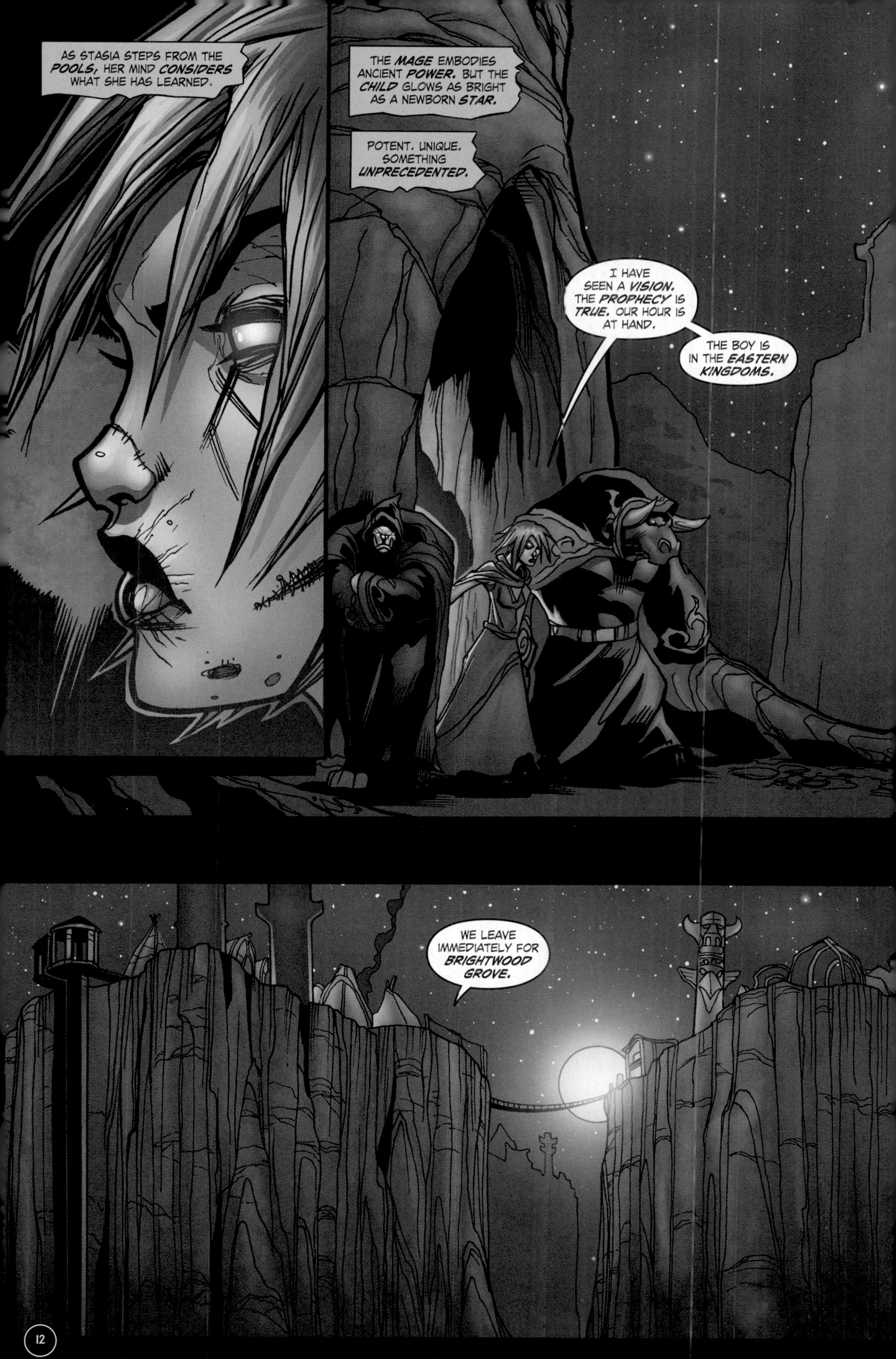
AS STASIA STEPS FROM THE POOLS, HER MIND CONSIDERS WHAT SHE HAS LEARNED.
THE MAGE EMBODIES ANCIENT POWER. BUT THE CHILD GLOWS AS BRIGHT AS A NEWBORN STAR.
POTENT. UNIQUE. SOMETHING UNPRECEDENTED.
I HAVE SEEN A VISION. THE PROPHECY IS TRUE. OUR HOUR IS AT HAND.
THE BOY IS IN THE EASTERN KINGDOMS.
WE LEAVE IMMEDIATELY FOR BRIGHTWOOD GROVE.

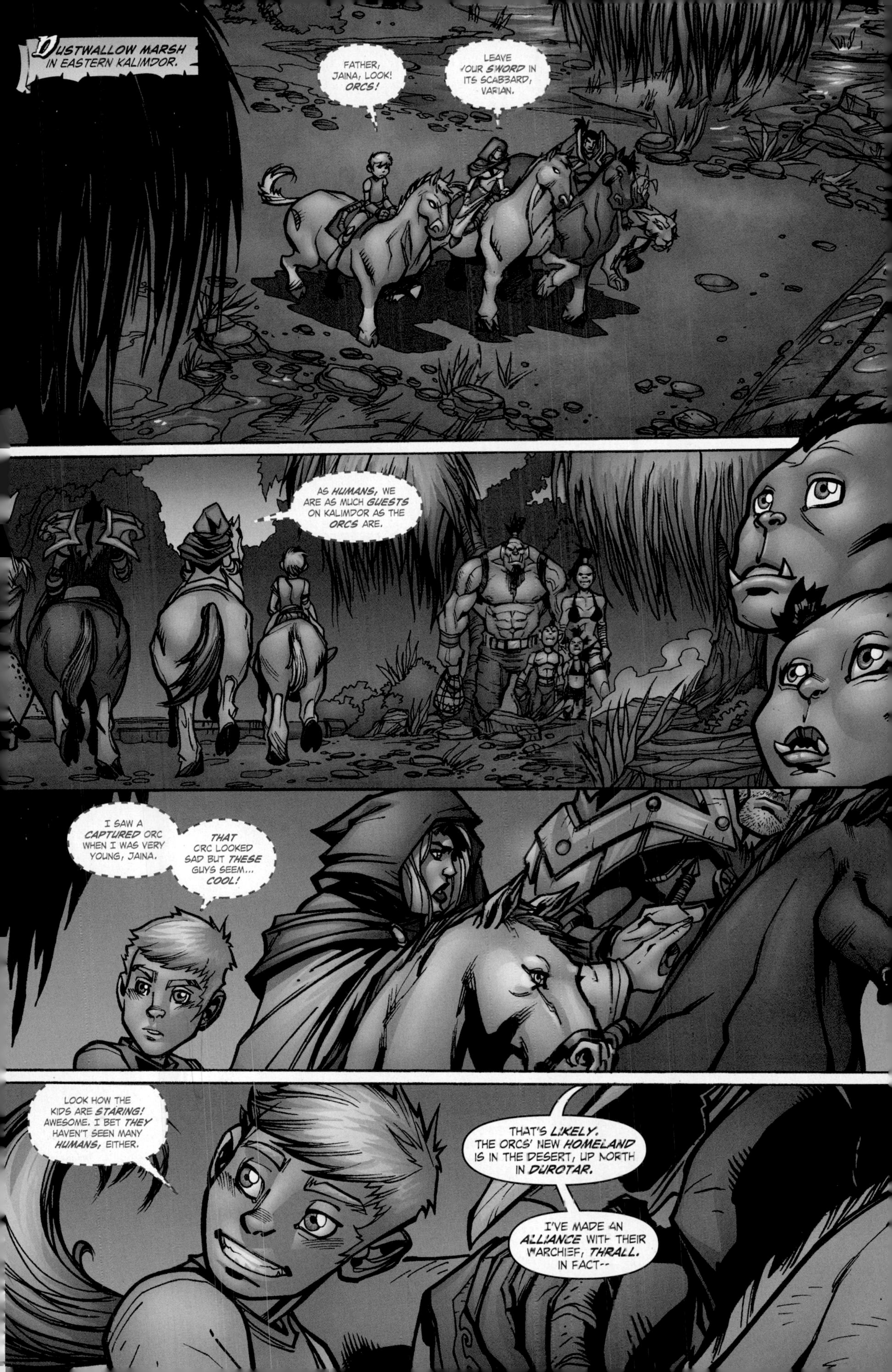

DUSTWALLOW MARSH IN EASTERN KALIMDOR.
FATHER, JAINA, LOOK! ORCS!
LEAVE YOUR SWORD IN ITS SCABBARD, VARIAN.
AS HUMANS, WE ARE AS MUCH GUESTS ON KALIMDOR AS THE ORCS ARE.
I SAW A CAPTURED ORC WHEN I WAS VERY YOUNG, JAINA.
THAT ORC LOOKED SAD BUT THESE GUYS SEEM... COOL!
LOOK HOW THE KIDS ARE STARING! AWESOME. I BET THEY HAVEN'T SEEN MANY HUMANS, EITHER.
THAT'S LIKELY. THE ORCS' NEW HOMELAND IS IN THE DESERT, UP NORTH IN DUROTAR.
I'VE MADE AN ALLIANCE WITH THEIR WARCHIEF, THRALL. IN FACT--

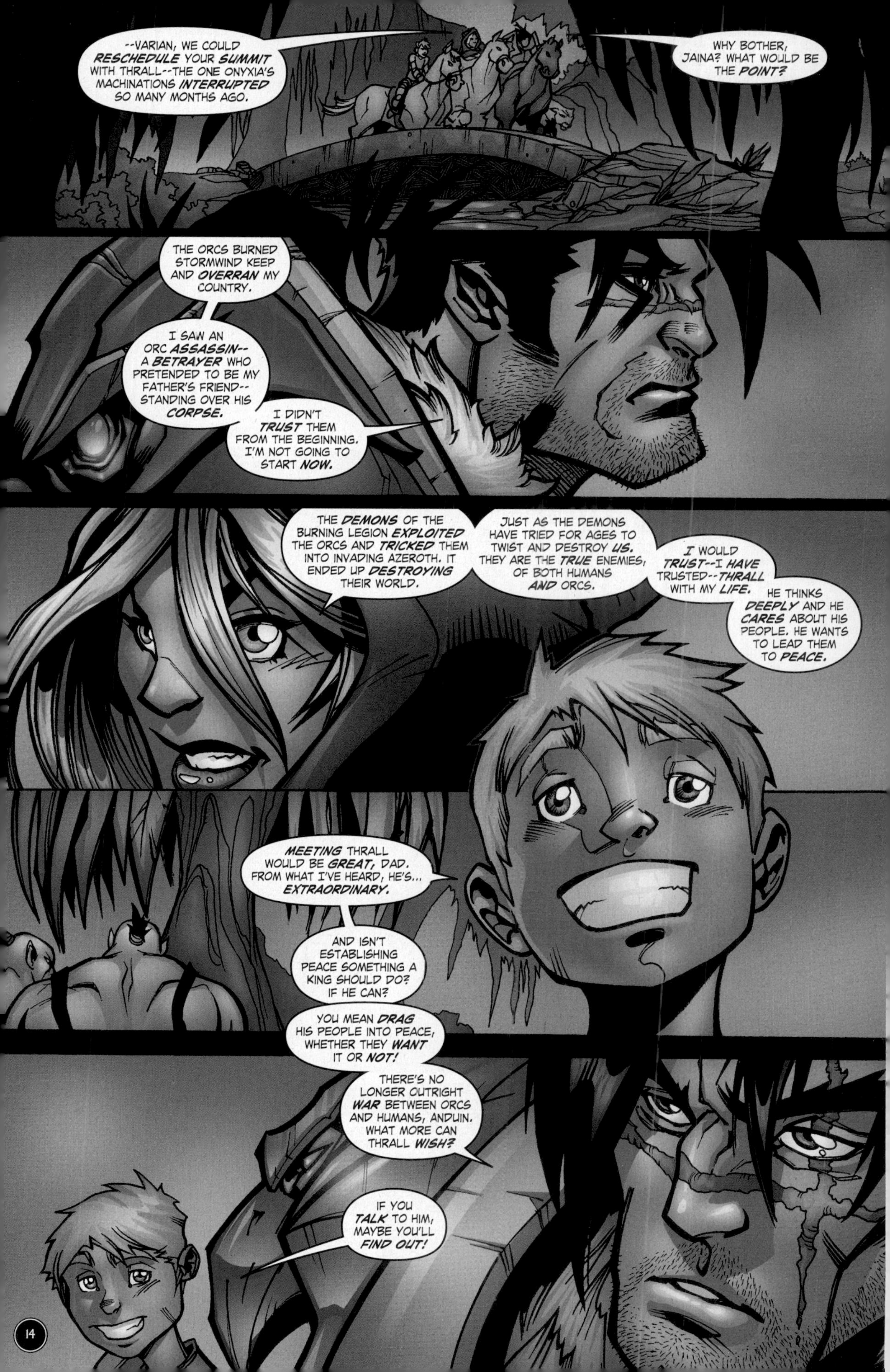
--VARIAN, WE COULD RESCHEDULE YOUR SUMMIT WITH THRALL--THE ONE ONYXIA'S MACHINATIONS INTERRUPTED SO MANY MONTHS AGO.
WHY BOTHER, JAINA? WHAT WOULD BE THE POINT?
THE ORCS BURNED STORMWIND KEEP AND OVERRAN MY COUNTRY.
I SAW AN ORC ASSASSIN--A BETRAYER WHO PRETENDED TO BE MY FATHER'S FRIEND--STANDING OVER HIS CORPSE.
I DIDN'T TRUST THEM FROM THE BEGINNING. I'M NOT GOING TO START NOW.
THE DEMONS OF THE BURNING LEGION EXPLOITED THE ORCS AND TRICKED THEM INTO INVADING AZEROTH. IT ENDED UP DESTROYING THEIR WORLD.
JUST AS THE DEMONS HAVE TRIED FOR AGES TO TWIST AND DESTROY US. THEY ARE THE TRUE ENEMIES, OF BOTH HUMANS AND ORCS.
I WOULD TRUST--I HAVE TRUSTED--THRALL WITH MY LIFE.
HE THINKS DEEPLY AND HE CARES ABOUT HIS PEOPLE. HE WANTS TO LEAD THEM TO PEACE.
MEETING THRALL WOULD BE GREAT, DAD. FROM WHAT I'VE HEARD, HE'S... EXTRAORDINARY.
AND ISN'T ESTABLISHING PEACE SOMETHING A KING SHOULD DO? IF HE CAN?
YOU MEAN DRAG HIS PEOPLE INTO PEACE, WHETHER THEY WANT IT OR NOT!
THERE'S NO LONGER OUTRIGHT WAR BETWEEN ORCS AND HUMANS, ANDUIN. WHAT MORE CAN THRALL WISH?
IF YOU TALK TO HIM, MAYBE YOU'LL FIND OUT!

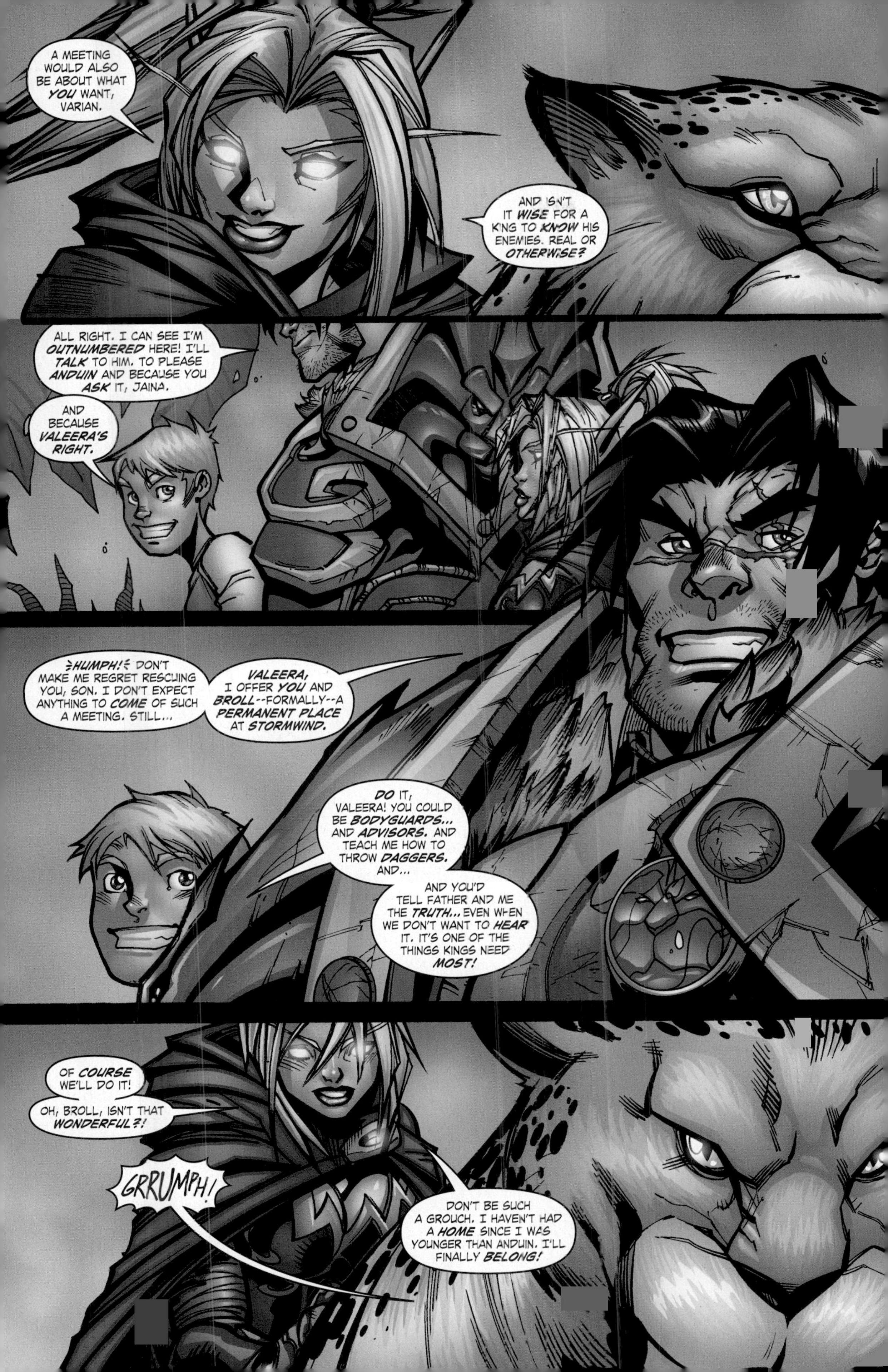
A MEETING WOULD ALSO BE ABOUT WHAT YOU WANT, VARIAN.
AND ISN'T IT WISE FOR A KING TO KNOW HIS ENEMIES. REAL OR OTHERWISE?
ALL RIGHT. I CAN SEE I'M OUTNUMBERED HERE! I'LL TALK TO HIM. TO PLEASE ANDUIN AND BECAUSE YOU ASK IT, JAINA.
AND BECAUSE VALEERA'S RIGHT.
HUMPH! DON'T MAKE ME REGRET RESCUING YOU, SON. I DON'T EXPECT ANYTHING TO COME OF SUCH A MEETING. STILL...
VALEERA, I OFFER YOU AND BROLL--FORMALLY--A PERMANENT PLACE AT STORMWIND.
DO IT, VALEERA! YOU COULD BE BODYGUARDS... AND ADVISORS. AND TEACH ME HOW TO THROW DAGGERS. AND...
AND YOU'D TELL FATHER AND ME THE TRUTH... EVEN WHEN WE DON'T WANT TO HEAR IT. IT'S ONE OF THE THINGS KINGS NEED MOST!
OF COURSE WE'LL DO IT!
OH, BROLL, ISN'T THAT WONDERFUL?!
GRRUMPH!
DON'T BE SUCH A GROUCH. I HAVEN'T HAD A HOME SINCE I WAS YOUNGER THAN ANDUIN. I'LL FINALLY BELONG!

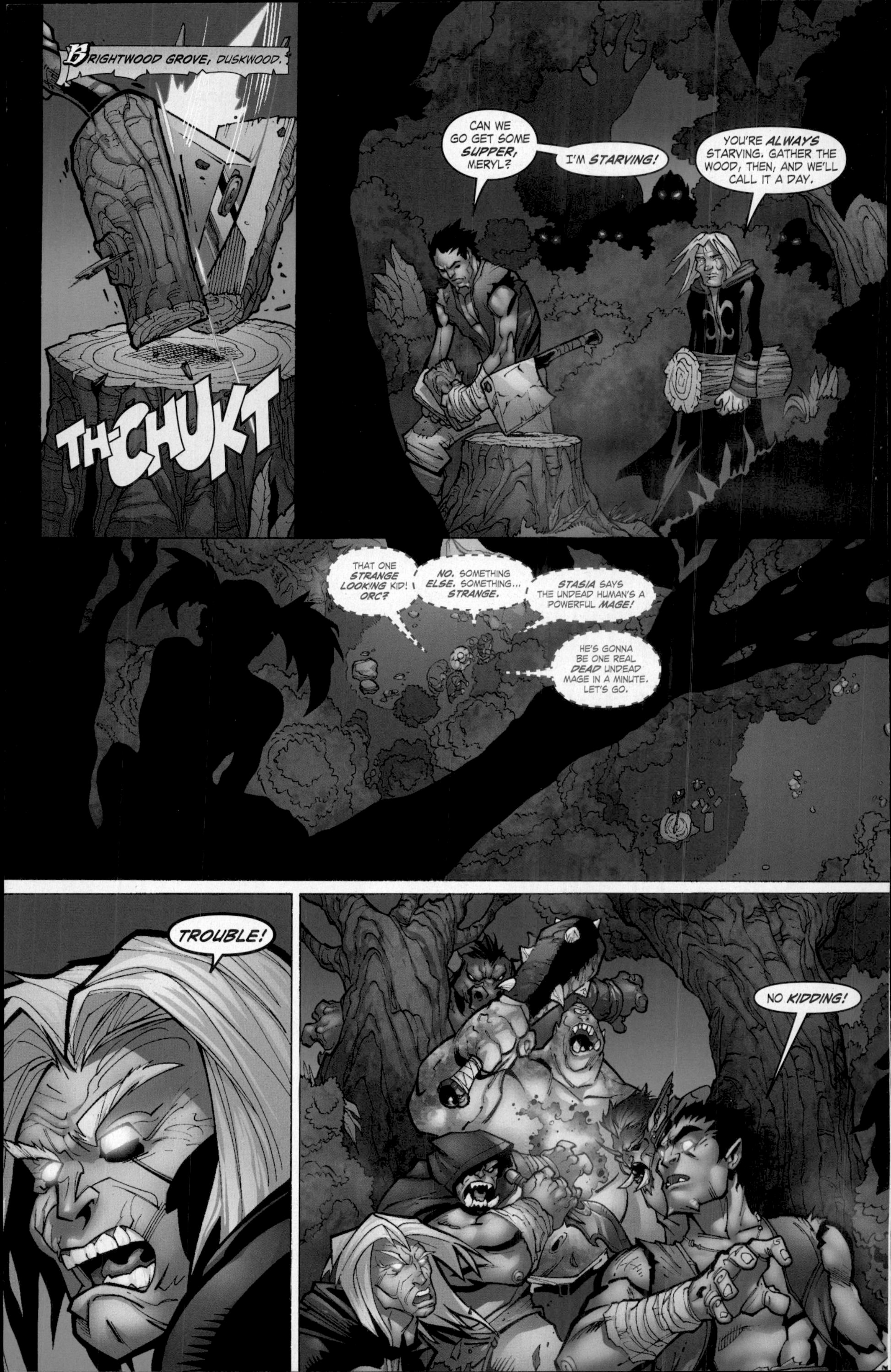
BRIGHTWOOD GROVE, DUSKWOOD.
TH-CHUKT
CAN WE GO GET SOME SUPPER, MERYL?
I'M STARVING!
YOU'RE ALWAYS STARVING. GATHER THE WOOD, THEN, AND WE'LL CALL IT A DAY.
THAT ONE STRANGE LOOKING KID! ORC?
NO. SOMETHING ELSE. SOMETHING... STRANGE.
STASIA SAYS THE UNDEAD HUMAN'S A POWERFUL MAGE!
HE'S GONNA BE ONE REAL DEAD UNDEAD MAGE IN A MINUTE. LET'S GO.
TROUBLE!
NO KIDDING!

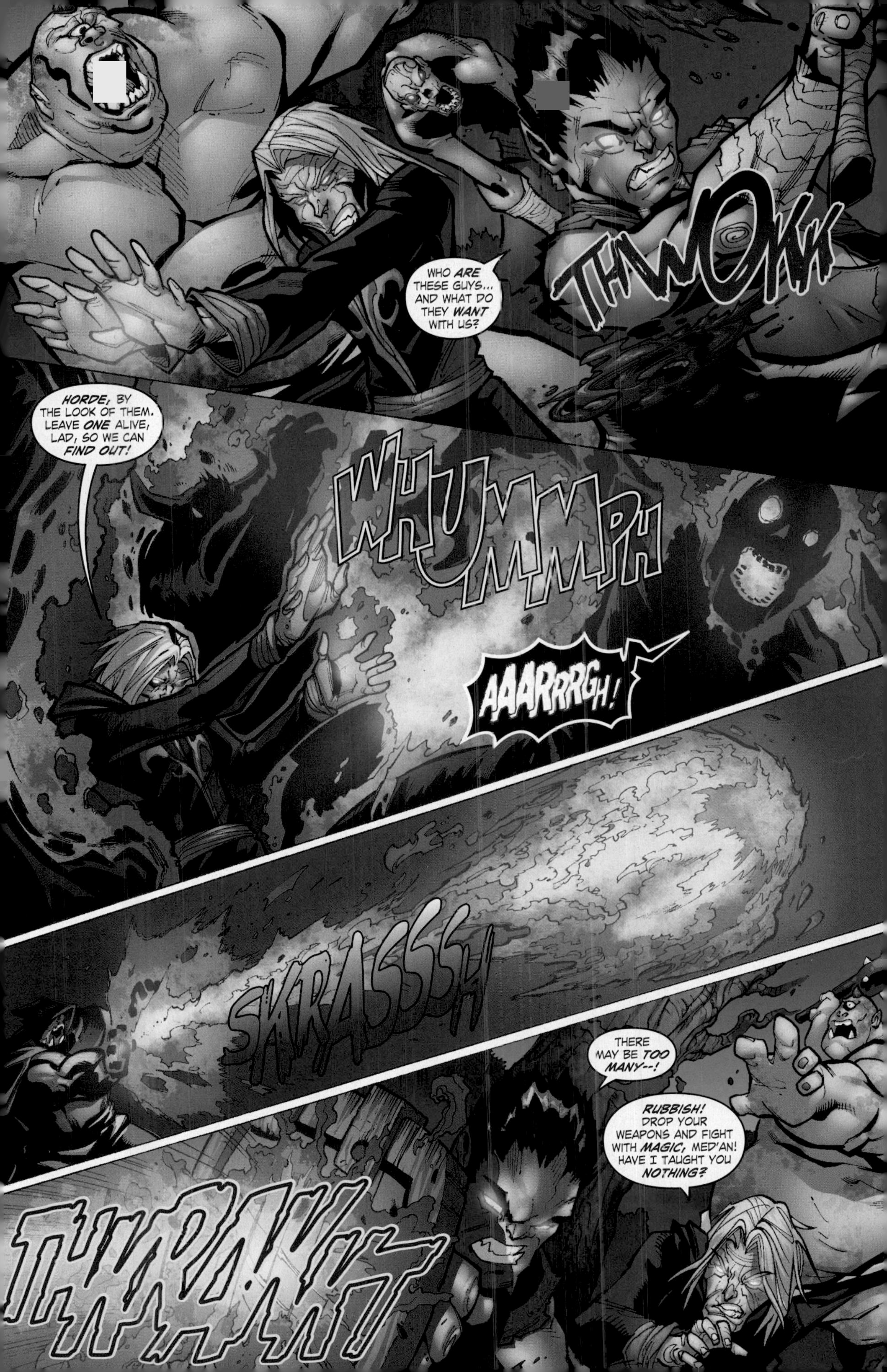
WHO ARE THESE GUYS... AND WHAT DO THEY WANT WITH US?
THWOKK
HORDE, BY THE LOOK OF THEM. LEAVE ONE ALIVE, LAD, SO WE CAN FIND OUT!
WHUMMMPH
AAARRRGH!
SKRASSSSH
THERE MAY BE TOO MANY--!
RUBBISH! DROP YOUR WEAPONS AND FIGHT WITH MAGIC, MED'AN! HAVE I TAUGHT YOU NOTHING?

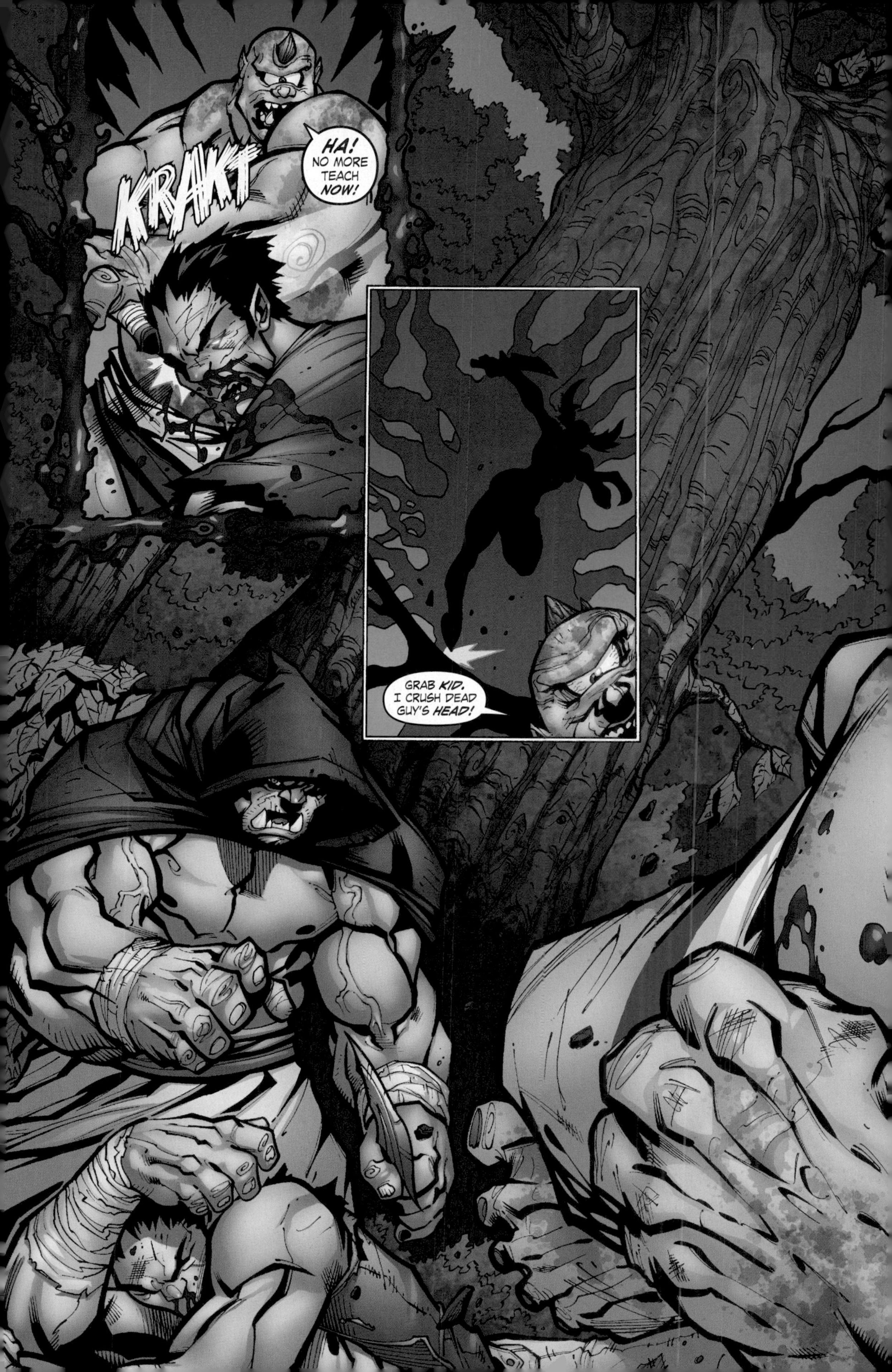
HA! NO MORE TEACH NOW!
KRAKT
GRAB KID. I CRUSH DEAD GUY'S HEAD!

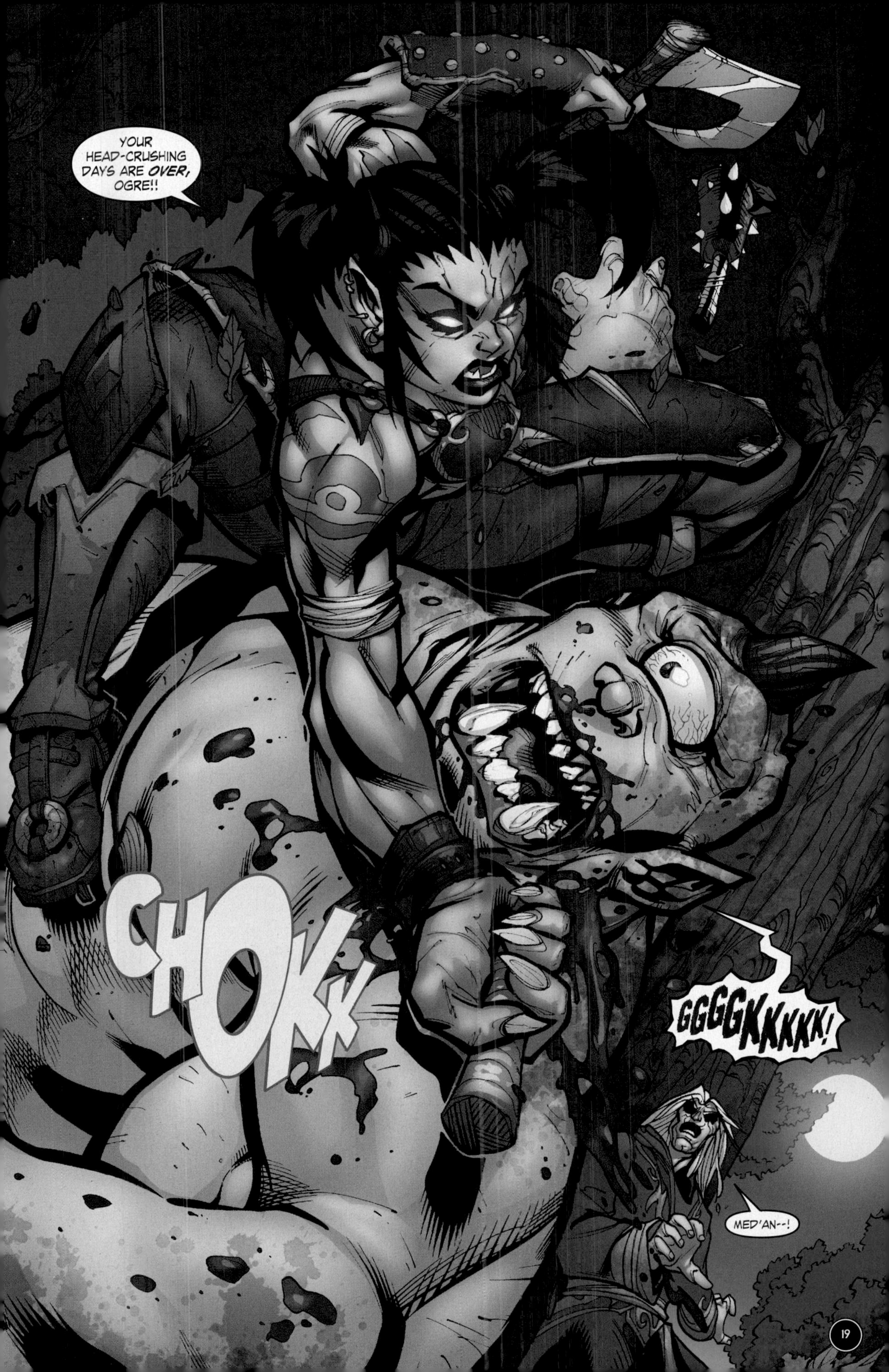
YOUR HEAD-CRUSHING DAYS ARE *OVER*, OGRE!!
CHOKK
GGGGKKKKK!
MED'AN--!

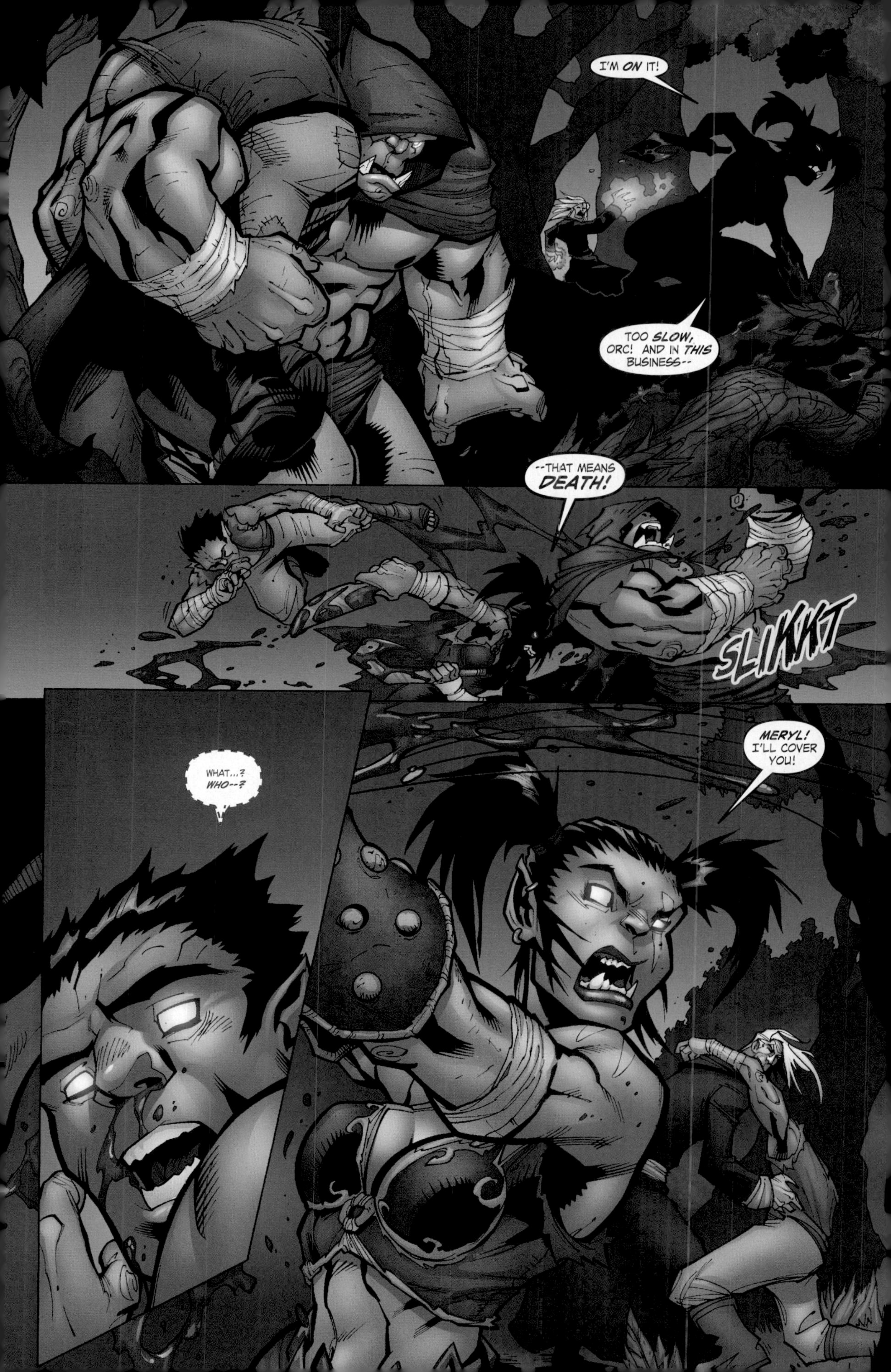

I'M ON IT!
TOO SLOW, ORC! AND IN THIS BUSINESS--
--THAT MEANS DEATH!
SLIKKT
WHAT...? WHO--?
MERYL! I'LL COVER YOU!

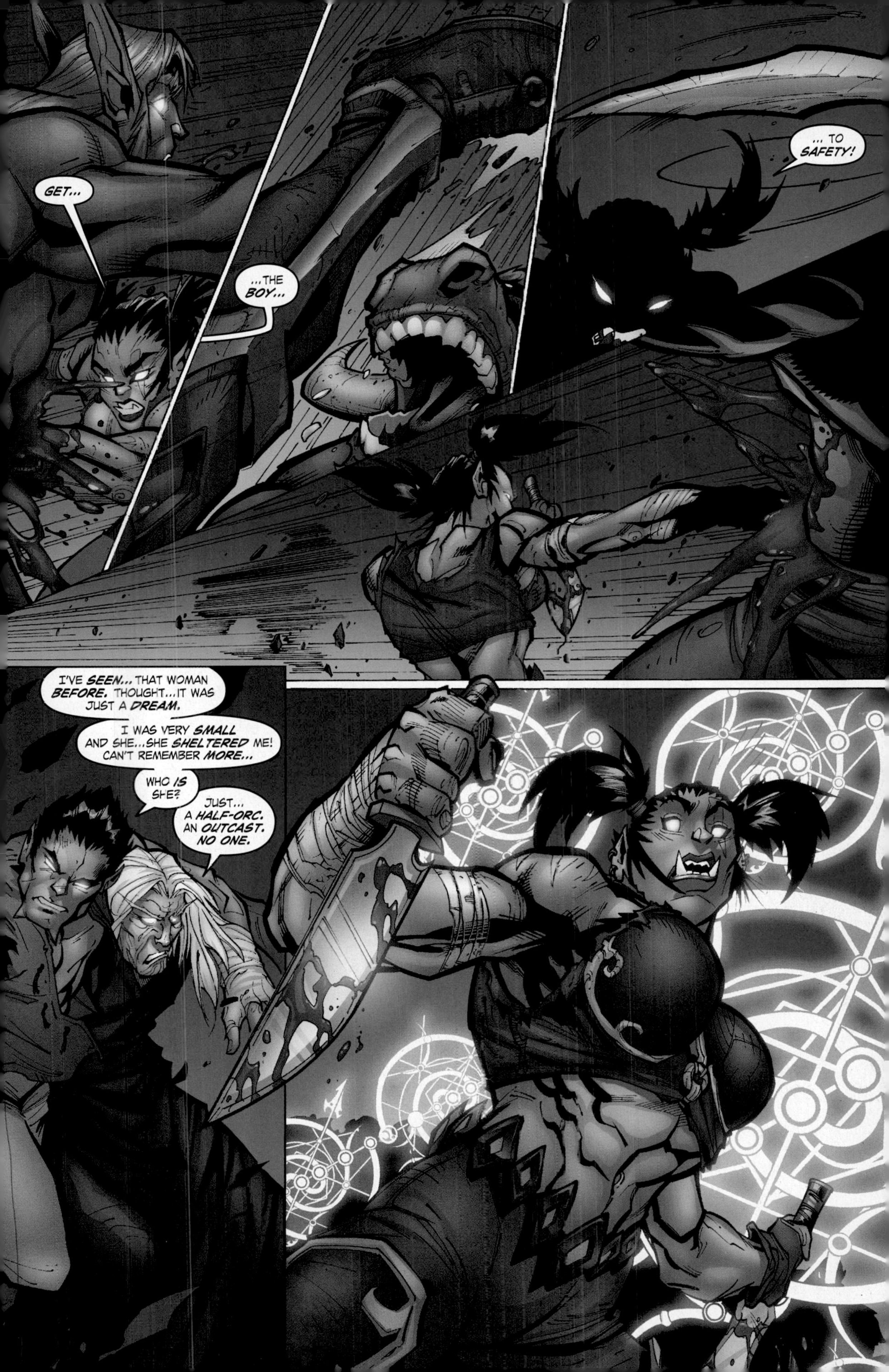
GET...
...THE BOY...
... TO SAFETY!
I'VE SEEN... THAT WOMAN BEFORE. THOUGHT...IT WAS JUST A DREAM.
I WAS VERY SMALL AND SHE...SHE SHELTERED ME! CAN'T REMEMBER MORE...
WHO IS SHE?
JUST... A HALF-ORC. AN OUTCAST. NO ONE.

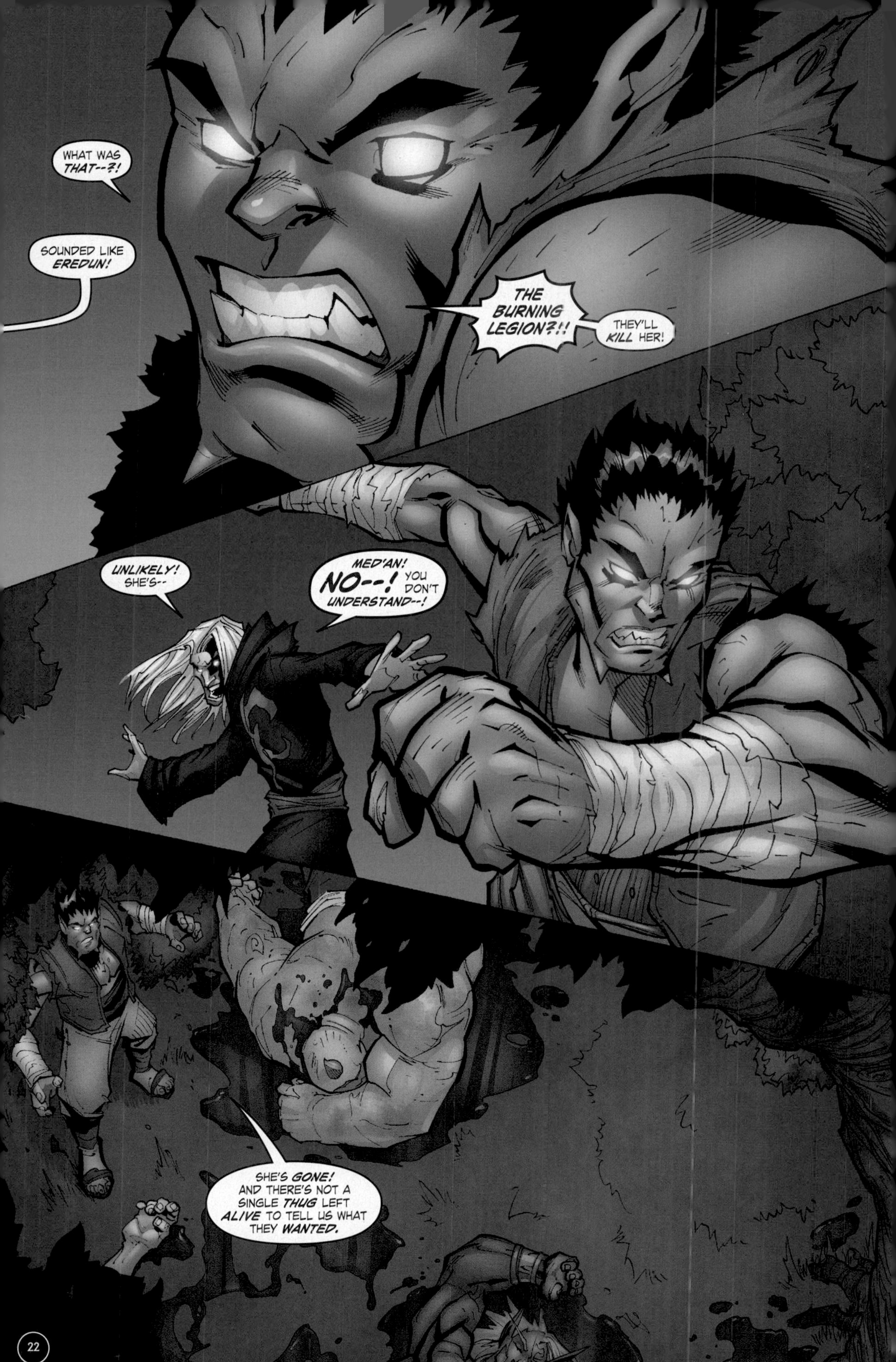
WHAT WAS THAT--?!
SOUNDED LIKE EREDUN!
THE BURNING LEGION?!!
THEY'LL KILL HER!
UNLIKELY! SHE'S--
MED'AN! NO--! YOU DON'T UNDERSTAND--!
SHE'S GONE! AND THERE'S NOT A SINGLE THUG LEFT ALIVE TO TELL US WHAT THEY WANTED.

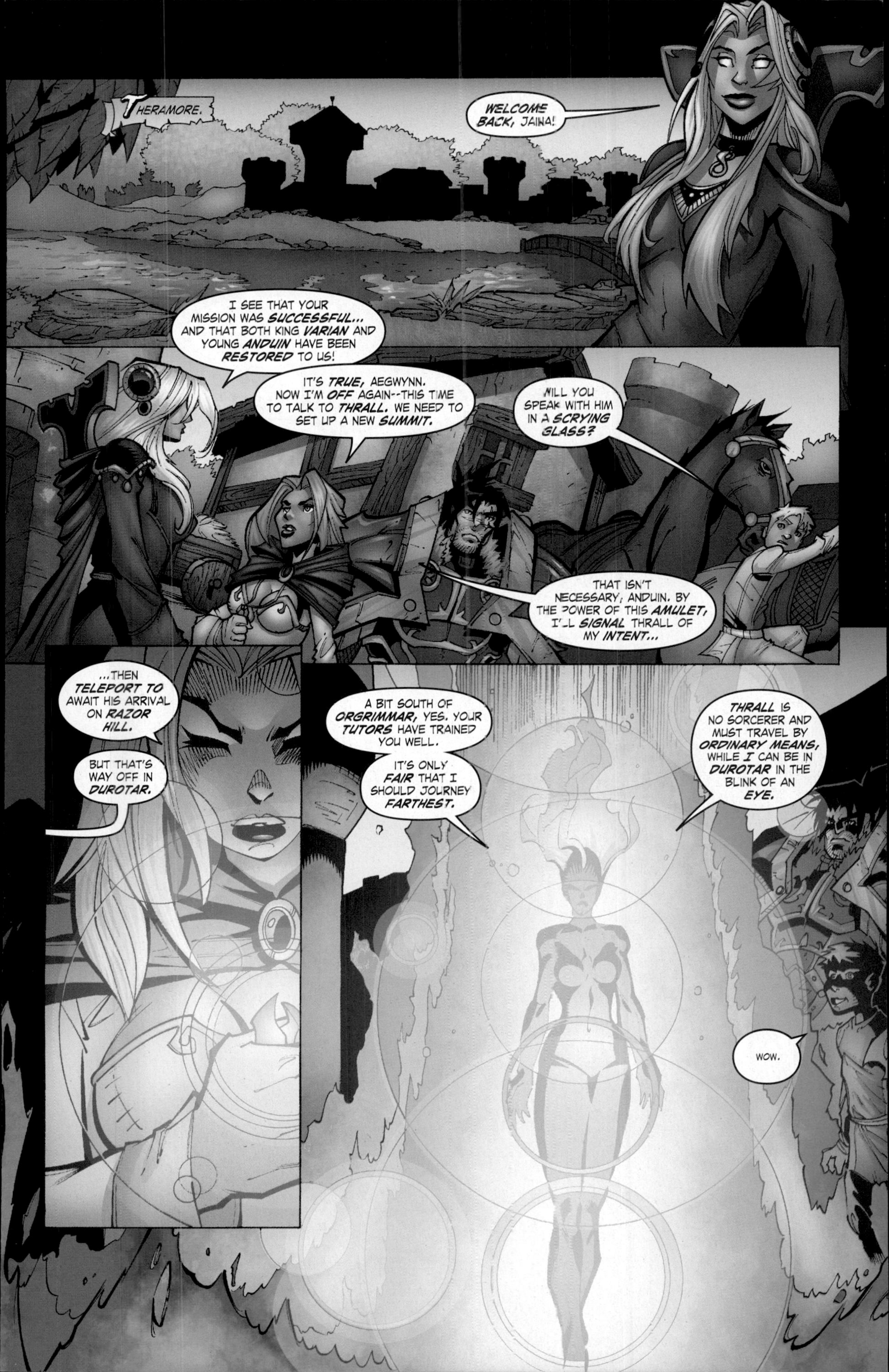
THERAMORE.
WELCOME BACK, JAINA!
I SEE THAT YOUR MISSION WAS SUCCESSFUL... AND THAT BOTH KING VARIAN AND YOUNG ANDUIN HAVE BEEN RESTORED TO US!
IT'S TRUE, AEGWYNN. NOW I'M OFF AGAIN--THIS TIME TO TALK TO THRALL. WE NEED TO SET UP A NEW SUMMIT.
WILL YOU SPEAK WITH HIM IN A SCRYING GLASS?
THAT ISN'T NECESSARY, ANDUIN. BY THE POWER OF THIS AMULET, I'LL SIGNAL THRALL OF MY INTENT...
...THEN TELEPORT TO AWAIT HIS ARRIVAL ON RAZOR HILL.
BUT THAT'S WAY OFF IN DUROTAR.
A BIT SOUTH OF ORGRIMMAR, YES. YOUR TUTORS HAVE TRAINED YOU WELL.
IT'S ONLY FAIR THAT I SHOULD JOURNEY FARTHEST.
THRALL IS NO SORCERER AND MUST TRAVEL BY ORDINARY MEANS, WHILE I CAN BE IN DUROTAR IN THE BLINK OF AN EYE.
WOW.

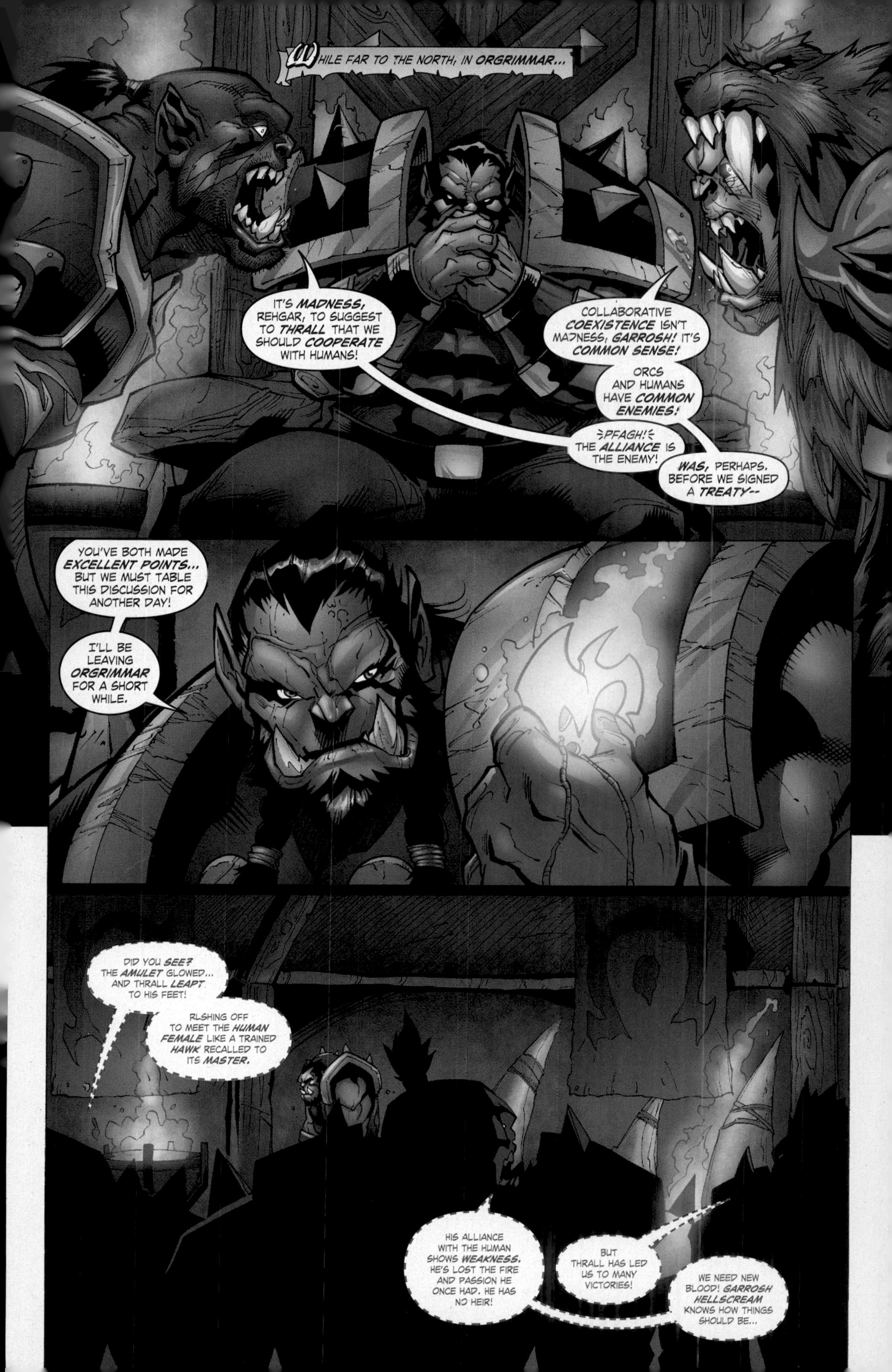
WHILE FAR TO THE NORTH, IN ORGRIMMAR...
IT'S MADNESS, REHGAR, TO SUGGEST TO THRALL THAT WE SHOULD COOPERATE WITH HUMANS!
COLLABORATIVE COEXISTENCE ISN'T MADNESS, GARROSH! IT'S COMMON SENSE!
ORCS AND HUMANS HAVE COMMON ENEMIES!
PFAGH! THE ALLIANCE IS THE ENEMY!
WAS, PERHAPS. BEFORE WE SIGNED A TREATY--
YOU'VE BOTH MADE EXCELLENT POINTS... BUT WE MUST TABLE THIS DISCUSSION FOR ANOTHER DAY!
I'LL BE LEAVING ORGRIMMAR FOR A SHORT WHILE.
DID YOU SEE? THE AMULET GLOWED... AND THRALL LEAPT TO HIS FEET!
RLSHING OFF TO MEET THE HUMAN FEMALE LIKE A TRAINED HAWK RECALLED TO ITS MASTER.
HIS ALLIANCE WITH THE HUMAN SHOWS WEAKNESS. HE'S LOST THE FIRE AND PASSION HE ONCE HAD. HE HAS NO HEIR!
BUT THRALL HAS LED US TO MANY VICTORIES!
WE NEED NEW BLOOD! GARROSH HELLSCREAM KNOWS HOW THINGS SHOULD BE...

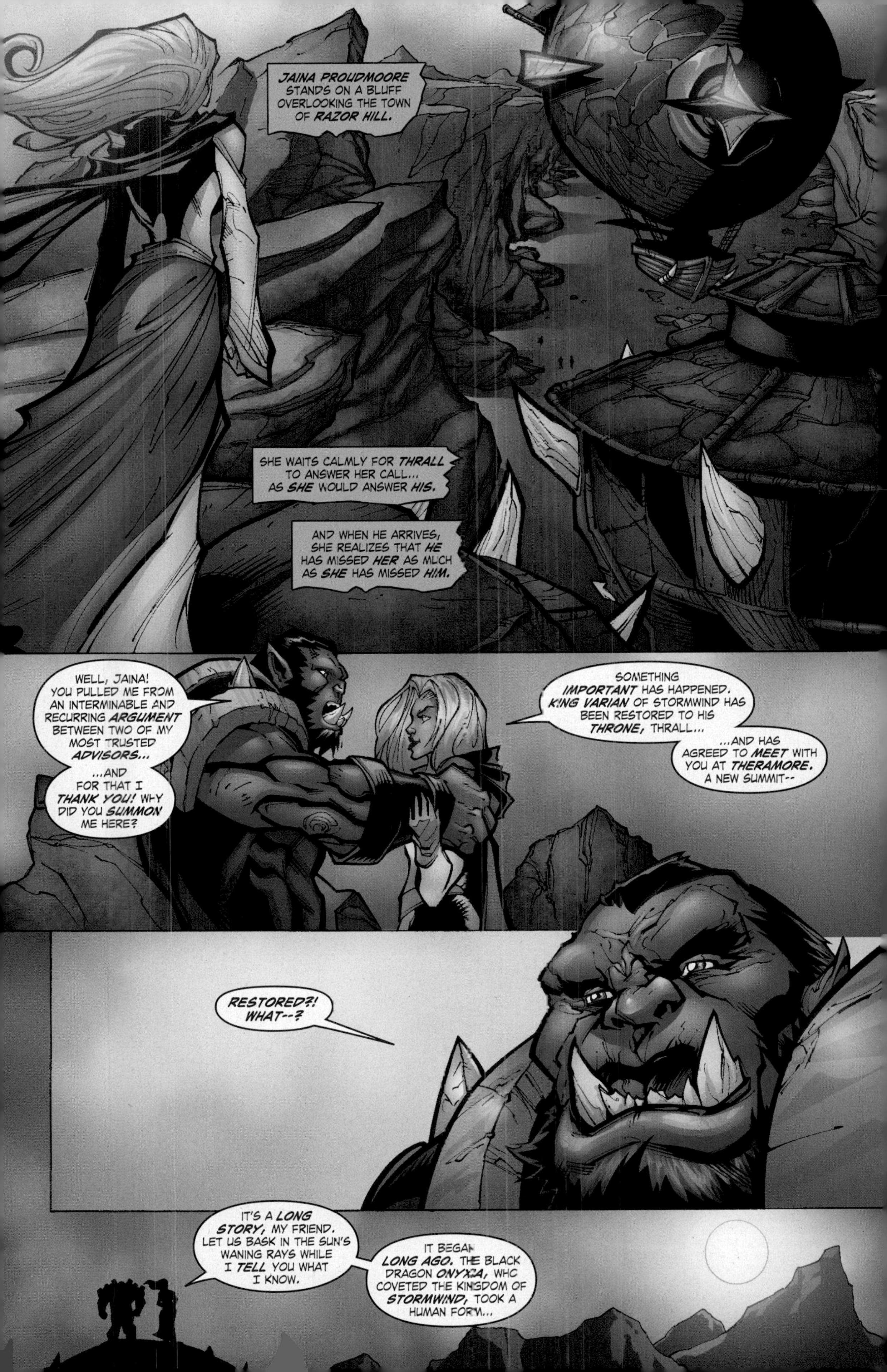
JAINA PROUDMOORE STANDS ON A BLUFF OVERLOOKING THE TOWN OF RAZOR HILL.
SHE WAITS CALMLY FOR THRALL TO ANSWER HER CALL... AS SHE WOULD ANSWER HIS.
AND WHEN HE ARRIVES, SHE REALIZES THAT HE HAS MISSED HER AS MUCH AS SHE HAS MISSED HIM.
WELL, JAINA! YOU PULLED ME FROM AN INTERMINABLE AND RECURRING ARGUMENT BETWEEN TWO OF MY MOST TRUSTED ADVISORS...
...AND FOR THAT I THANK YOU! WHY DID YOU SUMMON ME HERE?
SOMETHING IMPORTANT HAS HAPPENED. KING VARIAN OF STORMWIND HAS BEEN RESTORED TO HIS THRONE, THRALL...
...AND HAS AGREED TO MEET WITH YOU AT THERAMORE. A NEW SUMMIT--
RESTORED?! WHAT--?
IT'S A LONG STORY, MY FRIEND. LET US BASK IN THE SUN'S WANING RAYS WHILE I TELL YOU WHAT I KNOW.
IT BEGAN LONG AGO. THE BLACK DRAGON ONYXIA, WHO COVETED THE KINGDOM OF STORMWIND, TOOK A HUMAN FORM...

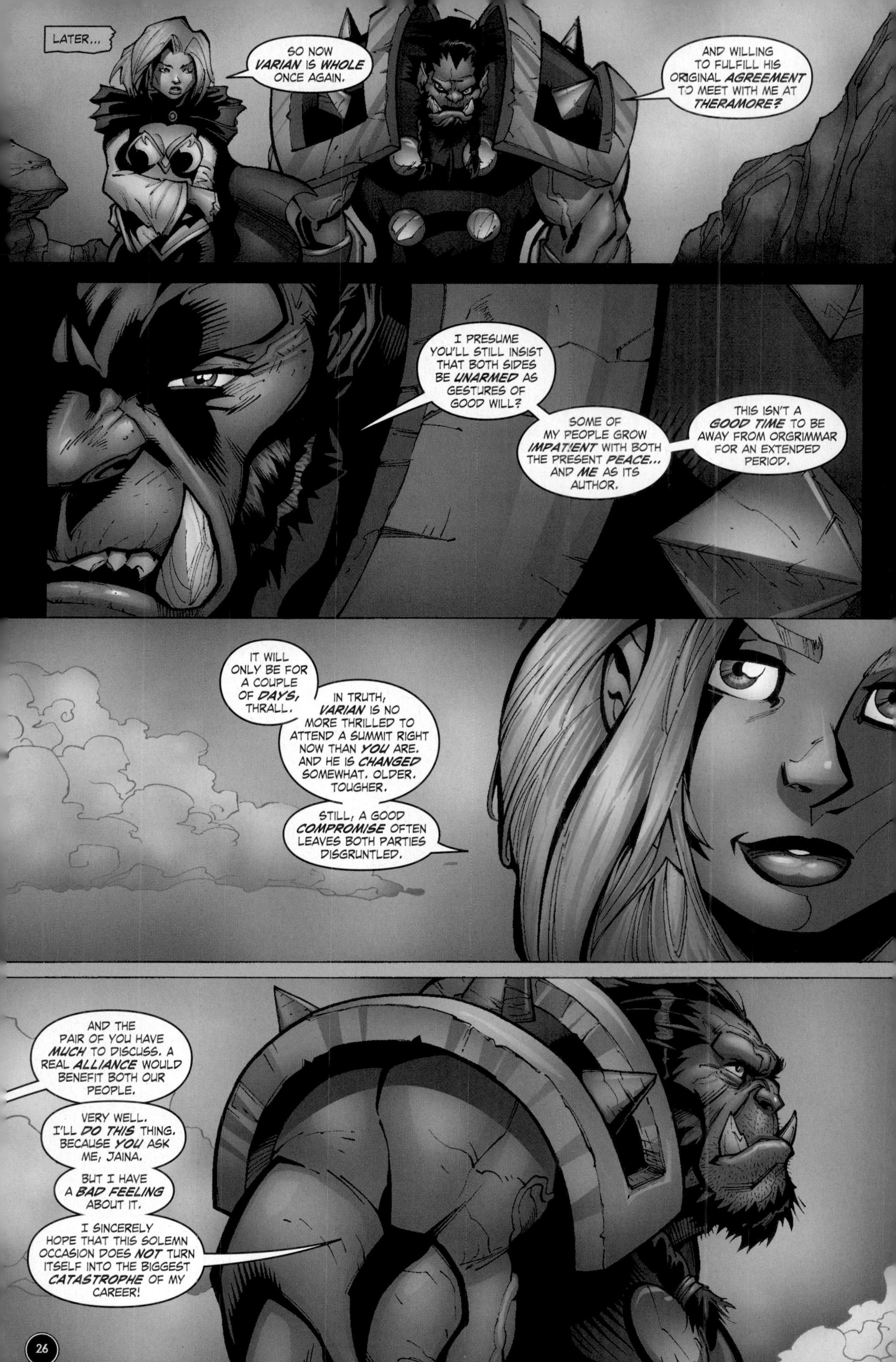
LATER...
SO NOW VARIAN IS WHOLE ONCE AGAIN.
AND WILLING TO FULFILL HIS ORIGINAL AGREEMENT TO MEET WITH ME AT THERAMORE?
I PRESUME YOU'LL STILL INSIST THAT BOTH SIDES BE UNARMED AS GESTURES OF GOOD WILL?
SOME OF MY PEOPLE GROW IMPATIENT WITH BOTH THE PRESENT PEACE... AND ME AS ITS AUTHOR.
THIS ISN'T A GOOD TIME TO BE AWAY FROM ORGRIMMAR FOR AN EXTENDED PERIOD.
IT WILL ONLY BE FOR A COUPLE OF DAYS, THRALL.
IN TRUTH, VARIAN IS NO MORE THRILLED TO ATTEND A SUMMIT RIGHT NOW THAN YOU ARE. AND HE IS CHANGED SOMEWHAT. OLDER. TOUGHER.
STILL, A GOOD COMPROMISE OFTEN LEAVES BOTH PARTIES DISGRUNTLED.
AND THE PAIR OF YOU HAVE MUCH TO DISCUSS. A REAL ALLIANCE WOULD BENEFIT BOTH OUR PEOPLE.
VERY WELL. I'LL DO THIS THING. BECAUSE YOU ASK ME, JAINA.
BUT I HAVE A BAD FEELING ABOUT IT.
I SINCERELY HOPE THAT THIS SOLEMN OCCASION DOES NOT TURN ITSELF INTO THE BIGGEST CATASTROPHE OF MY CAREER!

CHAPTER 2

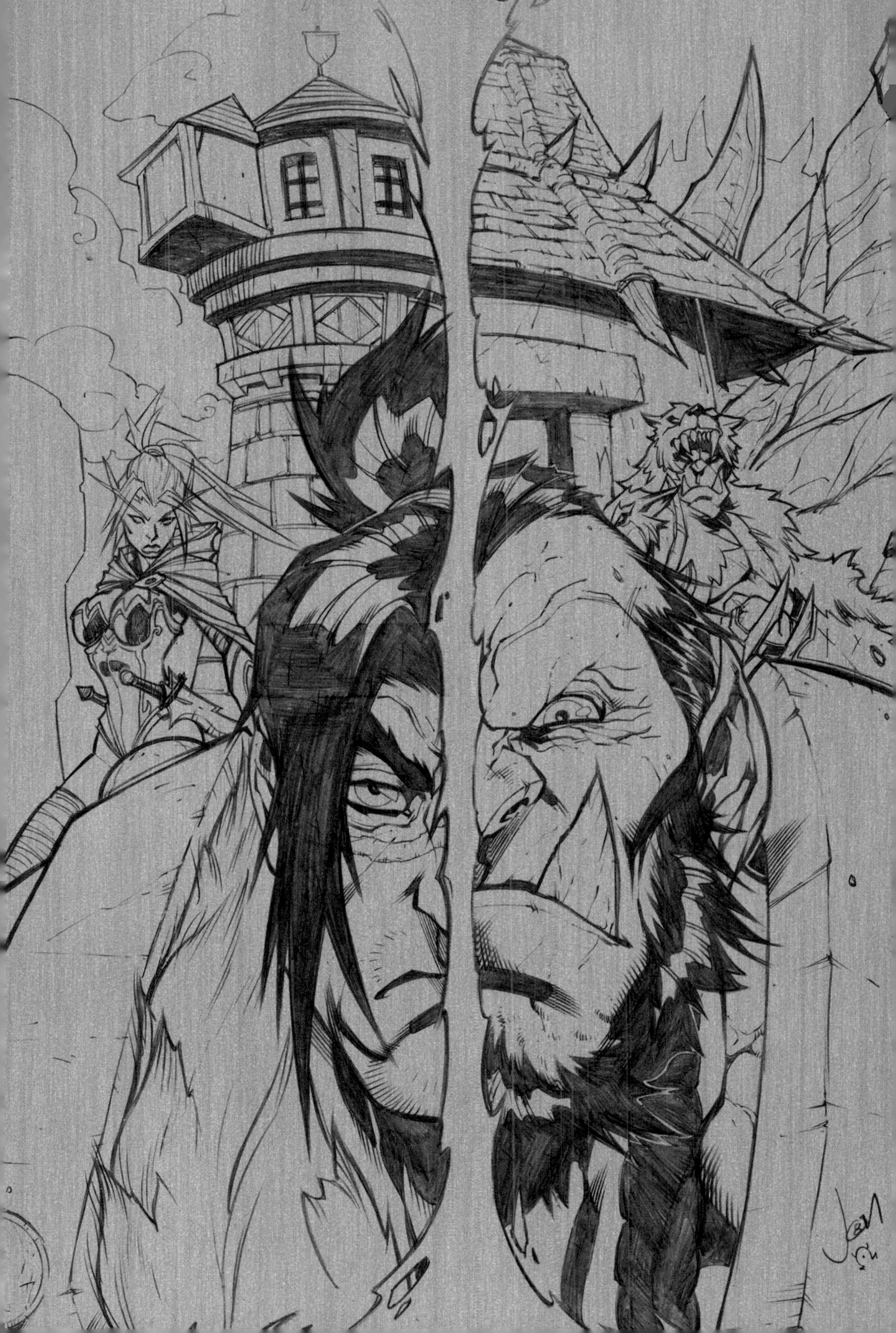

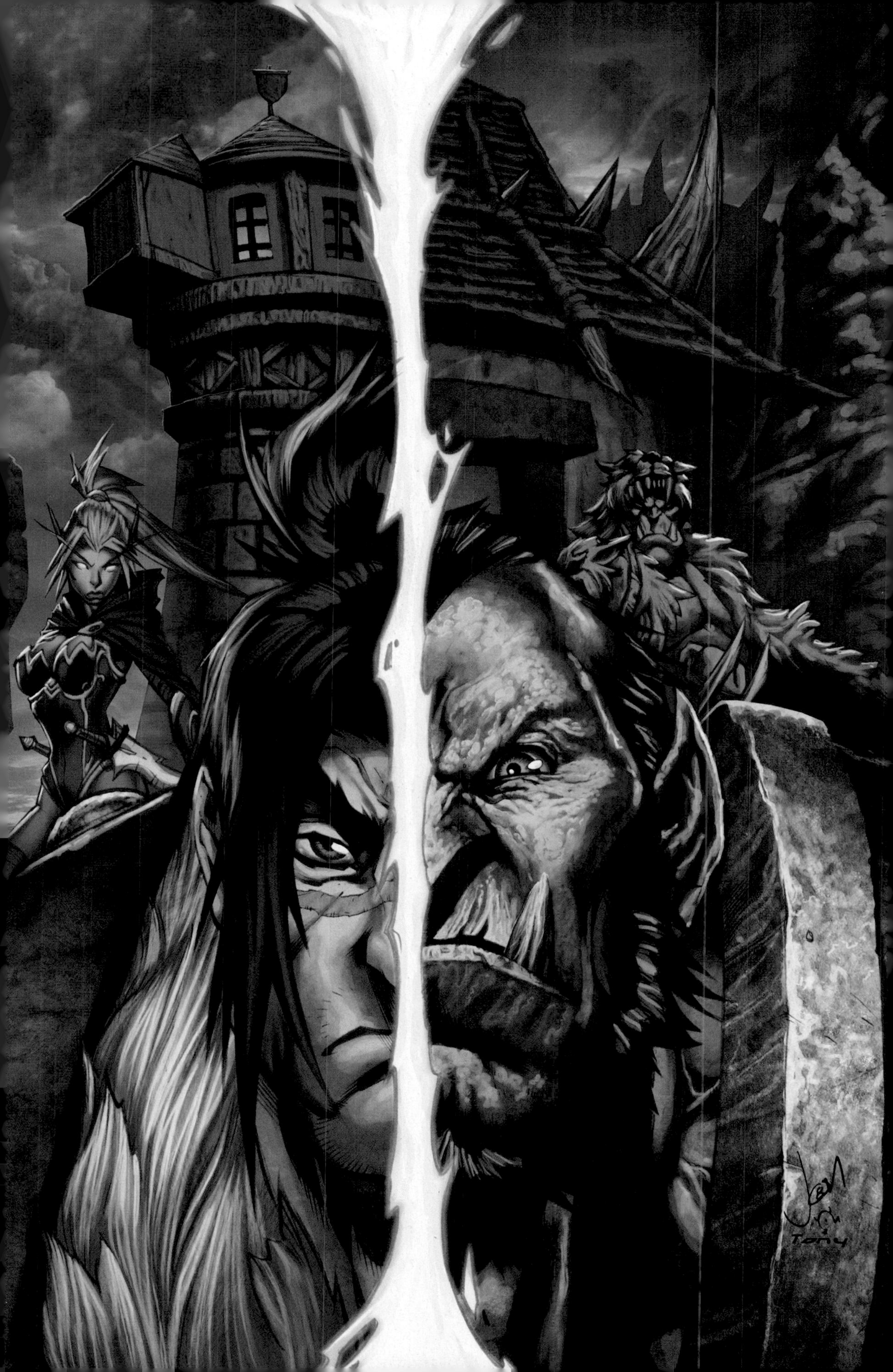

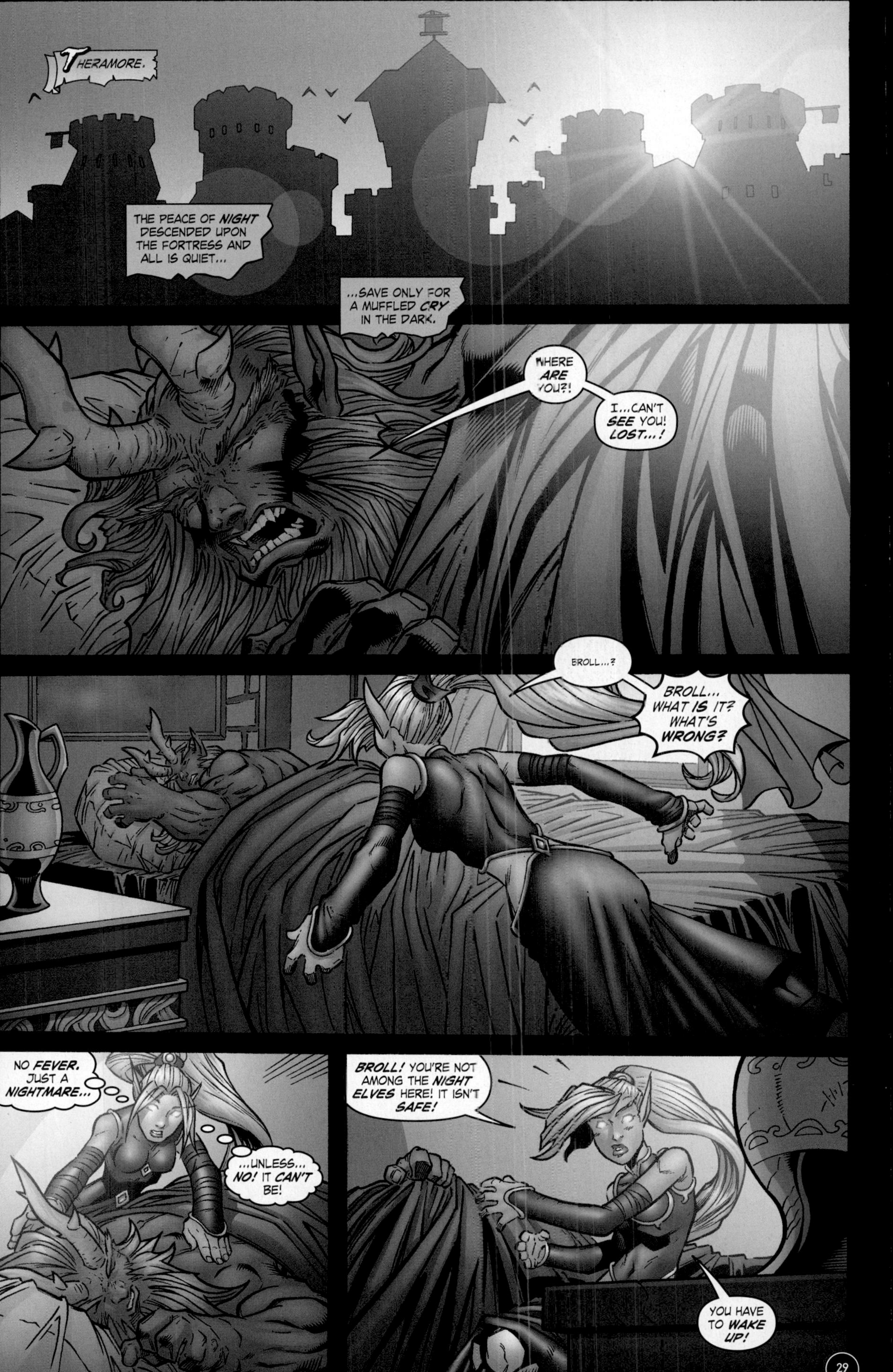
THERAMORE.
THE PEACE OF NIGHT DESCENDED UPON THE FORTRESS AND ALL IS QUIET...
...SAVE ONLY FOR A MUFFLED CRY IN THE DARK.
WHERE ARE YOU?!
I...CAN'T SEE YOU! LOST...!
BROLL...?
BROLL... WHAT IS IT? WHAT'S WRONG?
NO FEVER. JUST A NIGHTMARE...
...UNLESS... NO! IT CAN'T BE!
BROLL! YOU'RE NOT AMONG THE NIGHT ELVES HERE! IT ISN'T SAFE!
YOU HAVE TO WAKE UP!

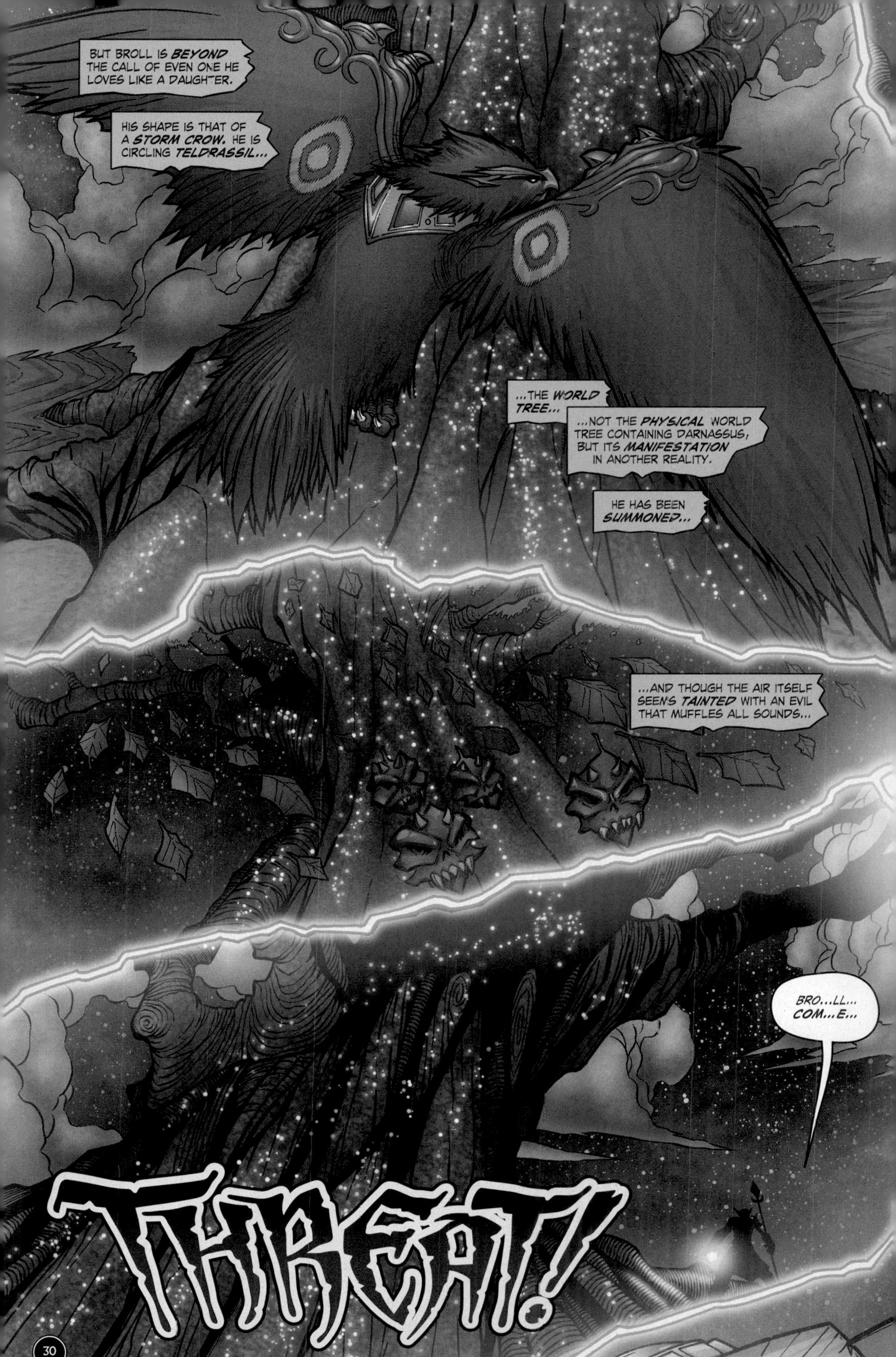

BUT BROLL IS BEYOND THE CALL OF EVEN ONE HE LOVES LIKE A DAUGHTER.
HIS SHAPE IS THAT OF A STORM CROW. HE IS CIRCLING TELDRASSIL...
...THE WORLD TREE...
...NOT THE PHYSICAL WORLD TREE CONTAINING DARNASSUS, BUT ITS MANIFESTATION IN ANOTHER REALITY.
HE HAS BEEN SUMMONED...
...AND THOUGH THE AIR ITSELF SEEMS TAINTED WITH AN EVIL THAT MUFFLES ALL SOUNDS...
BRO...LL... COM...E...
THREAT!

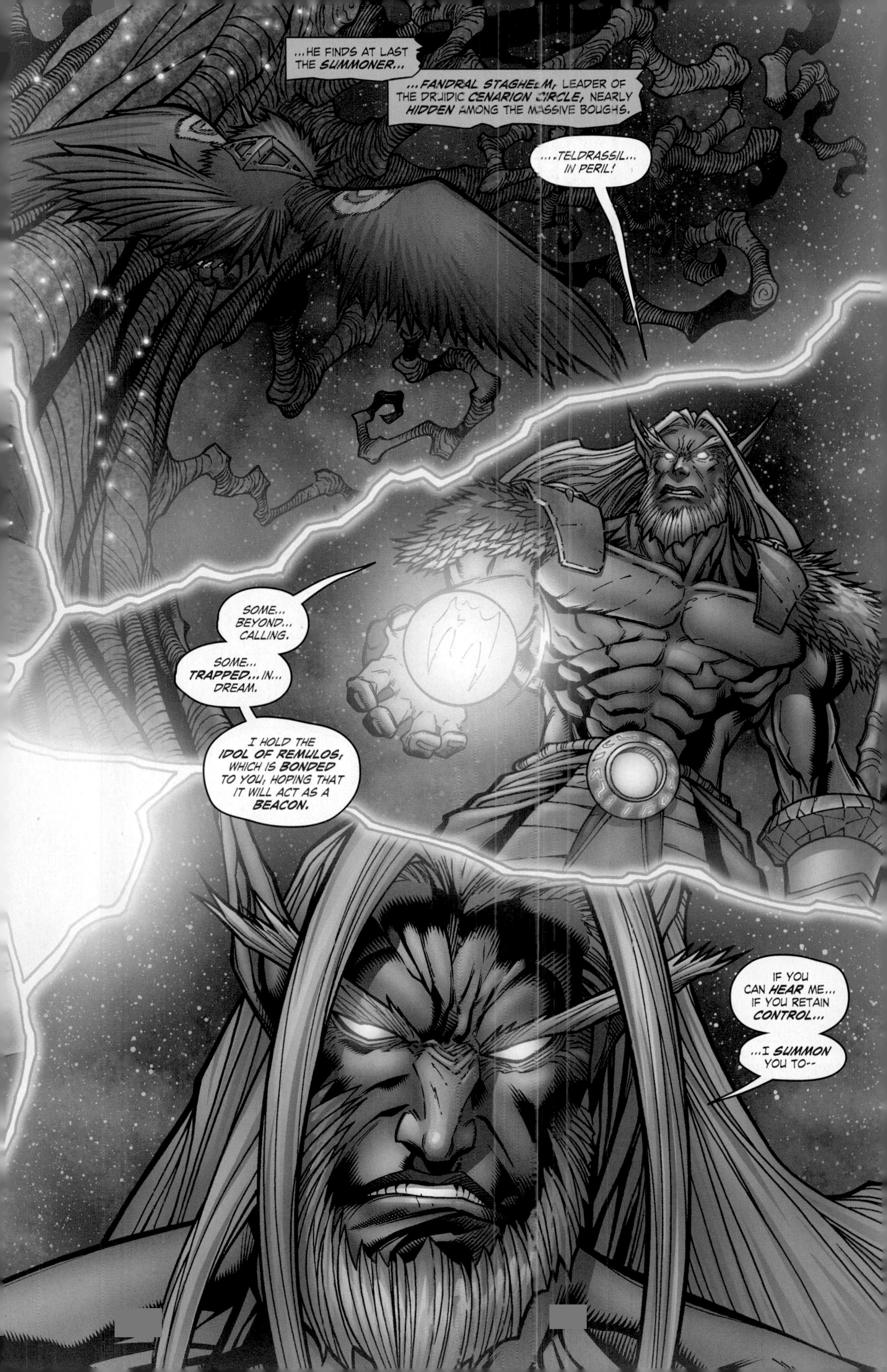

...HE FINDS AT LAST THE SUMMONER...
...FANDRAL STAGHELM, LEADER OF THE DRUIDIC CENARION CIRCLE, NEARLY HIDDEN AMONG THE MASSIVE BOUGHS.
....TELDRASSIL... IN PERIL!
SOME... BEYOND... CALLING.
SOME... TRAPPED... IN... DREAM.
I HOLD THE IDOL OF REMULOS, WHICH IS BONDED TO YOU, HOPING THAT IT WILL ACT AS A BEACON.
IF YOU CAN HEAR ME... IF YOU RETAIN CONTROL...
...I SUMMON YOU TO--

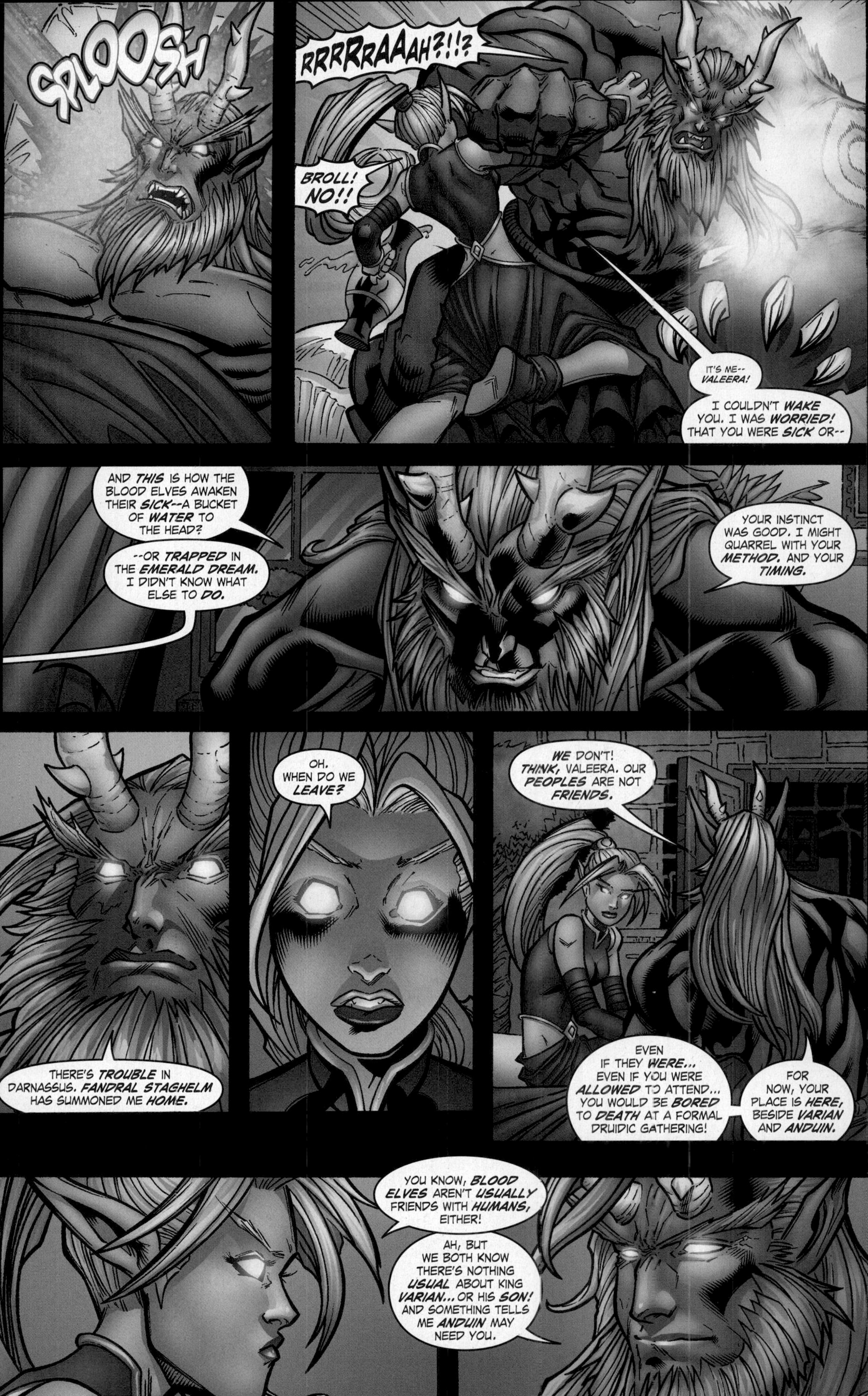
SPLOOSH
RRRRAAAH?!!?
BROLL! NO!!
IT'S ME-- VALEERA!
I COULDN'T WAKE YOU. I WAS WORRIED! THAT YOU WERE SICK OR--
AND THIS IS HOW THE BLOOD ELVES AWAKEN THEIR SICK--A BUCKET OF WATER TO THE HEAD?
--OR TRAPPED IN THE EMERALD DREAM. I DIDN'T KNOW WHAT ELSE TO DO.
YOUR INSTINCT WAS GOOD. I MIGHT QUARREL WITH YOUR METHOD. AND YOUR TIMING.
THERE'S TROUBLE IN DARNASSUS. FANDRAL STAGHELM HAS SUMMONED ME HOME.
OH. WHEN DO WE LEAVE?
WE DON'T! THINK, VALEERA. OUR PEOPLES ARE NOT FRIENDS.
EVEN IF THEY WERE... EVEN IF YOU WERE ALLOWED TO ATTEND... YOU WOULD BE BORED TO DEATH AT A FORMAL DRUIDIC GATHERING!
FOR NOW, YOUR PLACE IS HERE, BESIDE VARIAN AND ANDUIN.
YOU KNOW, BLOOD ELVES AREN'T USUALLY FRIENDS WITH HUMANS, EITHER!
AH, BUT WE BOTH KNOW THERE'S NOTHING USUAL ABOUT KING VARIAN... OR HIS SON! AND SOMETHING TELLS ME ANDUIN MAY NEED YOU.

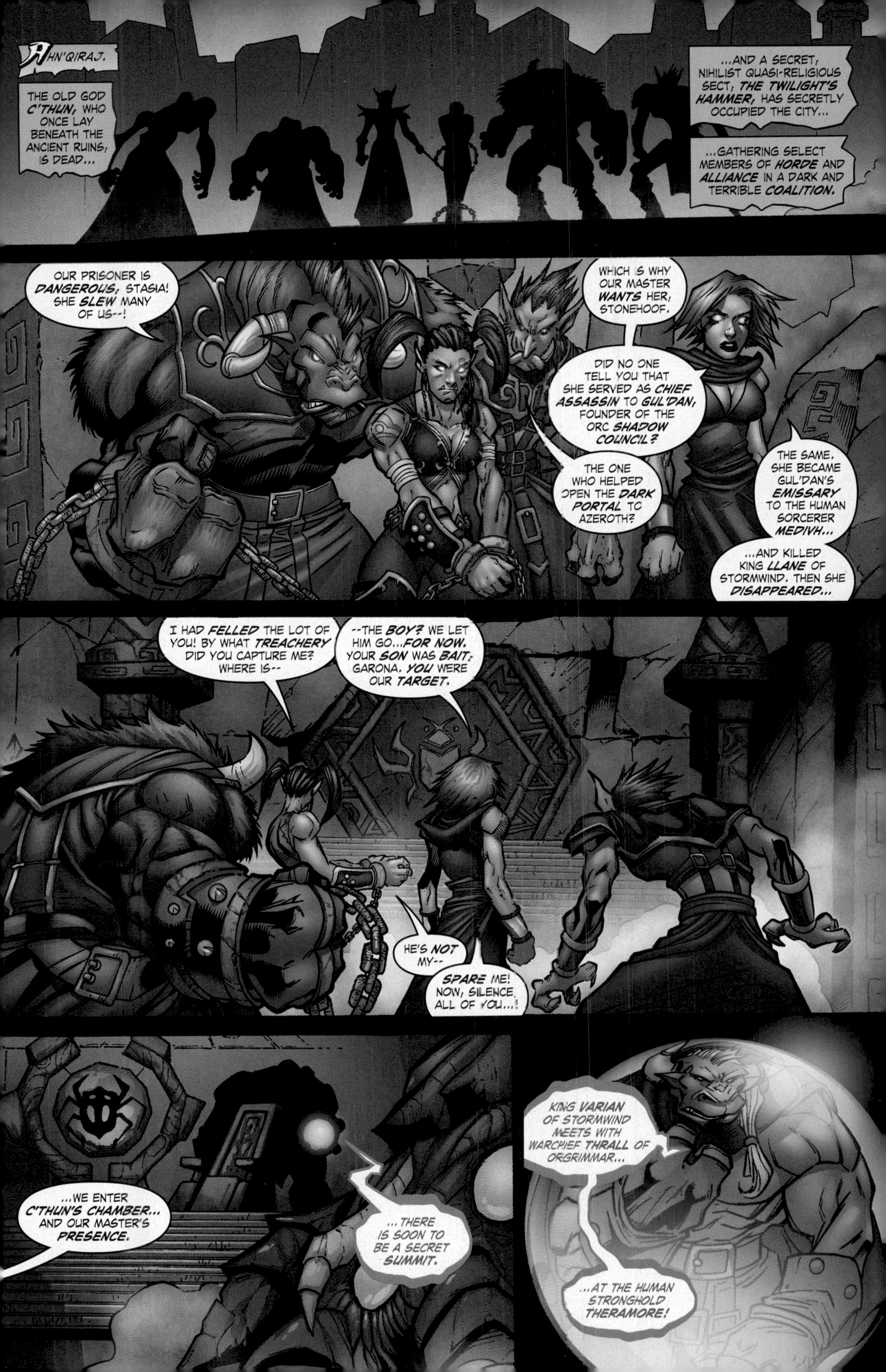
AHN'QIRAJ.
THE OLD GOD C'THUN, WHO ONCE LAY BENEATH THE ANCIENT RUINS, IS DEAD...
...AND A SECRET, NIHILIST QUASI-RELIGIOUS SECT, THE TWILIGHT'S HAMMER, HAS SECRETLY OCCUPIED THE CITY...
...GATHERING SELECT MEMBERS OF HORDE AND ALLIANCE IN A DARK AND TERRIBLE COALITION.
OUR PRISONER IS DANGEROUS, STASIA! SHE SLEW MANY OF US--!
WHICH IS WHY OUR MASTER WANTS HER, STONEHOOF.
DID NO ONE TELL YOU THAT SHE SERVED AS CHIEF ASSASSIN TO GUL'DAN, FOUNDER OF THE ORC SHADOW COUNCIL?
THE ONE WHO HELPED OPEN THE DARK PORTAL TO AZEROTH?
THE SAME. SHE BECAME GUL'DAN'S EMISSARY TO THE HUMAN SORCERER MEDIVH...
...AND KILLED KING LLANE OF STORMWIND. THEN SHE DISAPPEARED...
I HAD FELLED THE LOT OF YOU! BY WHAT TREACHERY DID YOU CAPTURE ME? WHERE IS--
--THE BOY? WE LET HIM GO...FOR NOW. YOUR SON WAS BAIT, GARONA. YOU WERE OUR TARGET.
HE'S NOT MY--
SPARE ME! NOW, SILENCE, ALL OF YOU...!
...WE ENTER C'THUN'S CHAMBER... AND OUR MASTER'S PRESENCE.
...THERE IS SOON TO BE A SECRET SUMMIT.
KING VARIAN OF STORMWIND MEETS WITH WARCHIEF THRALL OF ORGRIMMAR...
...AT THE HUMAN STRONGHOLD THERAMORE!

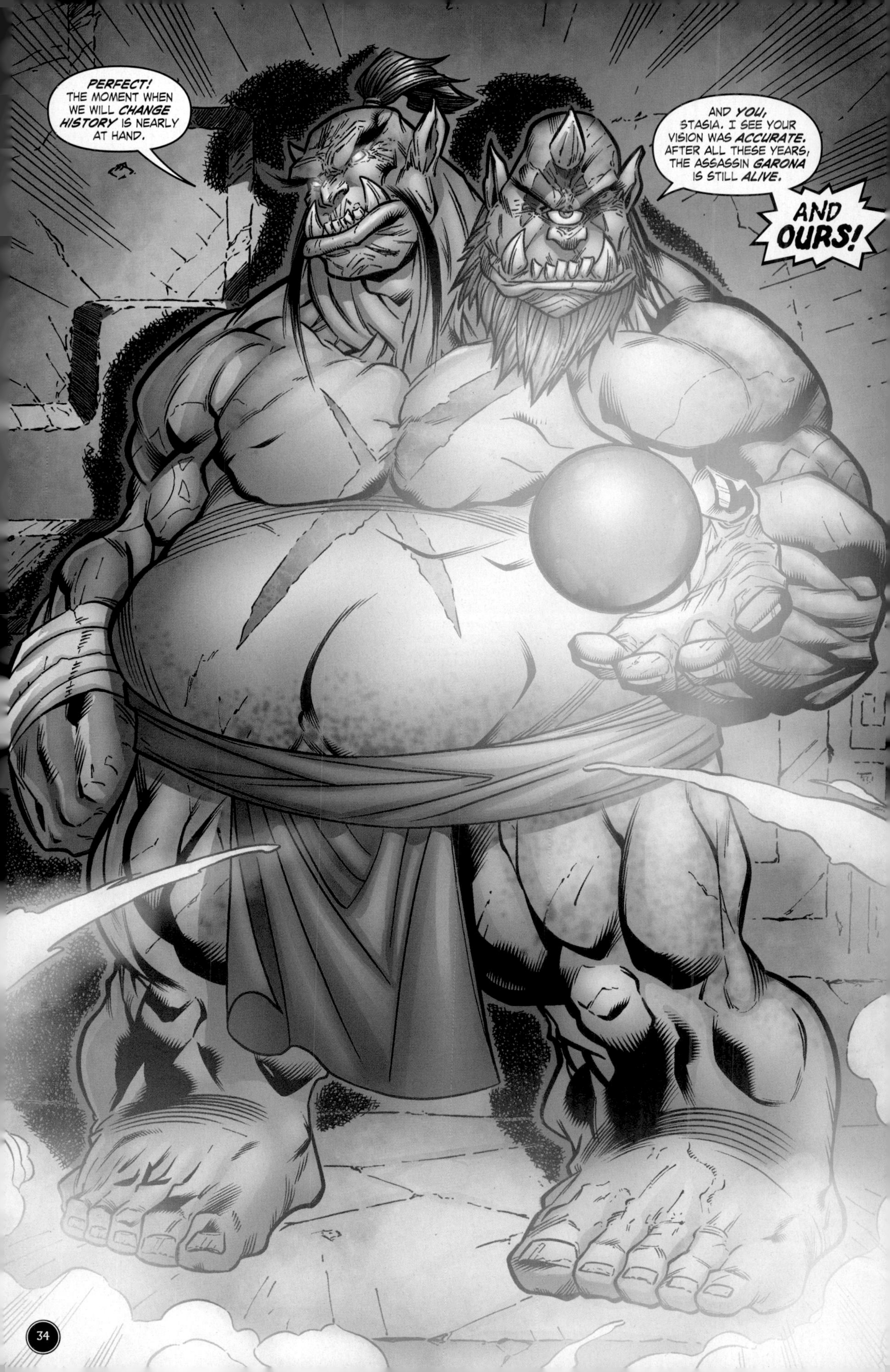
PERFECT! THE MOMENT WHEN WE WILL CHANGE HISTORY IS NEARLY AT HAND.
AND YOU, STASIA. I SEE YOUR VISION WAS ACCURATE. AFTER ALL THESE YEARS, THE ASSASSIN GARONA IS STILL ALIVE.
AND OURS!

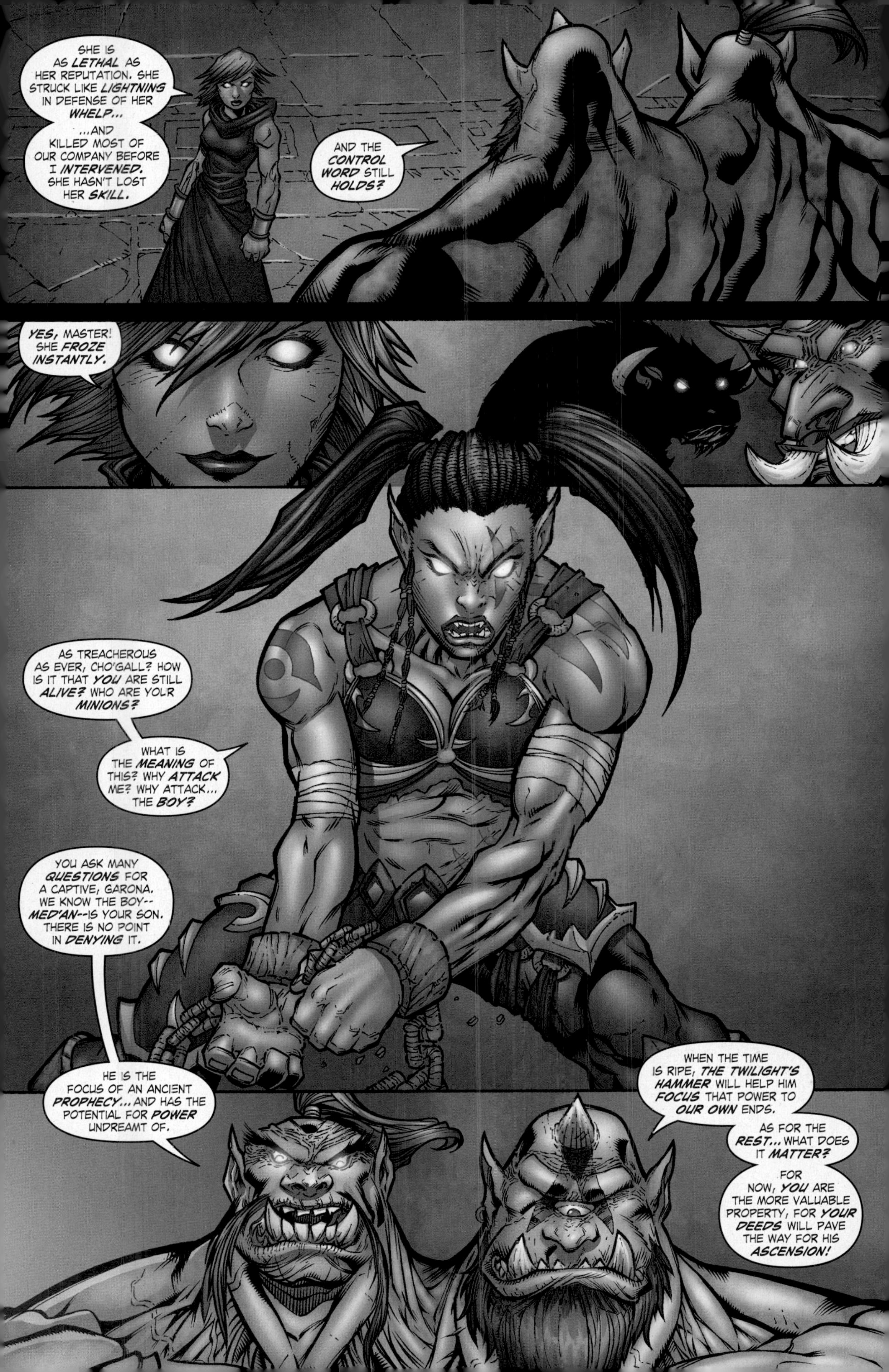

SHE IS AS LETHAL AS HER REPUTATION. SHE STRUCK LIKE LIGHTNING IN DEFENSE OF HER WHELP...
...AND KILLED MOST OF OUR COMPANY BEFORE I INTERVENED. SHE HASN'T LOST HER SKILL.
AND THE CONTROL WORD STILL HOLDS?
YES, MASTER! SHE FROZE INSTANTLY.
AS TREACHEROUS AS EVER, CHO'GALL? HOW IS IT THAT YOU ARE STILL ALIVE? WHO ARE YOUR MINIONS?
WHAT IS THE MEANING OF THIS? WHY ATTACK ME? WHY ATTACK... THE BOY?
YOU ASK MANY QUESTIONS FOR A CAPTIVE, GARONA. WE KNOW THE BOY-- MED'AN--IS YOUR SON. THERE IS NO POINT IN DENYING IT.
HE IS THE FOCUS OF AN ANCIENT PROPHECY... AND HAS THE POTENTIAL FOR POWER UNDREAMT OF.
WHEN THE TIME IS RIPE, THE TWILIGHT'S HAMMER WILL HELP HIM FOCUS THAT POWER TO OUR OWN ENDS.
AS FOR THE REST... WHAT DOES IT MATTER?
FOR NOW, YOU ARE THE MORE VALUABLE PROPERTY, FOR YOUR DEEDS WILL PAVE THE WAY FOR HIS ASCENSION!

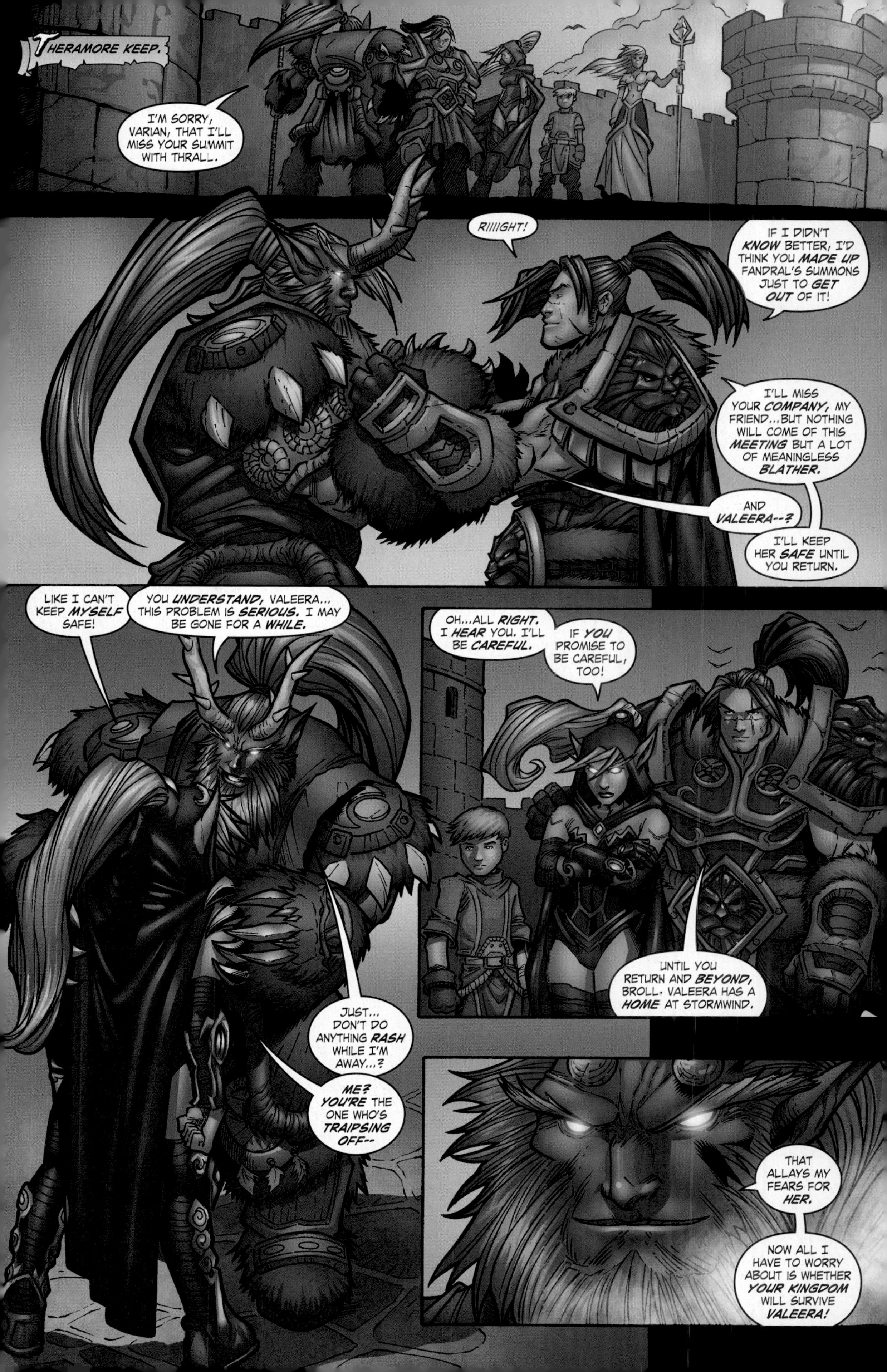
THERAMORE KEEP.
I'M SORRY, VARIAN, THAT I'LL MISS YOUR SUMMIT WITH THRALL.
RIIIIGHT!
IF I DIDN'T KNOW BETTER, I'D THINK YOU MADE UP FANDRAL'S SUMMONS JUST TO GET OUT OF IT!
I'LL MISS YOUR COMPANY, MY FRIEND...BUT NOTHING WILL COME OF THIS MEETING BUT A LOT OF MEANINGLESS BLATHER.
AND VALEERA--?
I'LL KEEP HER SAFE UNTIL YOU RETURN.
LIKE I CAN'T KEEP MYSELF SAFE!
YOU UNDERSTAND, VALEERA... THIS PROBLEM IS SERIOUS. I MAY BE GONE FOR A WHILE.
JUST... DON'T DO ANYTHING RASH WHILE I'M AWAY...?
ME? YOU'RE THE ONE WHO'S TRAIPSING OFF--
OH...ALL RIGHT. I HEAR YOU. I'LL BE CAREFUL.
IF YOU PROMISE TO BE CAREFUL, TOO!
UNTIL YOU RETURN AND BEYOND, BROLL. VALEERA HAS A HOME AT STORMWIND.
THAT ALLAYS MY FEARS FOR HER.
NOW ALL I HAVE TO WORRY ABOUT IS WHETHER YOUR KINGDOM WILL SURVIVE VALEERA!

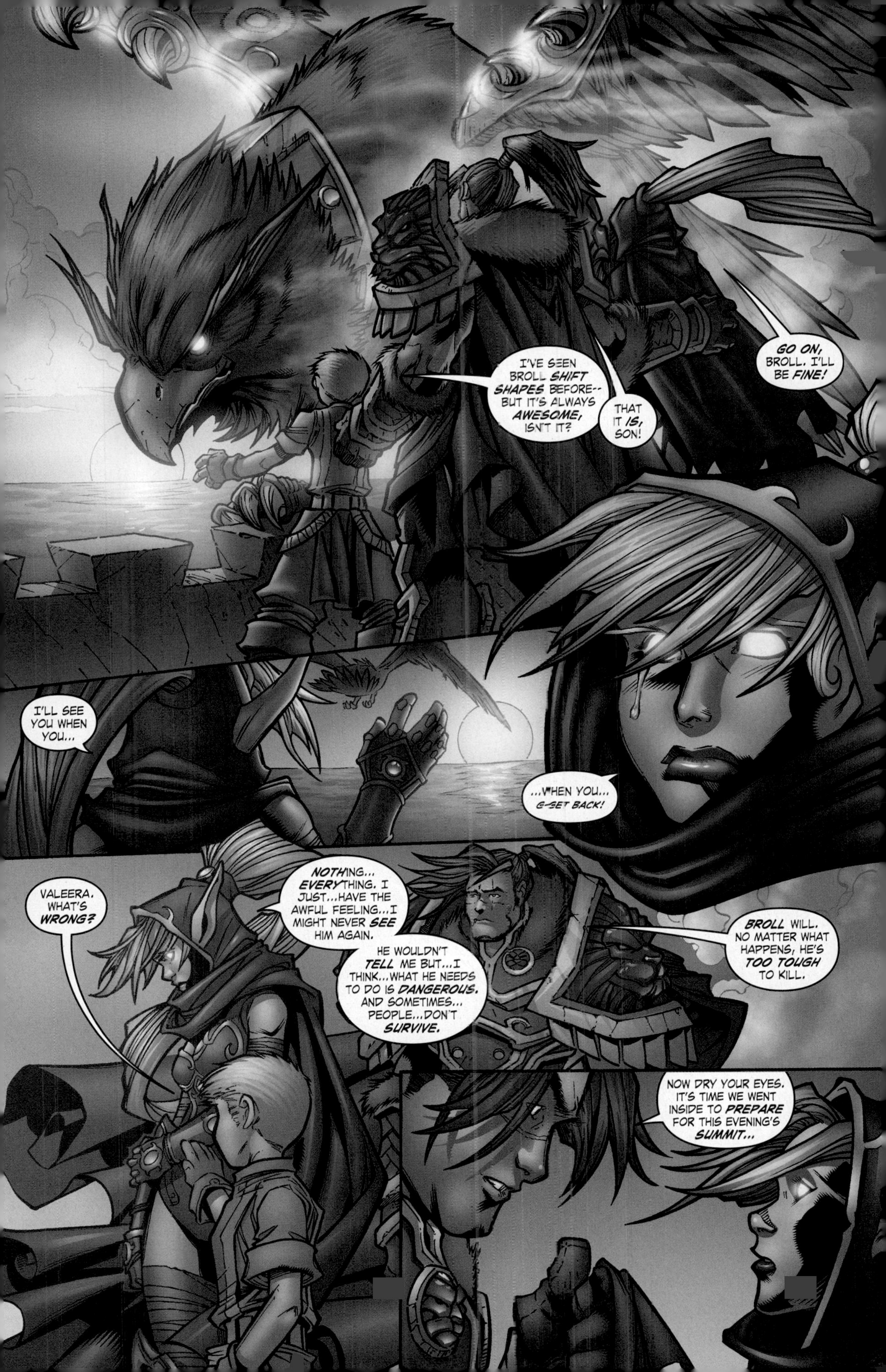
I'VE SEEN BROLL SHIFT SHAPES BEFORE-- BUT IT'S ALWAYS AWESOME, ISN'T IT?
THAT IT IS, SON!
GO ON, BROLL. I'LL BE FINE!
I'LL SEE YOU WHEN YOU...
...WHEN YOU... G-GET BACK!
VALEERA. WHAT'S WRONG?
NOTHING... EVERYTHING. I JUST...HAVE THE AWFUL FEELING...I MIGHT NEVER SEE HIM AGAIN.
HE WOULDN'T TELL ME BUT...I THINK...WHAT HE NEEDS TO DO IS DANGEROUS. AND SOMETIMES... PEOPLE...DON'T SURVIVE.
BROLL WILL. NO MATTER WHAT HAPPENS, HE'S TOO TOUGH TO KILL.
NOW DRY YOUR EYES. IT'S TIME WE WENT INSIDE TO PREPARE FOR THIS EVENING'S SUMMIT...

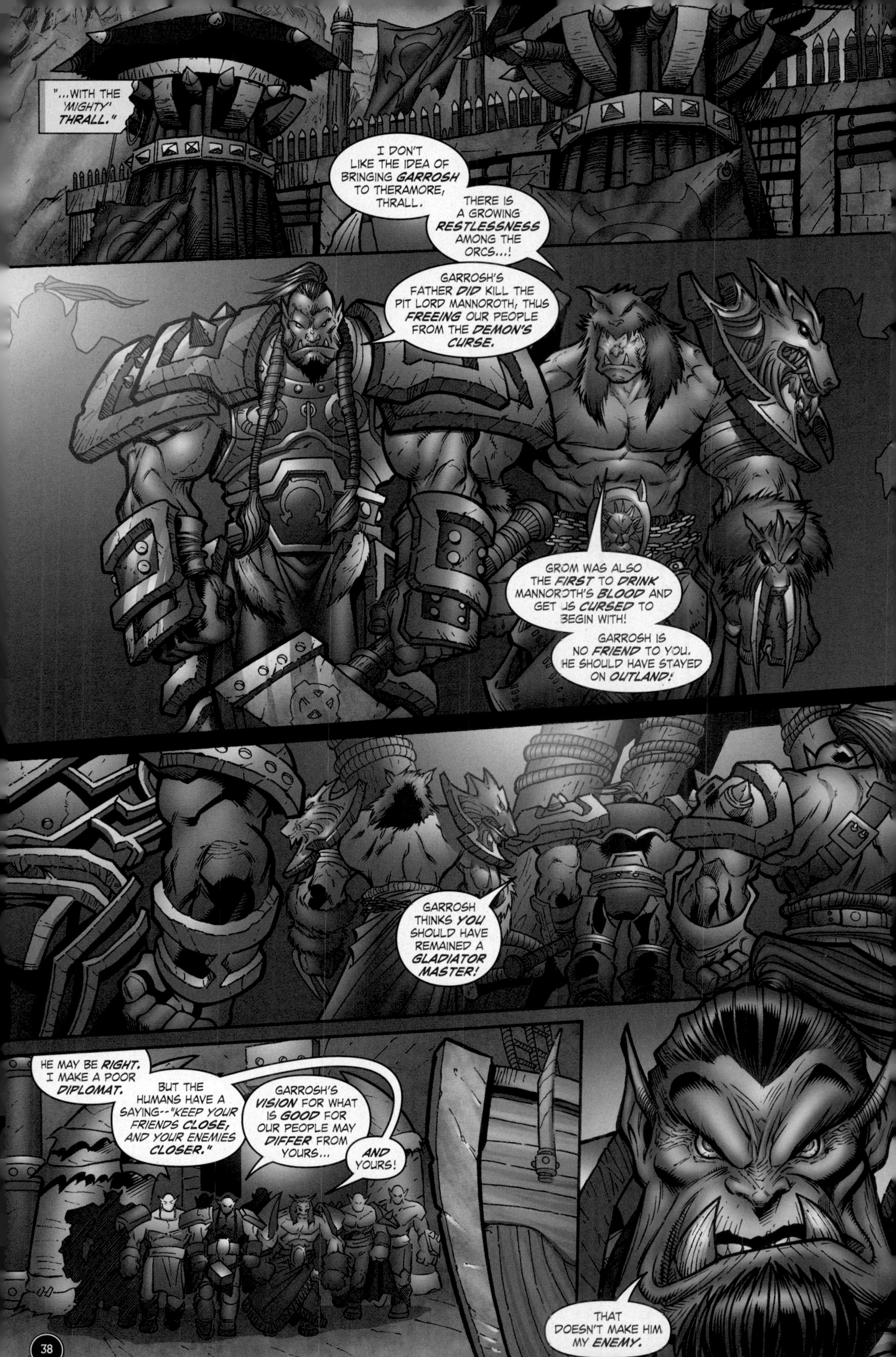
"...WITH THE 'MIGHTY' THRALL."
I DON'T LIKE THE IDEA OF BRINGING GARROSH TO THERAMORE, THRALL.
THERE IS A GROWING RESTLESSNESS AMONG THE ORCS...!
GARROSH'S FATHER DID KILL THE PIT LORD MANNOROTH, THUS FREEING OUR PEOPLE FROM THE DEMON'S CURSE.
GROM WAS ALSO THE FIRST TO DRINK MANNOROTH'S BLOOD AND GET US CURSED TO BEGIN WITH!
GARROSH IS NO FRIEND TO YOU. HE SHOULD HAVE STAYED ON OUTLAND!
GARROSH THINKS YOU SHOULD HAVE REMAINED A GLADIATOR MASTER!
HE MAY BE RIGHT. I MAKE A POOR DIPLOMAT.
BUT THE HUMANS HAVE A SAYING--"KEEP YOUR FRIENDS CLOSE, AND YOUR ENEMIES CLOSER."
GARROSH'S VISION FOR WHAT IS GOOD FOR OUR PEOPLE MAY DIFFER FROM YOURS...
AND YOURS!
THAT DOESN'T MAKE HIM MY ENEMY.

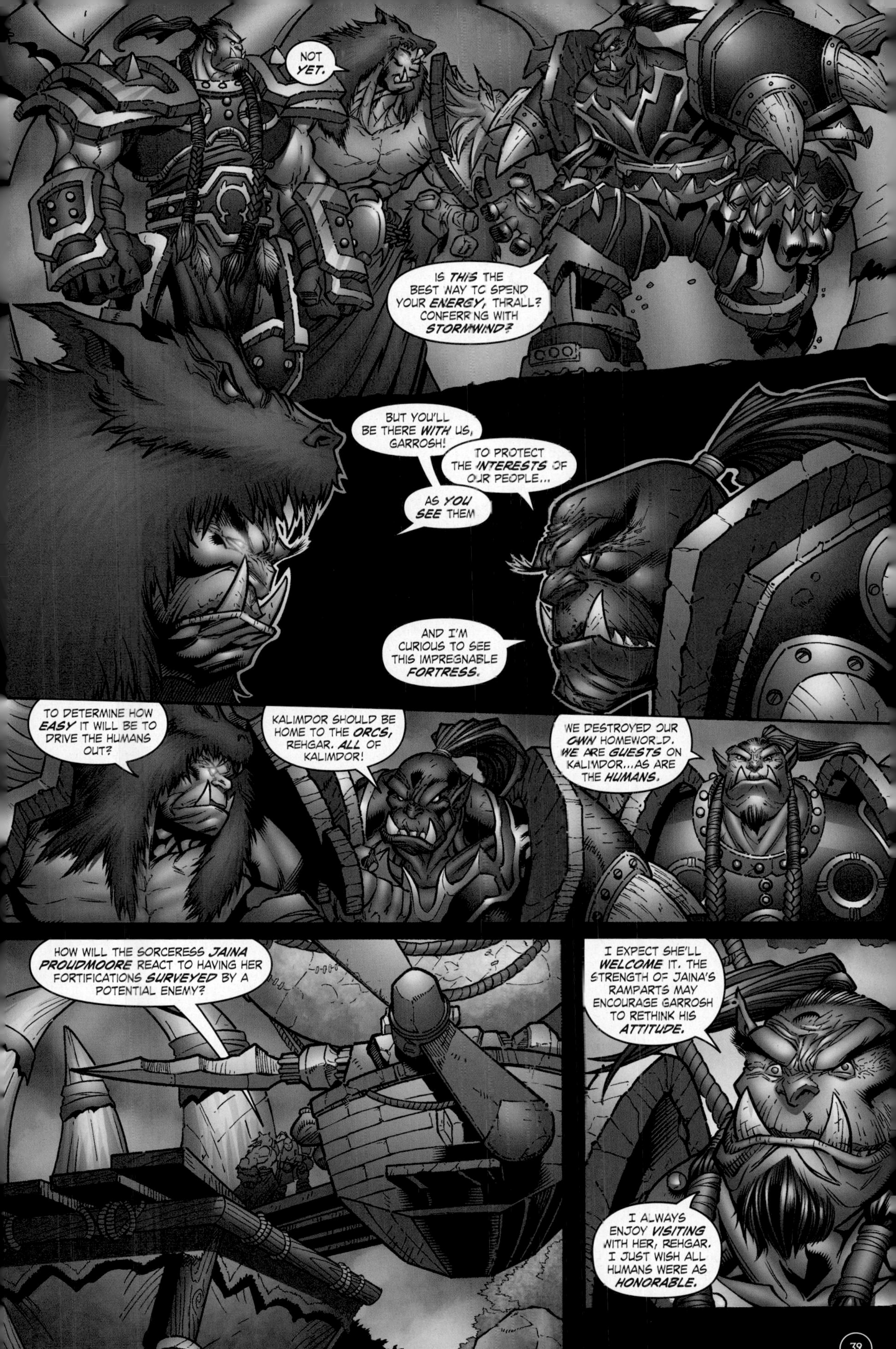
NOT YET.
IS THIS THE BEST WAY TO SPEND YOUR ENERGY, THRALL? CONFERRING WITH STORMWIND?
BUT YOU'LL BE THERE WITH US, GARROSH!
TO PROTECT THE INTERESTS OF OUR PEOPLE...
AS YOU SEE THEM
AND I'M CURIOUS TO SEE THIS IMPREGNABLE FORTRESS.
TO DETERMINE HOW EASY IT WILL BE TO DRIVE THE HUMANS OUT?
KALIMDOR SHOULD BE HOME TO THE ORCS, REHGAR. ALL OF KALIMDOR!
WE DESTROYED OUR OWN HOMEWORLD. WE ARE GUESTS ON KALIMDOR...AS ARE THE HUMANS.
HOW WILL THE SORCERESS JAINA PROUDMOORE REACT TO HAVING HER FORTIFICATIONS SURVEYED BY A POTENTIAL ENEMY?
I EXPECT SHE'LL WELCOME IT. THE STRENGTH OF JAINA'S RAMPARTS MAY ENCOURAGE GARROSH TO RETHINK HIS ATTITUDE.
I ALWAYS ENJOY VISITING WITH HER, REHGAR. I JUST WISH ALL HUMANS WERE AS HONORABLE.

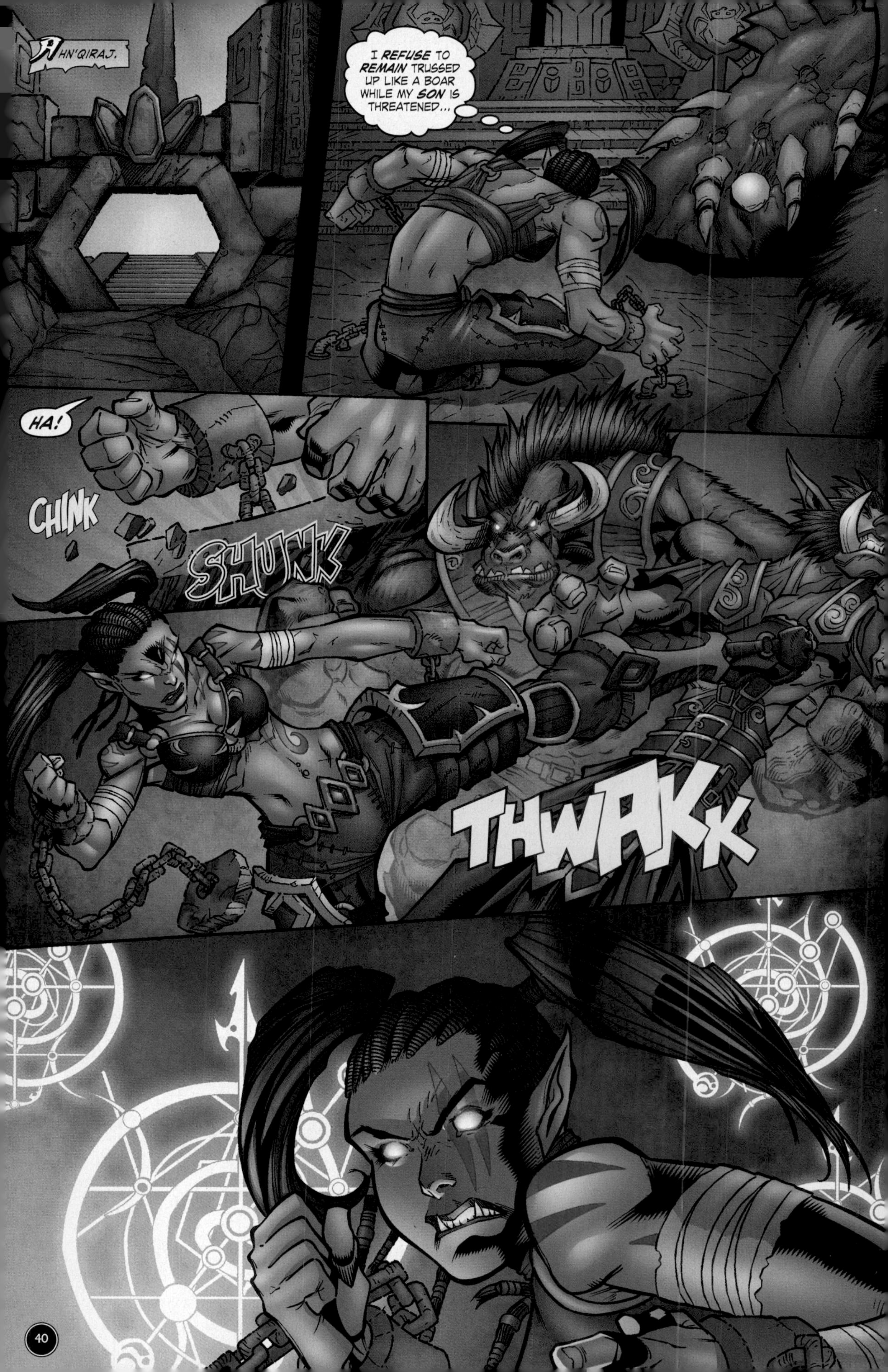
AHN'QIRAJ.
I REFUSE TO REMAIN TRUSSED UP LIKE A BOAR WHILE MY SON IS THREATENED...
HA!
CHINK
SHUNK
THWAKK

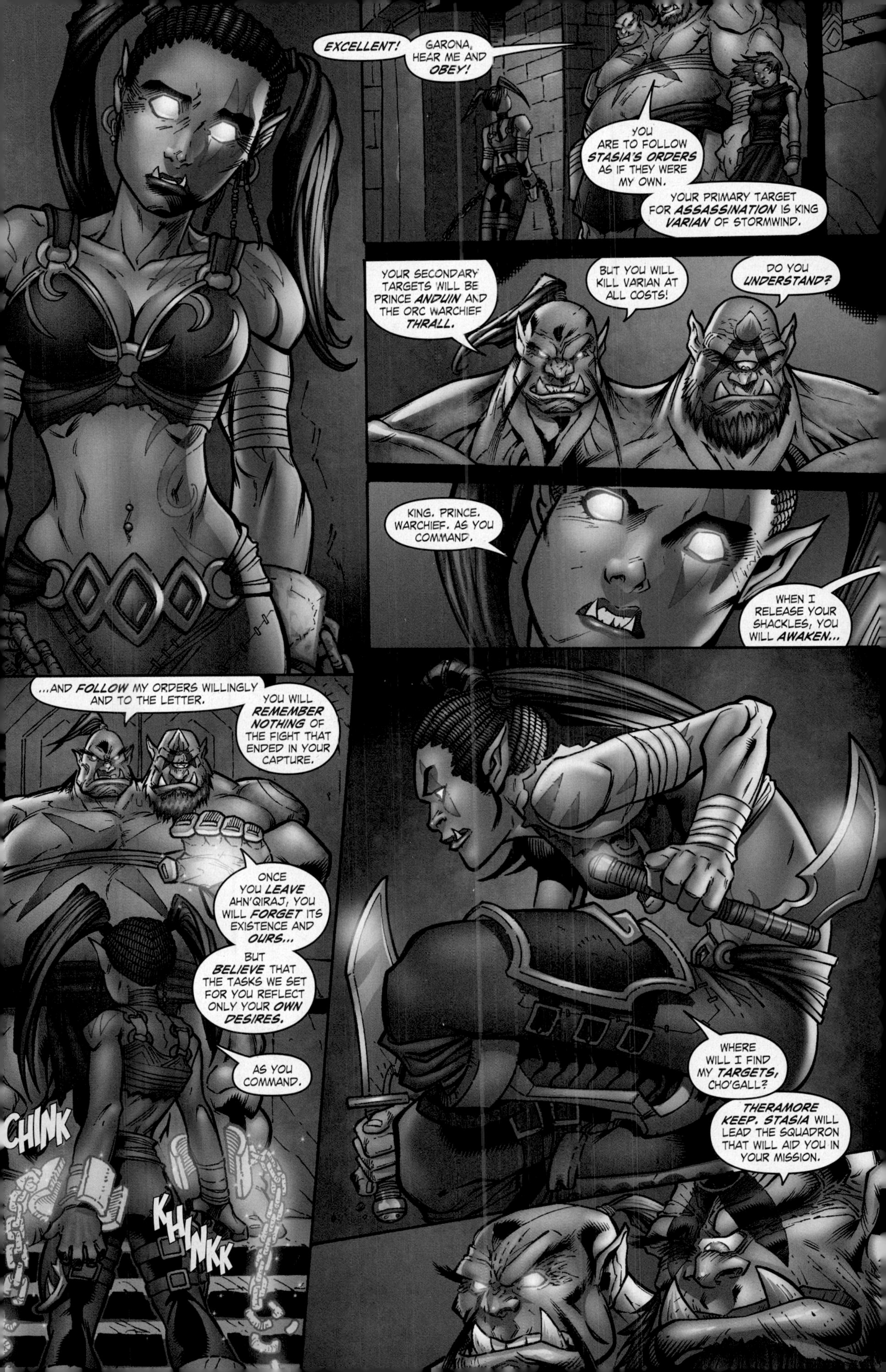

EXCELLENT!
GARONA, HEAR ME AND OBEY!
YOU ARE TO FOLLOW STASIA'S ORDERS AS IF THEY WERE MY OWN.
YOUR PRIMARY TARGET FOR ASSASSINATION IS KING VARIAN OF STORMWIND.
YOUR SECONDARY TARGETS WILL BE PRINCE ANDUIN AND THE ORC WARCHIEF THRALL.
BUT YOU WILL KILL VARIAN AT ALL COSTS!
DO YOU UNDERSTAND?
KING. PRINCE. WARCHIEF. AS YOU COMMAND.
WHEN I RELEASE YOUR SHACKLES, YOU WILL AWAKEN...
...AND FOLLOW MY ORDERS WILLINGLY AND TO THE LETTER.
YOU WILL REMEMBER NOTHING OF THE FIGHT THAT ENDED IN YOUR CAPTURE.
ONCE YOU LEAVE AHN'QIRAJ, YOU WILL FORGET ITS EXISTENCE AND OURS...
BUT BELIEVE THAT THE TASKS WE SET FOR YOU REFLECT ONLY YOUR OWN DESIRES.
AS YOU COMMAND.
CHINK
KHINKK
WHERE WILL I FIND MY TARGETS, CHO'GALL?
THERAMORE KEEP. STASIA WILL LEAD THE SQUADRON THAT WILL AID YOU IN YOUR MISSION.

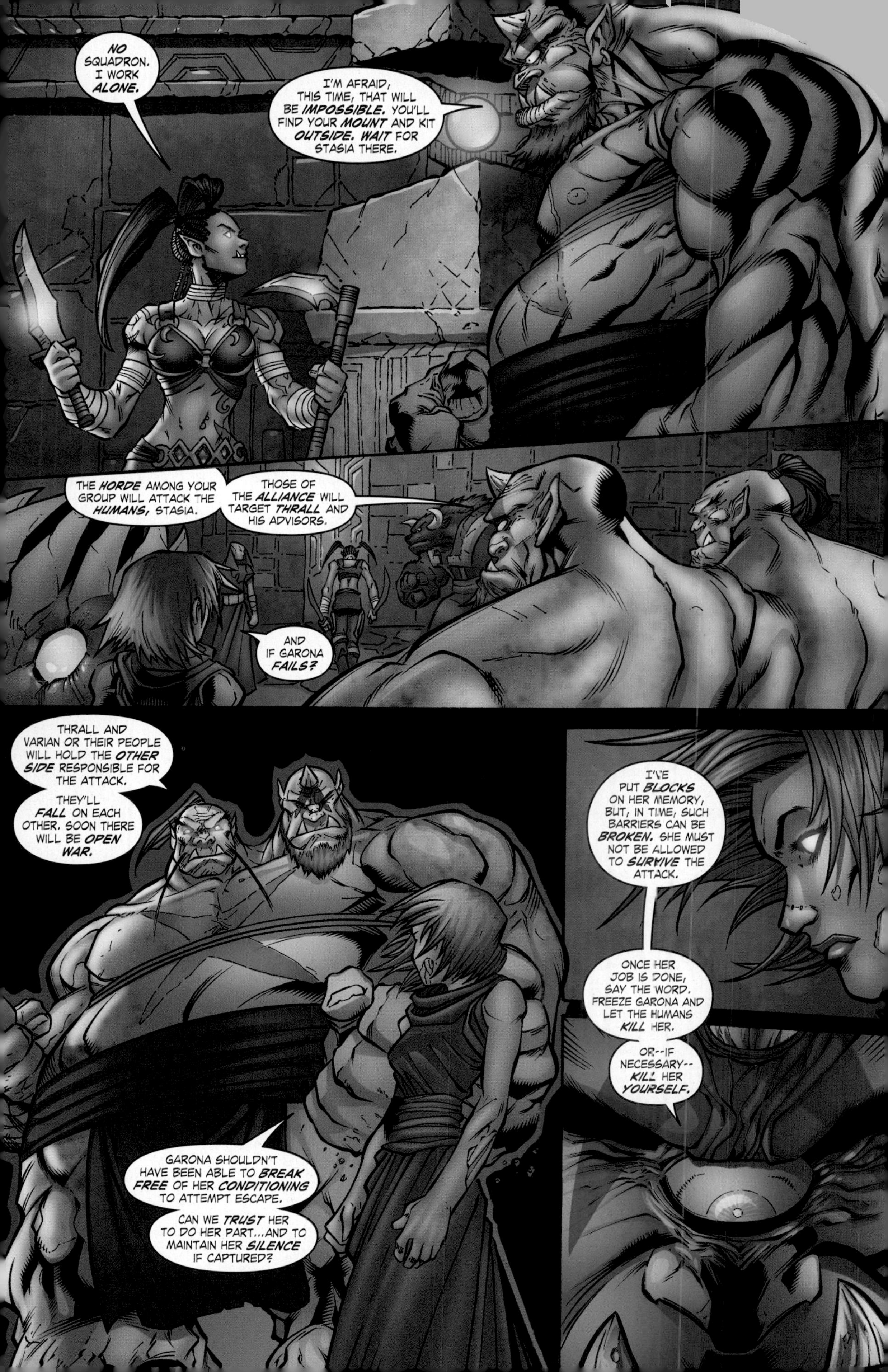
NO SQUADRON. I WORK ALONE.
I'M AFRAID, THIS TIME, THAT WILL BE IMPOSSIBLE. YOU'LL FIND YOUR MOUNT AND KIT OUTSIDE. WAIT FOR STASIA THERE.
THE HORDE AMONG YOUR GROUP WILL ATTACK THE HUMANS, STASIA.
THOSE OF THE ALLIANCE WILL TARGET THRALL AND HIS ADVISORS.
AND IF GARONA FAILS?
THRALL AND VARIAN OR THEIR PEOPLE WILL HOLD THE OTHER SIDE RESPONSIBLE FOR THE ATTACK.
THEY'LL FALL ON EACH OTHER. SOON THERE WILL BE OPEN WAR.
GARONA SHOULDN'T HAVE BEEN ABLE TO BREAK FREE OF HER CONDITIONING TO ATTEMPT ESCAPE.
CAN WE TRUST HER TO DO HER PART...AND TO MAINTAIN HER SILENCE IF CAPTURED?
I'VE PUT BLOCKS ON HER MEMORY, BUT, IN TIME, SUCH BARRIERS CAN BE BROKEN. SHE MUST NOT BE ALLOWED TO SURVIVE THE ATTACK.
ONCE HER JOB IS DONE, SAY THE WORD. FREEZE GARONA AND LET THE HUMANS KILL HER.
OR--IF NECESSARY--KILL HER YOURSELF.

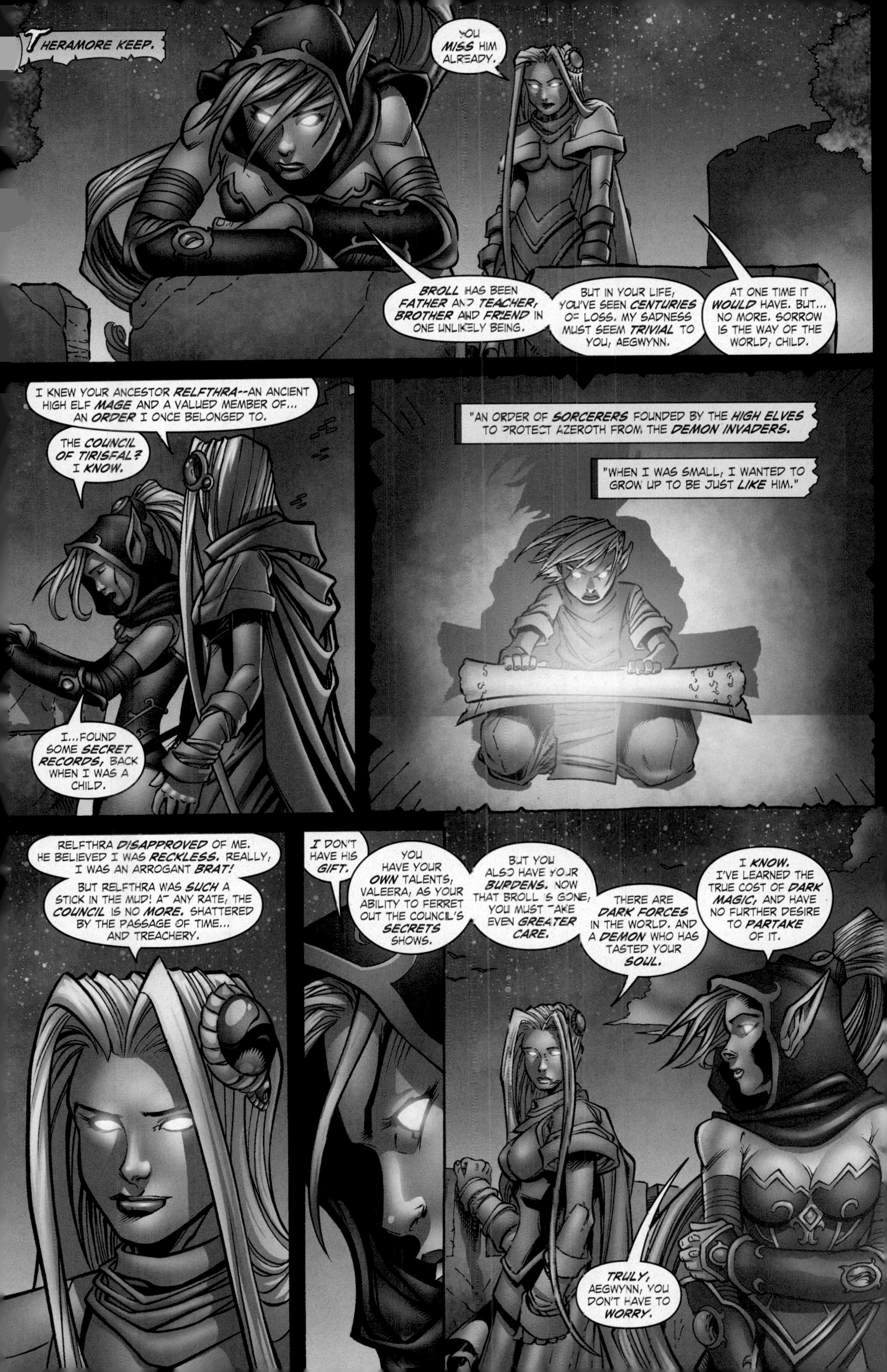
THERAMORE KEEP.
YOU MISS HIM ALREADY.
BROLL HAS BEEN FATHER AND TEACHER, BROTHER AND FRIEND IN ONE UNLIKELY BEING.
BUT IN YOUR LIFE, YOU'VE SEEN CENTURIES OF LOSS. MY SADNESS MUST SEEM TRIVIAL TO YOU, AEGWYNN.
AT ONE TIME IT WOULD HAVE. BUT... NO MORE. SORROW IS THE WAY OF THE WORLD, CHILD.
I KNEW YOUR ANCESTOR RELFTHRA--AN ANCIENT HIGH ELF MAGE AND A VALUED MEMBER OF... AN ORDER I ONCE BELONGED TO.
THE COUNCIL OF TIRISFAL? I KNOW.
I...FOUND SOME SECRET RECORDS, BACK WHEN I WAS A CHILD.
"AN ORDER OF SORCERERS FOUNDED BY THE HIGH ELVES TO PROTECT AZEROTH FROM THE DEMON INVADERS.
"WHEN I WAS SMALL, I WANTED TO GROW UP TO BE JUST LIKE HIM."
RELFTHRA DISAPPROVED OF ME. HE BELIEVED I WAS RECKLESS. REALLY, I WAS AN ARROGANT BRAT!
BUT RELFTHRA WAS SUCH A STICK IN THE MUD! AT ANY RATE, THE COUNCIL IS NO MORE. SHATTERED BY THE PASSAGE OF TIME... AND TREACHERY.
I DON'T HAVE HIS GIFT.
YOU HAVE YOUR OWN TALENTS, VALEERA, AS YOUR ABILITY TO FERRET OUT THE COUNCIL'S SECRETS SHOWS.
BUT YOU ALSO HAVE YOUR BURDENS. NOW THAT BROLL IS GONE, YOU MUST TAKE EVEN GREATER CARE.
THERE ARE DARK FORCES IN THE WORLD. AND A DEMON WHO HAS TASTED YOUR SOUL.
I KNOW. I'VE LEARNED THE TRUE COST OF DARK MAGIC, AND HAVE NO FURTHER DESIRE TO PARTAKE OF IT.
TRULY, AEGWYNN, YOU DON'T HAVE TO WORRY.

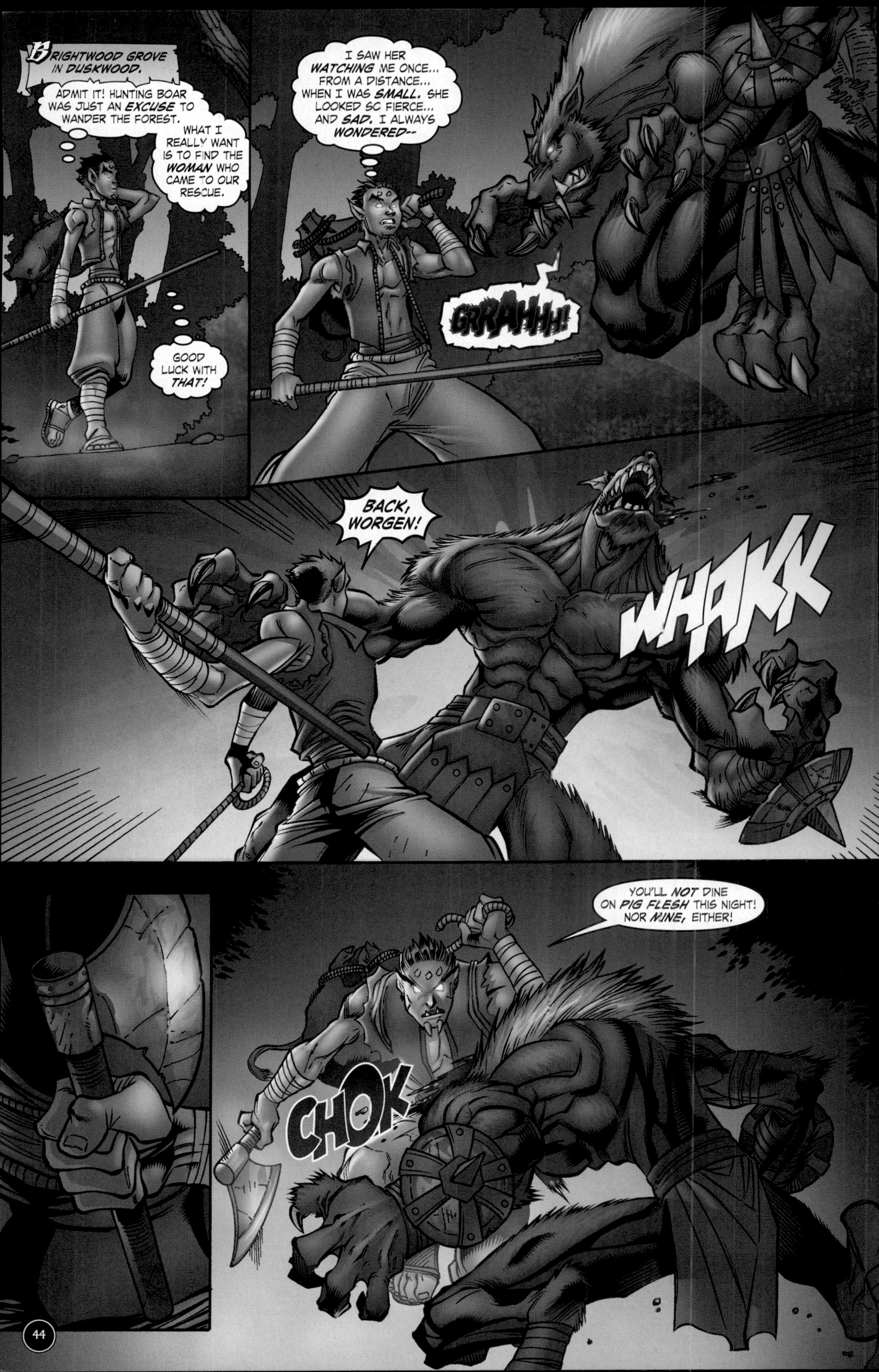
BRIGHTWOOD GROVE IN DUSKWOOD.
ADMIT IT! HUNTING BOAR WAS JUST AN EXCUSE TO WANDER THE FOREST.
WHAT I REALLY WANT IS TO FIND THE WOMAN WHO CAME TO OUR RESCUE.
GOOD LUCK WITH THAT!
I SAW HER WATCHING ME ONCE... FROM A DISTANCE... WHEN I WAS SMALL. SHE LOOKED SO FIERCE... AND SAD. I ALWAYS WONDERED--
GRRAHHH!
BACK, WORGEN!
WHAKK
YOU'LL NOT DINE ON PIG FLESH THIS NIGHT! NOR MINE, EITHER!
CHOK

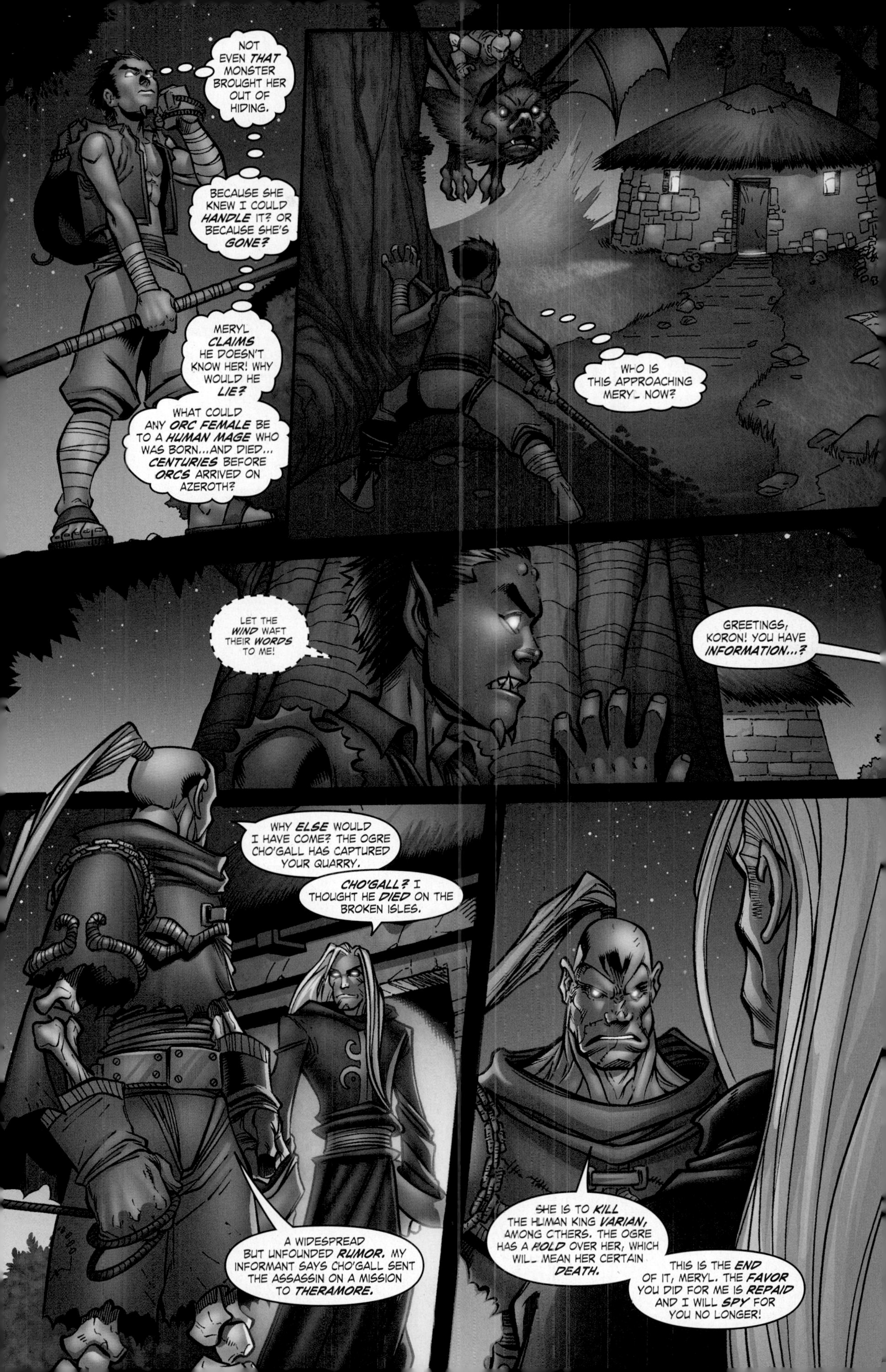
NOT EVEN THAT MONSTER BROUGHT HER OUT OF HIDING.
BECAUSE SHE KNEW I COULD HANDLE IT? OR BECAUSE SHE'S GONE?
MERYL CLAIMS HE DOESN'T KNOW HER! WHY WOULD HE LIE?
WHAT COULD ANY ORC FEMALE BE TO A HUMAN MAGE WHO WAS BORN...AND DIED... CENTURIES BEFORE ORCS ARRIVED ON AZEROTH?
WHO IS THIS APPROACHING MERYL NOW?
LET THE WIND WAFT THEIR WORDS TO ME!
GREETINGS, KORON! YOU HAVE INFORMATION...?
WHY ELSE WOULD I HAVE COME? THE OGRE CHO'GALL HAS CAPTURED YOUR QUARRY.
CHO'GALL? I THOUGHT HE DIED ON THE BROKEN ISLES.
A WIDESPREAD BUT UNFOUNDED RUMOR. MY INFORMANT SAYS CHO'GALL SENT THE ASSASSIN ON A MISSION TO THERAMORE.
SHE IS TO KILL THE HUMAN KING VARIAN, AMONG OTHERS. THE OGRE HAS A HOLD OVER HER, WHICH WILL MEAN HER CERTAIN DEATH.
THIS IS THE END OF IT, MERYL. THE FAVOR YOU DID FOR ME IS REPAID AND I WILL SPY FOR YOU NO LONGER!

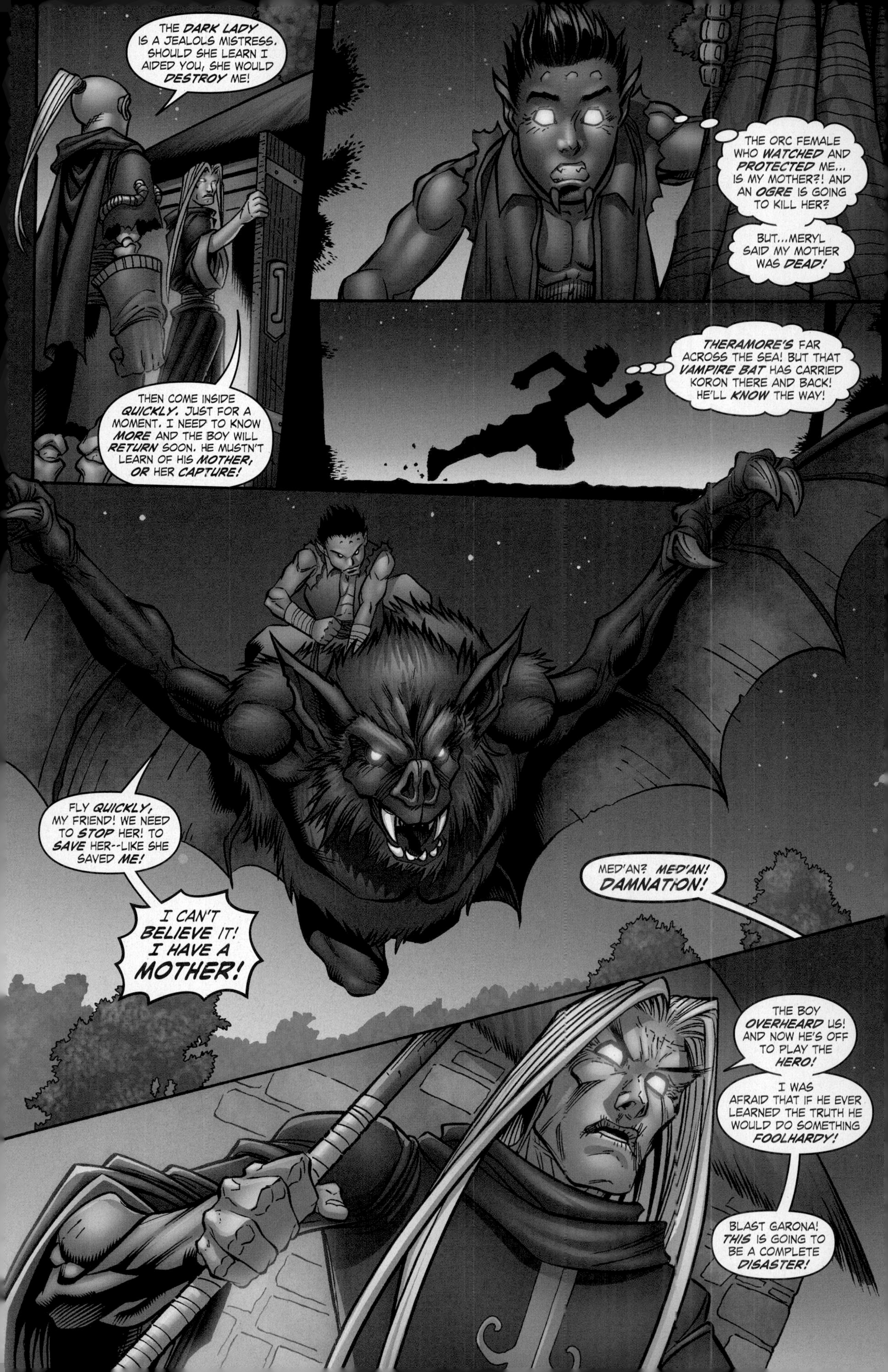
THE DARK LADY IS A JEALOLS MISTRESS. SHOULD SHE LEARN I AIDED YOU, SHE WOULD DESTROY ME!
THEN COME INSIDE QUICKLY. JUST FOR A MOMENT. I NEED TO KNOW MORE AND THE BOY WILL RETURN SOON. HE MUSTN'T LEARN OF HIS MOTHER, OR HER CAPTURE!
THE ORC FEMALE WHO WATCHED AND PROTECTED ME... IS MY MOTHER?! AND AN OGRE IS GOING TO KILL HER?
BUT...MERYL SAID MY MOTHER WAS DEAD!
THERAMORE'S FAR ACROSS THE SEA! BUT THAT VAMPIRE BAT HAS CARRIED KORON THERE AND BACK! HE'LL KNOW THE WAY!
FLY QUICKLY, MY FRIEND! WE NEED TO STOP HER! TO SAVE HER--LIKE SHE SAVED ME!
I CAN'T BELIEVE IT! I HAVE A MOTHER!
MED'AN? MED'AN! DAMNATION!
THE BOY OVERHEARD US! AND NOW HE'S OFF TO PLAY THE HERO!
I WAS AFRAID THAT IF HE EVER LEARNED THE TRUTH HE WOULD DO SOMETHING FOOLHARDY!
BLAST GARONA! THIS IS GOING TO BE A COMPLETE DISASTER!

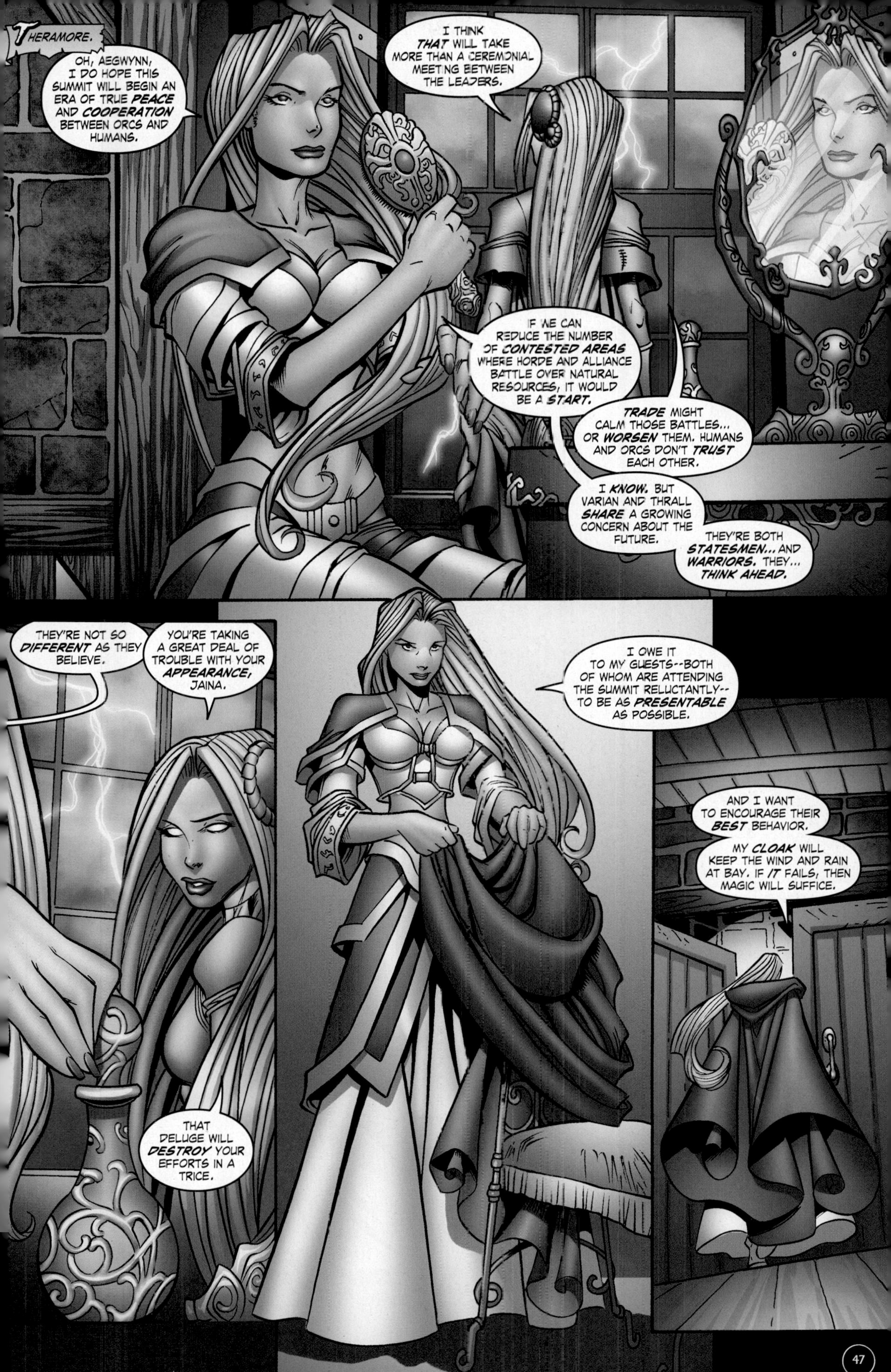
THERAMORE.
OH, AEGWYNN, I DO HOPE THIS SUMMIT WILL BEGIN AN ERA OF TRUE PEACE AND COOPERATION BETWEEN ORCS AND HUMANS.
I THINK THAT WILL TAKE MORE THAN A CEREMONIAL MEETING BETWEEN THE LEADERS.
IF WE CAN REDUCE THE NUMBER OF CONTESTED AREAS WHERE HORDE AND ALLIANCE BATTLE OVER NATURAL RESOURCES, IT WOULD BE A START.
TRADE MIGHT CALM THOSE BATTLES... OR WORSEN THEM. HUMANS AND ORCS DON'T TRUST EACH OTHER.
I KNOW. BUT VARIAN AND THRALL SHARE A GROWING CONCERN ABOUT THE FUTURE.
THEY'RE BOTH STATESMEN... AND WARRIORS. THEY... THINK AHEAD.
THEY'RE NOT SO DIFFERENT AS THEY BELIEVE.
YOU'RE TAKING A GREAT DEAL OF TROUBLE WITH YOUR APPEARANCE, JAINA.
THAT DELUGE WILL DESTROY YOUR EFFORTS IN A TRICE.
I OWE IT TO MY GUESTS--BOTH OF WHOM ARE ATTENDING THE SUMMIT RELUCTANTLY--TO BE AS PRESENTABLE AS POSSIBLE.
AND I WANT TO ENCOURAGE THEIR BEST BEHAVIOR.
MY CLOAK WILL KEEP THE WIND AND RAIN AT BAY. IF IT FAILS, THEN MAGIC WILL SUFFICE.

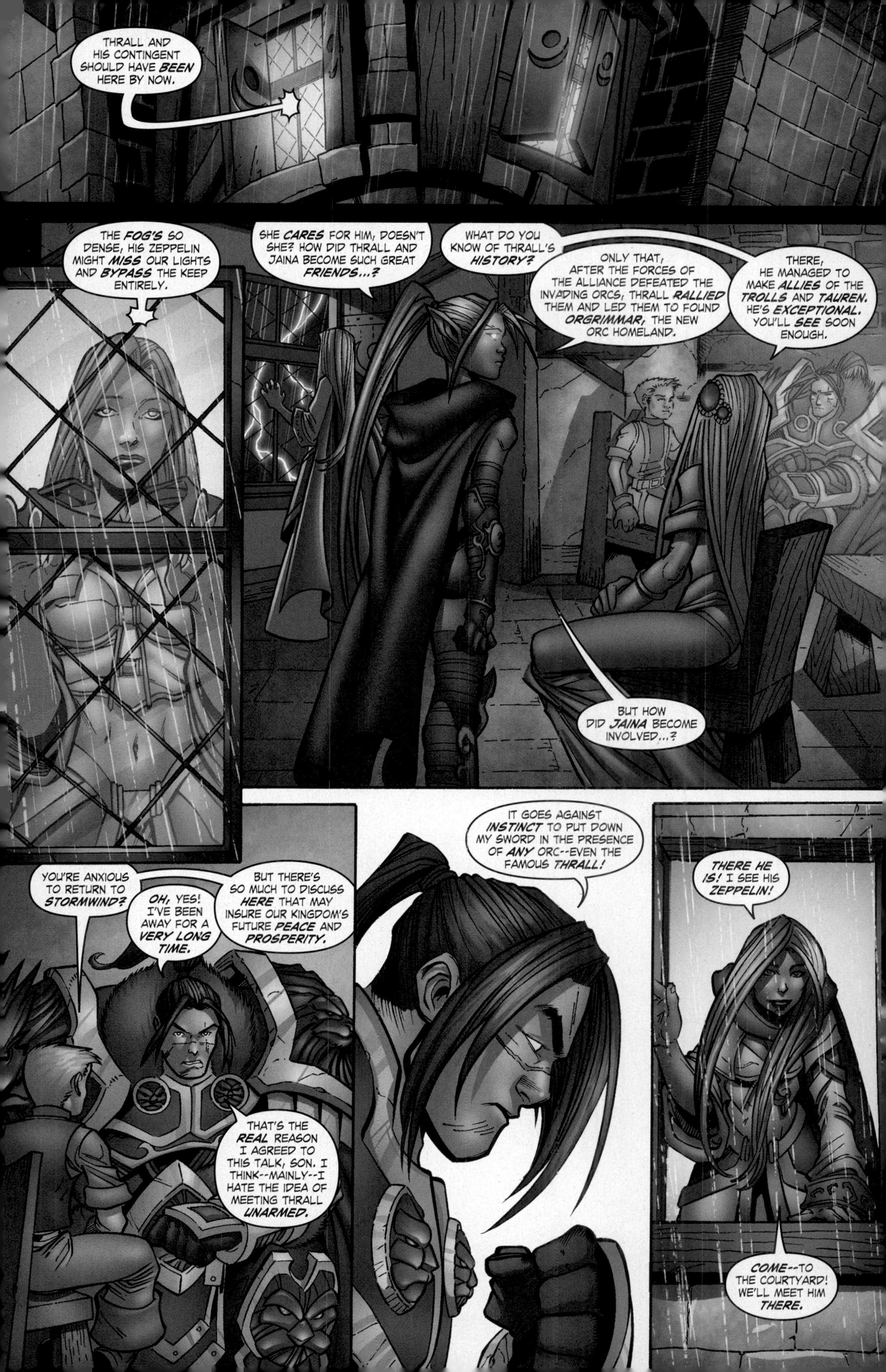
THRALL AND HIS CONTINGENT SHOULD HAVE BEEN HERE BY NOW.
THE FOG'S SO DENSE, HIS ZEPPELIN MIGHT MISS OUR LIGHTS AND BYPASS THE KEEP ENTIRELY.
SHE CARES FOR HIM, DOESN'T SHE? HOW DID THRALL AND JAINA BECOME SUCH GREAT FRIENDS...?
WHAT DO YOU KNOW OF THRALL'S HISTORY?
ONLY THAT, AFTER THE FORCES OF THE ALLIANCE DEFEATED THE INVADING ORCS, THRALL RALLIED THEM AND LED THEM TO FOUND ORGRIMMAR, THE NEW ORC HOMELAND.
THERE, HE MANAGED TO MAKE ALLIES OF THE TROLLS AND TAUREN. HE'S EXCEPTIONAL. YOU'LL SEE SOON ENOUGH.
BUT HOW DID JAINA BECOME INVOLVED...?
YOU'RE ANXIOUS TO RETURN TO STORMWIND?
OH, YES! I'VE BEEN AWAY FOR A VERY LONG TIME.
BUT THERE'S SO MUCH TO DISCUSS HERE THAT MAY INSURE OUR KINGDOM'S FUTURE PEACE AND PROSPERITY.
THAT'S THE REAL REASON I AGREED TO THIS TALK, SON. I THINK--MAINLY--I HATE THE IDEA OF MEETING THRALL UNARMED.
IT GOES AGAINST INSTINCT TO PUT DOWN MY SWORD IN THE PRESENCE OF ANY ORC--EVEN THE FAMOUS THRALL!
THERE HE IS! I SEE HIS ZEPPELIN!
COME--TO THE COURTYARD! WE'LL MEET HIM THERE.

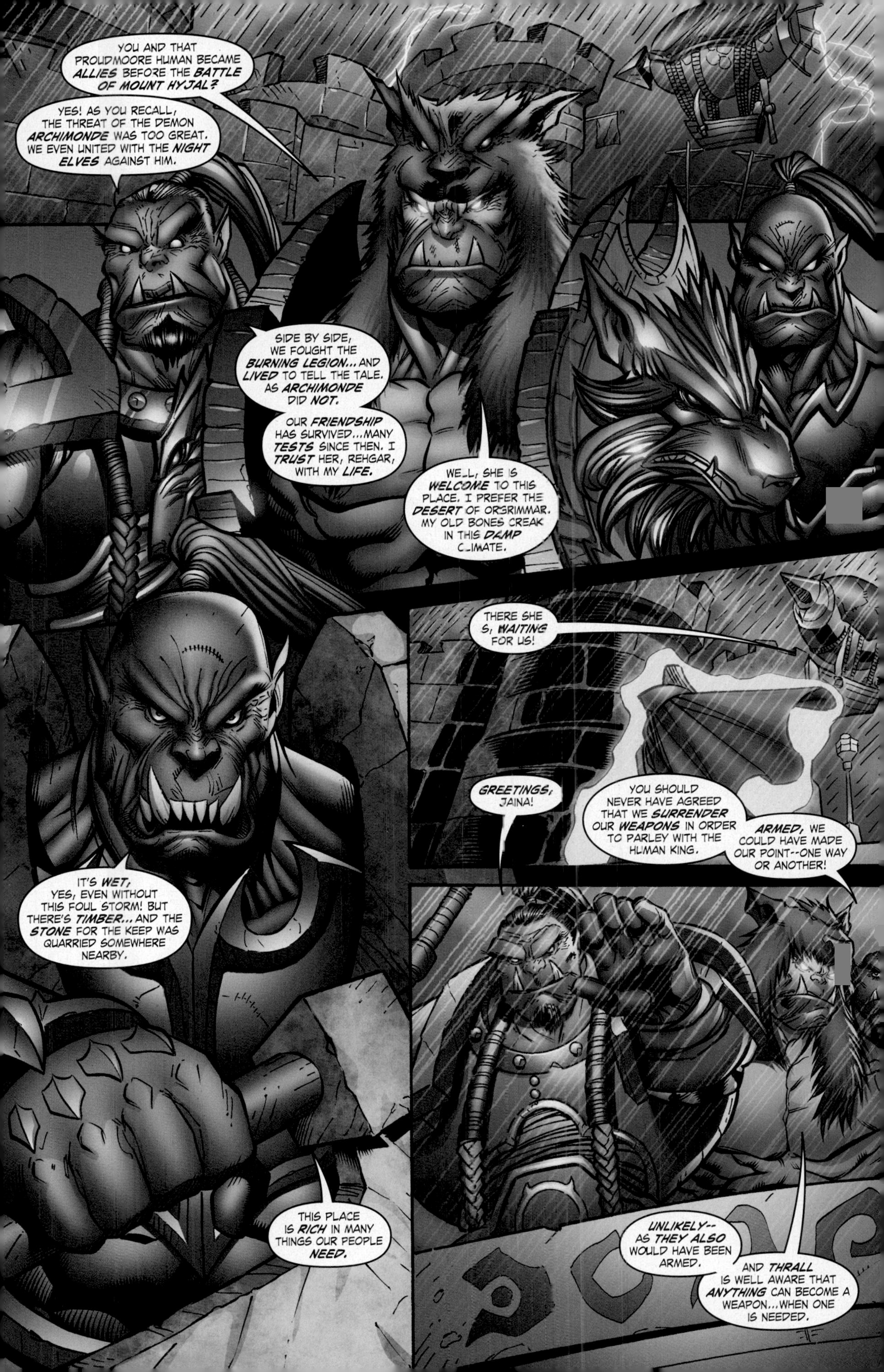
YOU AND THAT PROUDMOORE HUMAN BECAME ALLIES BEFORE THE BATTLE OF MOUNT HYJAL?
YES! AS YOU RECALL, THE THREAT OF THE DEMON ARCHIMONDE WAS TOO GREAT. WE EVEN UNITED WITH THE NIGHT ELVES AGAINST HIM.
SIDE BY SIDE, WE FOUGHT THE BURNING LEGION... AND LIVED TO TELL THE TALE. AS ARCHIMONDE DID NOT.
OUR FRIENDSHIP HAS SURVIVED... MANY TESTS SINCE THEN. I TRUST HER, REHGAR, WITH MY LIFE.
WELL, SHE IS WELCOME TO THIS PLACE. I PREFER THE DESERT OF ORGRIMMAR. MY OLD BONES CREAK IN THIS DAMP CLIMATE.
IT'S WET, YES, EVEN WITHOUT THIS FOUL STORM! BUT THERE'S TIMBER... AND THE STONE FOR THE KEEP WAS QUARRIED SOMEWHERE NEARBY.
THIS PLACE IS RICH IN MANY THINGS OUR PEOPLE NEED.
THERE SHE IS, WAITING FOR US!
GREETINGS, JAINA!
YOU SHOULD NEVER HAVE AGREED THAT WE SURRENDER OUR WEAPONS IN ORDER TO PARLEY WITH THE HUMAN KING.
ARMED, WE COULD HAVE MADE OUR POINT--ONE WAY OR ANOTHER!
UNLIKELY-- AS THEY ALSO WOULD HAVE BEEN ARMED.
AND THRALL IS WELL AWARE THAT ANYTHING CAN BECOME A WEAPON... WHEN ONE IS NEEDED.

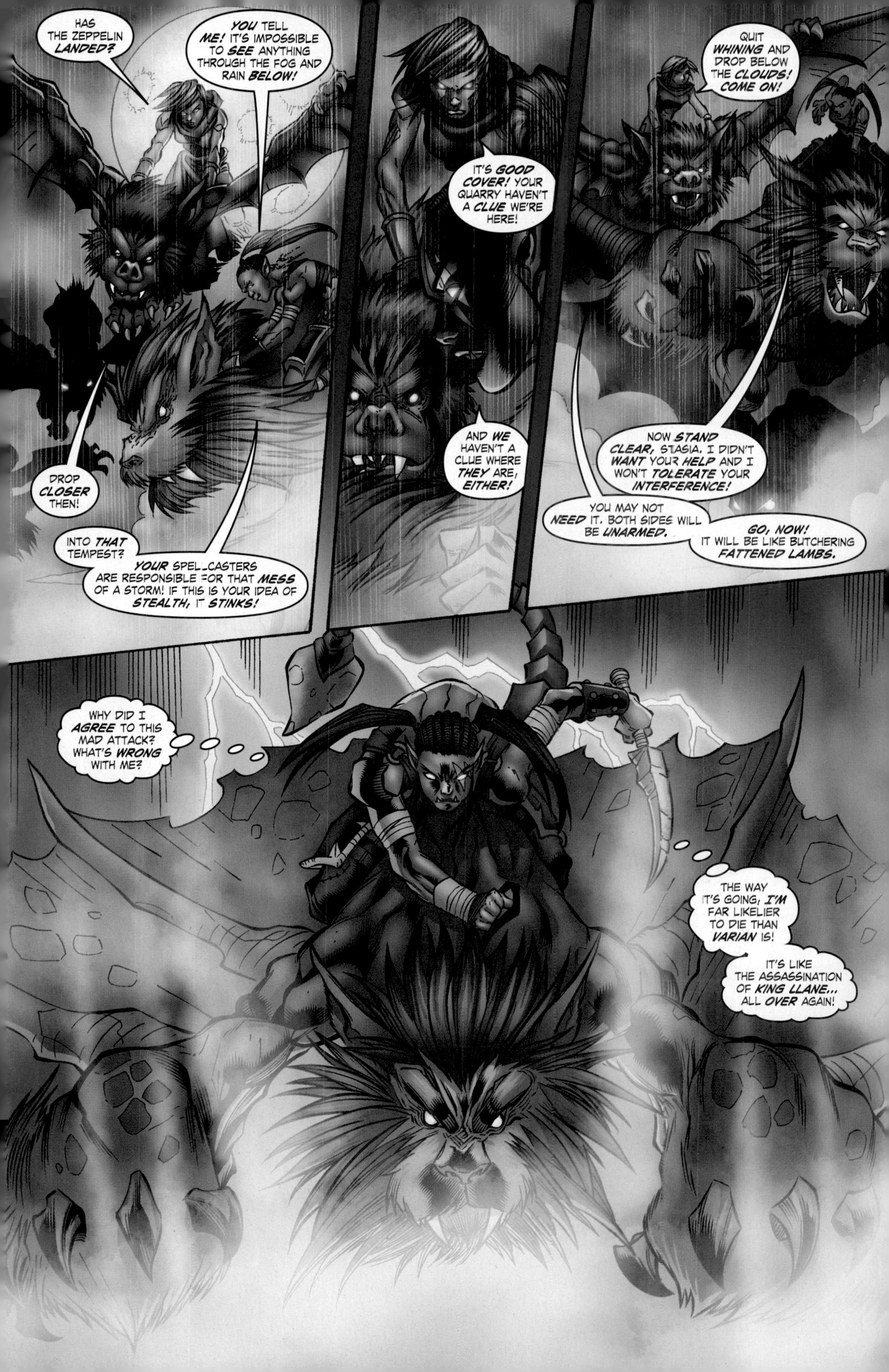
HAS THE ZEPPELIN LANDED?
YOU TELL ME! IT'S IMPOSSIBLE TO SEE ANYTHING THROUGH THE FOG AND RAIN BELOW!
DROP CLOSER THEN!
INTO THAT TEMPEST?
YOUR SPELLCASTERS ARE RESPONSIBLE FOR THAT MESS OF A STORM! IF THIS IS YOUR IDEA OF STEALTH, IT STINKS!
IT'S GOOD COVER! YOUR QUARRY HAVEN'T A CLUE WE'RE HERE!
AND WE HAVEN'T A CLUE WHERE THEY ARE, EITHER!
QUIT WHINING AND DROP BELOW THE CLOUDS! COME ON!
NOW STAND CLEAR, STASIA. I DIDN'T WANT YOUR HELP AND I WON'T TOLERATE YOUR INTERFERENCE!
YOU MAY NOT NEED IT. BOTH SIDES WILL BE UNARMED.
GO, NOW! IT WILL BE LIKE BUTCHERING FATTENED LAMBS.
WHY DID I AGREE TO THIS MAD ATTACK? WHAT'S WRONG WITH ME?
THE WAY IT'S GOING, I'M FAR LIKELIER TO DIE THAN VARIAN IS!
IT'S LIKE THE ASSASSINATION OF KING LLANE... ALL OVER AGAIN!

CHAPTER 3

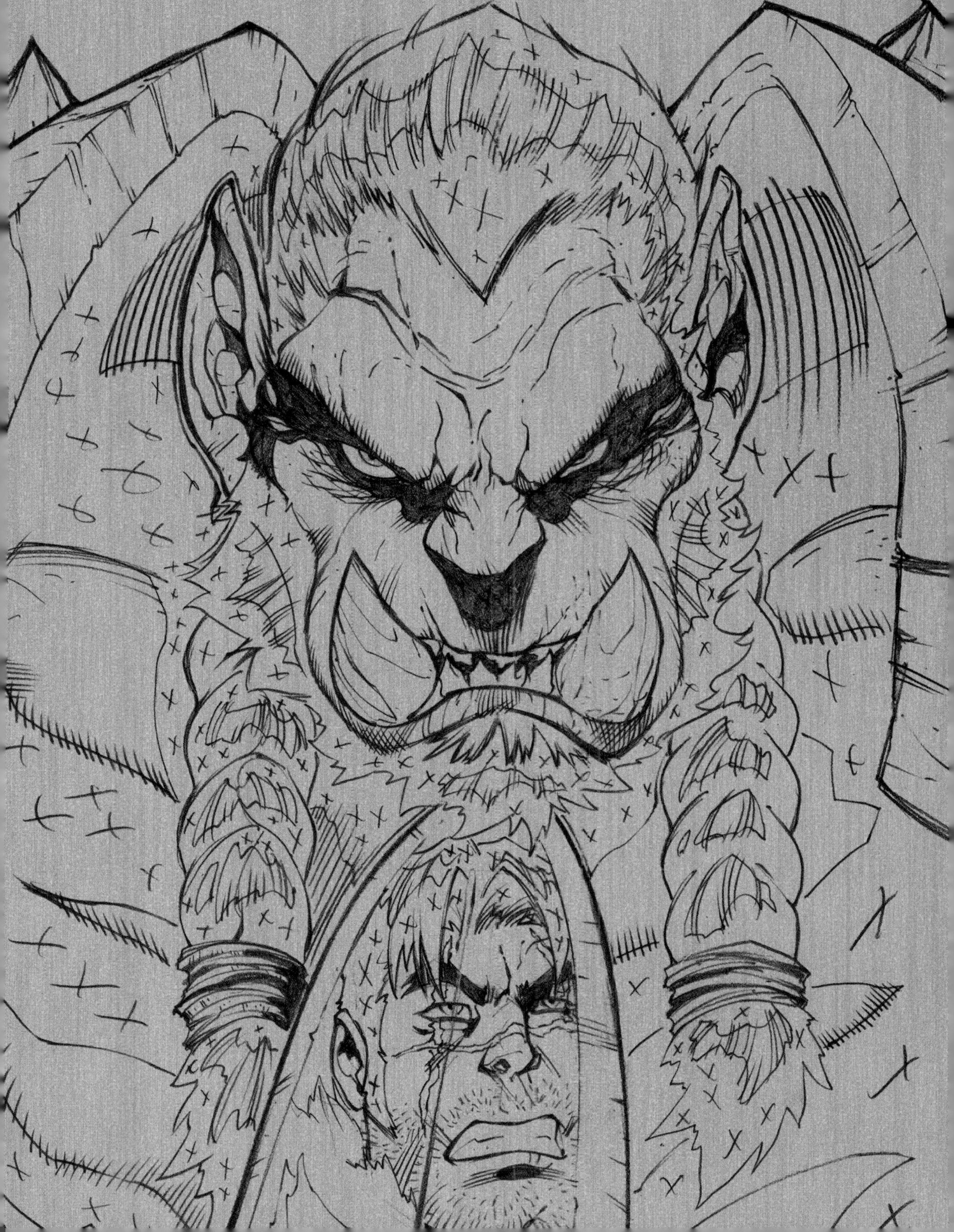

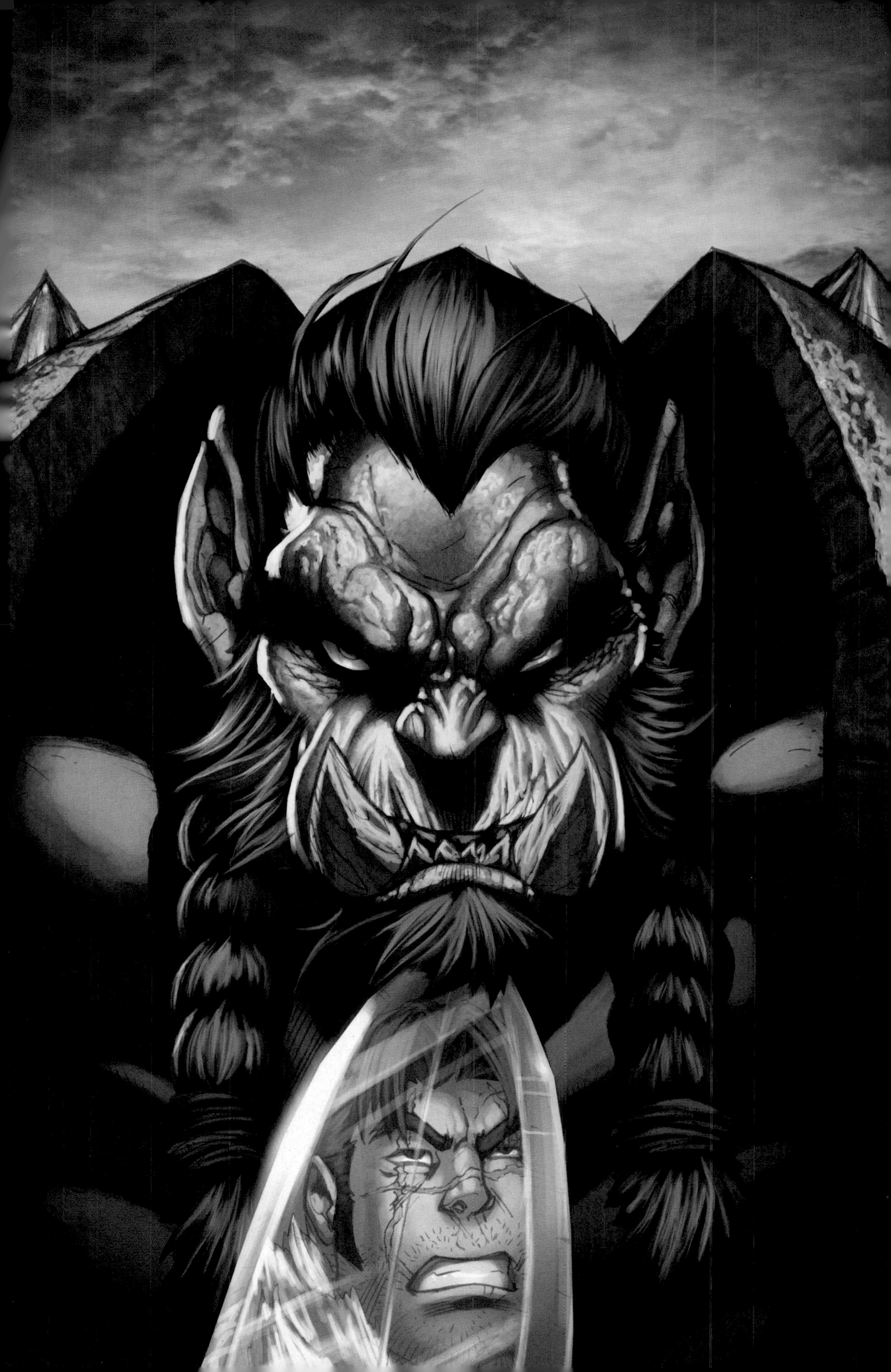

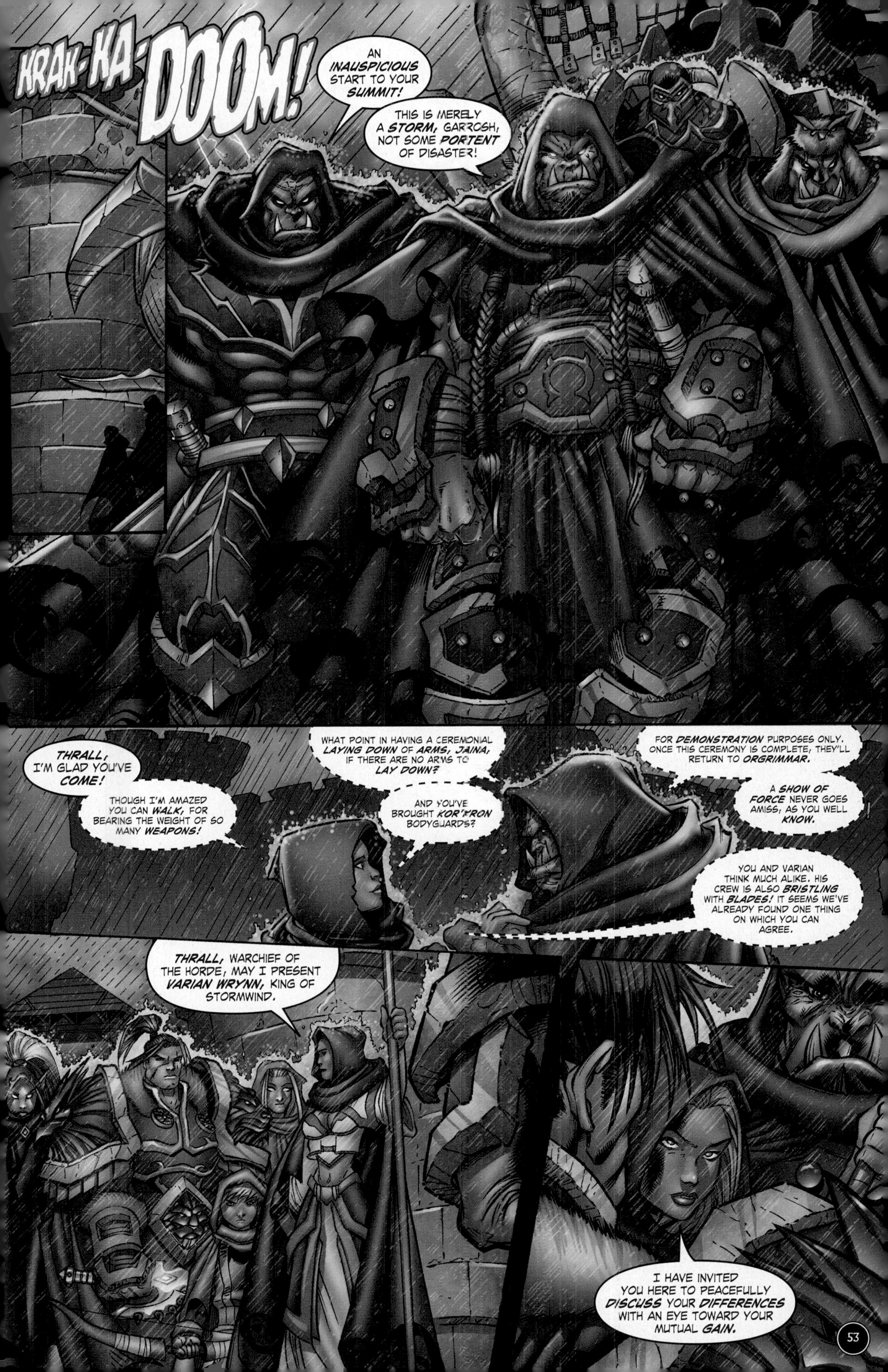
KRAK-KA-DOOM!
AN INAUSPICIOUS START TO YOUR SUMMIT!
THIS IS MERELY A STORM, GARROSH, NOT SOME PORTENT OF DISASTER!
THRALL, I'M GLAD YOU'VE COME!
THOUGH I'M AMAZED YOU CAN WALK, FOR BEARING THE WEIGHT OF SO MANY WEAPONS!
WHAT POINT IN HAVING A CEREMONIAL LAYING DOWN OF ARMS, JAINA, IF THERE ARE NO ARMS TO LAY DOWN?
AND YOU'VE BROUGHT KOR'KRON BODYGUARDS?
FOR DEMONSTRATION PURPOSES ONLY. ONCE THIS CEREMONY IS COMPLETE, THEY'LL RETURN TO ORGRIMMAR.
A SHOW OF FORCE NEVER GOES AMISS, AS YOU WELL KNOW.
YOU AND VARIAN THINK MUCH ALIKE. HIS CREW IS ALSO BRISTLING WITH BLADES! IT SEEMS WE'VE ALREADY FOUND ONE THING ON WHICH YOU CAN AGREE.
THRALL, WARCHIEF OF THE HORDE, MAY I PRESENT VARIAN WRYNN, KING OF STORMWIND.
I HAVE INVITED YOU HERE TO PEACEFULLY DISCUSS YOUR DIFFERENCES WITH AN EYE TOWARD YOUR MUTUAL GAIN.

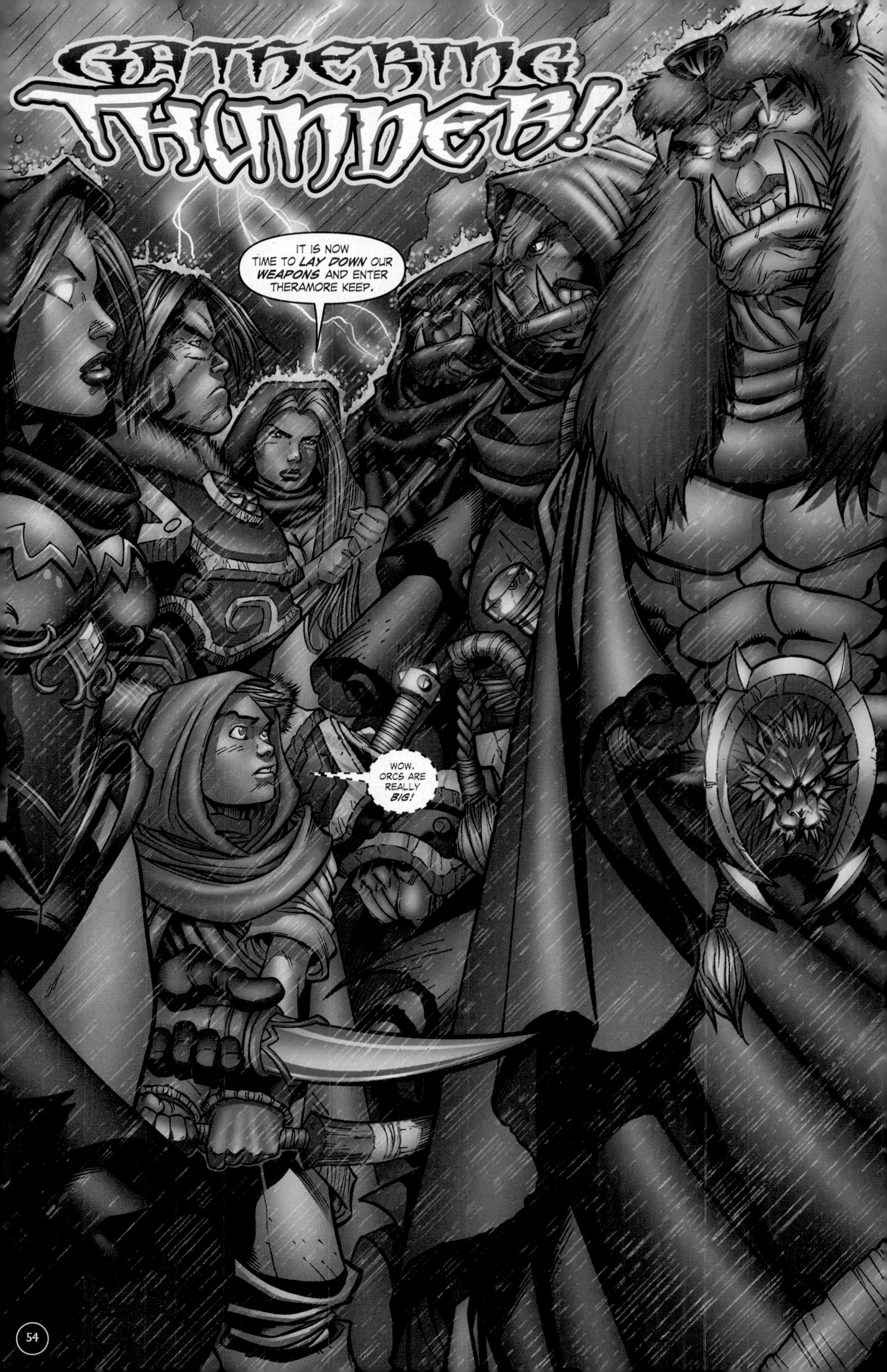
GATHERING THUNDER!
IT IS NOW TIME TO LAY DOWN OUR WEAPONS AND ENTER THERAMORE KEEP.
WOW. ORCS ARE REALLY BIG!

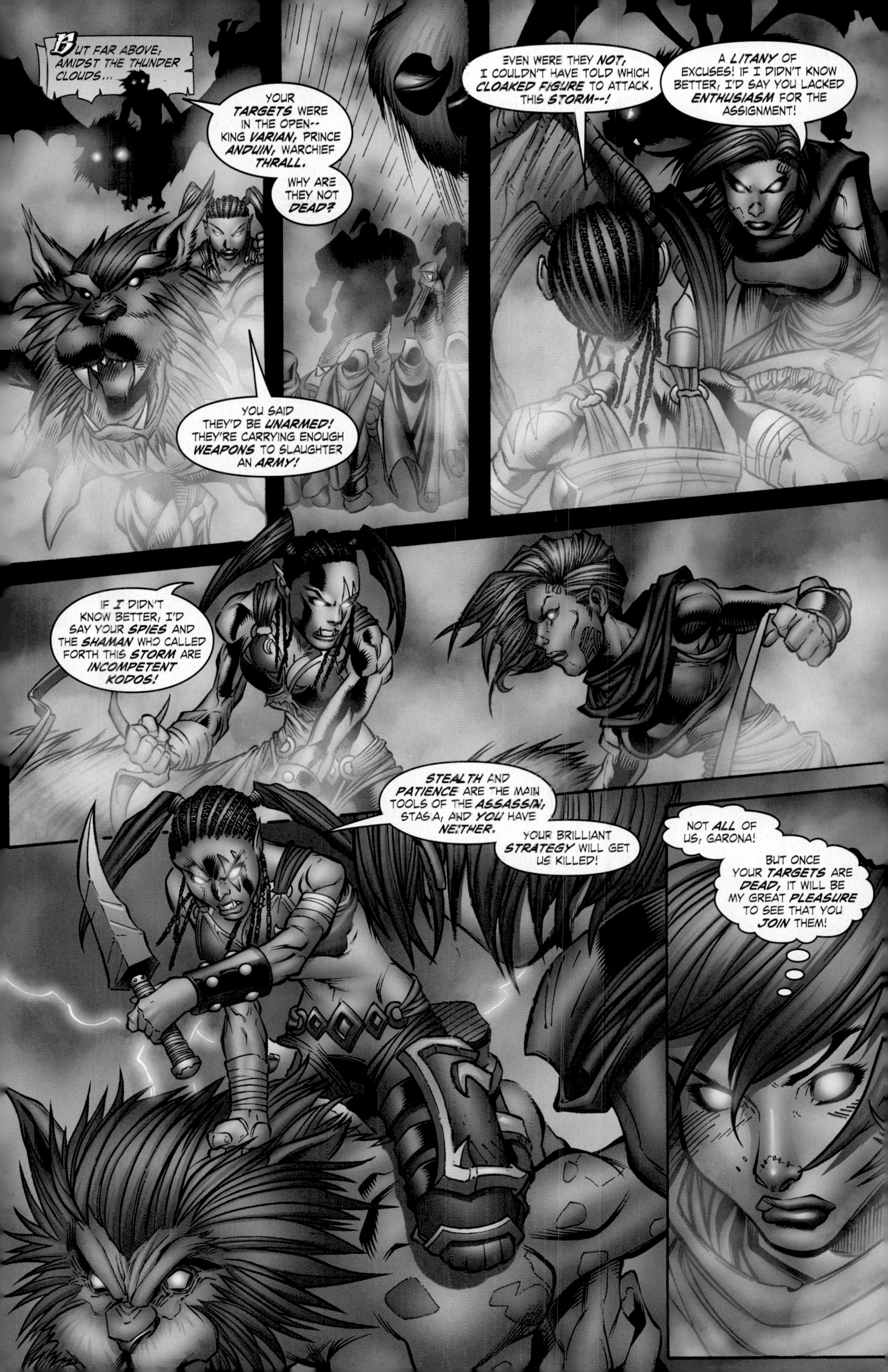

BUT FAR ABOVE, AMIDST THE THUNDER CLOUDS...
YOUR TARGETS WERE IN THE OPEN-- KING VARIAN, PRINCE ANDUIN, WARCHIEF THRALL.
WHY ARE THEY NOT DEAD?
YOU SAID THEY'D BE UNARMED! THEY'RE CARRYING ENOUGH WEAPONS TO SLAUGHTER AN ARMY!
EVEN WERE THEY NOT, I COULDN'T HAVE TOLD WHICH CLOAKED FIGURE TO ATTACK. THIS STORM--!
A LITANY OF EXCUSES! IF I DIDN'T KNOW BETTER, I'D SAY YOU LACKED ENTHUSIASM FOR THE ASSIGNMENT!
IF I DIDN'T KNOW BETTER, I'D SAY YOUR SPIES AND THE SHAMAN WHO CALLED FORTH THIS STORM ARE INCOMPETENT KODOS!
STEALTH AND PATIENCE ARE THE MAIN TOOLS OF THE ASSASSIN, STASIA, AND YOU HAVE NEITHER.
YOUR BRILLIANT STRATEGY WILL GET US KILLED!
NOT ALL OF US, GARONA!
BUT ONCE YOUR TARGETS ARE DEAD, IT WILL BE MY GREAT PLEASURE TO SEE THAT YOU JOIN THEM!

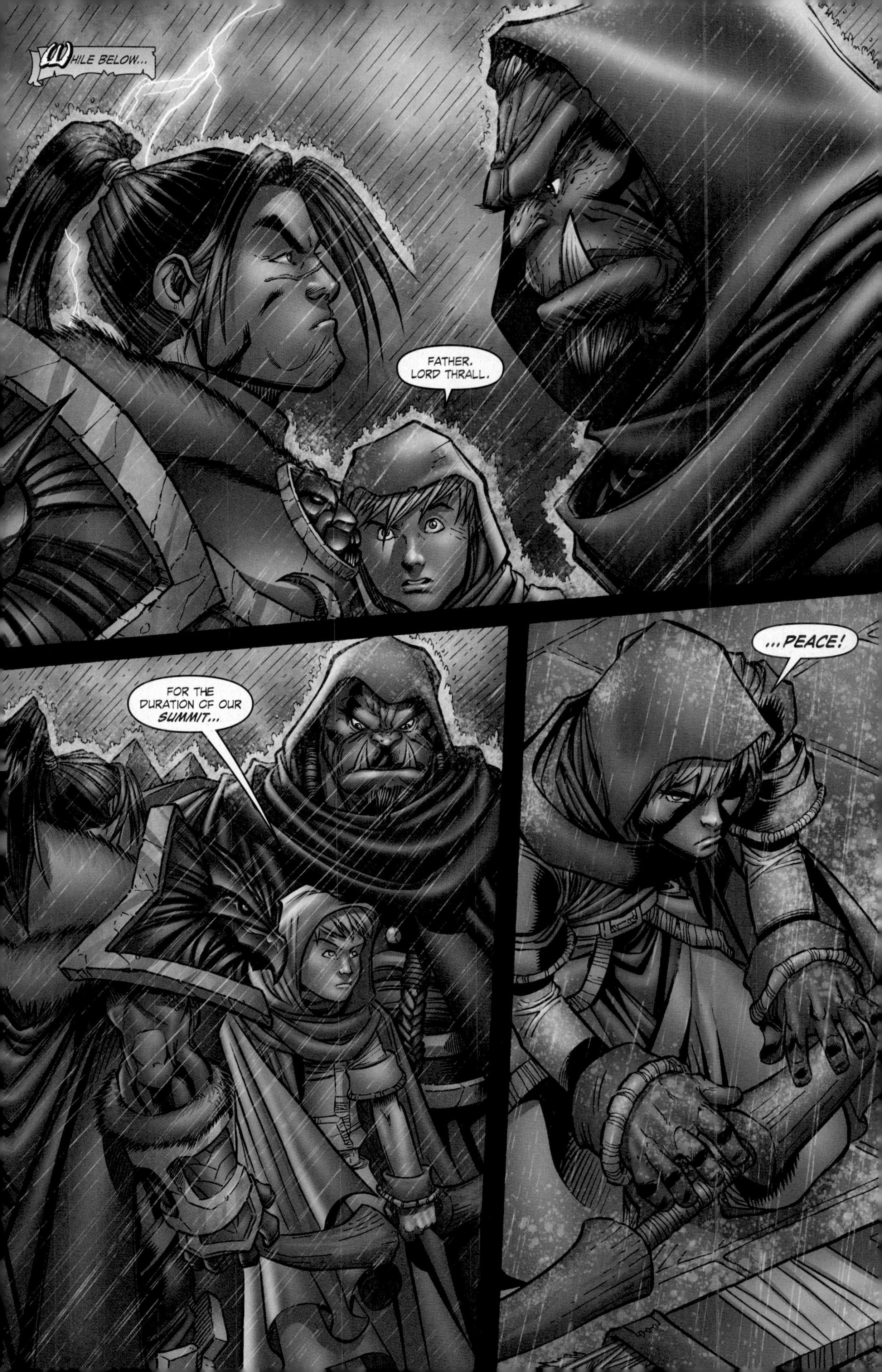
WHILE BELOW...
FATHER. LORD THRALL.
FOR THE DURATION OF OUR SUMMIT...
...PEACE!

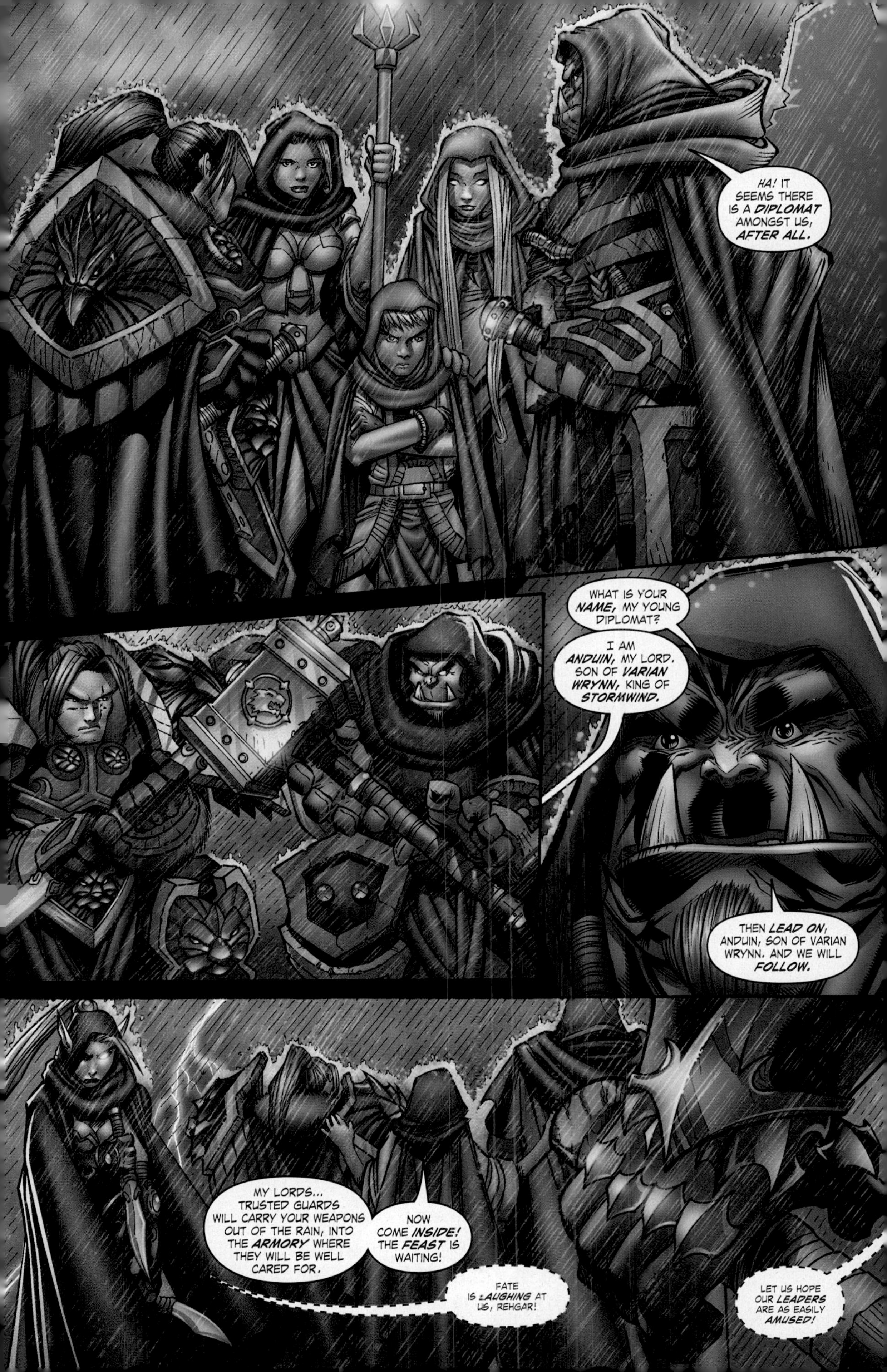
HA! IT SEEMS THERE IS A DIPLOMAT AMONGST US, AFTER ALL.
WHAT IS YOUR NAME, MY YOUNG DIPLOMAT?
I AM ANDUIN, MY LORD. SON OF VARIAN WRYNN, KING OF STORMWIND.
THEN LEAD ON, ANDUIN, SON OF VARIAN WRYNN. AND WE WILL FOLLOW.
MY LORDS... TRUSTED GUARDS WILL CARRY YOUR WEAPONS OUT OF THE RAIN, INTO THE ARMORY WHERE THEY WILL BE WELL CARED FOR.
NOW COME INSIDE! THE FEAST IS WAITING!
FATE IS LAUGHING AT US, REHGAR!
LET US HOPE OUR LEADERS ARE AS EASILY AMUSED!

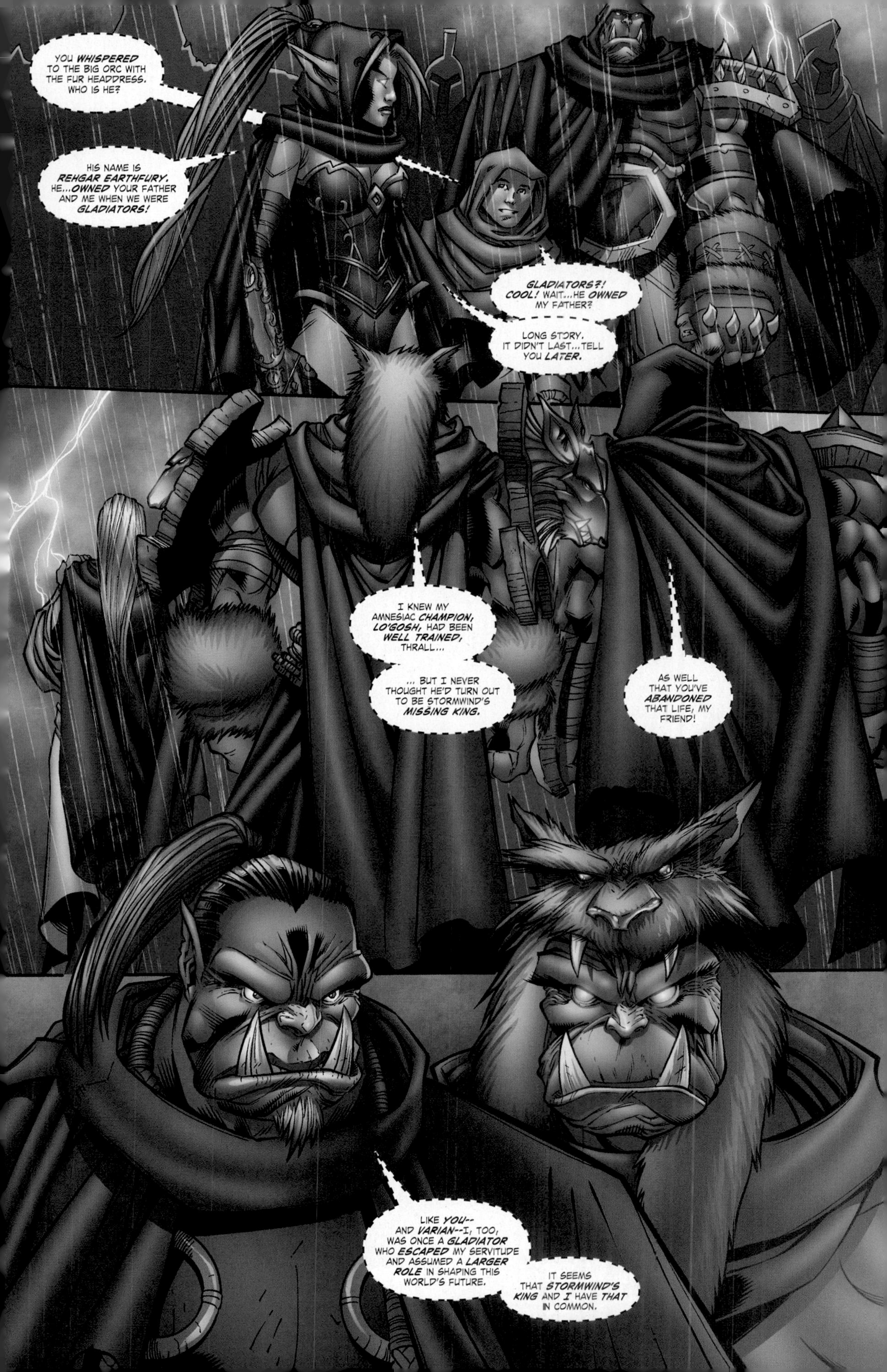

YOU WHISPERED TO THE BIG ORC WITH THE FUR HEADDRESS. WHO IS HE?
HIS NAME IS REHGAR EARTHFURY. HE...OWNED YOUR FATHER AND ME WHEN WE WERE GLADIATORS!
GLADIATORS?! COOL! WAIT...HE OWNED MY FATHER?
LONG STORY. IT DIDN'T LAST...TELL YOU LATER.
I KNEW MY AMNESIAC CHAMPION, LO'GOSH, HAD BEEN WELL TRAINED, THRALL...
... BUT I NEVER THOUGHT HE'D TURN OUT TO BE STORMWIND'S MISSING KING.
AS WELL THAT YOU'VE ABANDONED THAT LIFE, MY FRIEND!
LIKE YOU-- AND VARIAN--I, TOO, WAS ONCE A GLADIATOR WHO ESCAPED MY SERVITUDE AND ASSUMED A LARGER ROLE IN SHAPING THIS WORLD'S FUTURE.
IT SEEMS THAT STORMWIND'S KING AND I HAVE THAT IN COMMON.

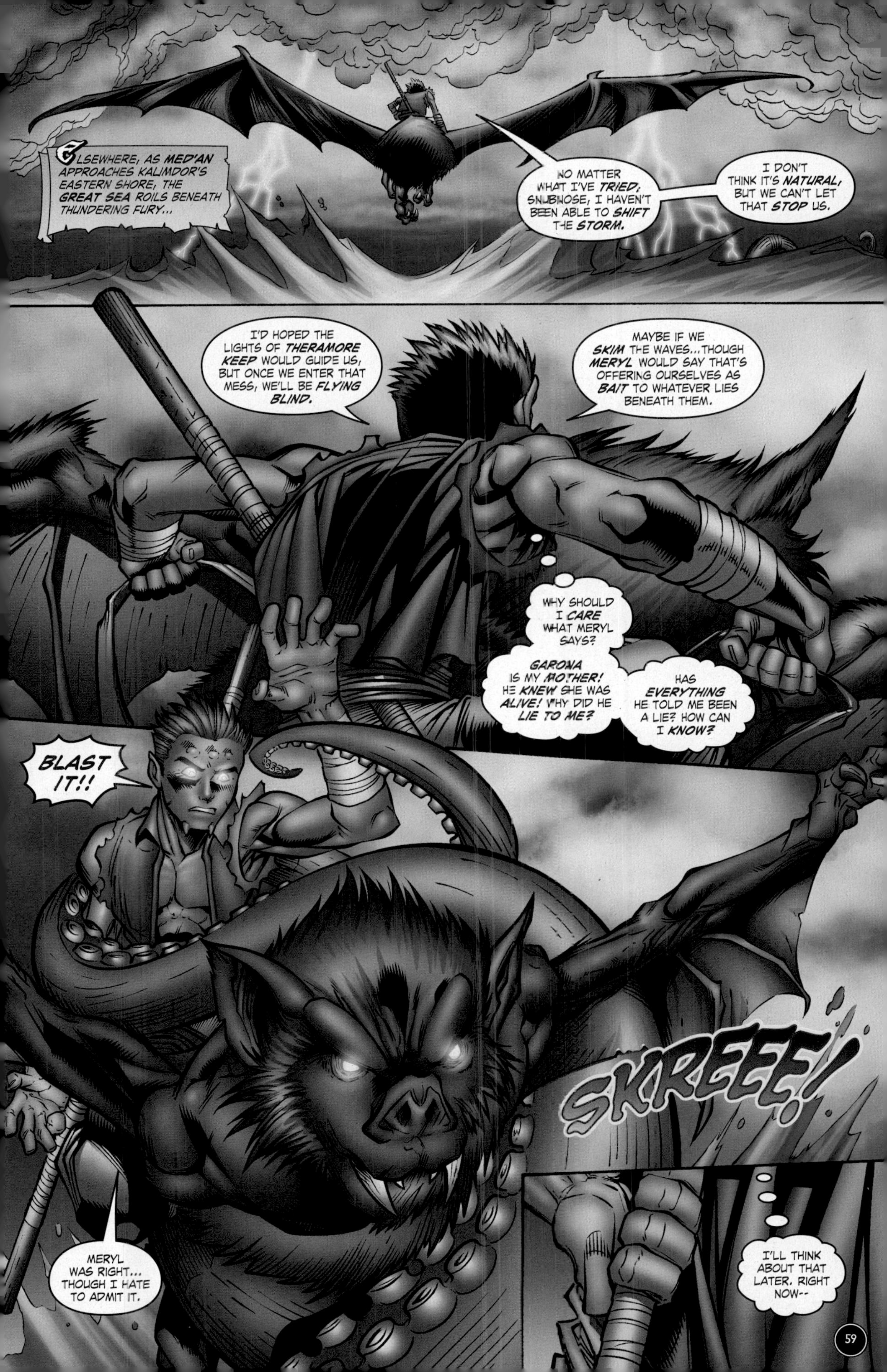

ELSEWHERE, AS MED'AN APPROACHES KALIMDOR'S EASTERN SHORE, THE GREAT SEA ROILS BENEATH THUNDERING FURY...
NO MATTER WHAT I'VE TRIED, SNUBNOSE, I HAVEN'T BEEN ABLE TO SHIFT THE STORM.
I DON'T THINK IT'S NATURAL, BUT WE CAN'T LET THAT STOP US.
I'D HOPED THE LIGHTS OF THERAMORE KEEP WOULD GUIDE US, BUT ONCE WE ENTER THAT MESS, WE'LL BE FLYING BLIND.
MAYBE IF WE SKIM THE WAVES...THOUGH MERYL WOULD SAY THAT'S OFFERING OURSELVES AS BAIT TO WHATEVER LIES BENEATH THEM.
WHY SHOULD I CARE WHAT MERYL SAYS?
GARONA IS MY MOTHER! HE KNEW SHE WAS ALIVE! WHY DID HE LIE TO ME?
HAS EVERYTHING HE TOLD ME BEEN A LIE? HOW CAN I KNOW?
BLAST IT!!
SKREEE!
MERYL WAS RIGHT... THOUGH I HATE TO ADMIT IT.
I'LL THINK ABOUT THAT LATER. RIGHT NOW--

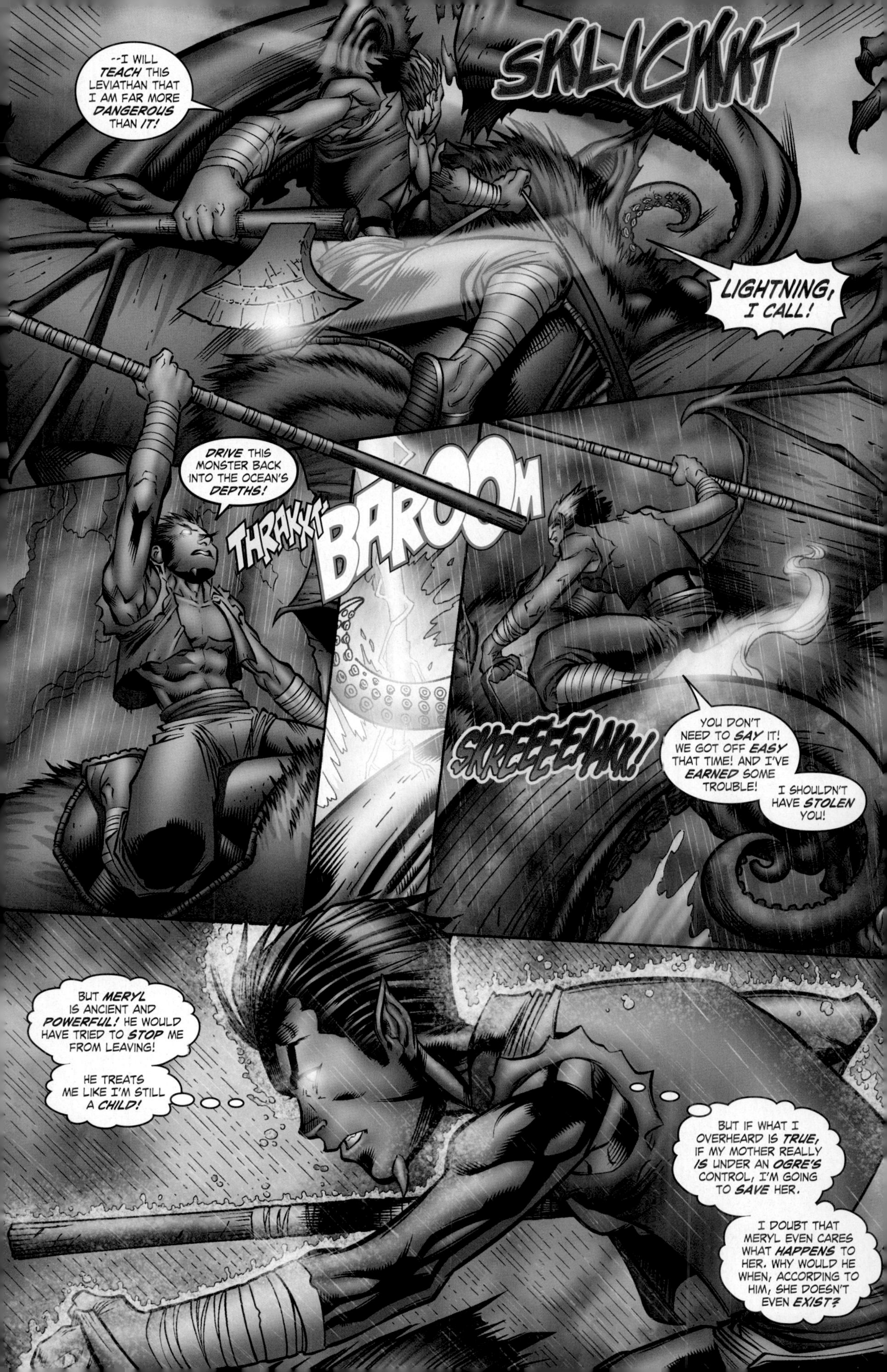

--I WILL TEACH THIS LEVIATHAN THAT I AM FAR MORE DANGEROUS THAN IT!
SKLICKKT
LIGHTNING, I CALL!
DRIVE THIS MONSTER BACK INTO THE OCEAN'S DEPTHS!
THRAKKT
BAROOOM
SKREEEEEAAKK!
YOU DON'T NEED TO SAY IT! WE GOT OFF EASY THAT TIME! AND I'VE EARNED SOME TROUBLE!
I SHOULDN'T HAVE STOLEN YOU!
BUT MERYL IS ANCIENT AND POWERFUL! HE WOULD HAVE TRIED TO STOP ME FROM LEAVING!
HE TREATS ME LIKE I'M STILL A CHILD!
BUT IF WHAT I OVERHEARD IS TRUE, IF MY MOTHER REALLY IS UNDER AN OGRE'S CONTROL, I'M GOING TO SAVE HER.
I DOUBT THAT MERYL EVEN CARES WHAT HAPPENS TO HER. WHY WOULD HE WHEN, ACCORDING TO HIM, SHE DOESN'T EVEN EXIST?

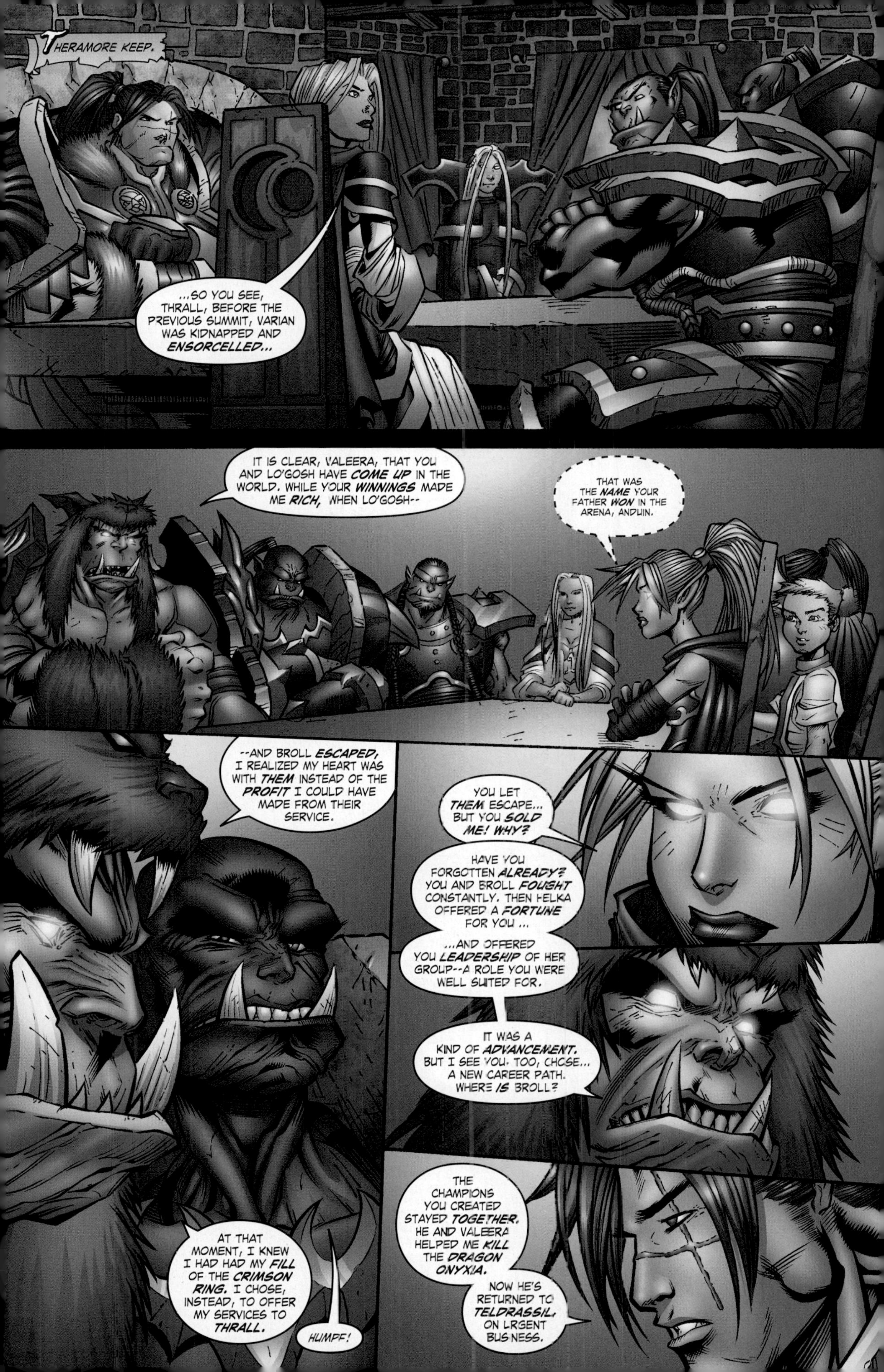
THERAMORE KEEP.
...SO YOU SEE, THRALL, BEFORE THE PREVIOUS SUMMIT, VARIAN WAS KIDNAPPED AND ENSORCELLED...
IT IS CLEAR, VALEERA, THAT YOU AND LO'GOSH HAVE COME UP IN THE WORLD. WHILE YOUR WINNINGS MADE ME RICH, WHEN LO'GOSH--
THAT WAS THE NAME YOUR FATHER WON IN THE ARENA, ANDUIN.
--AND BROLL ESCAPED, I REALIZED MY HEART WAS WITH THEM INSTEAD OF THE PROFIT I COULD HAVE MADE FROM THEIR SERVICE.
YOU LET THEM ESCAPE... BUT YOU SOLD ME! WHY?
HAVE YOU FORGOTTEN ALREADY? YOU AND BROLL FOUGHT CONSTANTLY. THEN HELKA OFFERED A FORTUNE FOR YOU ...
...AND OFFERED YOU LEADERSHIP OF HER GROUP--A ROLE YOU WERE WELL SUITED FOR.
IT WAS A KIND OF ADVANCEMENT. BUT I SEE YOU, TOO, CHOSE... A NEW CAREER PATH. WHERE IS BROLL?
THE CHAMPIONS YOU CREATED STAYED TOGETHER. HE AND VALEERA HELPED ME KILL THE DRAGON ONYXIA.
NOW HE'S RETURNED TO TELDRASSIL, ON URGENT BUSINESS.
AT THAT MOMENT, I KNEW I HAD HAD MY FILL OF THE CRIMSON RING. I CHOSE, INSTEAD, TO OFFER MY SERVICES TO THRALL.
HUMPF!

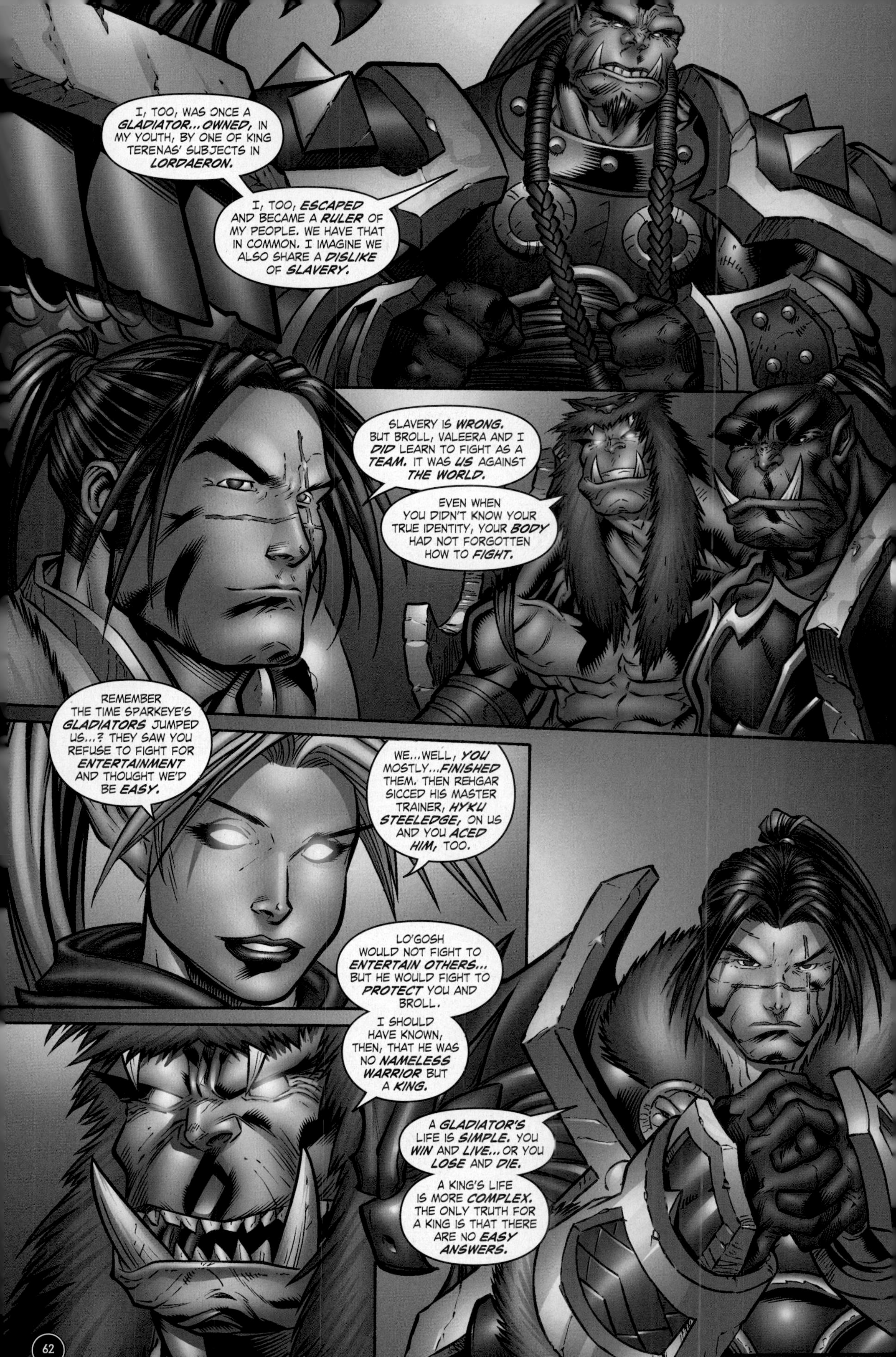
I, TOO, WAS ONCE A GLADIATOR...OWNED, IN MY YOUTH, BY ONE OF KING TERENAS' SUBJECTS IN LORDAERON.
I, TOO, ESCAPED AND BECAME A RULER OF MY PEOPLE. WE HAVE THAT IN COMMON. I IMAGINE WE ALSO SHARE A DISLIKE OF SLAVERY.
SLAVERY IS WRONG. BUT BROLL, VALEERA AND I DID LEARN TO FIGHT AS A TEAM. IT WAS US AGAINST THE WORLD.
EVEN WHEN YOU DIDN'T KNOW YOUR TRUE IDENTITY, YOUR BODY HAD NOT FORGOTTEN HOW TO FIGHT.
REMEMBER THE TIME SPARKEYE'S GLADIATORS JUMPED US...? THEY SAW YOU REFUSE TO FIGHT FOR ENTERTAINMENT AND THOUGHT WE'D BE EASY.
WE...WELL, YOU MOSTLY...FINISHED THEM. THEN REHGAR SICCED HIS MASTER TRAINER, HYKU STEELEDGE, ON US AND YOU ACED HIM, TOO.
LO'GOSH WOULD NOT FIGHT TO ENTERTAIN OTHERS... BUT HE WOULD FIGHT TO PROTECT YOU AND BROLL.
I SHOULD HAVE KNOWN, THEN, THAT HE WAS NO NAMELESS WARRIOR BUT A KING.
A GLADIATOR'S LIFE IS SIMPLE. YOU WIN AND LIVE...OR YOU LOSE AND DIE.
A KING'S LIFE IS MORE COMPLEX. THE ONLY TRUTH FOR A KING IS THAT THERE ARE NO EASY ANSWERS.

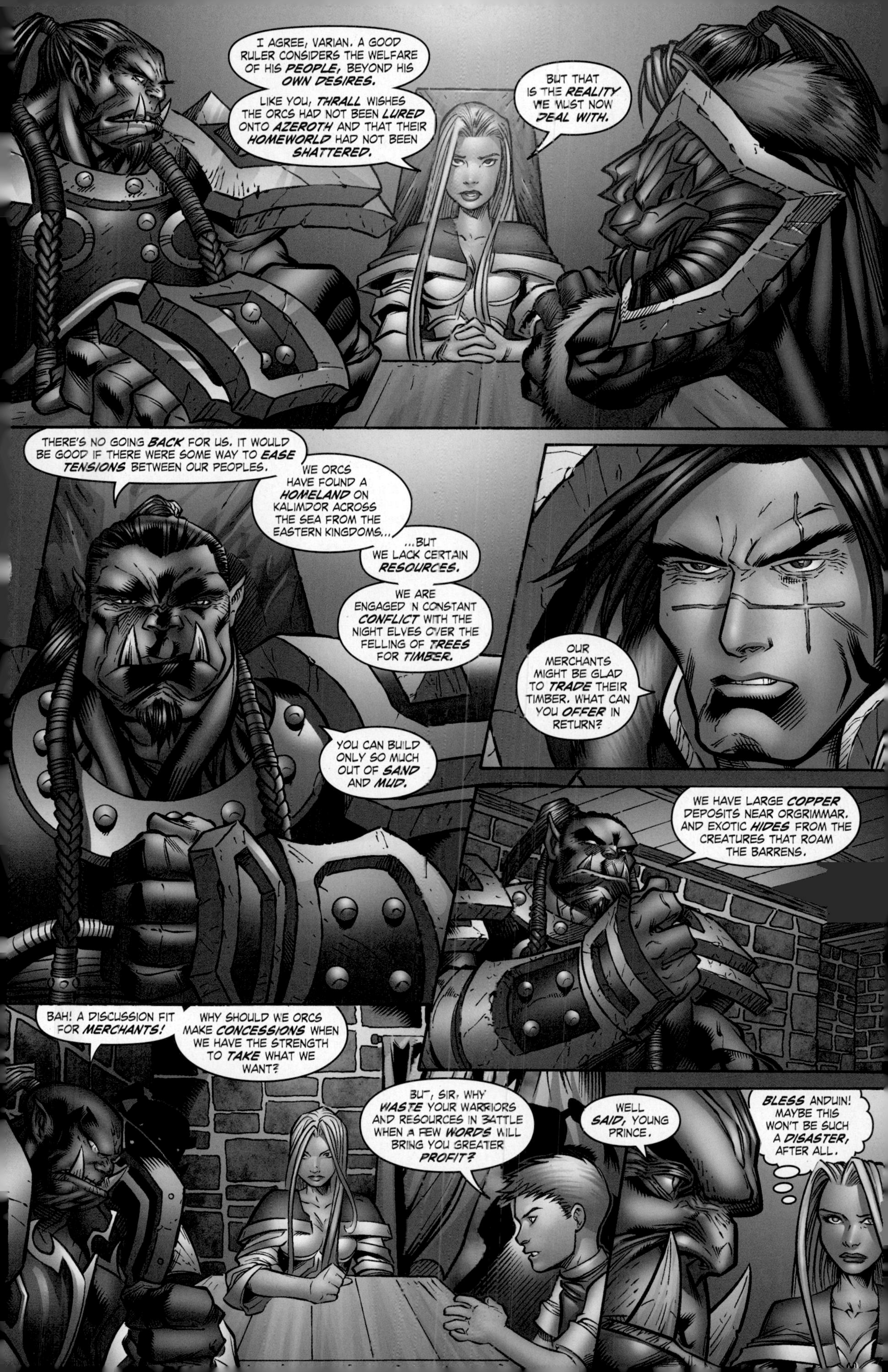
I AGREE, VARIAN. A GOOD RULER CONSIDERS THE WELFARE OF HIS PEOPLE, BEYOND HIS OWN DESIRES.
LIKE YOU, THRALL WISHES THE ORCS HAD NOT BEEN LURED ONTO AZEROTH AND THAT THEIR HOMEWORLD HAD NOT BEEN SHATTERED.
BUT THAT IS THE REALITY WE MUST NOW DEAL WITH.
THERE'S NO GOING BACK FOR US. IT WOULD BE GOOD IF THERE WERE SOME WAY TO EASE TENSIONS BETWEEN OUR PEOPLES.
WE ORCS HAVE FOUND A HOMELAND ON KALIMDOR ACROSS THE SEA FROM THE EASTERN KINGDOMS...
...BUT WE LACK CERTAIN RESOURCES.
WE ARE ENGAGED IN CONSTANT CONFLICT WITH THE NIGHT ELVES OVER THE FELLING OF TREES FOR TIMBER.
YOU CAN BUILD ONLY SO MUCH OUT OF SAND AND MUD.
OUR MERCHANTS MIGHT BE GLAD TO TRADE THEIR TIMBER. WHAT CAN YOU OFFER IN RETURN?
WE HAVE LARGE COPPER DEPOSITS NEAR ORGRIMMAR. AND EXOTIC HIDES FROM THE CREATURES THAT ROAM THE BARRENS.
BAH! A DISCUSSION FIT FOR MERCHANTS!
WHY SHOULD WE ORCS MAKE CONCESSIONS WHEN WE HAVE THE STRENGTH TO TAKE WHAT WE WANT?
BUT, SIR, WHY WASTE YOUR WARRIORS AND RESOURCES IN BATTLE WHEN A FEW WORDS WILL BRING YOU GREATER PROFIT?
WELL SAID, YOUNG PRINCE.
BLESS ANDUIN! MAYBE THIS WON'T BE SUCH A DISASTER, AFTER ALL.

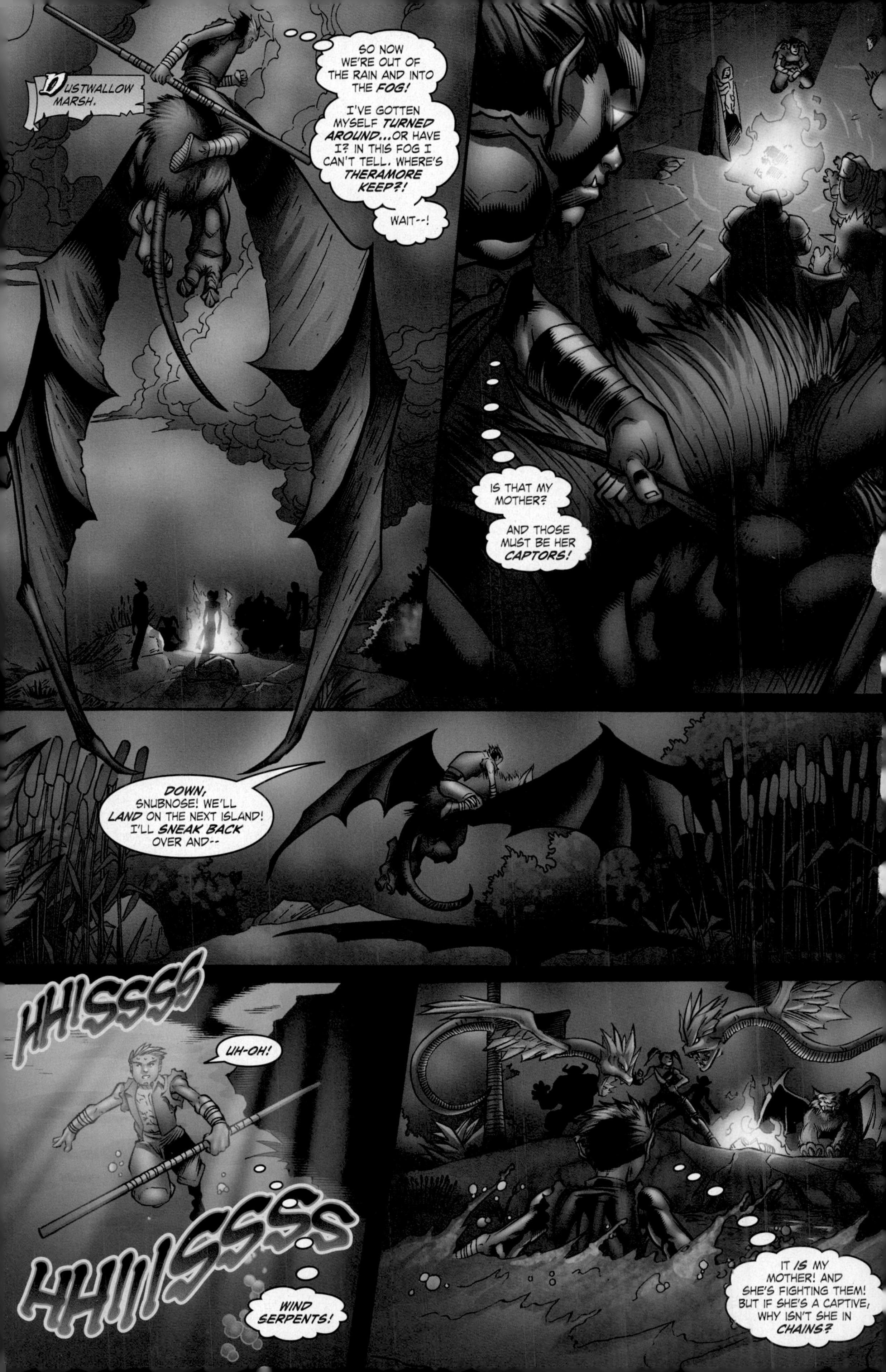
DUSTWALLOW MARSH.
SO NOW WE'RE OUT OF THE RAIN AND INTO THE FOG!
I'VE GOTTEN MYSELF TURNED AROUND...OR HAVE I? IN THIS FOG I CAN'T TELL. WHERE'S THERAMORE KEEP?!
WAIT--!
IS THAT MY MOTHER?
AND THOSE MUST BE HER CAPTORS!
DOWN, SNUBNOSE! WE'LL LAND ON THE NEXT ISLAND! I'LL SNEAK BACK OVER AND--
HHISSSS
UH-OH!
HHIIISSSS
WIND SERPENTS!
IT IS MY MOTHER! AND SHE'S FIGHTING THEM! BUT IF SHE'S A CAPTIVE, WHY ISN'T SHE IN CHAINS?

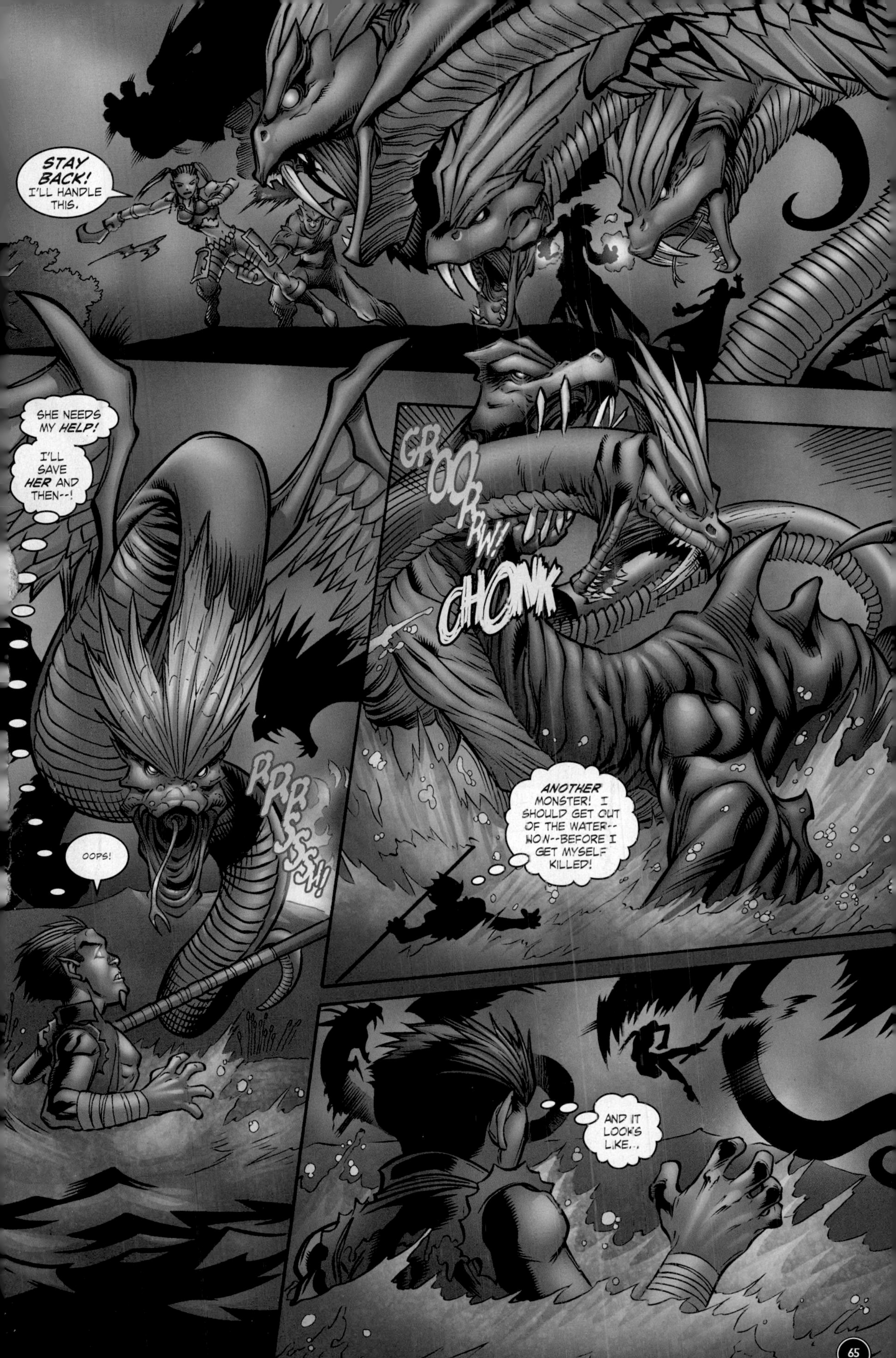
STAY BACK! I'LL HANDLE THIS.
SHE NEEDS MY HELP!
I'LL SAVE HER AND THEN--!
OOPS!
PPPSSSH!!
GROOORRW!
CHOMK
ANOTHER MONSTER! I SHOULD GET OUT OF THE WATER--NOW--BEFORE I GET MYSELF KILLED!
AND IT LOOKS LIKE...

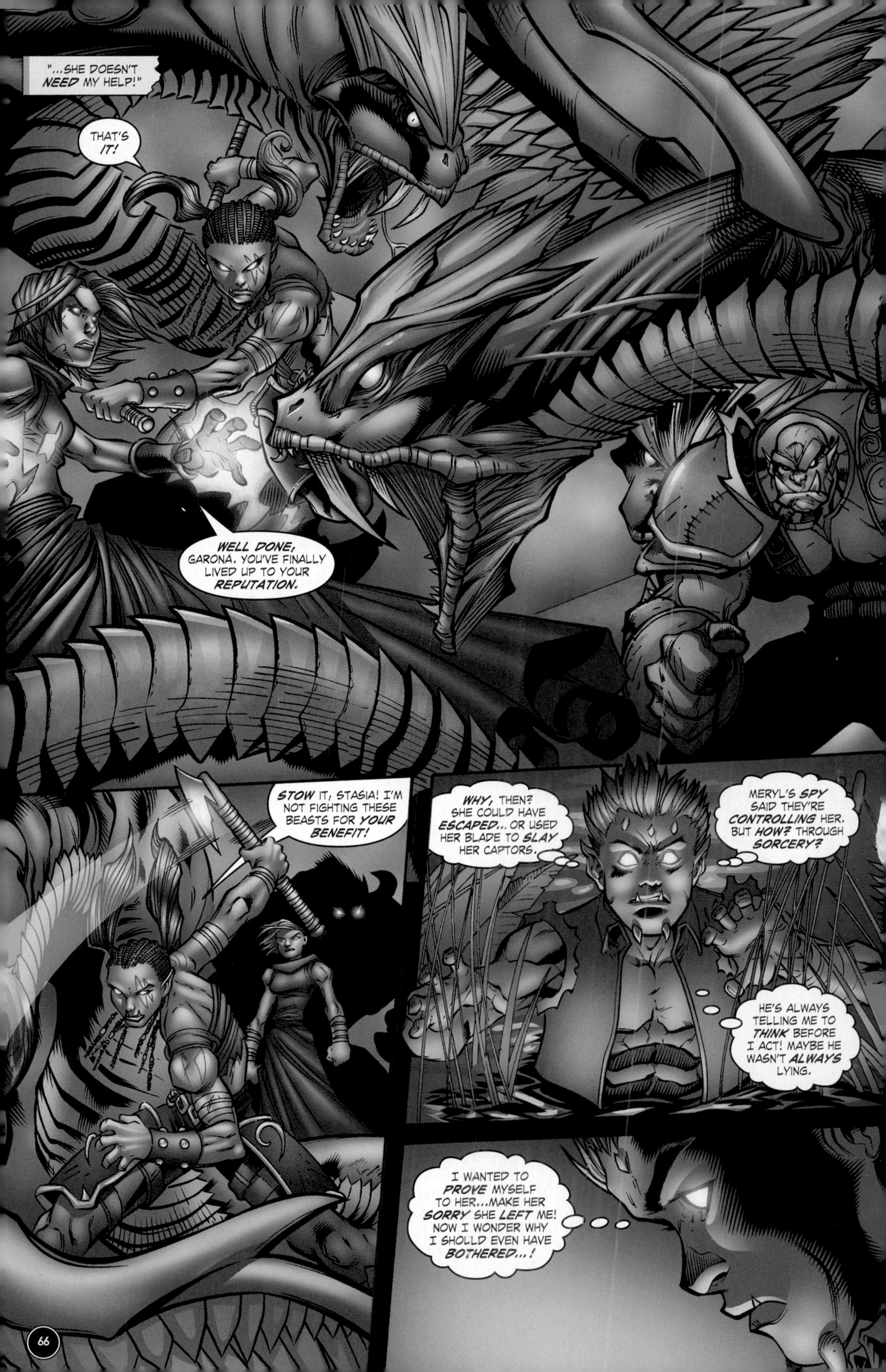

"...SHE DOESN'T NEED MY HELP!"
THAT'S IT!
WELL DONE, GARONA. YOU'VE FINALLY LIVED UP TO YOUR REPUTATION.
STOW IT, STASIA! I'M NOT FIGHTING THESE BEASTS FOR YOUR BENEFIT!
WHY, THEN? SHE COULD HAVE ESCAPED... OR USED HER BLADE TO SLAY HER CAPTORS.
MERYL'S SPY SAID THEY'RE CONTROLLING HER. BUT HOW? THROUGH SORCERY?
HE'S ALWAYS TELLING ME TO THINK BEFORE I ACT! MAYBE HE WASN'T ALWAYS LYING.
I WANTED TO PROVE MYSELF TO HER...MAKE HER SORRY SHE LEFT ME! NOW I WONDER WHY I SHOULD EVEN HAVE BOTHERED...!

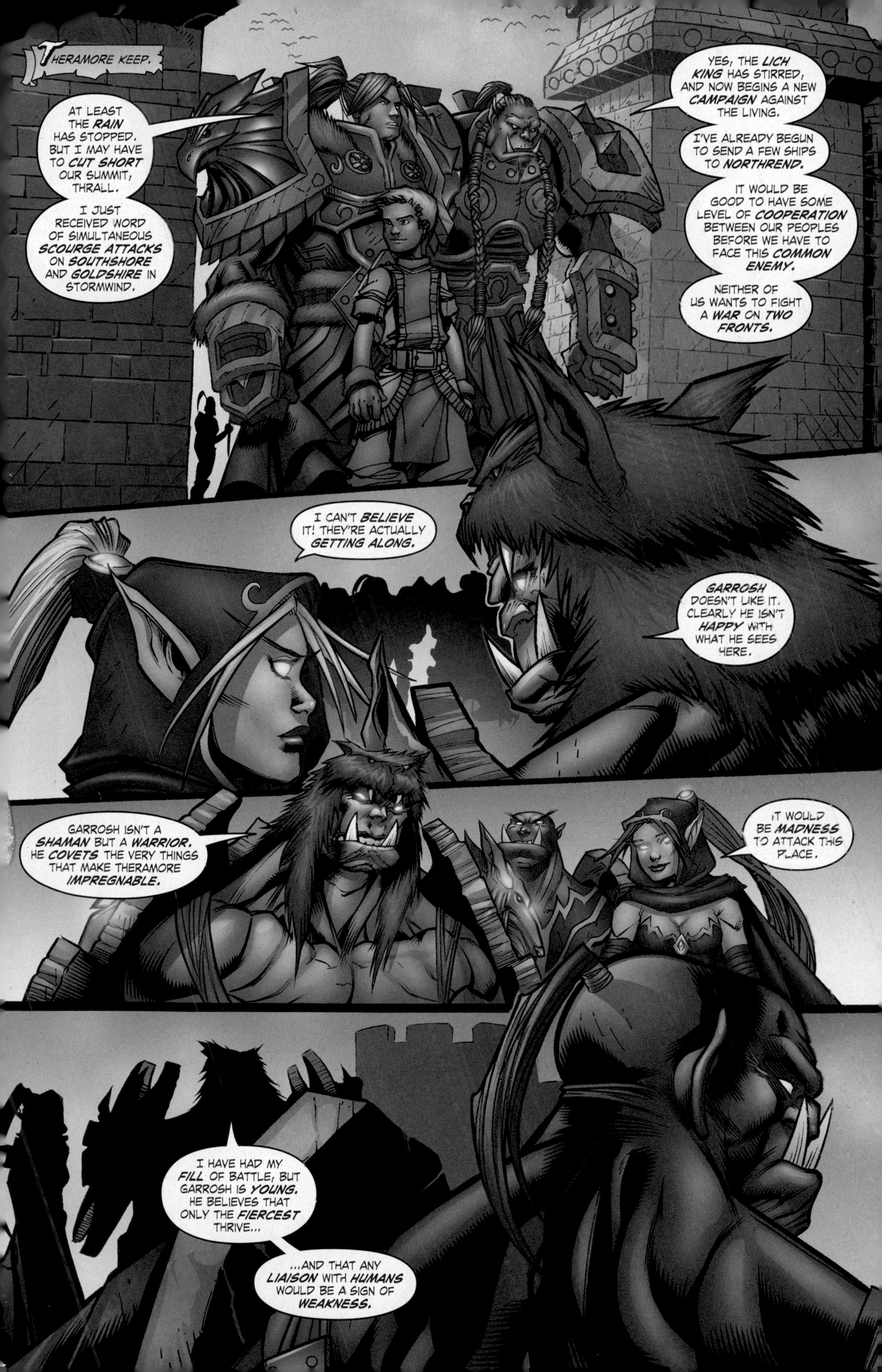
THERAMORE KEEP.
AT LEAST THE RAIN HAS STOPPED. BUT I MAY HAVE TO CUT SHORT OUR SUMMIT, THRALL.
I JUST RECEIVED WORD OF SIMULTANEOUS SCOURGE ATTACKS ON SOUTHSHORE AND GOLDSHIRE IN STORMWIND.
YES, THE LICH KING HAS STIRRED, AND NOW BEGINS A NEW CAMPAIGN AGAINST THE LIVING.
I'VE ALREADY BEGUN TO SEND A FEW SHIPS TO NORTHREND.
IT WOULD BE GOOD TO HAVE SOME LEVEL OF COOPERATION BETWEEN OUR PEOPLES BEFORE WE HAVE TO FACE THIS COMMON ENEMY.
NEITHER OF US WANTS TO FIGHT A WAR ON TWO FRONTS.
I CAN'T BELIEVE IT! THEY'RE ACTUALLY GETTING ALONG.
GARROSH DOESN'T LIKE IT. CLEARLY HE ISN'T HAPPY WITH WHAT HE SEES HERE.
GARROSH ISN'T A SHAMAN BUT A WARRIOR. HE COVETS THE VERY THINGS THAT MAKE THERAMORE IMPREGNABLE.
IT WOULD BE MADNESS TO ATTACK THIS PLACE.
I HAVE HAD MY FILL OF BATTLE, BUT GARROSH IS YOUNG. HE BELIEVES THAT ONLY THE FIERCEST THRIVE...
...AND THAT ANY LIAISON WITH HUMANS WOULD BE A SIGN OF WEAKNESS.

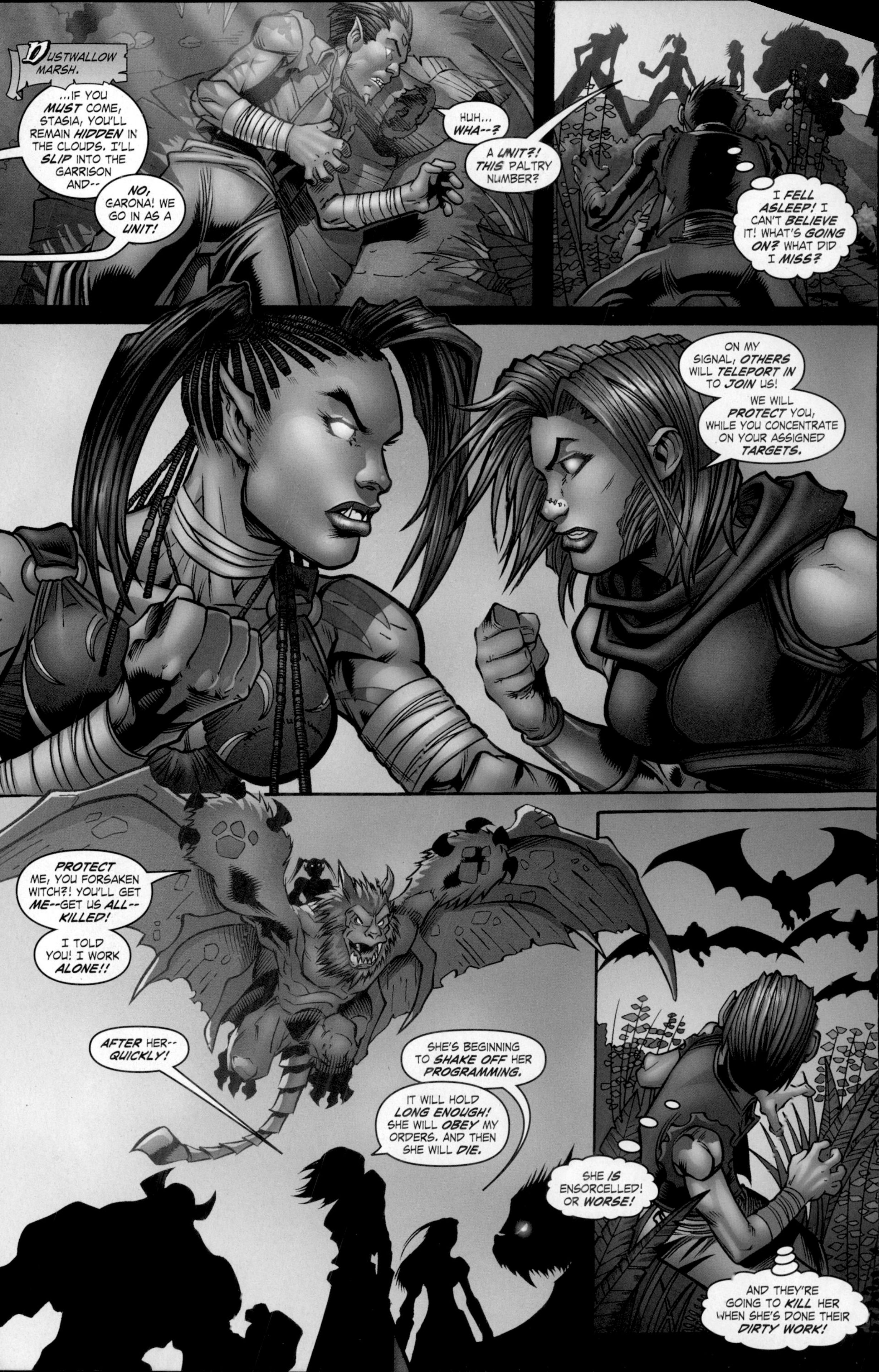

DUSTWALLOW MARSH.
...IF YOU MUST COME, STASIA, YOU'LL REMAIN HIDDEN IN THE CLOUDS. I'LL SLIP INTO THE GARRISON AND--
NO, GARONA! WE GO IN AS A UNIT!
HUH... WHA--?
A UNIT?! THIS PALTRY NUMBER?
I FELL ASLEEP! I CAN'T BELIEVE IT! WHAT'S GOING ON? WHAT DID I MISS?
ON MY SIGNAL, OTHERS WILL TELEPORT IN TO JOIN US!
WE WILL PROTECT YOU, WHILE YOU CONCENTRATE ON YOUR ASSIGNED TARGETS.
PROTECT ME, YOU FORSAKEN WITCH?! YOU'LL GET ME--GET US ALL--KILLED!
I TOLD YOU! I WORK ALONE!!
AFTER HER--QUICKLY!
SHE'S BEGINNING TO SHAKE OFF HER PROGRAMMING.
IT WILL HOLD LONG ENOUGH! SHE WILL OBEY MY ORDERS. AND THEN SHE WILL DIE.
SHE IS ENSORCELLED! OR WORSE!
AND THEY'RE GOING TO KILL HER WHEN SHE'S DONE THEIR DIRTY WORK!

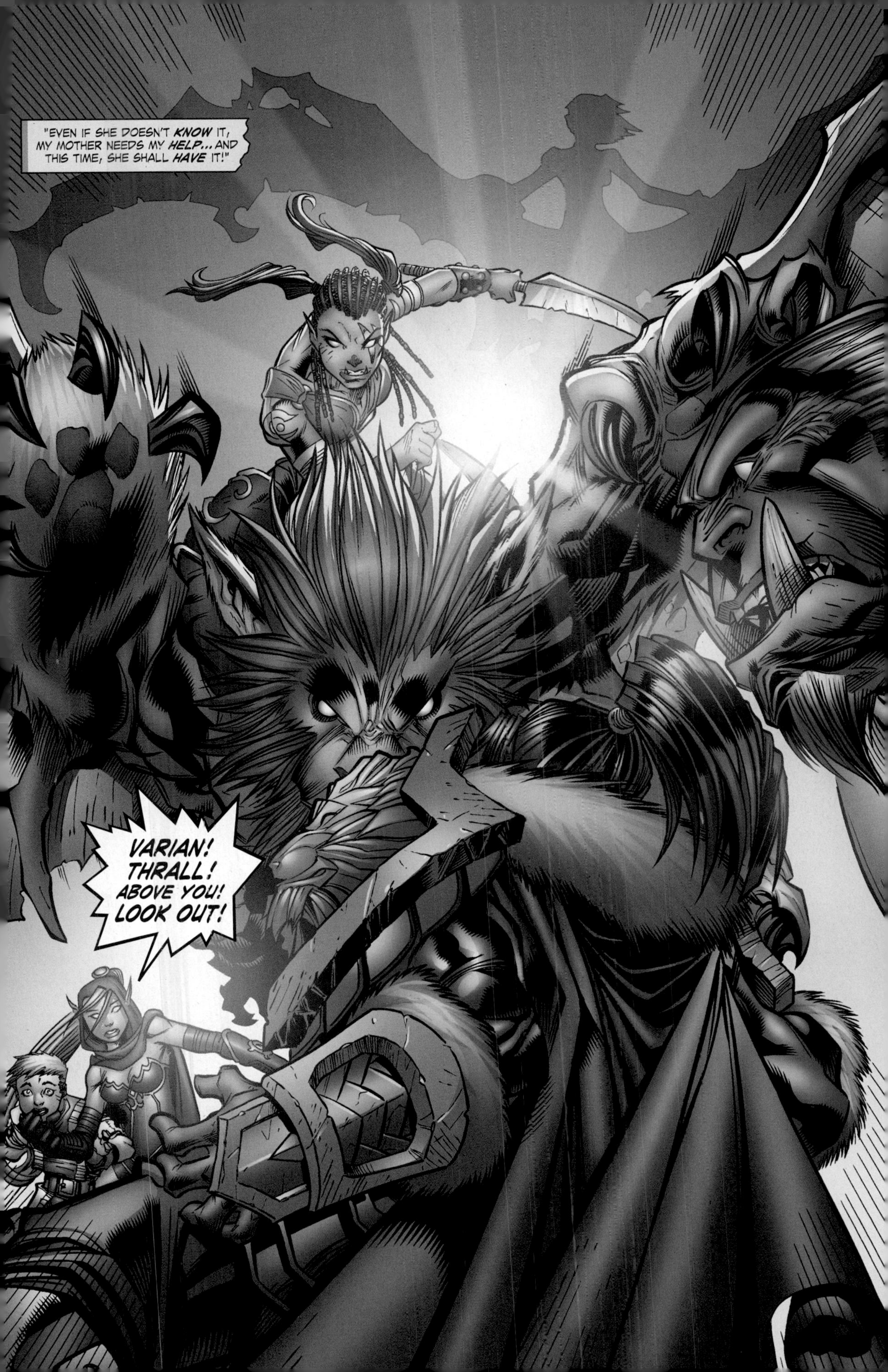
"EVEN IF SHE DOESN'T KNOW IT, MY MOTHER NEEDS MY HELP... AND THIS TIME, SHE SHALL HAVE IT!"
VARIAN! THRALL! ABOVE YOU! LOOK OUT!

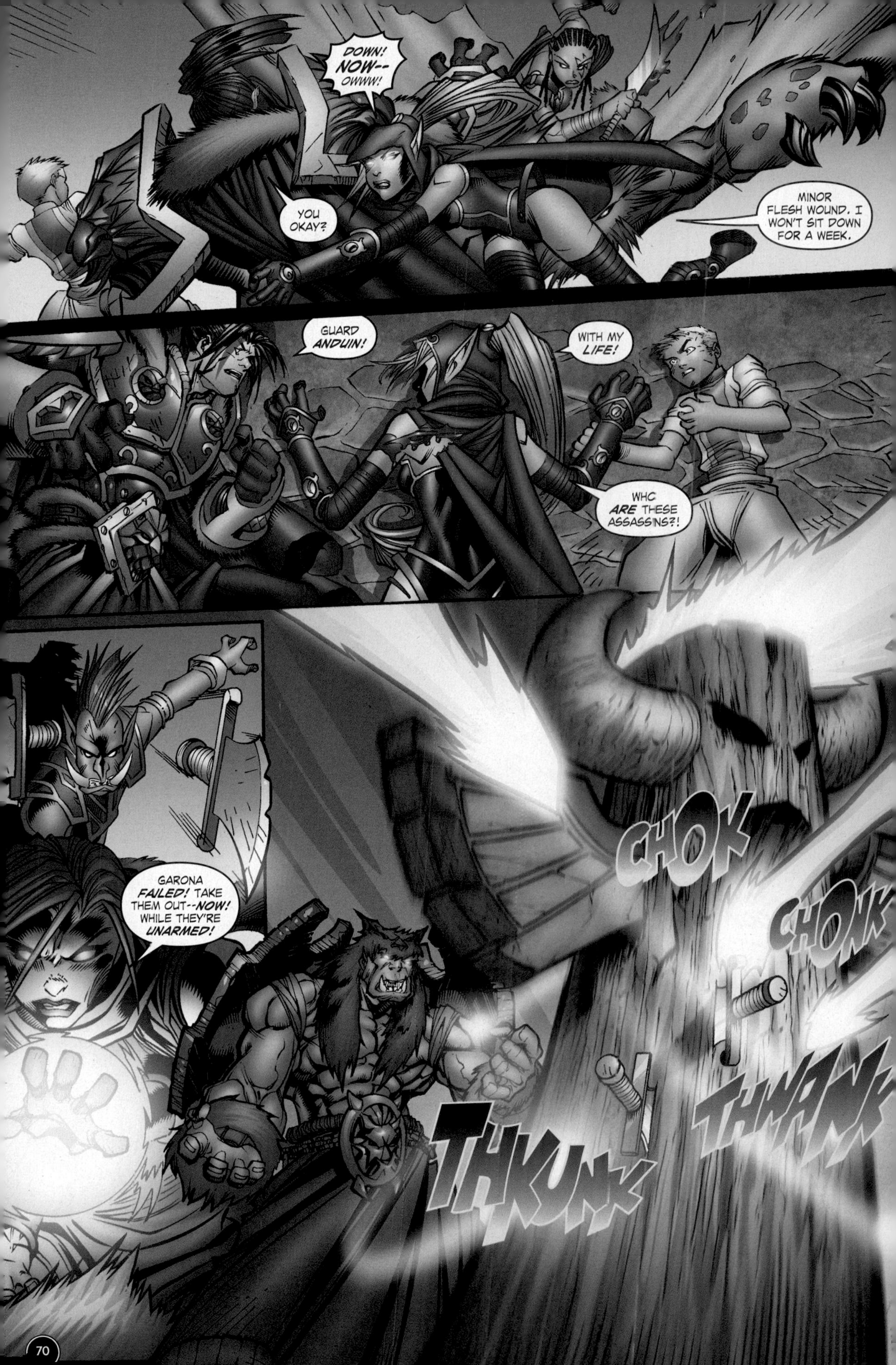
DOWN! NOW-- OWWW!
YOU OKAY?
MINOR FLESH WOUND. I WON'T SIT DOWN FOR A WEEK.
GUARD ANDUIN!
WITH MY LIFE!
WHC ARE THESE ASSASSINS?!
GARONA FAILED! TAKE THEM OUT--NOW! WHILE THEY'RE UNARMED!
CHOK
CHONK
THUNK
THWANK

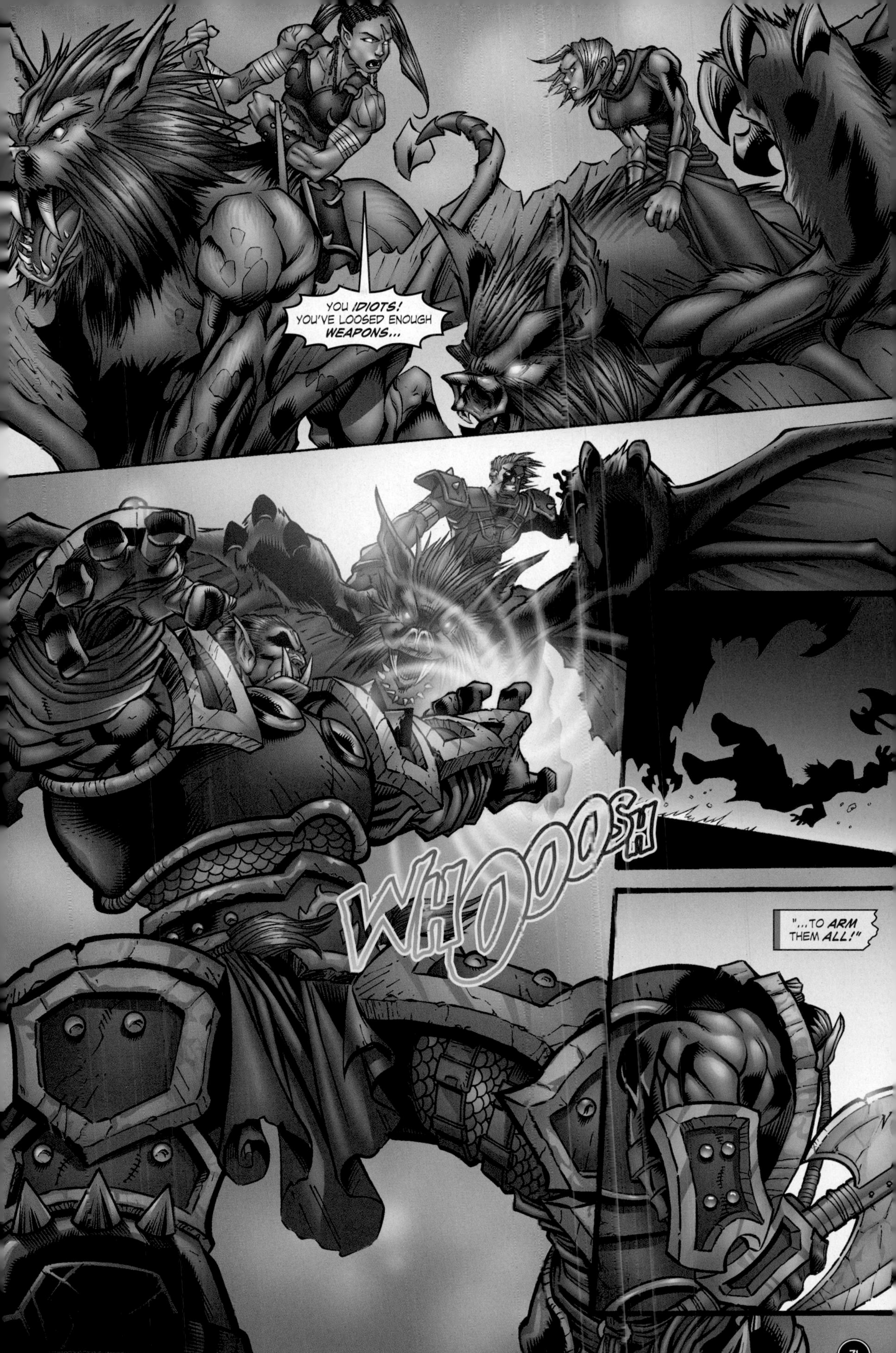
YOU IDIOTS! YOU'VE LOOSED ENOUGH WEAPONS...
WHOOOOSH
"...TO ARM THEM ALL!"

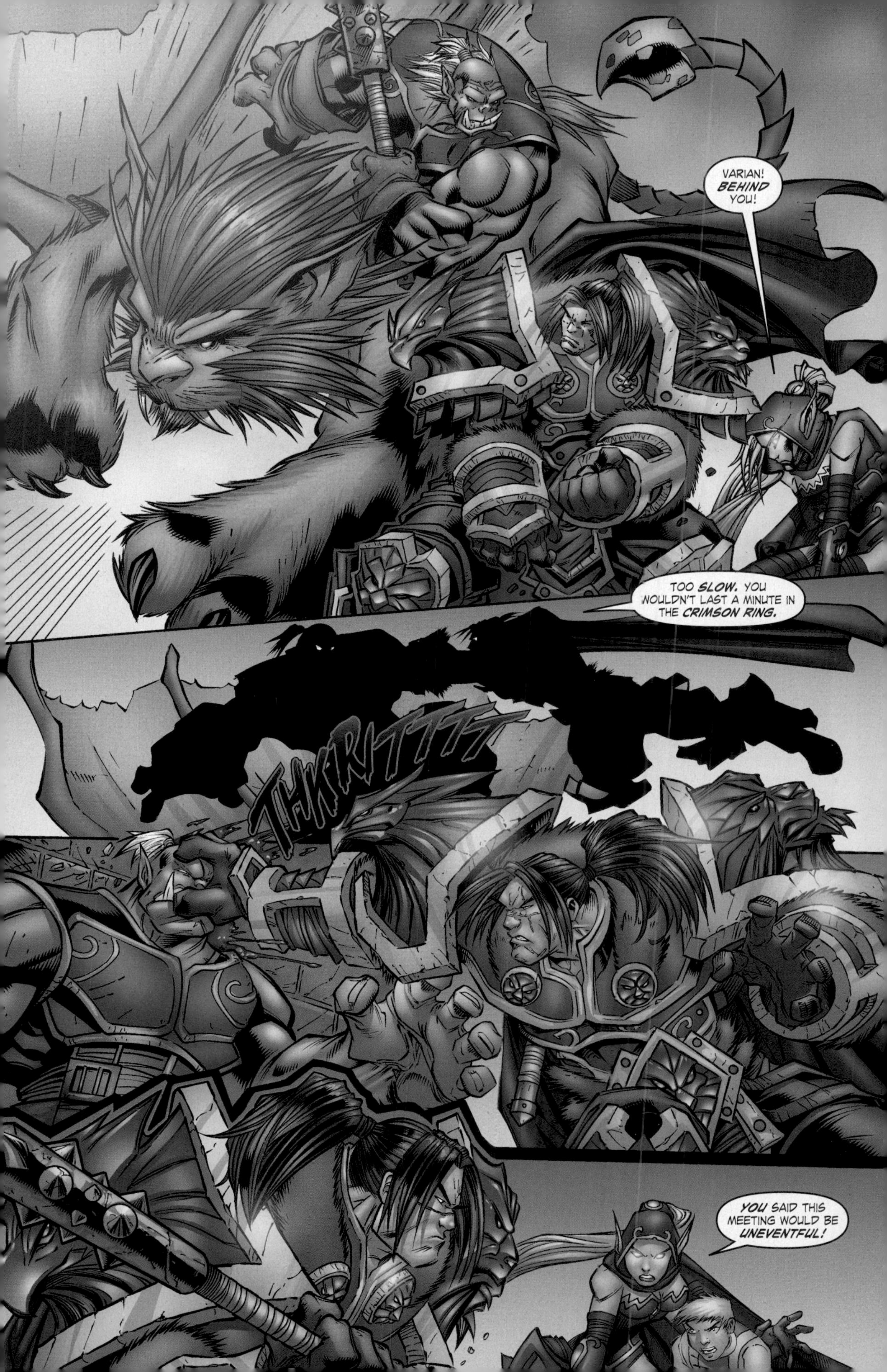
VARIAN! BEHIND YOU!
TOO SLOW. YOU WOULDN'T LAST A MINUTE IN THE CRIMSON RING.
THKRITTTT
YOU SAID THIS MEETING WOULD BE UNEVENTFUL!

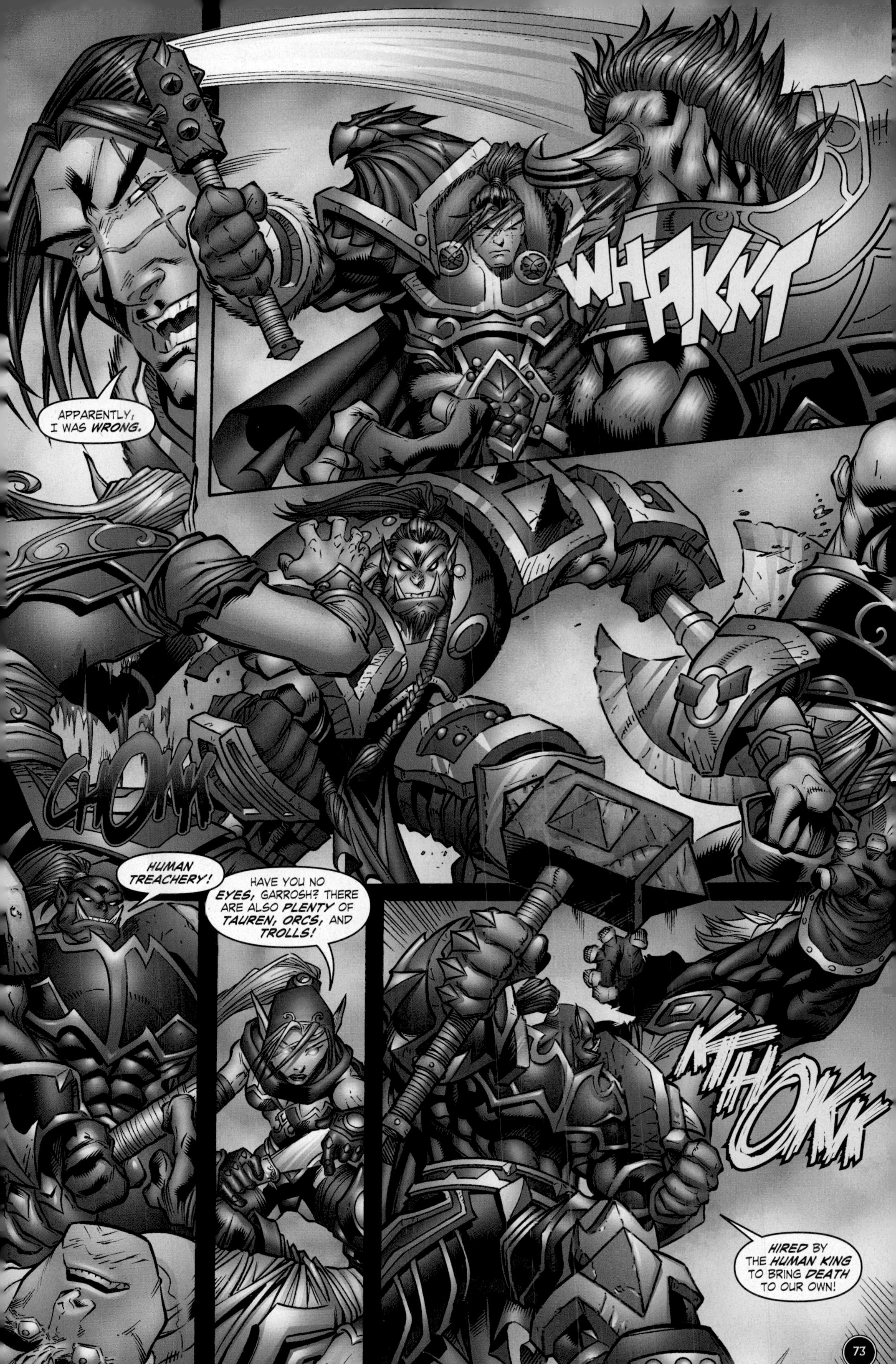
APPARENTLY, I WAS WRONG.
WHAKKT
CHOKK
HUMAN TREACHERY!
HAVE YOU NO EYES, GARROSH? THERE ARE ALSO PLENTY OF TAUREN, ORCS, AND TROLLS!
KTHOKK
HIRED BY THE HUMAN KING TO BRING DEATH TO OUR OWN!

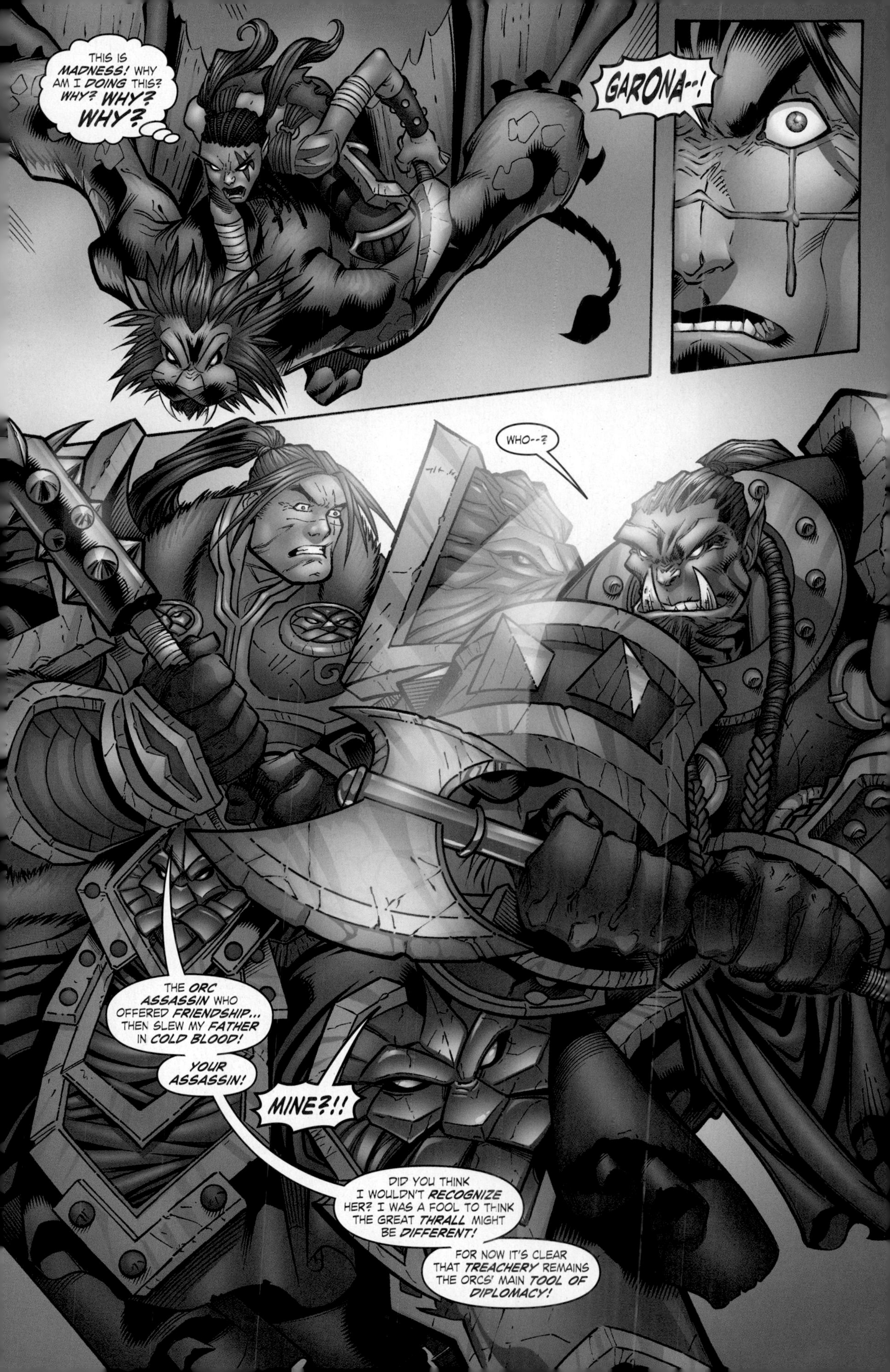
THIS IS MADNESS! WHY AM I DOING THIS? WHY? WHY? WHY?
GARONA--!
WHO--?
THE ORC ASSASSIN WHO OFFERED FRIENDSHIP... THEN SLEW MY FATHER IN COLD BLOOD!
YOUR ASSASSIN!
MINE?!!
DID YOU THINK I WOULDN'T RECOGNIZE HER? I WAS A FOOL TO THINK THE GREAT THRALL MIGHT BE DIFFERENT!
FOR NOW IT'S CLEAR THAT TREACHERY REMAINS THE ORCS' MAIN TOOL OF DIPLOMACY!

CHAPTER 4

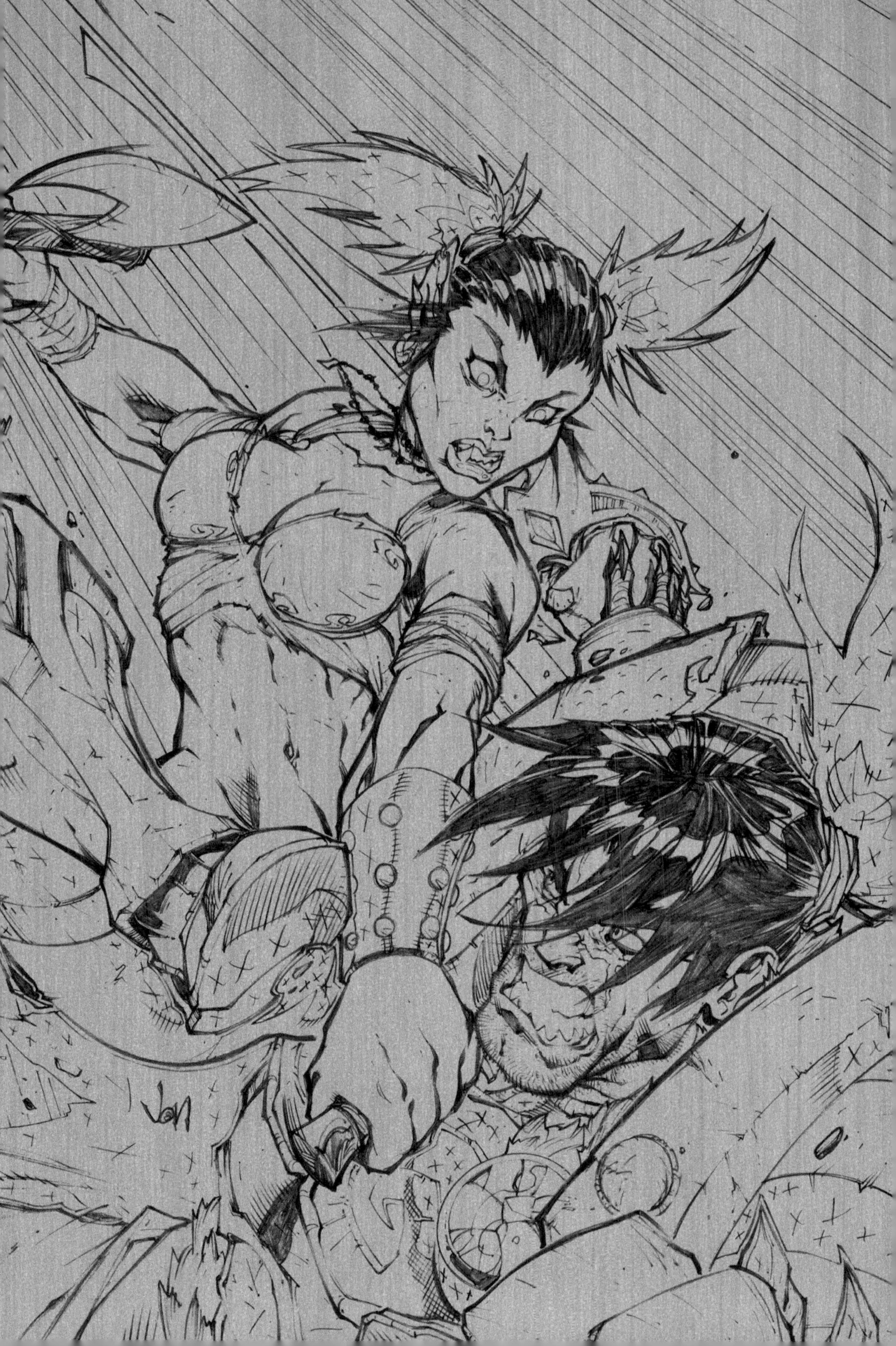

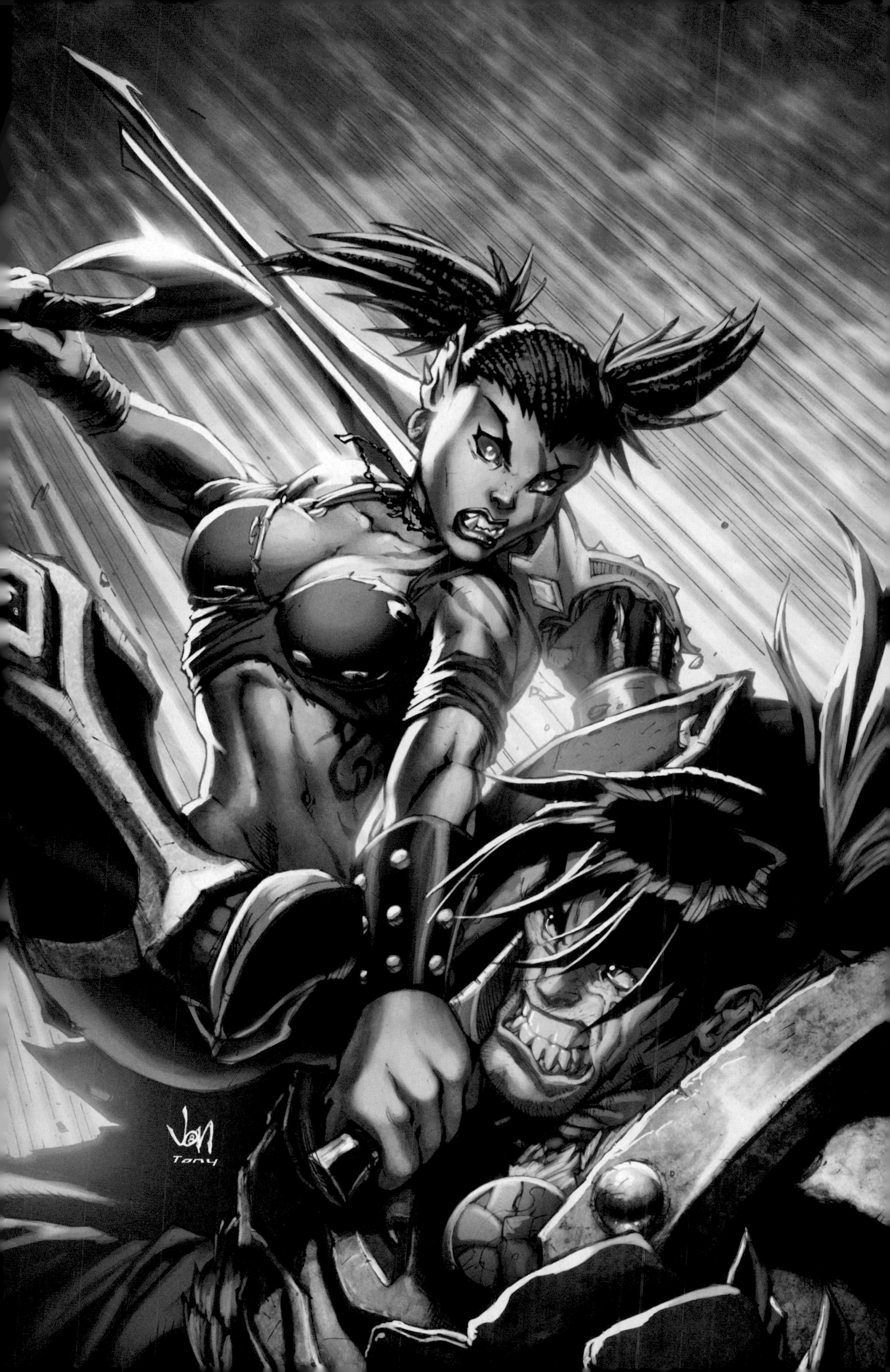

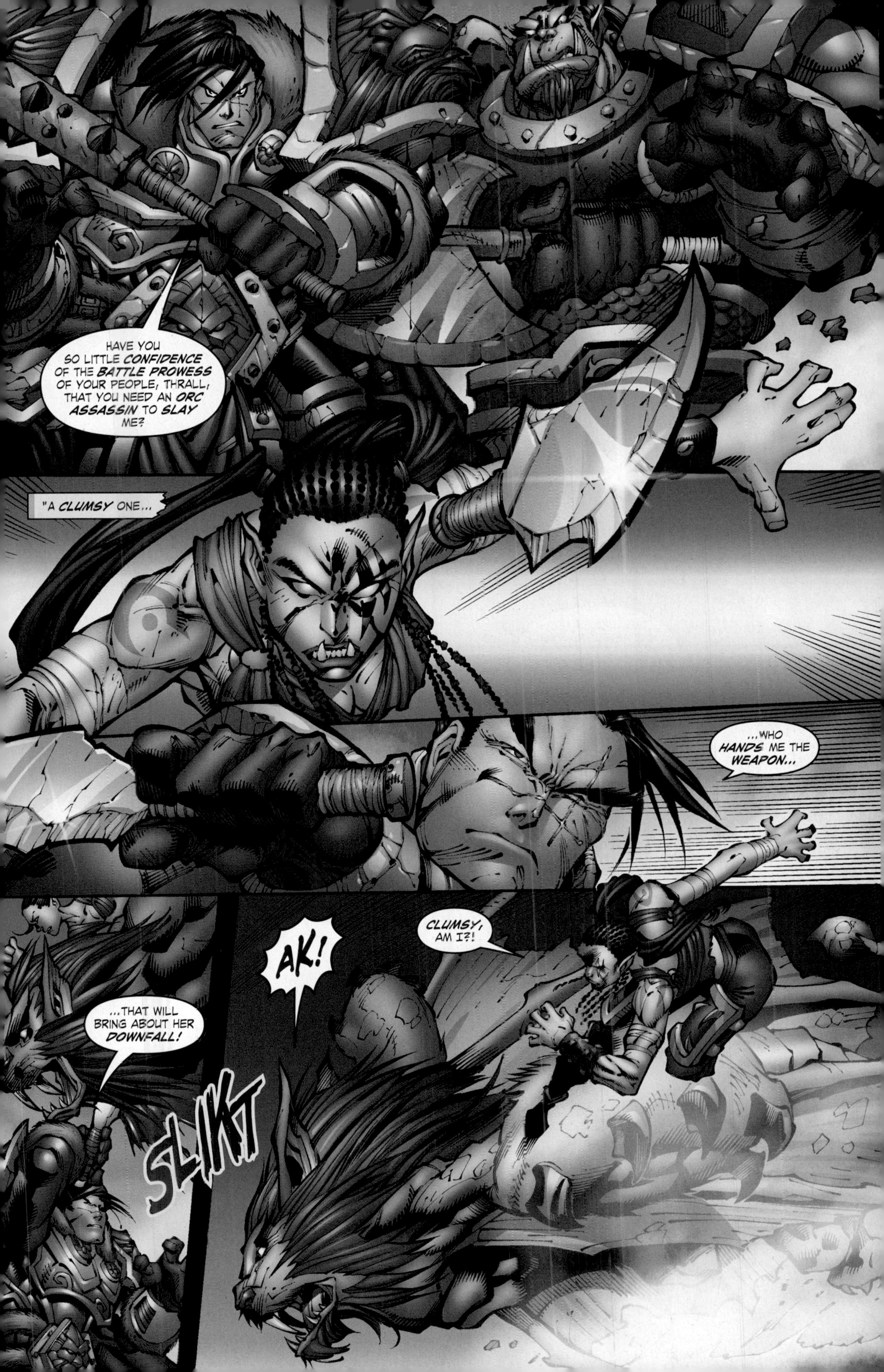
HAVE YOU SO LITTLE CONFIDENCE OF THE BATTLE PROWESS OF YOUR PEOPLE, THRALL, THAT YOU NEED AN ORC ASSASSIN TO SLAY ME?
"A CLUMSY ONE...
...WHO HANDS ME THE WEAPON...
...THAT WILL BRING ABOUT HER DOWNFALL!
AK!
CLUMSY, AM I?!
SLIKT

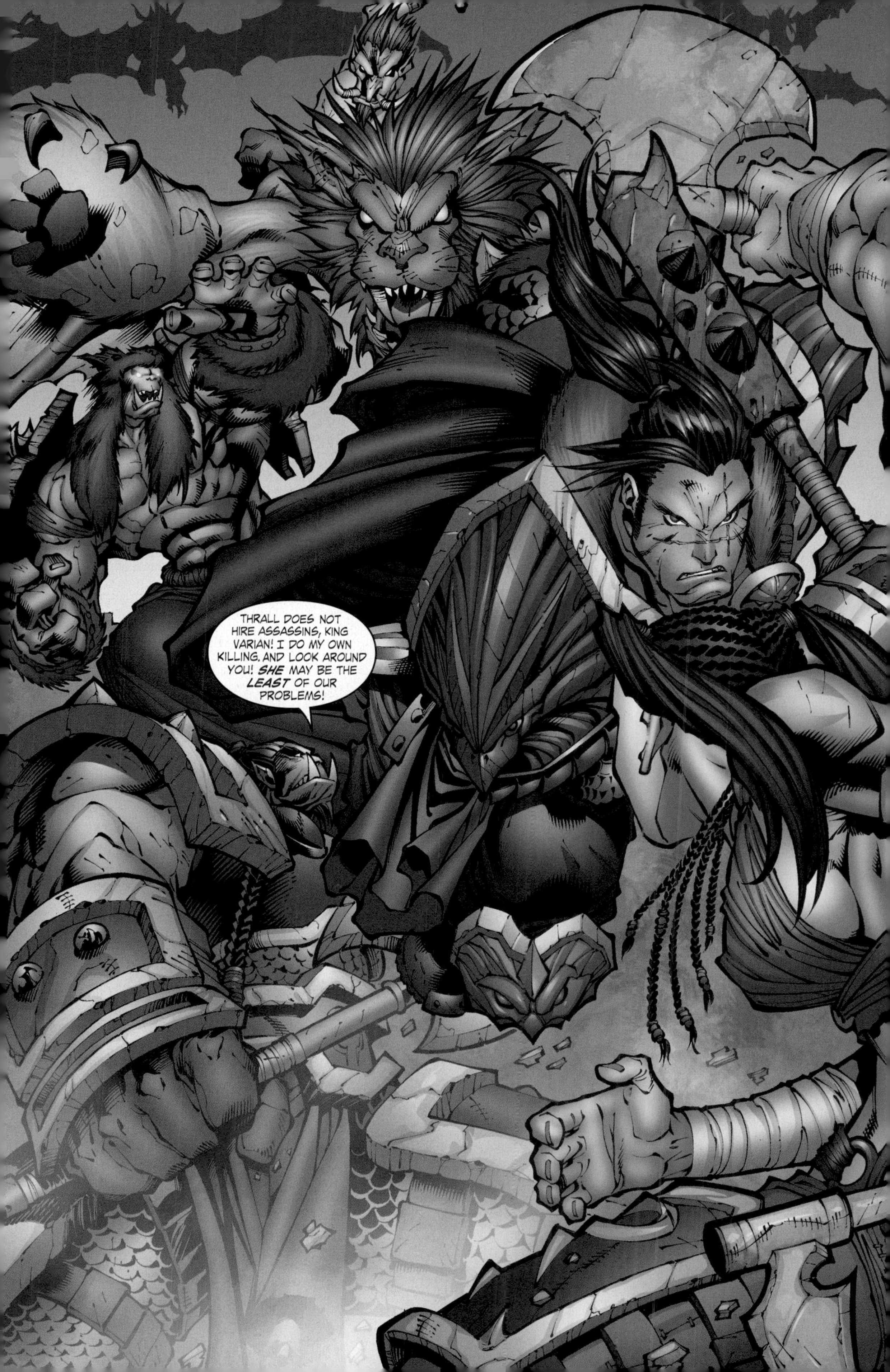
THRALL DOES NOT HIRE ASSASSINS, KING VARIAN! I DO MY OWN KILLING. AND LOOK AROUND YOU! *SHE* MAY BE THE *LEAST* OF OUR PROBLEMS!

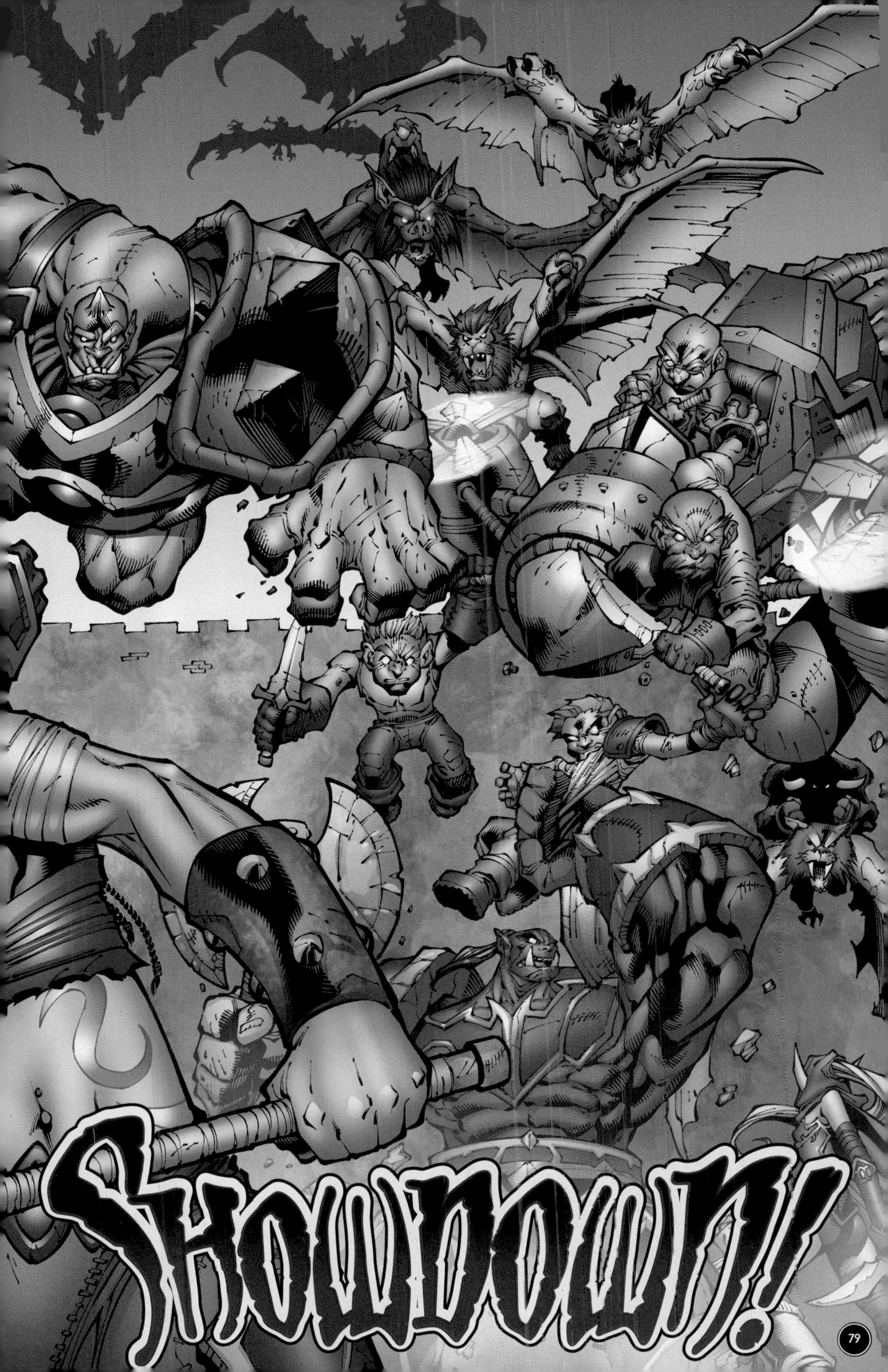
Showdown!

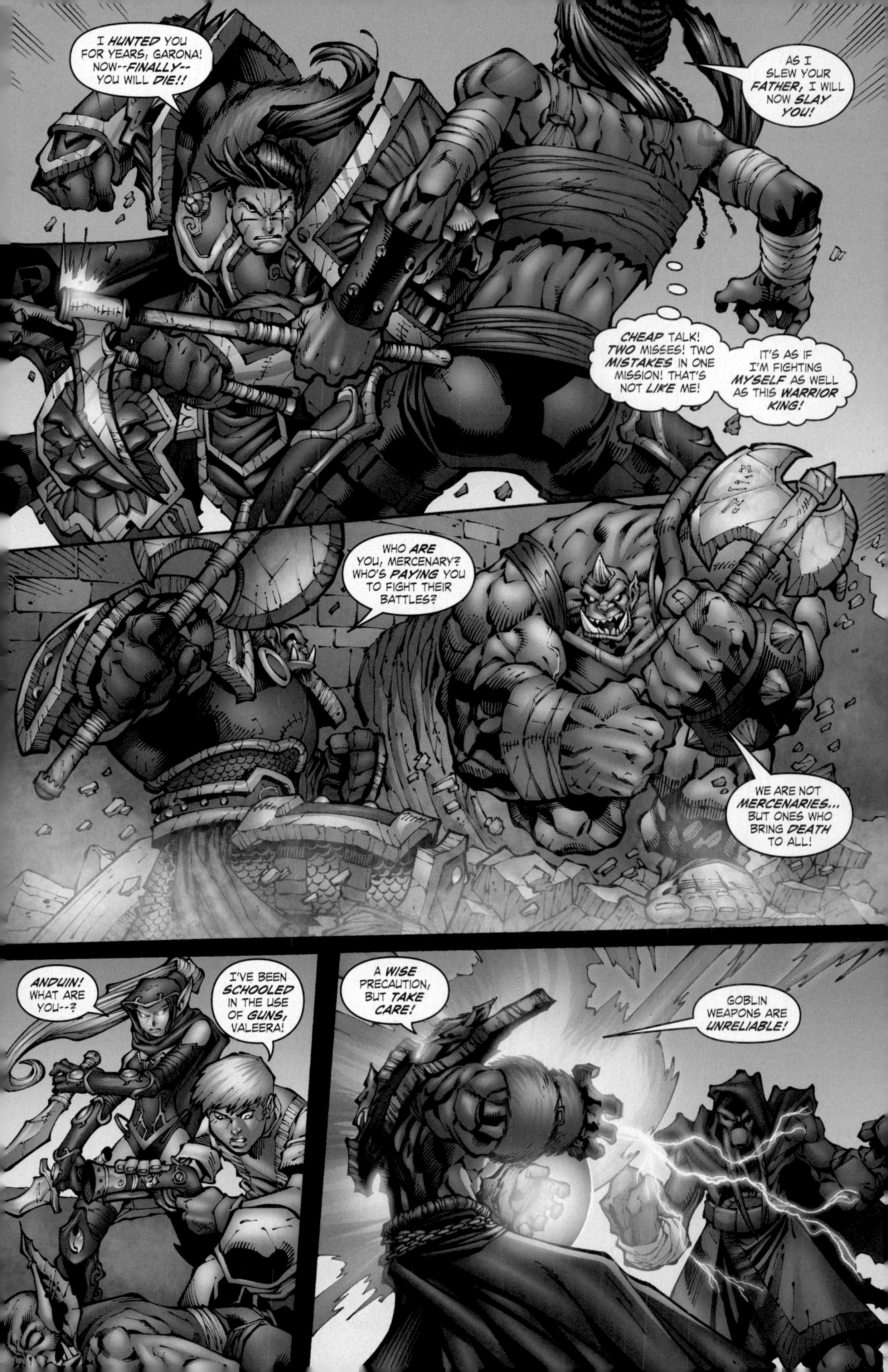
I HUNTED YOU FOR YEARS, GARONA! NOW--FINALLY--YOU WILL DIE!!
AS I SLEW YOUR FATHER, I WILL NOW SLAY YOU!
CHEAP TALK! TWO MISSES! TWO MISTAKES IN ONE MISSION! THAT'S NOT LIKE ME!
IT'S AS IF I'M FIGHTING MYSELF AS WELL AS THIS WARRIOR KING!
WHO ARE YOU, MERCENARY? WHO'S PAYING YOU TO FIGHT THEIR BATTLES?
WE ARE NOT MERCENARIES... BUT ONES WHO BRING DEATH TO ALL!
ANDUIN! WHAT ARE YOU--?
I'VE BEEN SCHOOLED IN THE USE OF GUNS, VALEERA!
A WISE PRECAUTION, BUT TAKE CARE!
GOBLIN WEAPONS ARE UNRELIABLE!

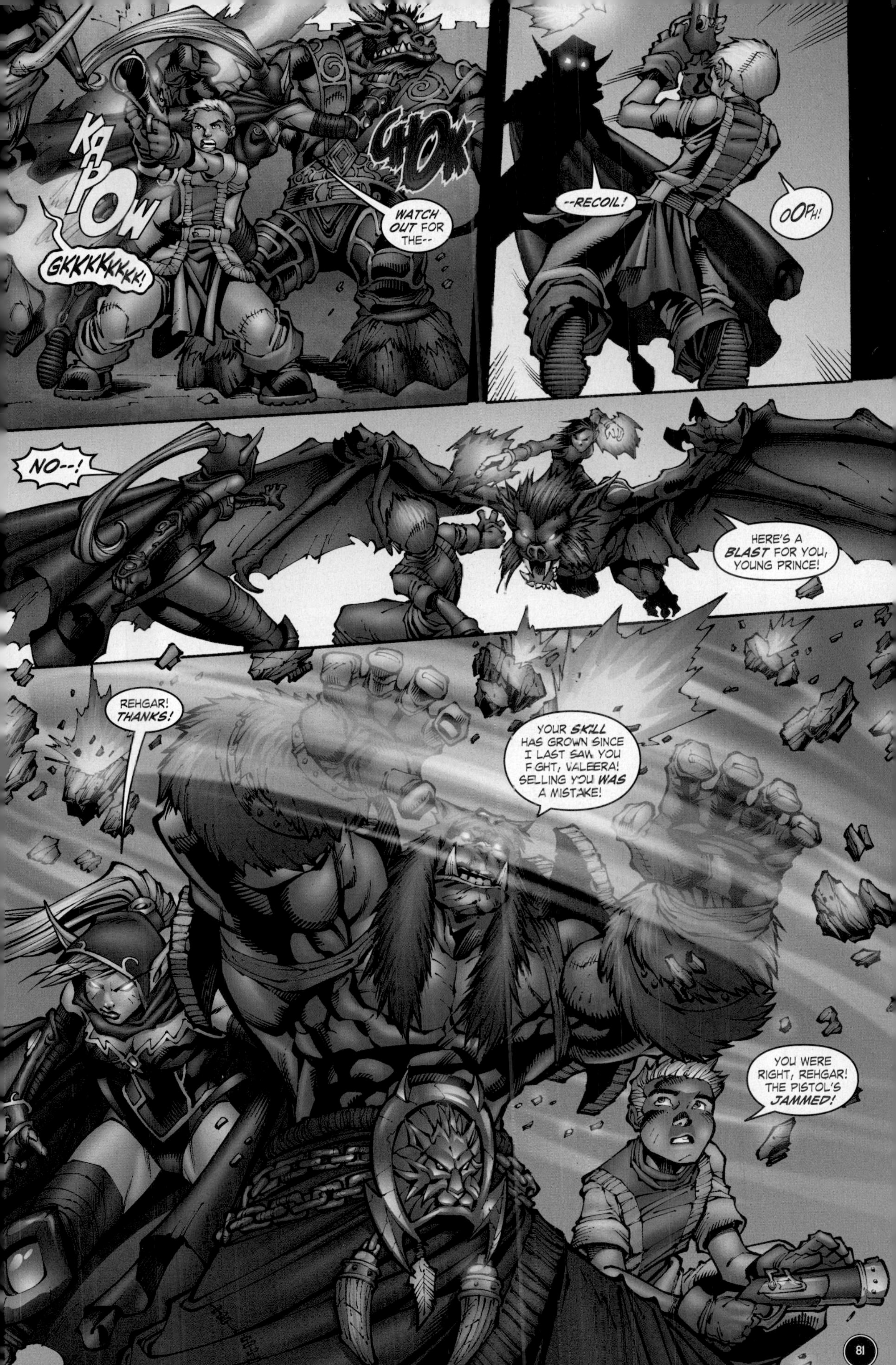
KA-POW
GKKKKKKKK!
CHOK
WATCH OUT FOR THE--
--RECOIL!
OOPH!
NO--!
HERE'S A BLAST FOR YOU, YOUNG PRINCE!
REHGAR! THANKS!
YOUR SKILL HAS GROWN SINCE I LAST SAW YOU FIGHT, VALEERA! SELLING YOU WAS A MISTAKE!
YOU WERE RIGHT, REHGAR! THE PISTOL'S JAMMED!

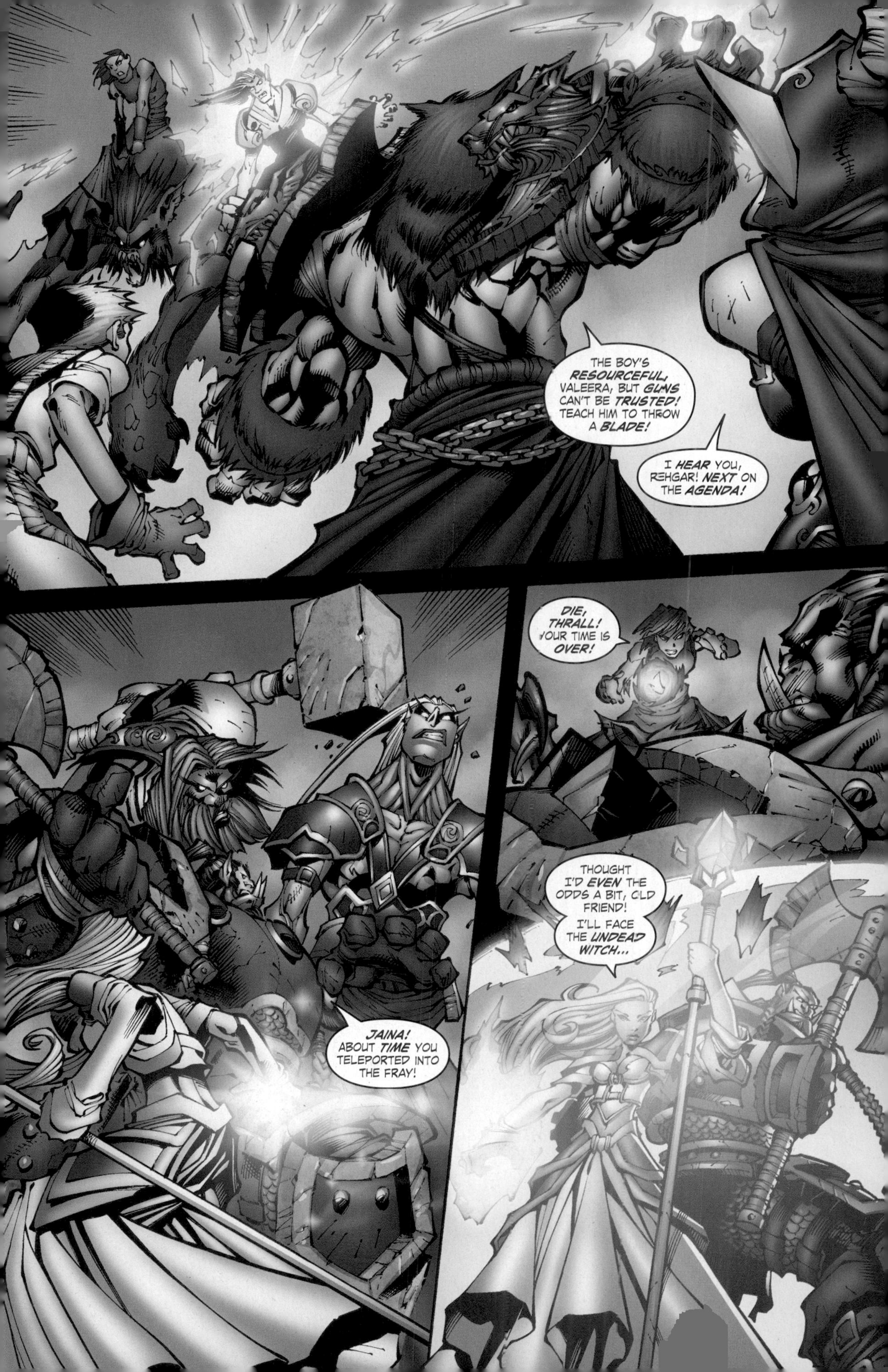
THE BOY'S RESOURCEFUL, VALEERA, BUT GUNS CAN'T BE TRUSTED! TEACH HIM TO THROW A BLADE!
I HEAR YOU, REHGAR! NEXT ON THE AGENDA!
JAINA! ABOUT TIME YOU TELEPORTED INTO THE FRAY!
DIE, THRALL! YOUR TIME IS OVER!
THOUGHT I'D EVEN THE ODDS A BIT, OLD FRIEND!
I'LL FACE THE UNDEAD WITCH...

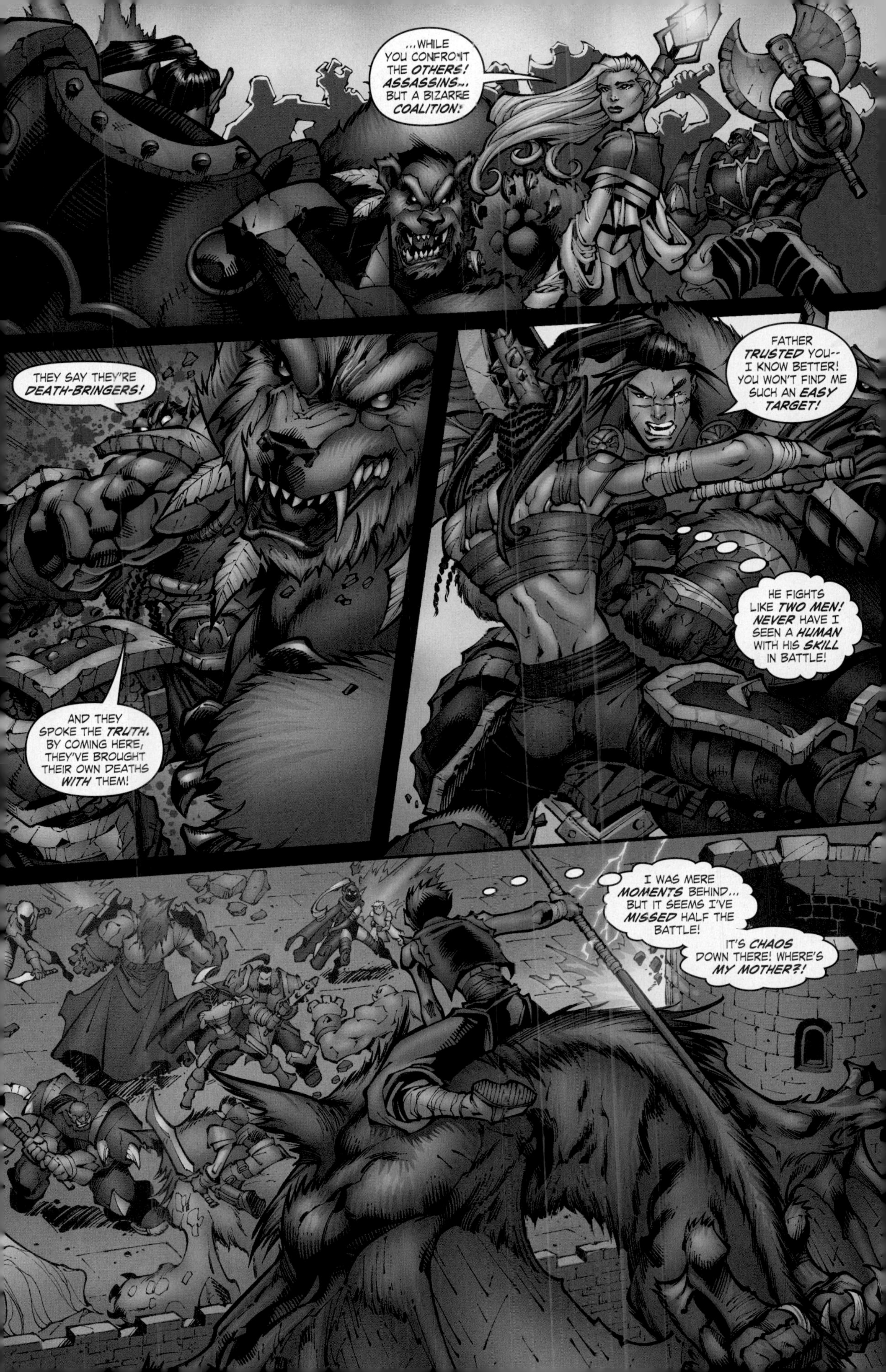
...WHILE YOU CONFRONT THE *OTHERS! ASSASSINS*... BUT A BIZARRE *COALITION!*
THEY SAY THEY'RE *DEATH-BRINGERS!*
AND THEY SPOKE THE *TRUTH.* BY COMING HERE, THEY'VE BROUGHT THEIR OWN DEATHS *WITH* THEM!
FATHER *TRUSTED* YOU-- I KNOW BETTER! YOU WON'T FIND ME SUCH AN *EASY TARGET!*
HE FIGHTS LIKE *TWO MEN! NEVER* HAVE I SEEN A *HUMAN* WITH HIS *SKILL* IN BATTLE!
I WAS MERE *MOMENTS* BEHIND... BUT IT SEEMS I'VE *MISSED* HALF THE BATTLE!
IT'S *CHAOS* DOWN THERE! WHERE'S *MY MOTHER?!*

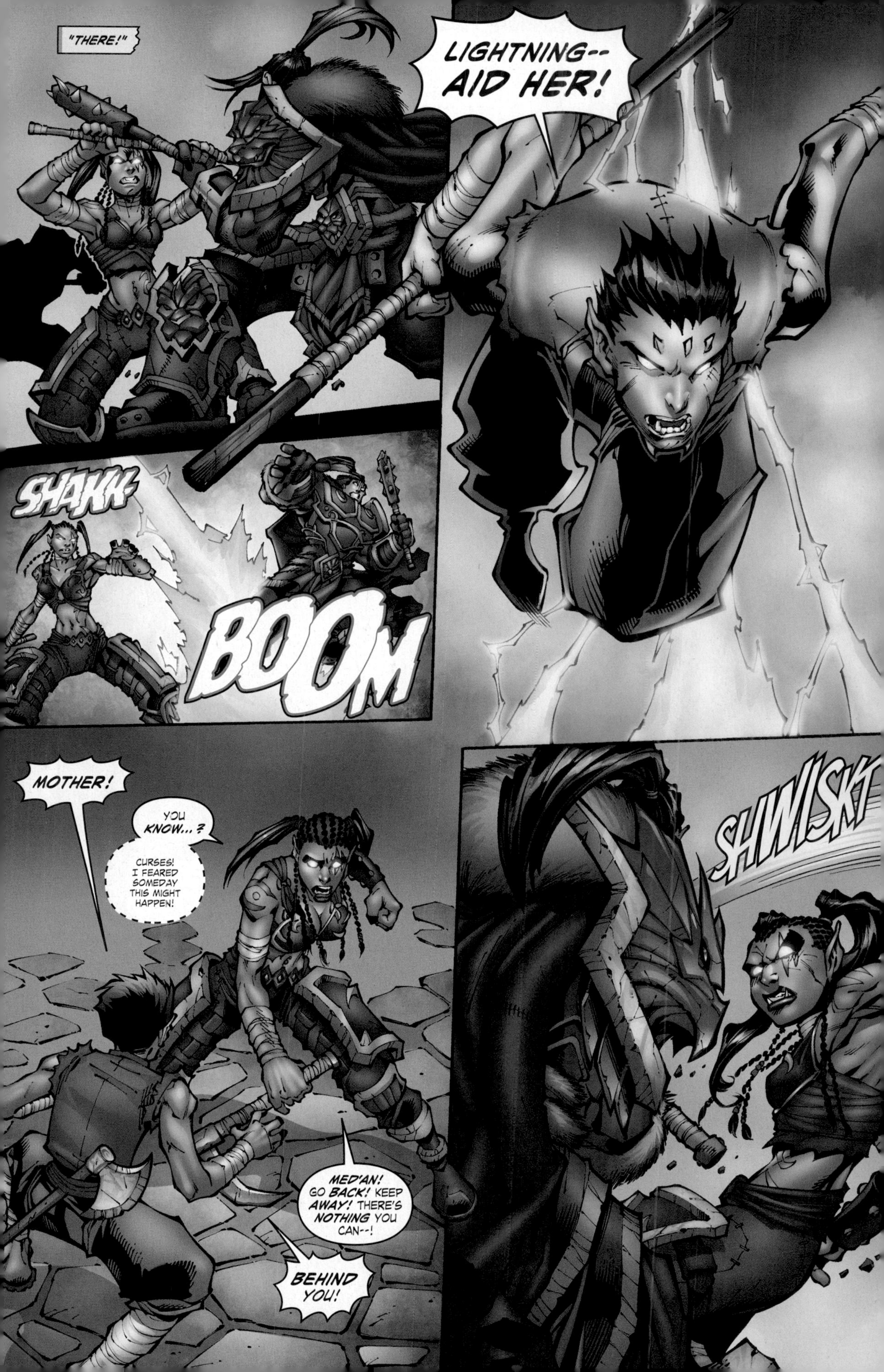
"THERE!"
LIGHTNING-- AID HER!
SHAKK
BOOM
MOTHER!
YOU KNOW...?
CURSES! I FEARED SOMEDAY THIS MIGHT HAPPEN!
MED'AN! GO BACK! KEEP AWAY! THERE'S NOTHING YOU CAN--!
BEHIND YOU!
SHWISKT

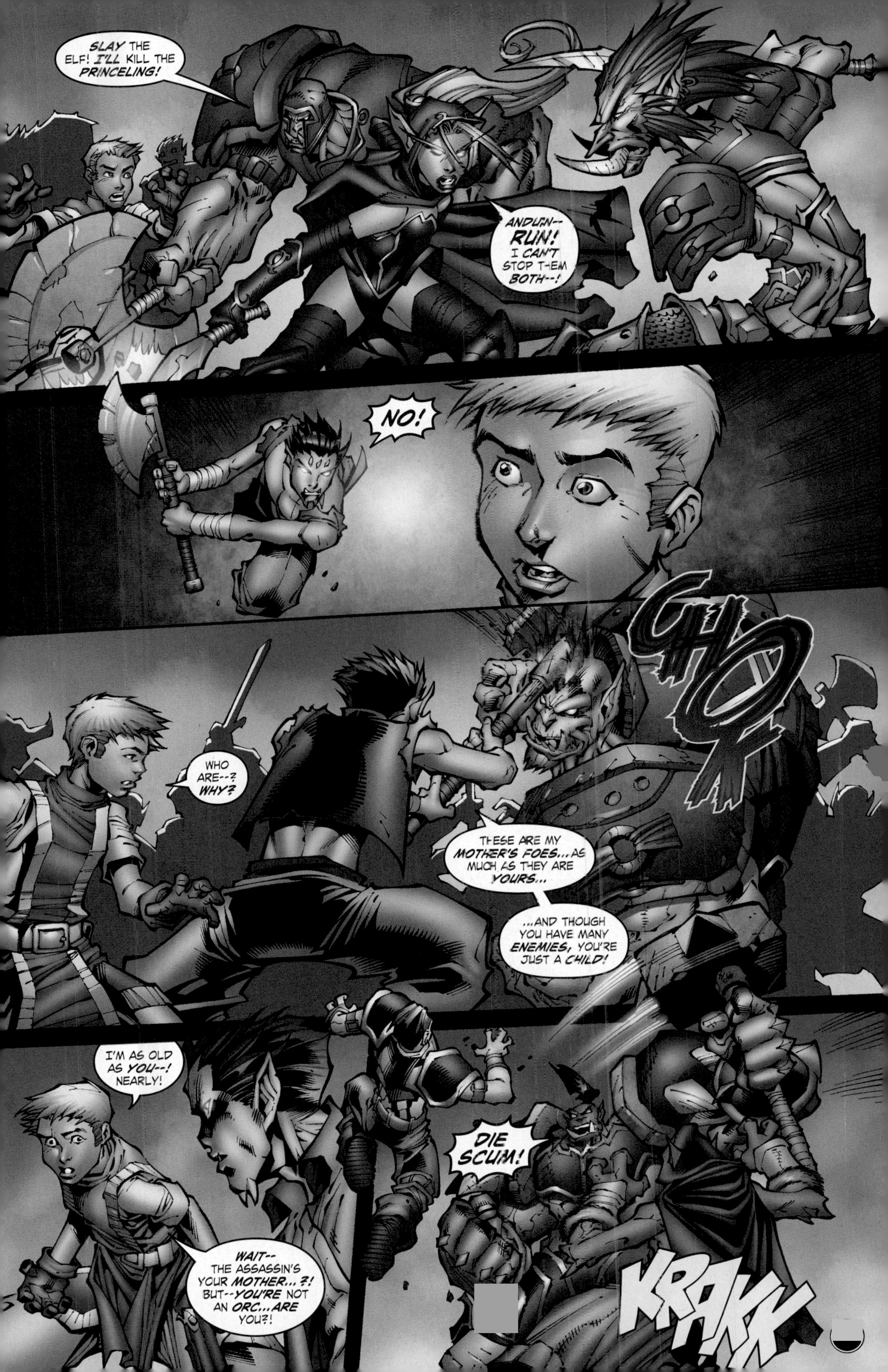
SLAY THE ELF! I'LL KILL THE PRINCELING!
ANDUIN--RUN! I CAN'T STOP THEM BOTH--!
NO!
CHOK
WHO ARE--? WHY?
THESE ARE MY MOTHER'S FOES...AS MUCH AS THEY ARE YOURS...
...AND THOUGH YOU HAVE MANY ENEMIES, YOU'RE JUST A CHILD!
I'M AS OLD AS YOU--! NEARLY!
DIE SCUM!
WAIT--THE ASSASSIN'S YOUR MOTHER...?! BUT--YOU'RE NOT AN ORC...ARE YOU?!
KRAKK

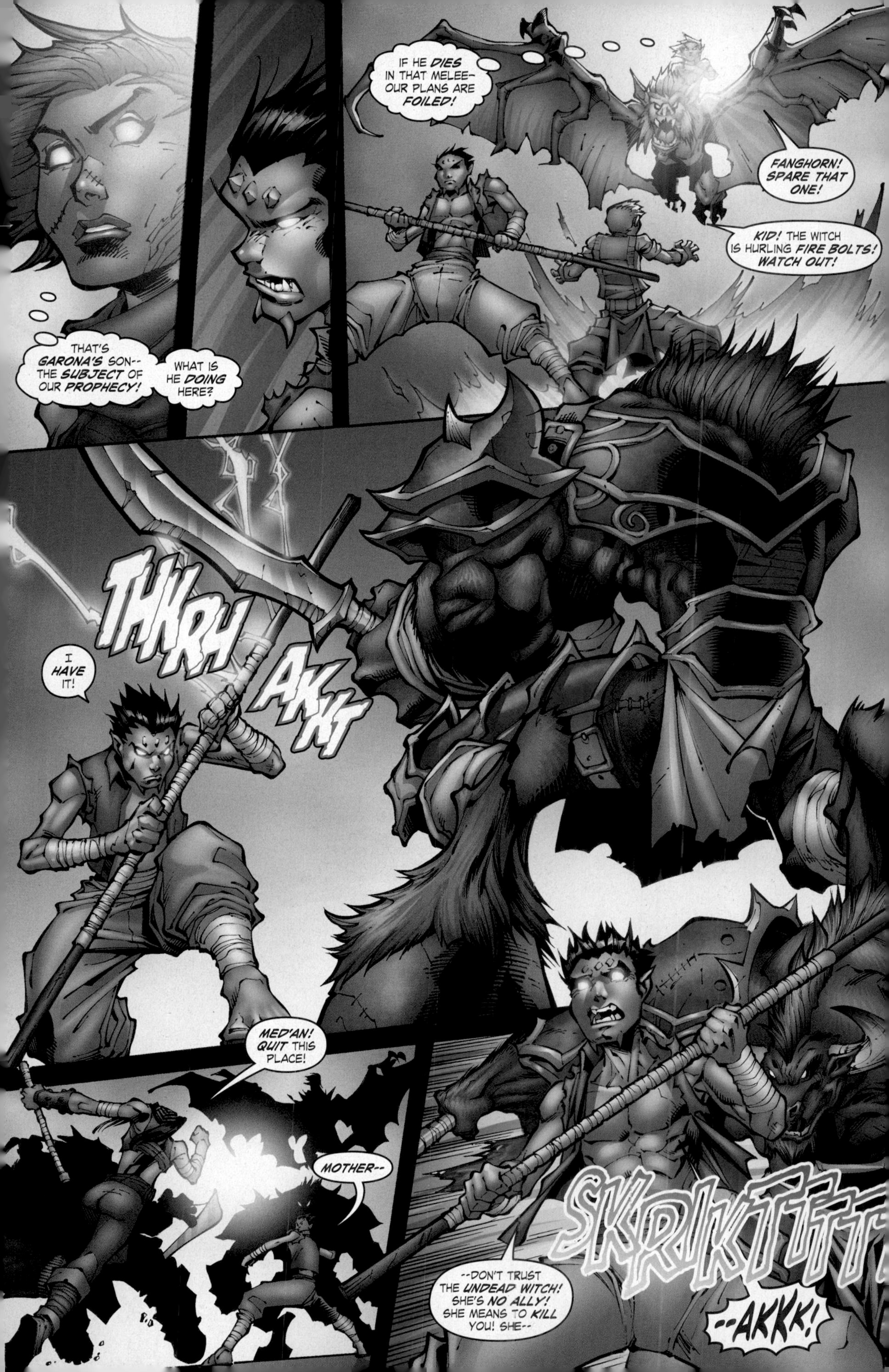
THAT'S GARONA'S SON--THE SUBJECT OF OUR PROPHECY!
WHAT IS HE DOING HERE?
IF HE DIES IN THAT MELEE--OUR PLANS ARE FOILED!
FANGHORN! SPARE THAT ONE!
KID! THE WITCH IS HURLING FIRE BOLTS! WATCH OUT!
THKRH
AKKT
I HAVE IT!
MED'AN! QUIT THIS PLACE!
MOTHER--
--DON'T TRUST THE UNDEAD WITCH! SHE'S NO ALLY! SHE MEANS TO KILL YOU! SHE--
SKRIKTTT
--AKKK!

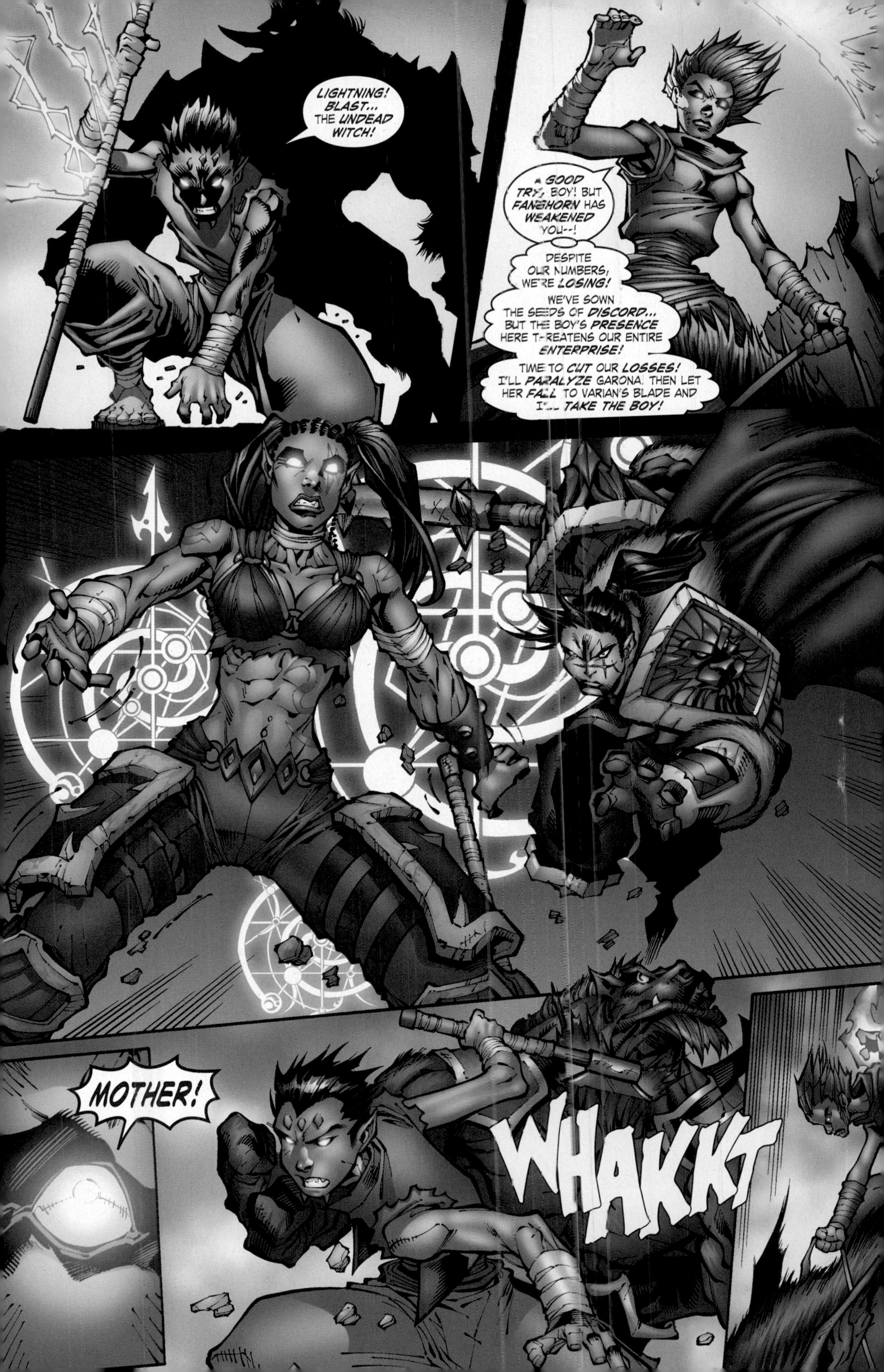
LIGHTNING! BLAST... THE UNDEAD WITCH!
A GOOD TRY, BOY! BUT FANGHORN HAS WEAKENED YOU--!
DESPITE OUR NUMBERS, WE'RE LOSING!
WE'VE SOWN THE SEEDS OF DISCORD... BUT THE BOY'S PRESENCE HERE THREATENS OUR ENTIRE ENTERPRISE!
TIME TO CUT OUR LOSSES! I'LL PARALYZE GARONA, THEN LET HER FALL TO VARIAN'S BLADE AND I'LL TAKE THE BOY!
MOTHER!
WHAKKT

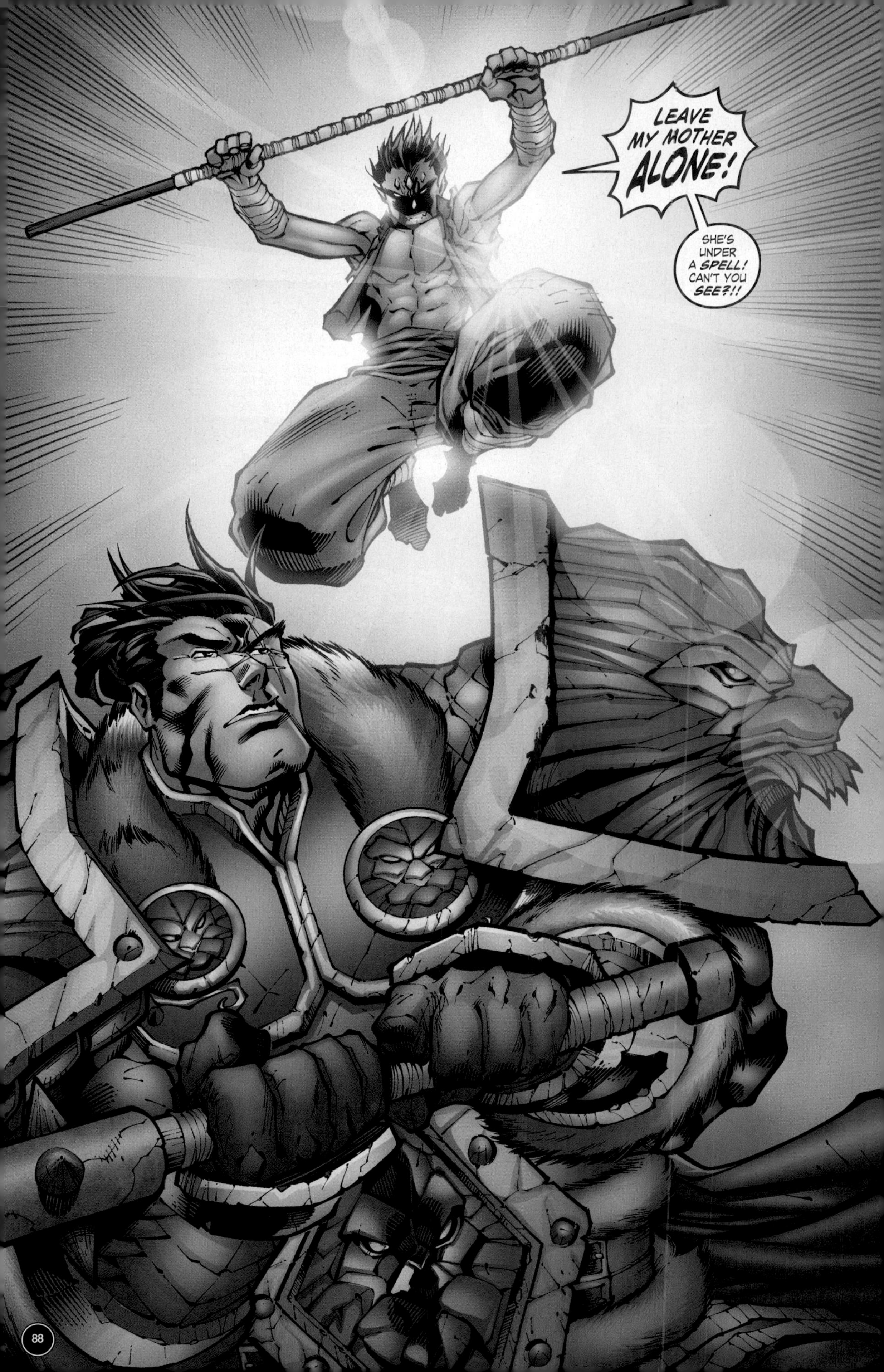
LEAVE MY MOTHER ALONE!
SHE'S UNDER A SPELL! CAN'T YOU SEE?!!

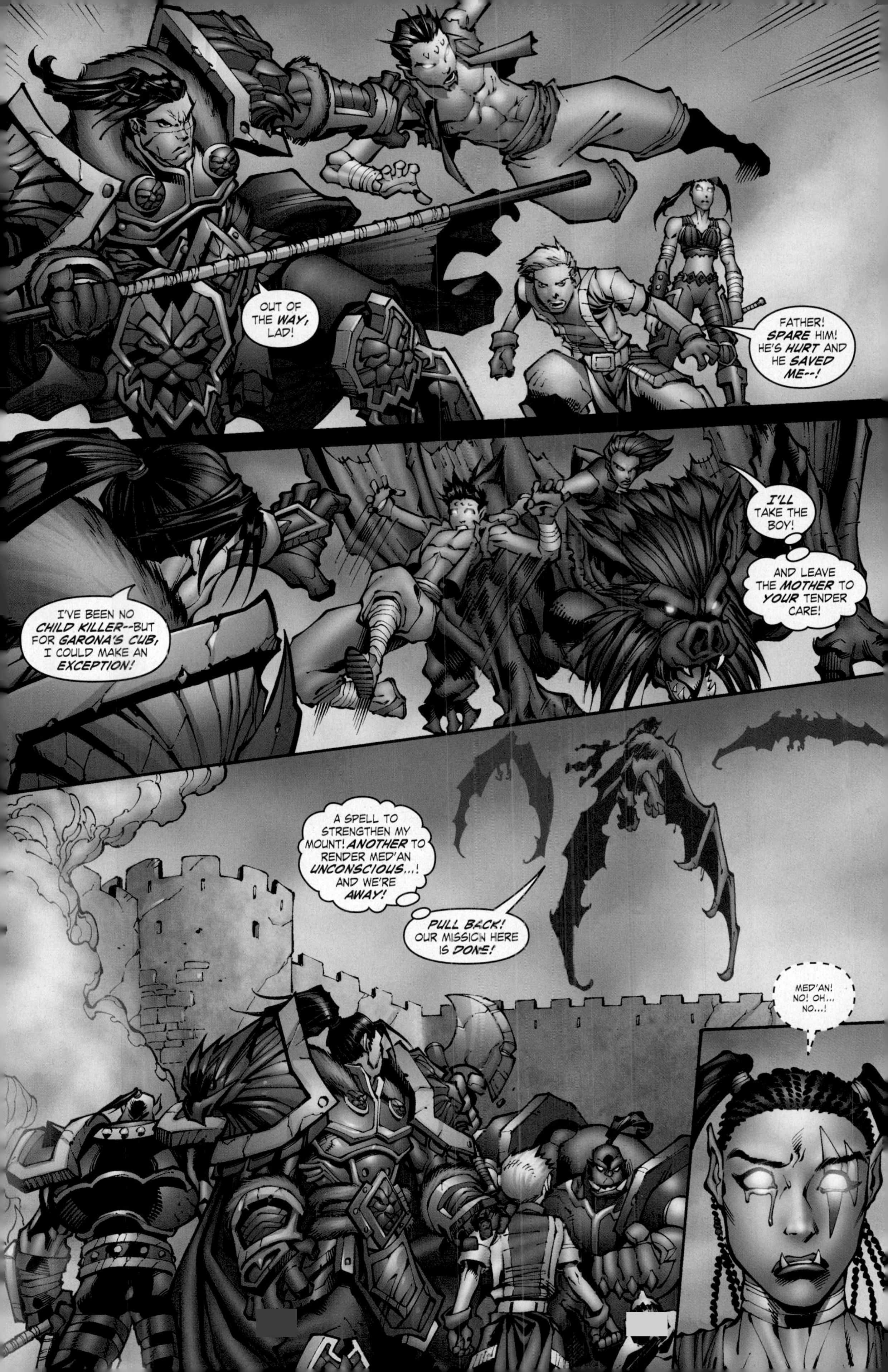

OUT OF THE WAY, LAD!
FATHER! SPARE HIM! HE'S HURT AND HE SAVED ME--!
I'VE BEEN NO CHILD KILLER--BUT FOR GARONA'S CUB, I COULD MAKE AN EXCEPTION!
I'LL TAKE THE BOY!
AND LEAVE THE MOTHER TO YOUR TENDER CARE!
A SPELL TO STRENGTHEN MY MOUNT! ANOTHER TO RENDER MED'AN UNCONSCIOUS...! AND WE'RE AWAY!
PULL BACK! OUR MISSION HERE IS DONE!
MED'AN! NO! OH... NO...!

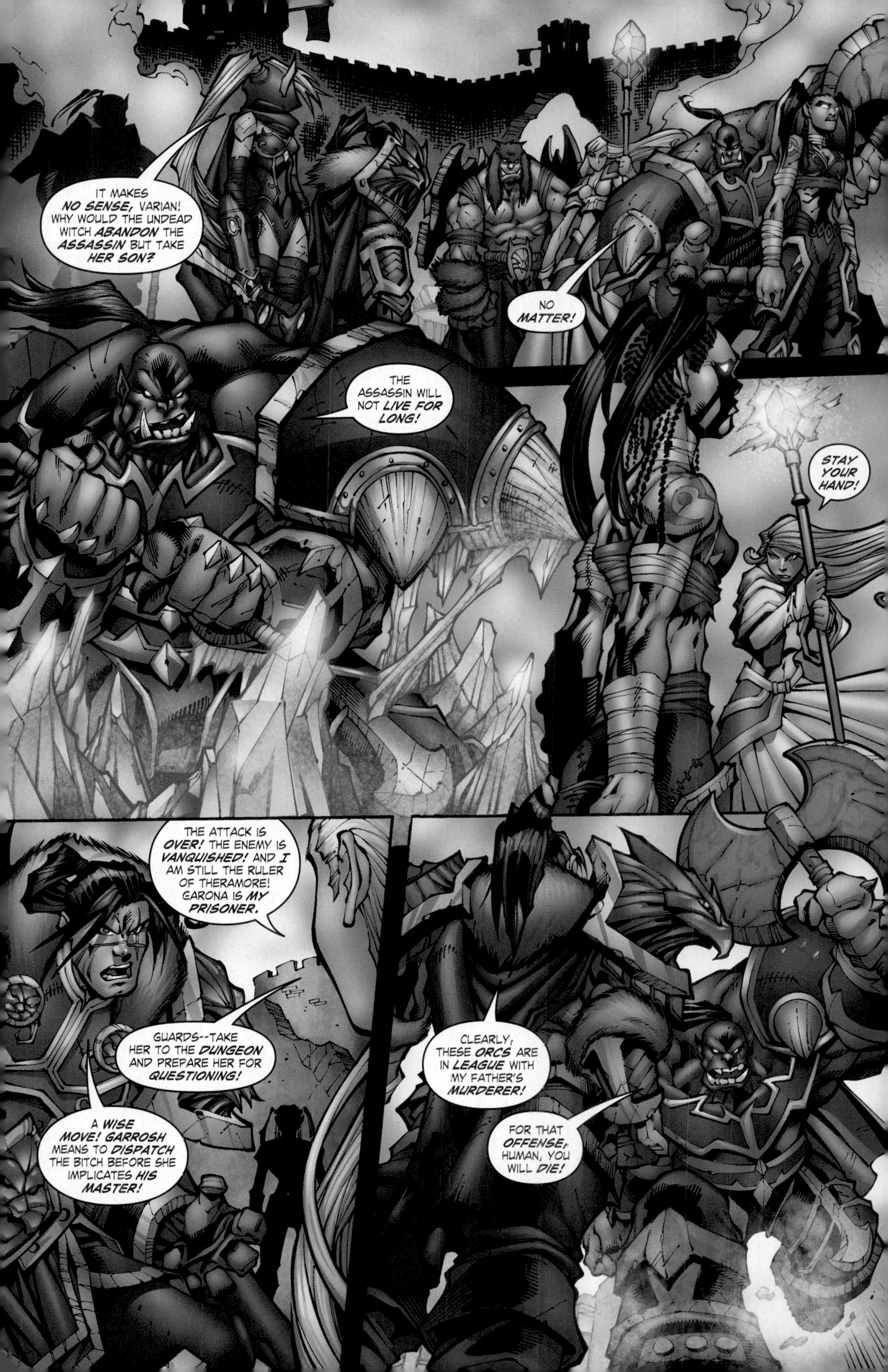
IT MAKES NO SENSE, VARIAN! WHY WOULD THE UNDEAD WITCH ABANDON THE ASSASSIN BUT TAKE HER SON?
NO MATTER!
THE ASSASSIN WILL NOT LIVE FOR LONG!
STAY YOUR HAND!
THE ATTACK IS OVER! THE ENEMY IS VANQUISHED! AND I AM STILL THE RULER OF THERAMORE! GARONA IS MY PRISONER.
GUARDS--TAKE HER TO THE DUNGEON AND PREPARE HER FOR QUESTIONING!
A WISE MOVE! GARROSH MEANS TO DISPATCH THE BITCH BEFORE SHE IMPLICATES HIS MASTER!
CLEARLY, THESE ORCS ARE IN LEAGUE WITH MY FATHER'S MURDERER!
FOR THAT OFFENSE, HUMAN, YOU WILL DIE!

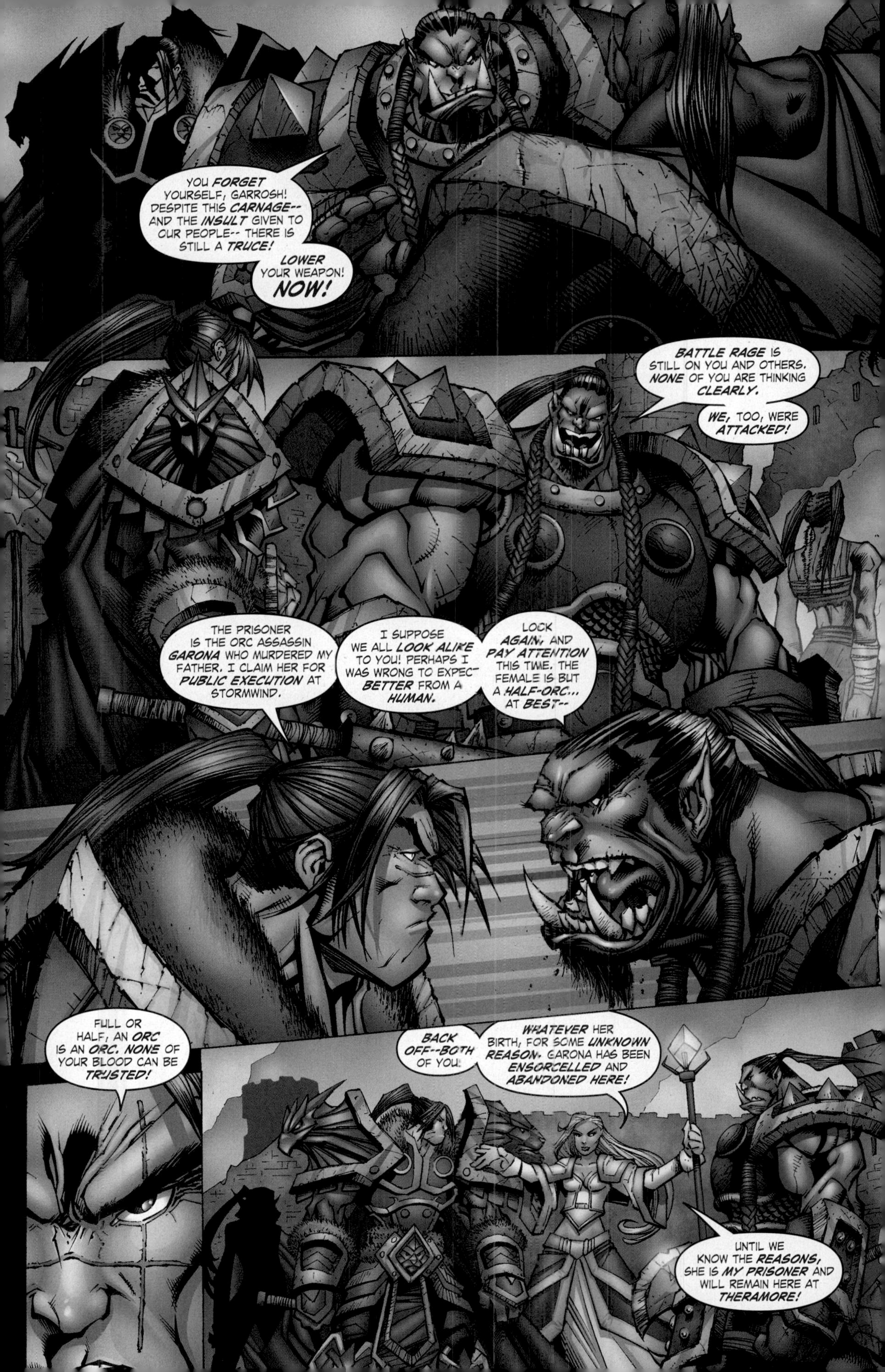
YOU FORGET YOURSELF, GARROSH! DESPITE THIS CARNAGE-- AND THE INSULT GIVEN TO OUR PEOPLE-- THERE IS STILL A TRUCE!
LOWER YOUR WEAPON! NOW!
BATTLE RAGE IS STILL ON YOU AND OTHERS. NONE OF YOU ARE THINKING CLEARLY.
WE, TOO, WERE ATTACKED!
THE PRISONER IS THE ORC ASSASSIN GARONA WHO MURDERED MY FATHER. I CLAIM HER FOR PUBLIC EXECUTION AT STORMWIND.
I SUPPOSE WE ALL LOOK ALIKE TO YOU! PERHAPS I WAS WRONG TO EXPECT BETTER FROM A HUMAN.
LOOK AGAIN, AND PAY ATTENTION THIS TIME. THE FEMALE IS BUT A HALF-ORC... AT BEST--
FULL OR HALF, AN ORC IS AN ORC. NONE OF YOUR BLOOD CAN BE TRUSTED!
BACK OFF--BOTH OF YOU!
WHATEVER HER BIRTH, FOR SOME UNKNOWN REASON, GARONA HAS BEEN ENSORCELLED AND ABANDONED HERE!
UNTIL WE KNOW THE REASONS, SHE IS MY PRISONER AND WILL REMAIN HERE AT THERAMORE!

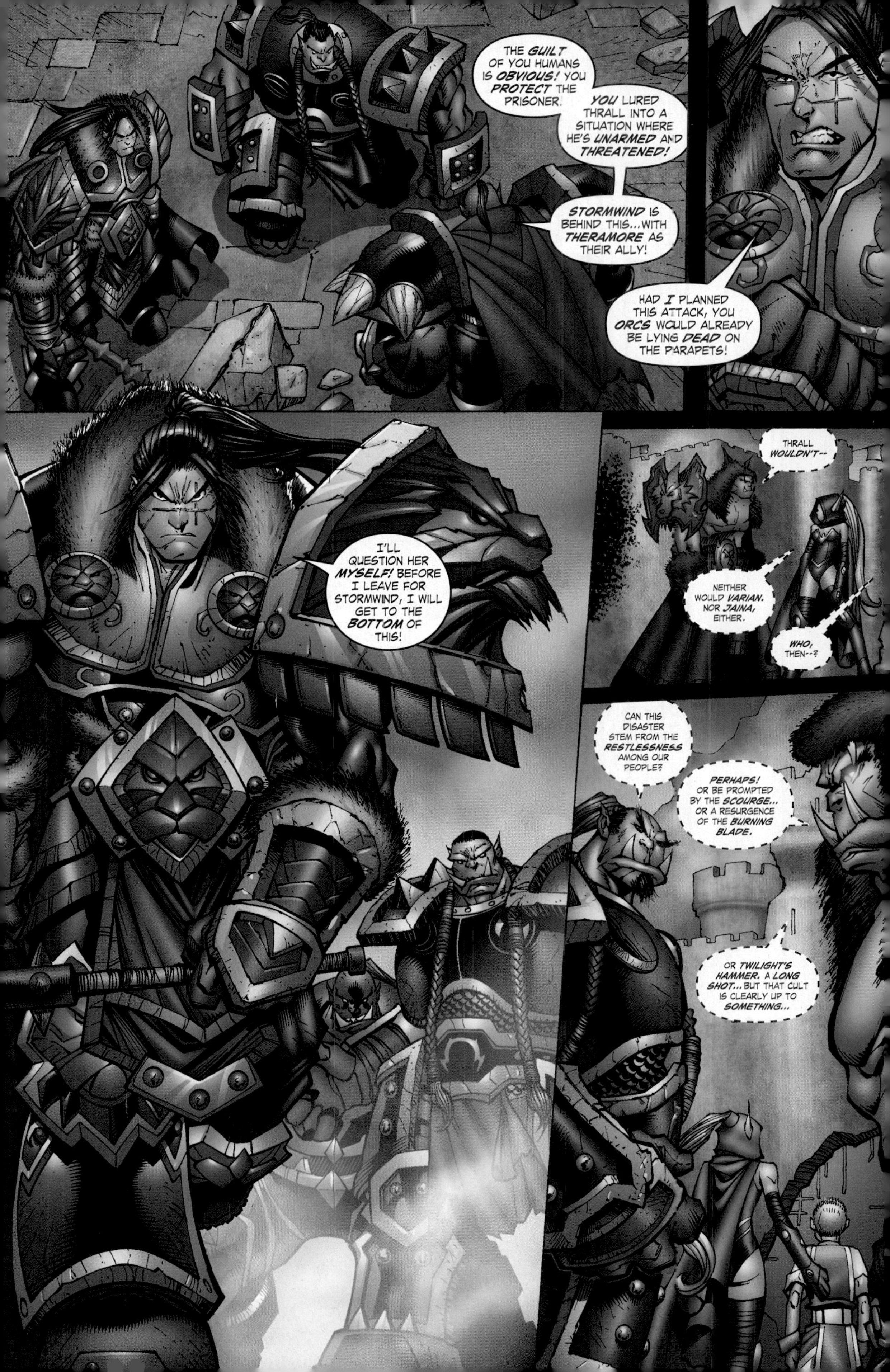
THE GUILT OF YOU HUMANS IS OBVIOUS! YOU PROTECT THE PRISONER.
YOU LURED THRALL INTO A SITUATION WHERE HE'S UNARMED AND THREATENED!
STORMWIND IS BEHIND THIS...WITH THERAMORE AS THEIR ALLY!
HAD I PLANNED THIS ATTACK, YOU ORCS WOULD ALREADY BE LYING DEAD ON THE PARAPETS!
I'LL QUESTION HER MYSELF! BEFORE I LEAVE FOR STORMWIND, I WILL GET TO THE BOTTOM OF THIS!
THRALL WOULDN'T--
NEITHER WOULD VARIAN. NOR JAINA, EITHER.
WHO, THEN--?
CAN THIS DISASTER STEM FROM THE RESTLESSNESS AMONG OUR PEOPLE?
PERHAPS! OR BE PROMPTED BY THE SCOURGE... OR A RESURGENCE OF THE BURNING BLADE.
OR TWILIGHT'S HAMMER. A LONG SHOT... BUT THAT CULT IS CLEARLY UP TO SOMETHING...

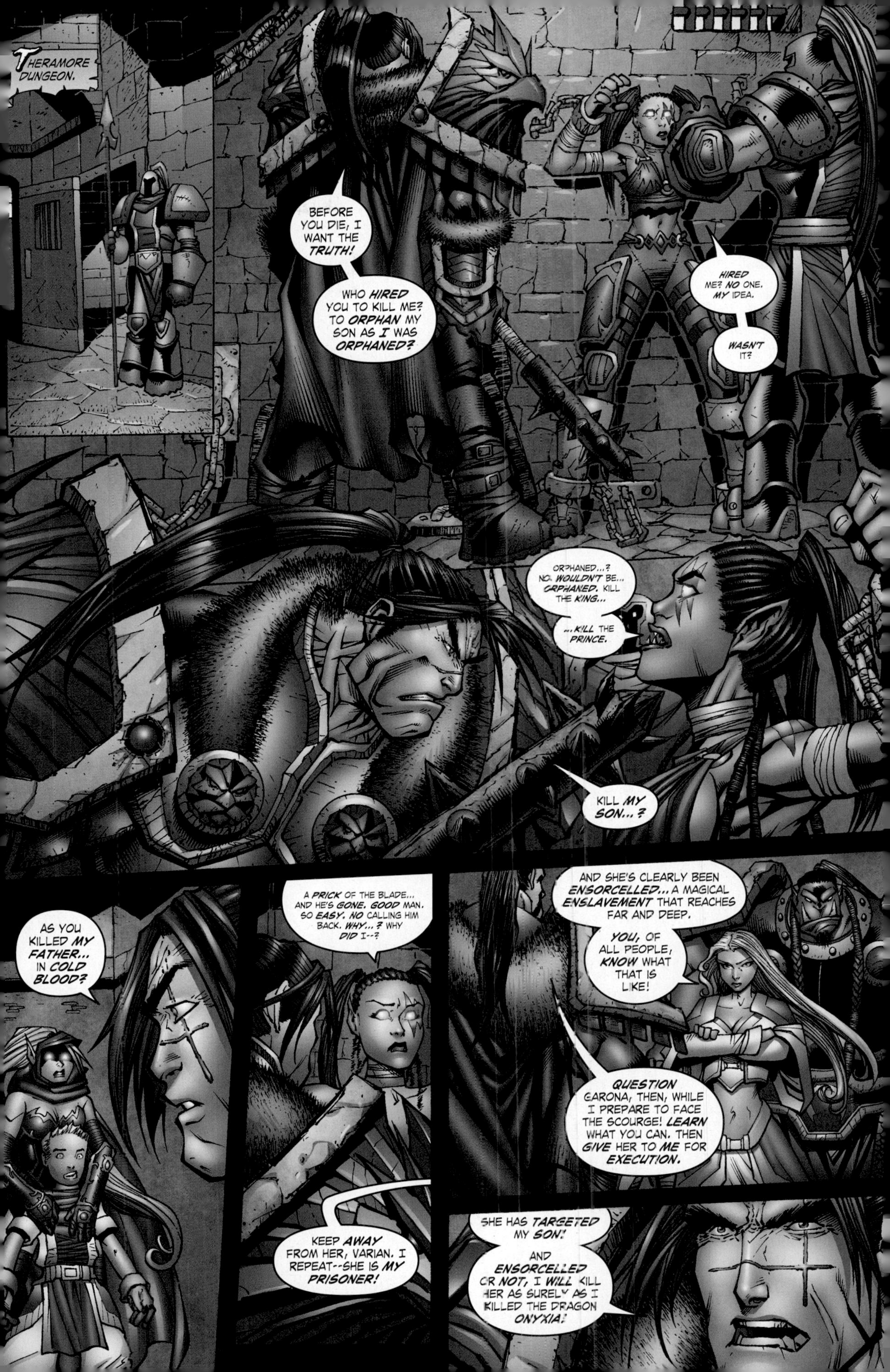
THERAMORE DUNGEON.
BEFORE YOU DIE, I WANT THE TRUTH!
WHO HIRED YOU TO KILL ME? TO ORPHAN MY SON AS I WAS ORPHANED?
HIRED ME? NO ONE. MY IDEA.
WASN'T IT?
ORPHANED...? NO. WOULDN'T BE... ORPHANED. KILL THE KING...
...KILL THE PRINCE.
KILL MY SON...?
AS YOU KILLED MY FATHER... IN COLD BLOOD?
A PRICK OF THE BLADE... AND HE'S GONE. GOOD MAN. SO EASY. NO CALLING HIM BACK. WHY...? WHY DID I--?
AND SHE'S CLEARLY BEEN ENSORCELLED... A MAGICAL ENSLAVEMENT THAT REACHES FAR AND DEEP.
YOU, OF ALL PEOPLE, KNOW WHAT THAT IS LIKE!
QUESTION GARONA, THEN, WHILE I PREPARE TO FACE THE SCOURGE! LEARN WHAT YOU CAN. THEN GIVE HER TO ME FOR EXECUTION.
KEEP AWAY FROM HER, VARIAN. I REPEAT--SHE IS MY PRISONER!
SHE HAS TARGETED MY SON!
AND ENSORCELLED OR NOT, I WILL KILL HER AS SURELY AS I KILLED THE DRAGON ONYXIA!

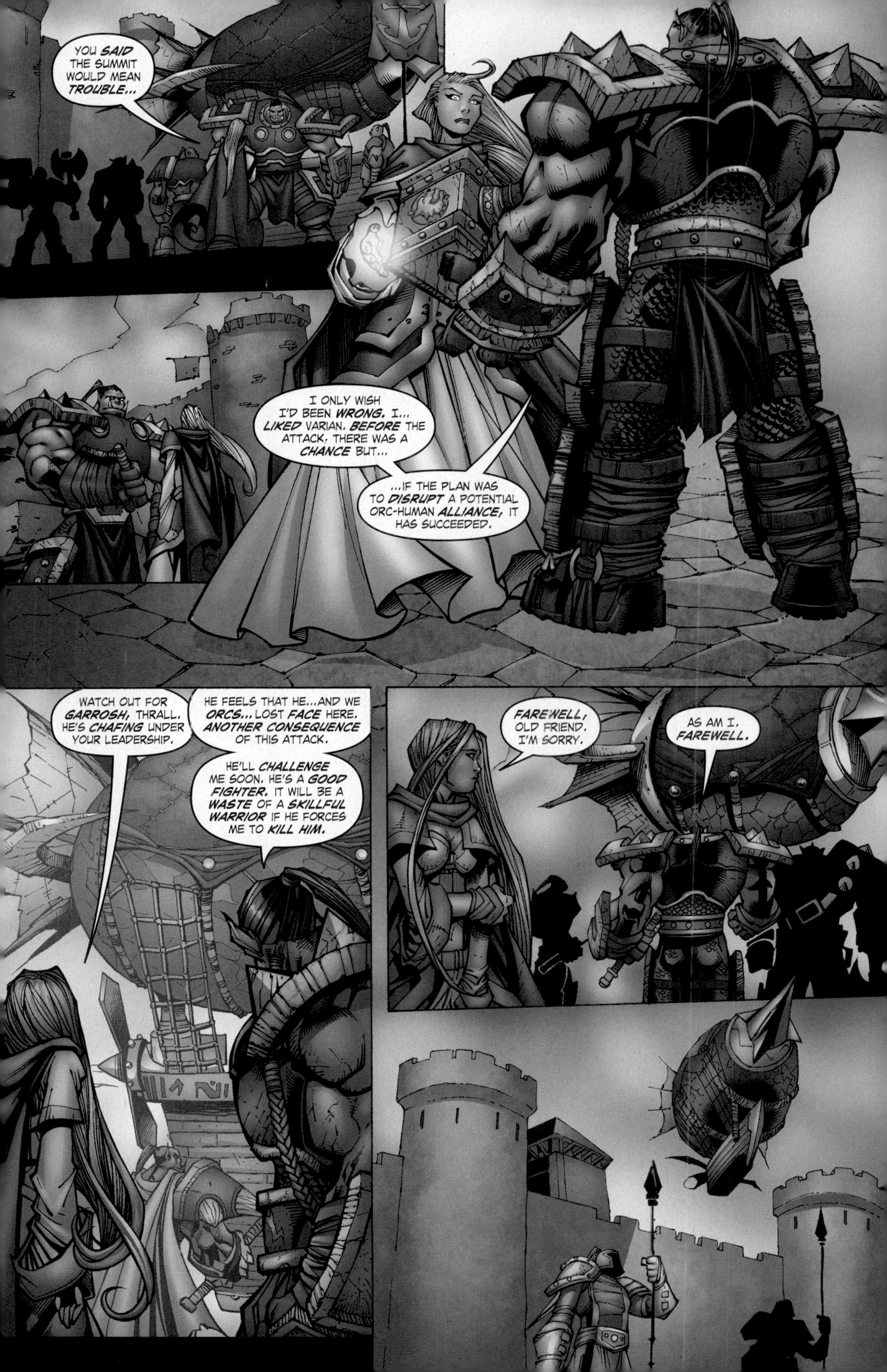
YOU SAID THE SUMMIT WOULD MEAN TROUBLE...
I ONLY WISH I'D BEEN WRONG. I... LIKED VARIAN. BEFORE THE ATTACK, THERE WAS A CHANCE BUT...
...IF THE PLAN WAS TO DISRUPT A POTENTIAL ORC-HUMAN ALLIANCE, IT HAS SUCCEEDED.
WATCH OUT FOR GARROSH, THRALL. HE'S CHAFING UNDER YOUR LEADERSHIP.
HE FEELS THAT HE...AND WE ORCS...LOST FACE HERE. ANOTHER CONSEQUENCE OF THIS ATTACK.
HE'LL CHALLENGE ME SOON. HE'S A GOOD FIGHTER. IT WILL BE A WASTE OF A SKILLFUL WARRIOR IF HE FORCES ME TO KILL HIM.
FAREWELL, OLD FRIEND. I'M SORRY.
AS AM I. FAREWELL.

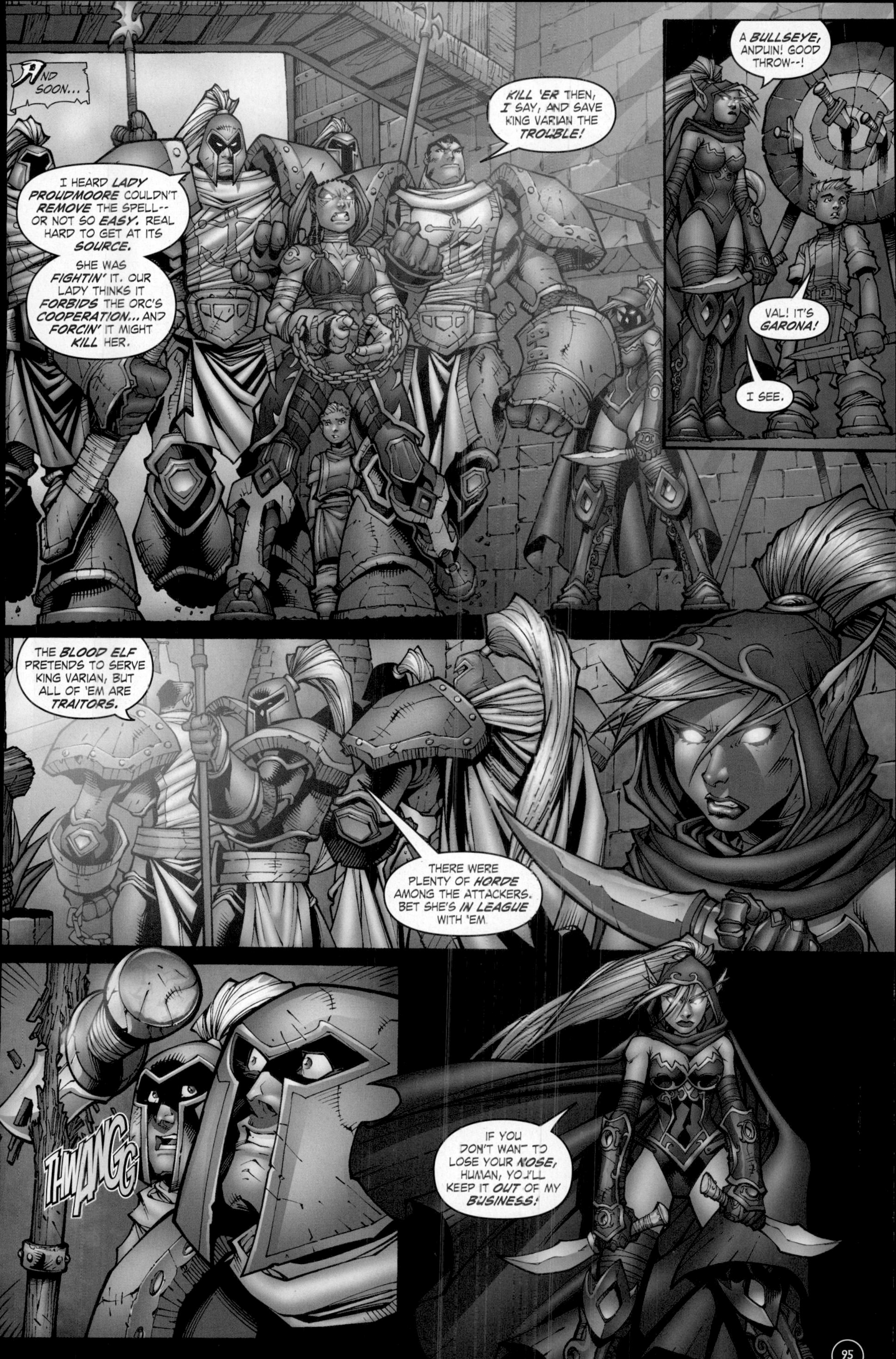
AND SOON...
A BULLSEYE, ANDUIN! GOOD THROW--!
KILL 'ER THEN, I SAY, AND SAVE KING VARIAN THE TROUBLE!
I HEARD LADY PROUDMOORE COULDN'T REMOVE THE SPELL-- OR NOT SO EASY. REAL HARD TO GET AT ITS SOURCE.
SHE WAS FIGHTIN' IT. OUR LADY THINKS IT FORBIDS THE ORC'S COOPERATION... AND FORCIN' IT MIGHT KILL HER.
VAL! IT'S GARONA!
I SEE.
THE BLOOD ELF PRETENDS TO SERVE KING VARIAN, BUT ALL OF 'EM ARE TRAITORS.
THERE WERE PLENTY OF HORDE AMONG THE ATTACKERS. BET SHE'S IN LEAGUE WITH 'EM.
THWANGG
IF YOU DON'T WANT TO LOSE YOUR NOSE, HUMAN, YOU'LL KEEP IT OUT OF MY BUSINESS!

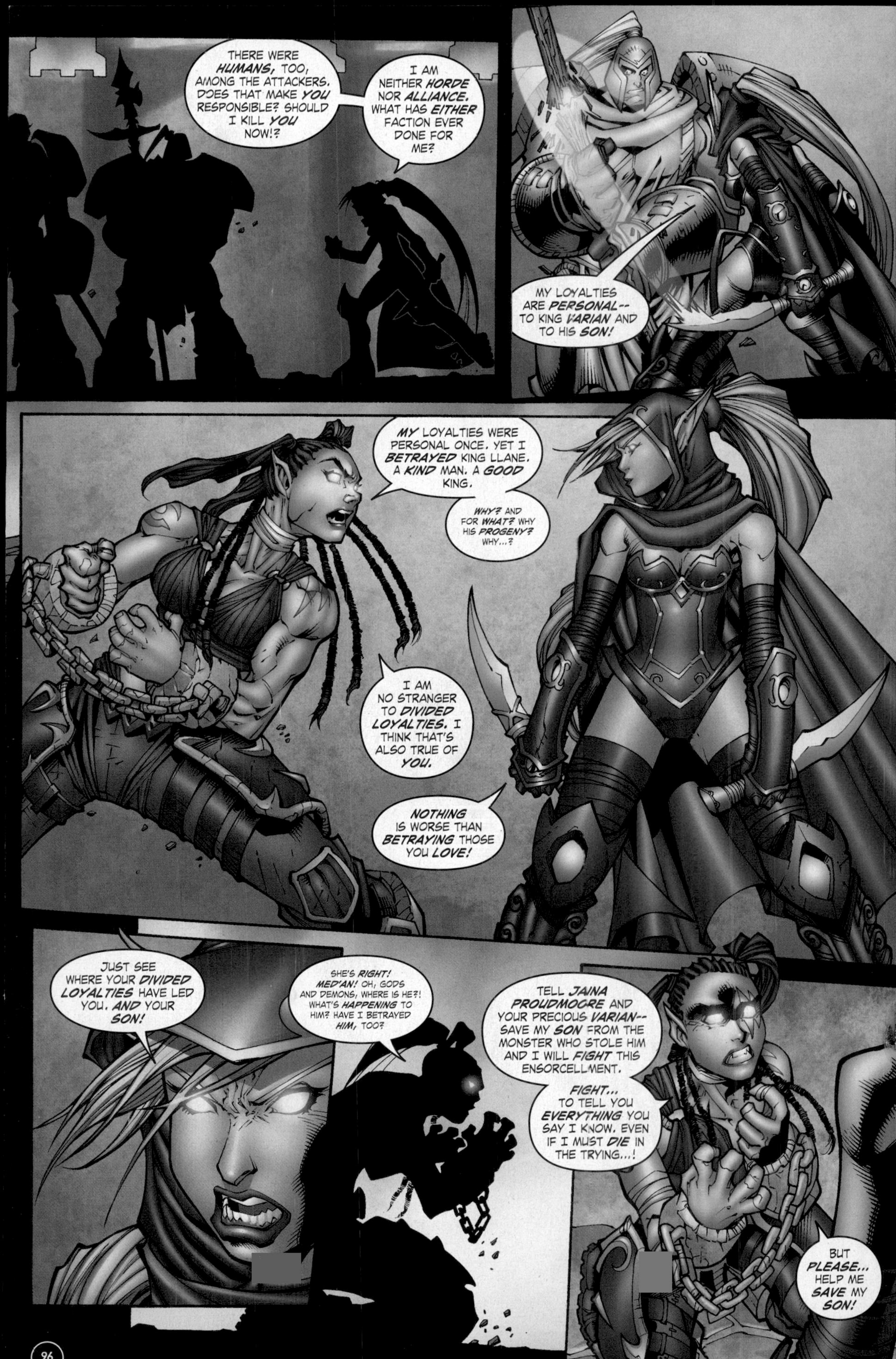

THERE WERE HUMANS, TOO, AMONG THE ATTACKERS. DOES THAT MAKE YOU RESPONSIBLE? SHOULD I KILL YOU NOW!?
I AM NEITHER HORDE NOR ALLIANCE. WHAT HAS EITHER FACTION EVER DONE FOR ME?
MY LOYALTIES ARE PERSONAL-- TO KING VARIAN AND TO HIS SON!
MY LOYALTIES WERE PERSONAL ONCE. YET I BETRAYED KING LLANE. A KIND MAN. A GOOD KING.
WHY? AND FOR WHAT? WHY HIS PROGENY? WHY...?
I AM NO STRANGER TO DIVIDED LOYALTIES. I THINK THAT'S ALSO TRUE OF YOU.
NOTHING IS WORSE THAN BETRAYING THOSE YOU LOVE!
JUST SEE WHERE YOUR DIVIDED LOYALTIES HAVE LED YOU. AND YOUR SON!
SHE'S RIGHT! MED'AN! OH, GODS AND DEMONS, WHERE IS HE?! WHAT'S HAPPENING TO HIM? HAVE I BETRAYED HIM, TOO?
TELL JAINA PROUDMOORE AND YOUR PRECIOUS VARIAN-- SAVE MY SON FROM THE MONSTER WHO STOLE HIM AND I WILL FIGHT THIS ENSORCELLMENT.
FIGHT... TO TELL YOU EVERYTHING YOU SAY I KNOW. EVEN IF I MUST DIE IN THE TRYING...!
BUT PLEASE... HELP ME SAVE MY SON!

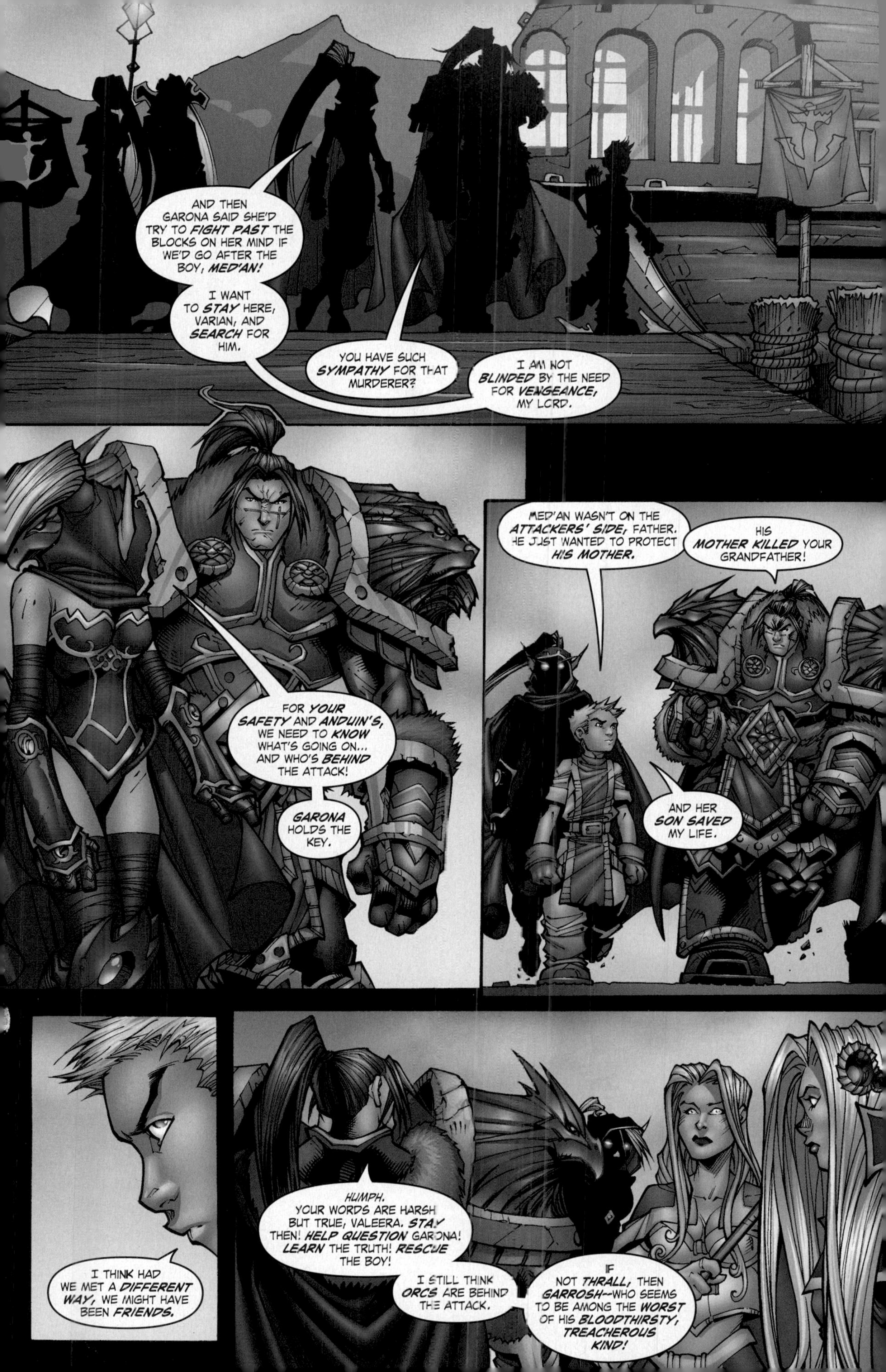
AND THEN GARONA SAID SHE'D TRY TO FIGHT PAST THE BLOCKS ON HER MIND IF WE'D GO AFTER THE BOY, MED'AN!
I WANT TO STAY HERE, VARIAN, AND SEARCH FOR HIM.
YOU HAVE SUCH SYMPATHY FOR THAT MURDERER?
I AM NOT BLINDED BY THE NEED FOR VENGEANCE, MY LORD.
FOR YOUR SAFETY AND ANDUIN'S, WE NEED TO KNOW WHAT'S GOING ON... AND WHO'S BEHIND THE ATTACK!
GARONA HOLDS THE KEY.
MED'AN WASN'T ON THE ATTACKERS' SIDE, FATHER. HE JUST WANTED TO PROTECT HIS MOTHER.
HIS MOTHER KILLED YOUR GRANDFATHER!
AND HER SON SAVED MY LIFE.
I THINK HAD WE MET A DIFFERENT WAY, WE MIGHT HAVE BEEN FRIENDS.
HUMPH. YOUR WORDS ARE HARSH BUT TRUE, VALEERA. STAY THEN! HELP QUESTION GARONA! LEARN THE TRUTH! RESCUE THE BOY!
I STILL THINK ORCS ARE BEHIND THE ATTACK.
IF NOT THRALL, THEN GARROSH--WHO SEEMS TO BE AMONG THE WORST OF HIS BLOODTHIRSTY, TREACHEROUS KIND!

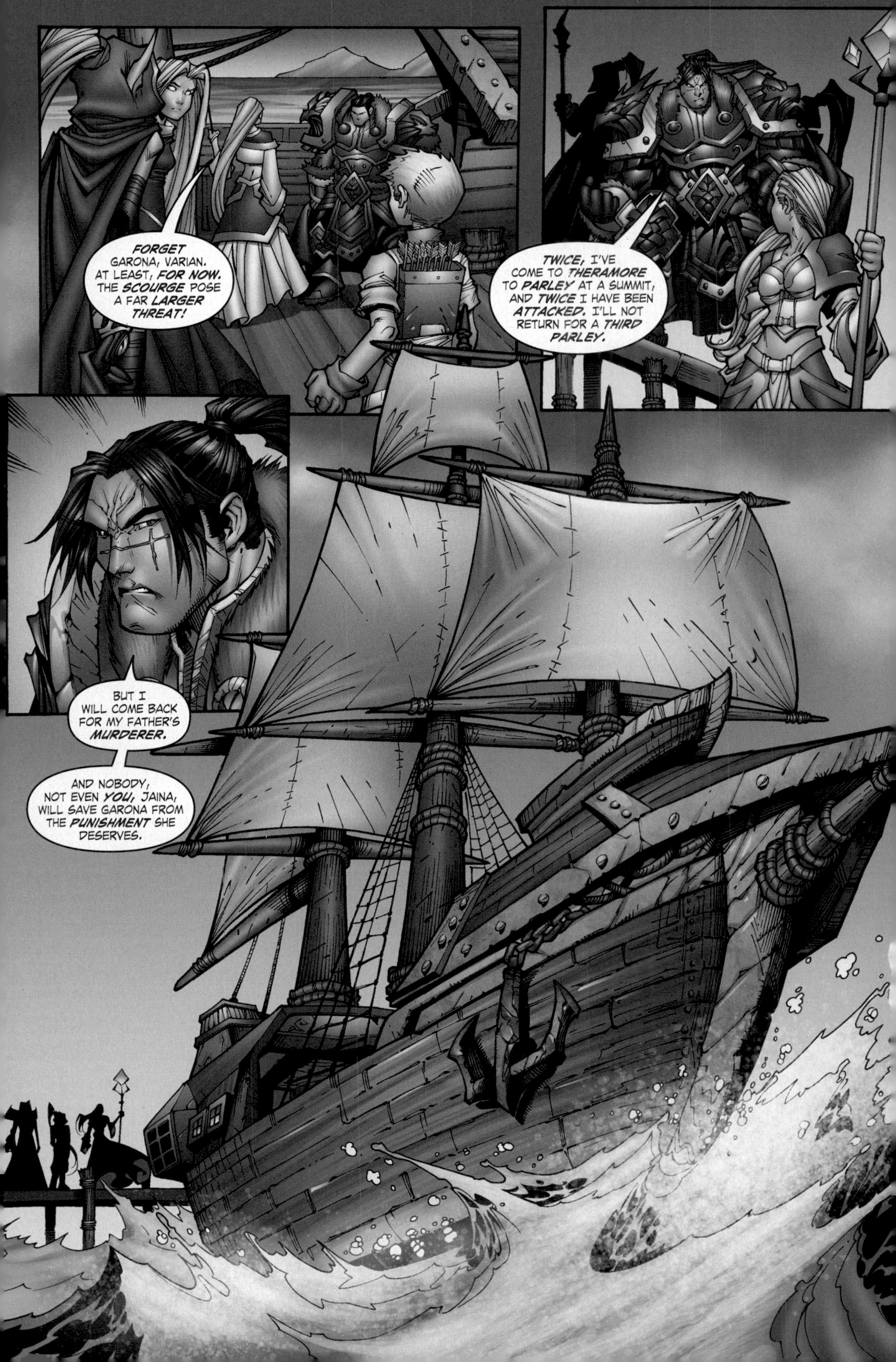

FORGET GARONA, VARIAN. AT LEAST, FOR NOW. THE SCOURGE POSE A FAR LARGER THREAT!
TWICE, I'VE COME TO THERAMORE TO PARLEY AT A SUMMIT, AND TWICE I HAVE BEEN ATTACKED. I'LL NOT RETURN FOR A THIRD PARLEY.
BUT I WILL COME BACK FOR MY FATHER'S MURDERER.
AND NOBODY, NOT EVEN YOU, JAINA, WILL SAVE GARONA FROM THE PUNISHMENT SHE DESERVES.

CHAPTER 5

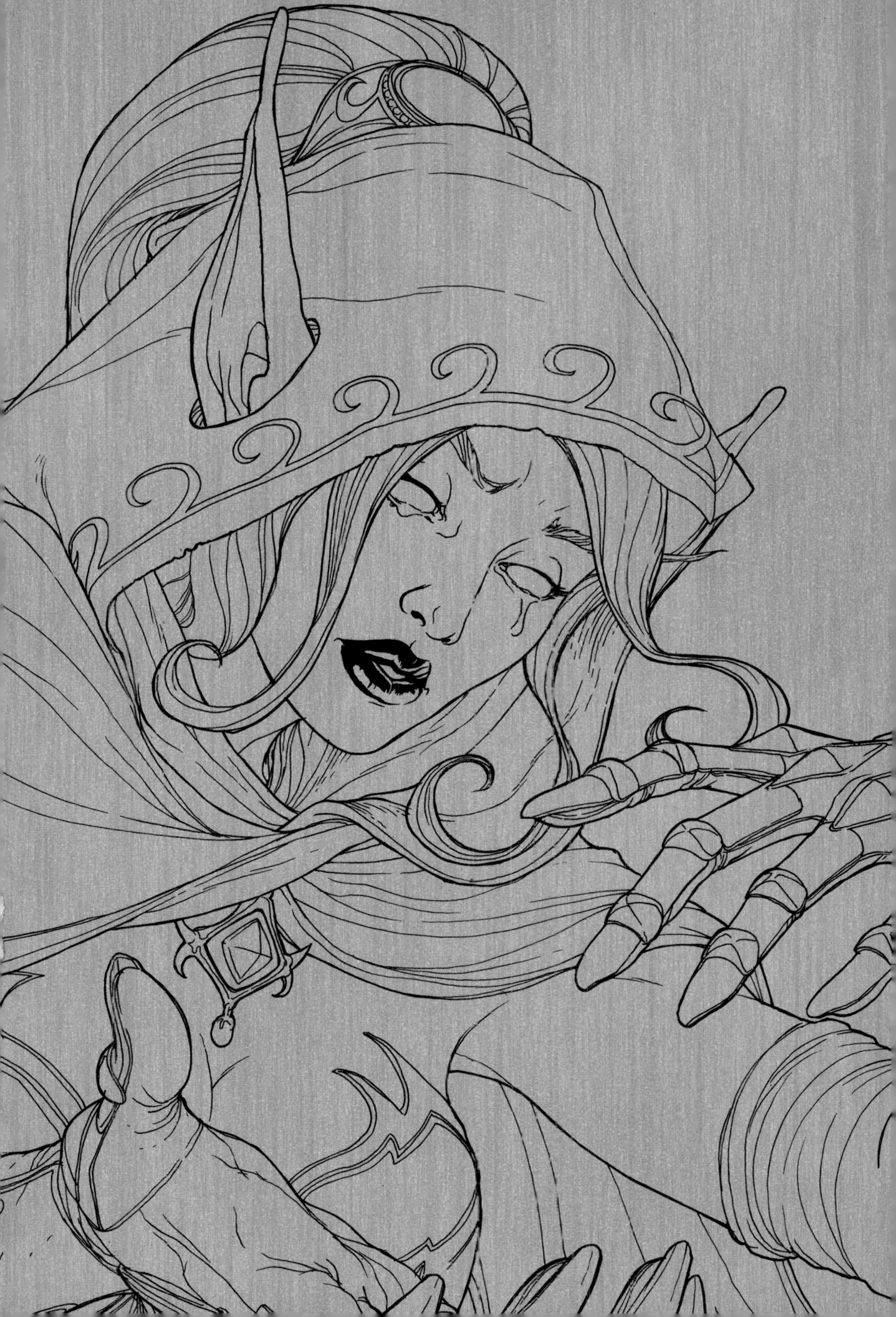

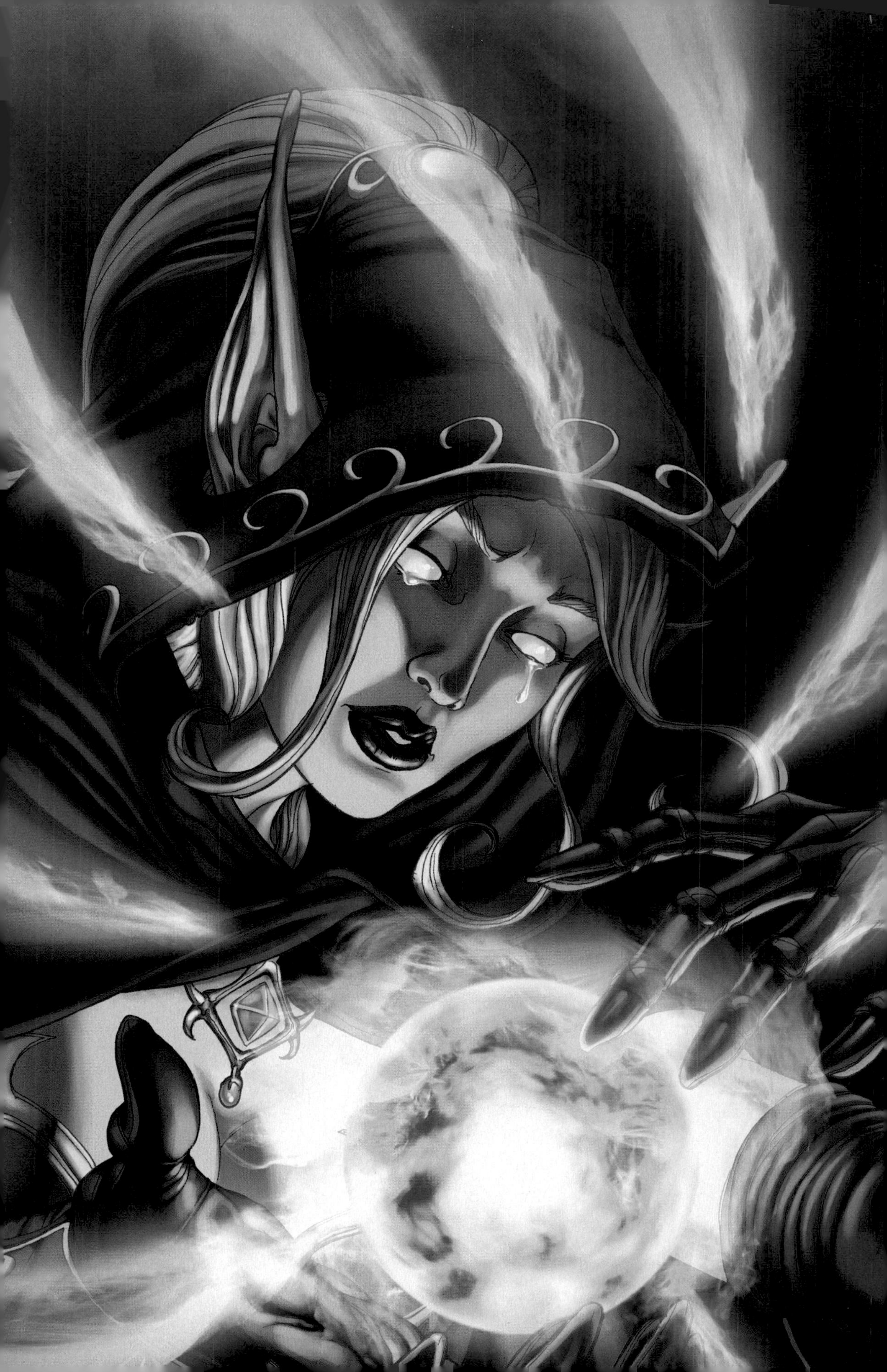

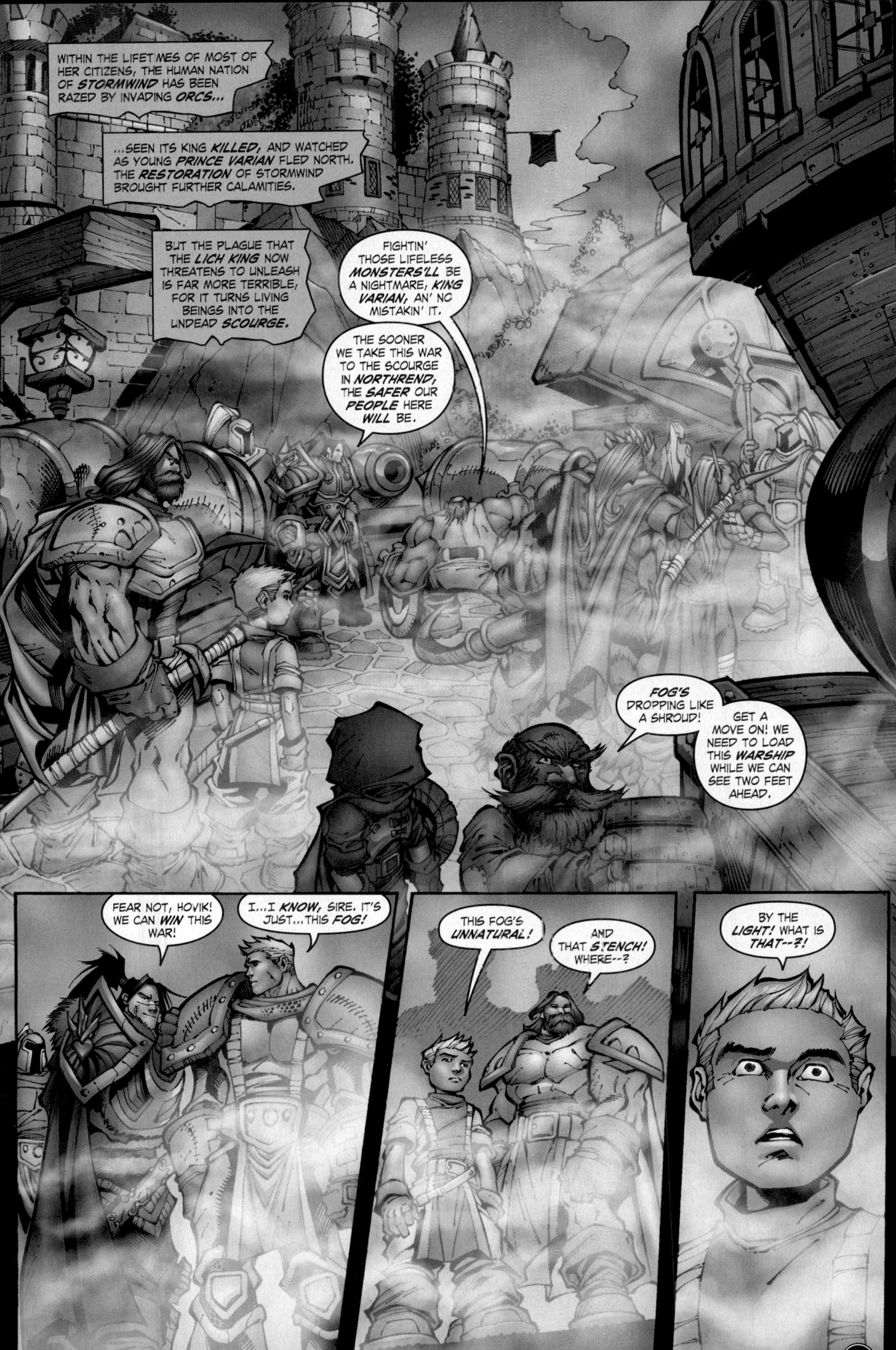

WITHIN THE LIFETIMES OF MOST OF HER CITIZENS, THE HUMAN NATION OF STORMWIND HAS BEEN RAZED BY INVADING ORCS...
...SEEN ITS KING KILLED, AND WATCHED AS YOUNG PRINCE VARIAN FLED NORTH. THE RESTORATION OF STORMWIND BROUGHT FURTHER CALAMITIES.
BUT THE PLAGUE THAT THE LICH KING NOW THREATENS TO UNLEASH IS FAR MORE TERRIBLE, FOR IT TURNS LIVING BEINGS INTO THE UNDEAD SCOURGE.
FIGHTIN' THOSE LIFELESS MONSTERS'LL BE A NIGHTMARE, KING VARIAN, AN' NO MISTAKIN' IT.
THE SOONER WE TAKE THIS WAR TO THE SCOURGE IN NORTHREND, THE SAFER OUR PEOPLE HERE WILL BE.
FOG'S DROPPING LIKE A SHROUD!
GET A MOVE ON! WE NEED TO LOAD THIS WARSHIP WHILE WE CAN SEE TWO FEET AHEAD.
FEAR NOT, HOVIK! WE CAN WIN THIS WAR!
I...I KNOW, SIRE. IT'S JUST...THIS FOG!
THIS FOG'S UNNATURAL!
AND THAT STENCH! WHERE--?
BY THE LIGHT! WHAT IS THAT--?!

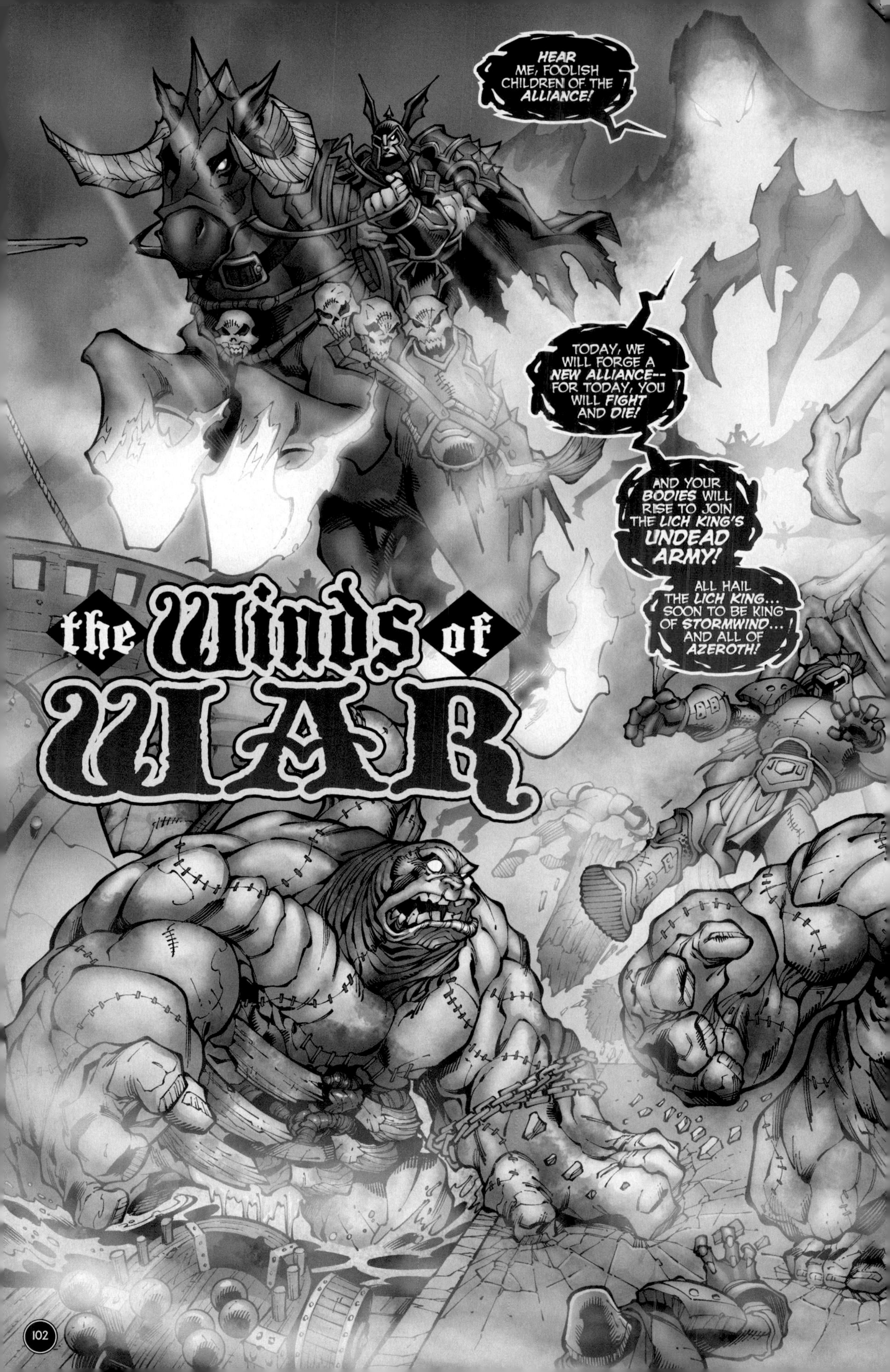
HEAR ME, FOOLISH CHILDREN OF THE ALLIANCE!
TODAY, WE WILL FORGE A NEW ALLIANCE-- FOR TODAY, YOU WILL FIGHT AND DIE!
AND YOUR BODIES WILL RISE TO JOIN THE LICH KING'S UNDEAD ARMY!
ALL HAIL THE LICH KING... SOON TO BE KING OF STORMWIND... AND ALL OF AZEROTH!
the Winds of WAR

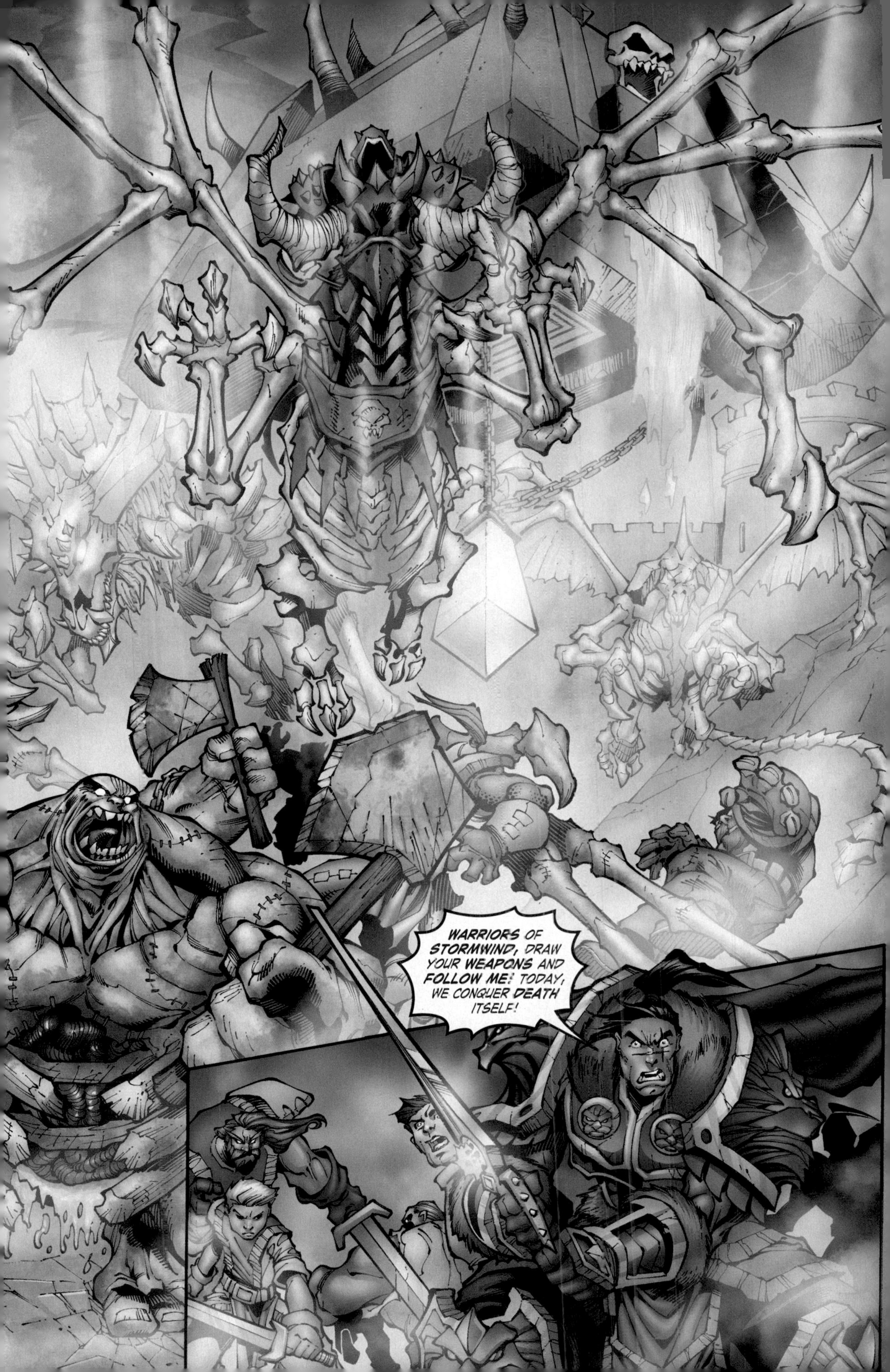
WARRIORS OF STORMWIND, DRAW YOUR WEAPONS AND FOLLOW ME! TODAY, WE CONQUER DEATH ITSELF!

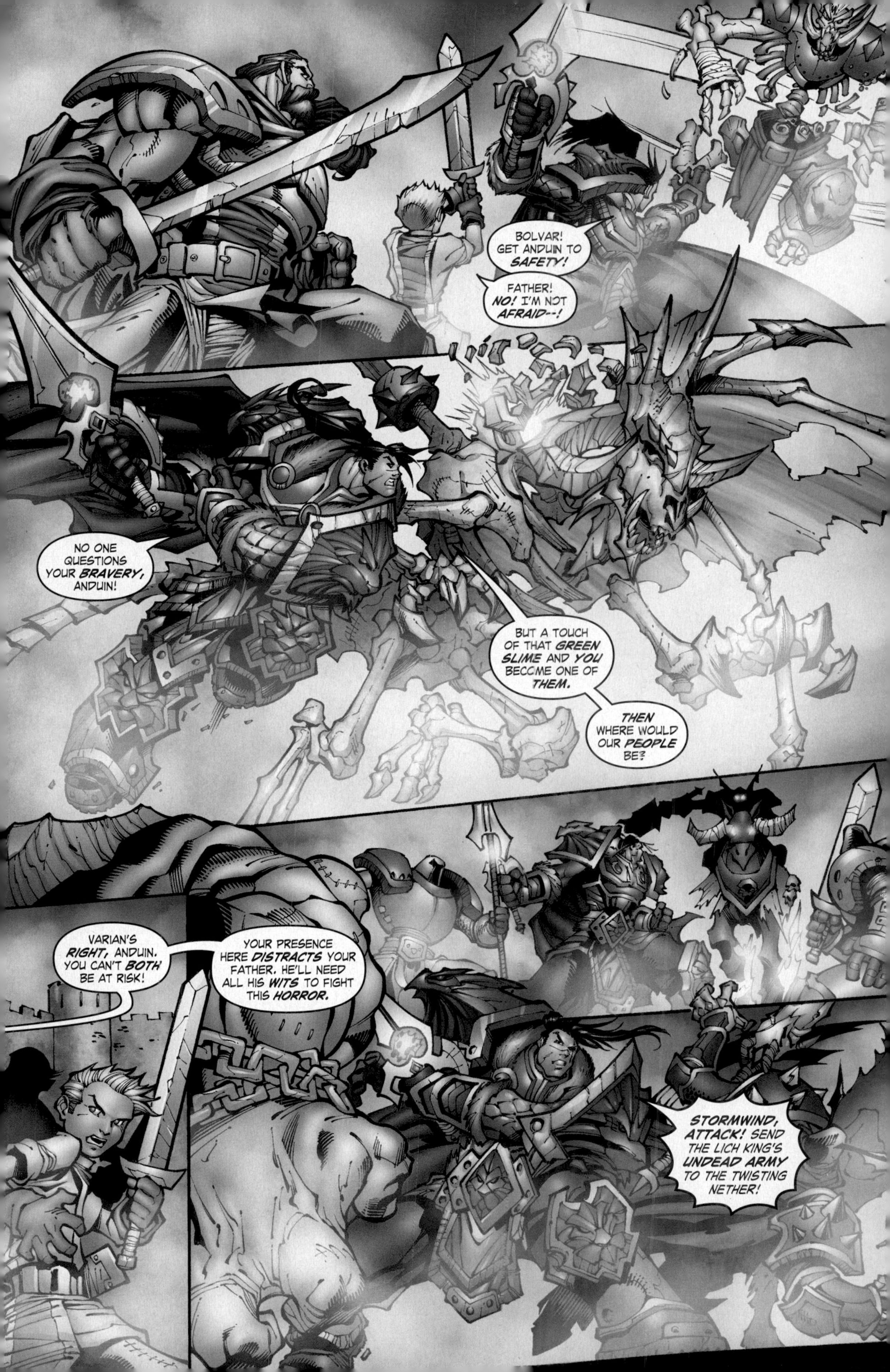
BOLVAR! GET ANDUIN TO SAFETY!
FATHER! NO! I'M NOT AFRAID--!
NO ONE QUESTIONS YOUR BRAVERY, ANDUIN!
BUT A TOUCH OF THAT GREEN SLIME AND YOU BECOME ONE OF THEM.
THEN WHERE WOULD OUR PEOPLE BE?
VARIAN'S RIGHT, ANDUIN. YOU CAN'T BOTH BE AT RISK!
YOUR PRESENCE HERE DISTRACTS YOUR FATHER. HE'LL NEED ALL HIS WITS TO FIGHT THIS HORROR.
STORMWIND, ATTACK! SEND THE LICH KING'S UNDEAD ARMY TO THE TWISTING NETHER!

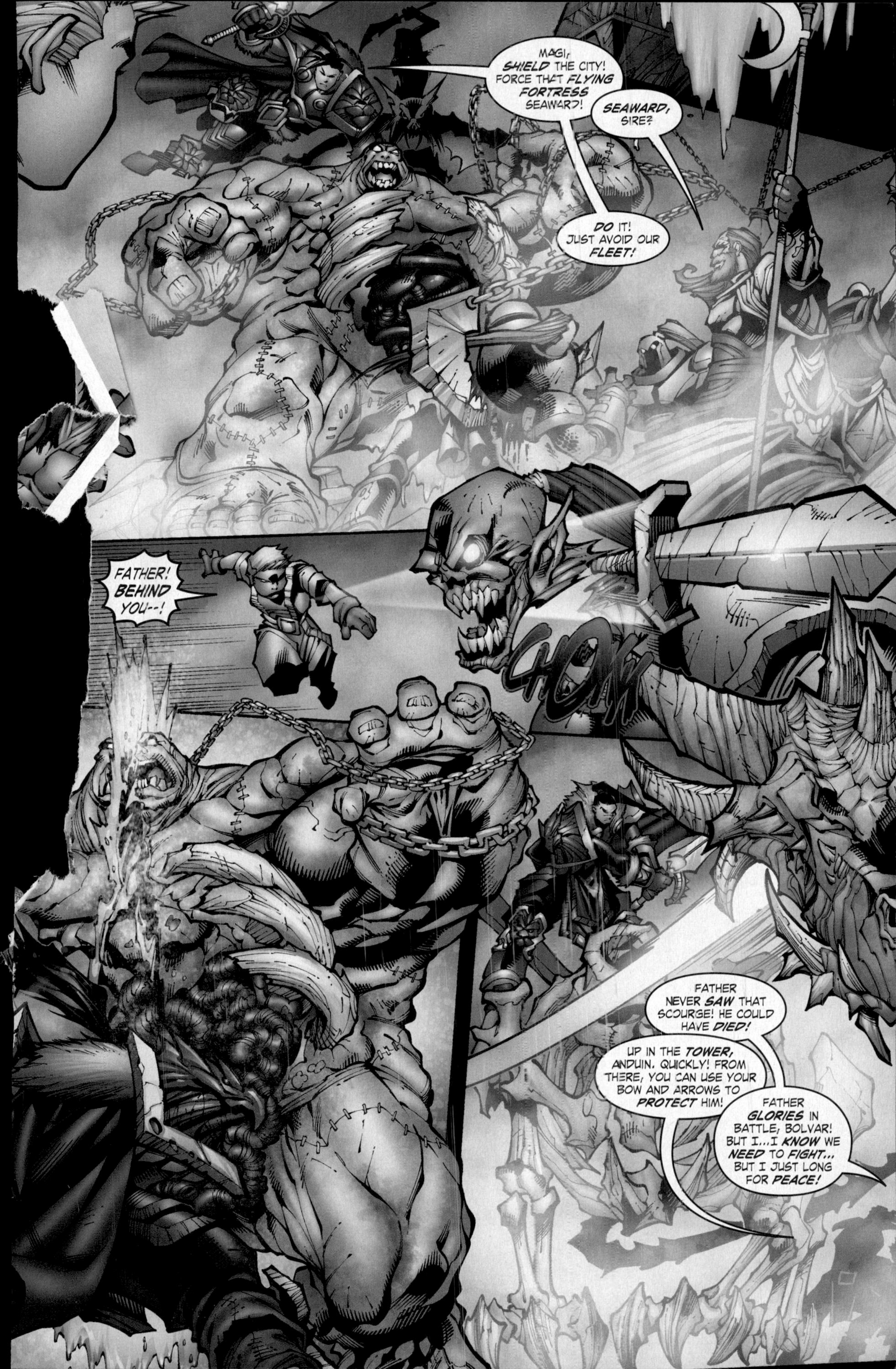
MAGI, SHIELD THE CITY! FORCE THAT FLYING FORTRESS SEAWARD?!
SEAWARD, SIRE?
DO IT! JUST AVOID OUR FLEET!
FATHER! BEHIND YOU--!
CHOM
FATHER NEVER SAW THAT SCOURGE! HE COULD HAVE DIED!
UP IN THE TOWER, ANDUIN. QUICKLY! FROM THERE, YOU CAN USE YOUR BOW AND ARROWS TO PROTECT HIM!
FATHER GLORIES IN BATTLE, BOLVAR! BUT I...I KNOW WE NEED TO FIGHT... BUT I JUST LONG FOR PEACE!

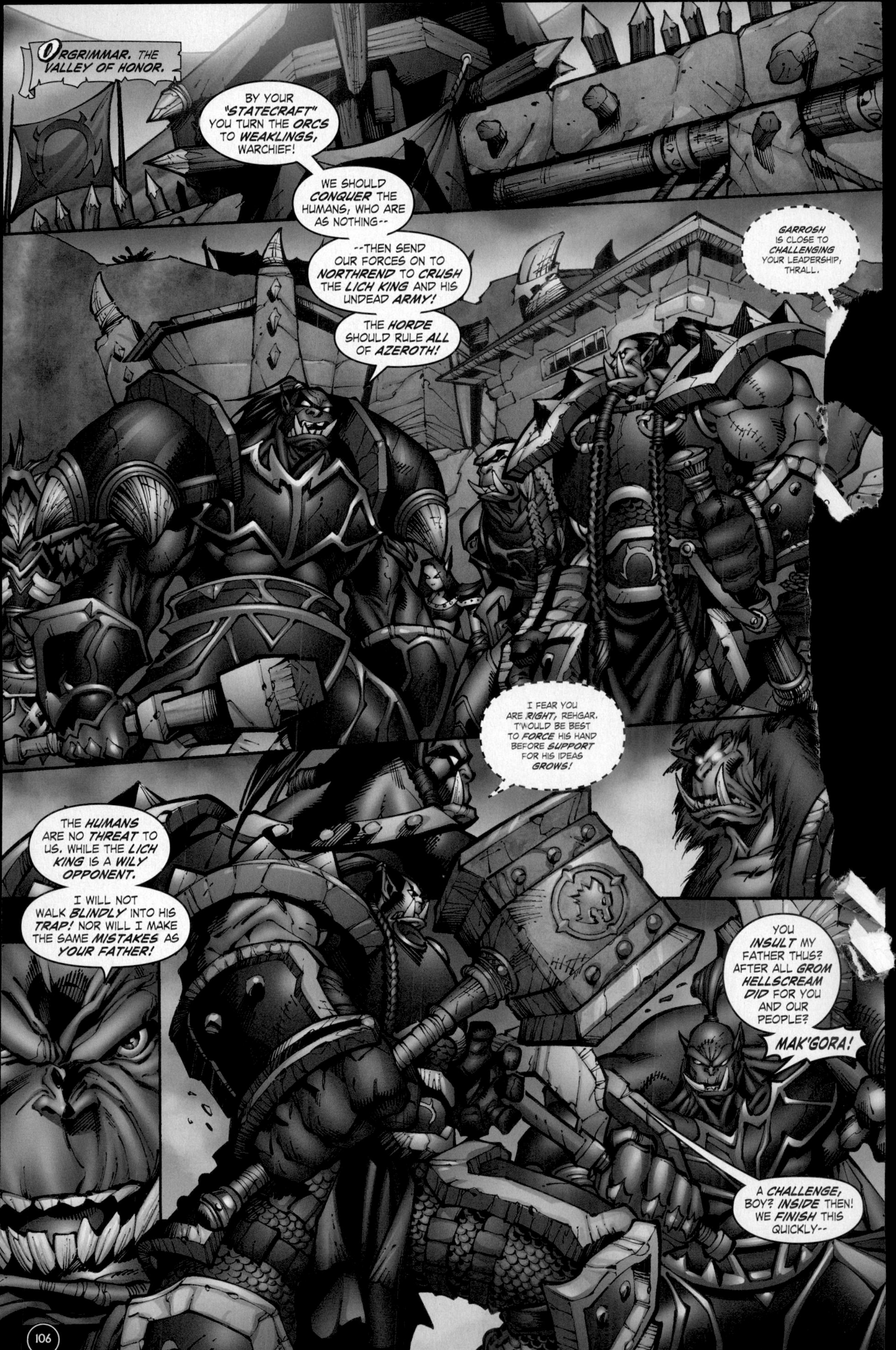

ORGRIMMAR. THE VALLEY OF HONOR.
BY YOUR "STATECRAFT" YOU TURN THE ORCS TO WEAKLINGS, WARCHIEF!
WE SHOULD CONQUER THE HUMANS, WHO ARE AS NOTHING--
--THEN SEND OUR FORCES ON TO NORTHREND TO CRUSH THE LICH KING AND HIS UNDEAD ARMY!
THE HORDE SHOULD RULE ALL OF AZEROTH!
GARROSH IS CLOSE TO CHALLENGING YOUR LEADERSHIP, THRALL.
I FEAR YOU ARE RIGHT, REHGAR. T'WOULD BE BEST TO FORCE HIS HAND BEFORE SUPPORT FOR HIS IDEAS GROWS!
THE HUMANS ARE NO THREAT TO US, WHILE THE LICH KING IS A WILY OPPONENT.
I WILL NOT WALK BLINDLY INTO HIS TRAP! NOR WILL I MAKE THE SAME MISTAKES AS YOUR FATHER!
YOU INSULT MY FATHER THUS? AFTER ALL GROM HELLSCREAM DID FOR YOU AND OUR PEOPLE?
MAK'GORA!
A CHALLENGE, BOY? INSIDE THEN! WE FINISH THIS QUICKLY--

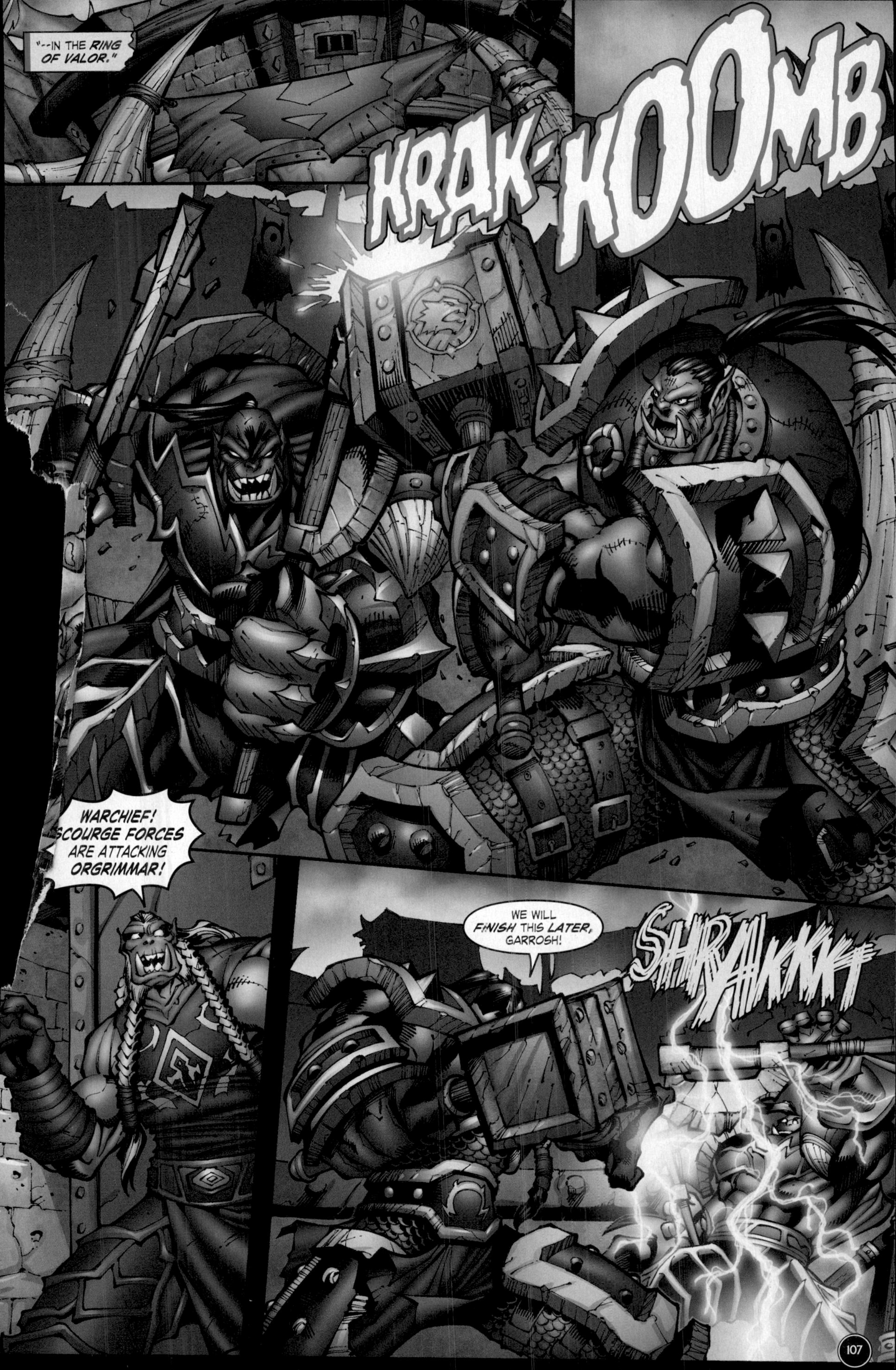
"--IN THE RING OF VALOR."
KRAK-KOOMB
WARCHIEF! SCOURGE FORCES ARE ATTACKING ORGRIMMAR!
WE WILL FINISH THIS LATER, GARROSH!
SHRAKKKT

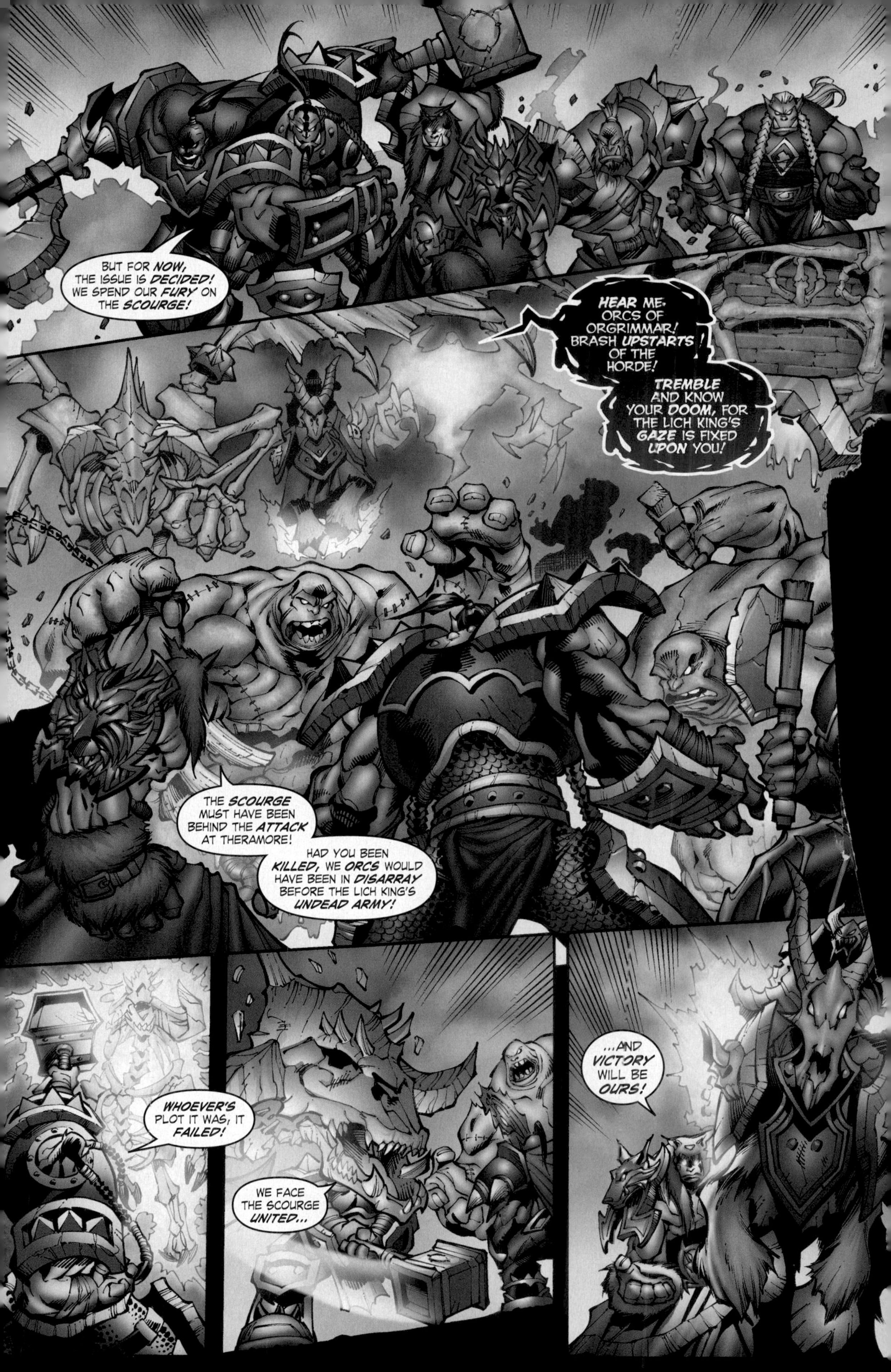
BUT FOR NOW, THE ISSUE IS DECIDED! WE SPEND OUR FURY ON THE SCOURGE!
HEAR ME, ORCS OF ORGRIMMAR! BRASH UPSTARTS OF THE HORDE!
TREMBLE AND KNOW YOUR DOOM, FOR THE LICH KING'S GAZE IS FIXED UPON YOU!
THE SCOURGE MUST HAVE BEEN BEHIND THE ATTACK AT THERAMORE!
HAD YOU BEEN KILLED, WE ORCS WOULD HAVE BEEN IN DISARRAY BEFORE THE LICH KING'S UNDEAD ARMY!
WHOEVER'S PLOT IT WAS, IT FAILED!
WE FACE THE SCOURGE UNITED...
...AND VICTORY WILL BE OURS!

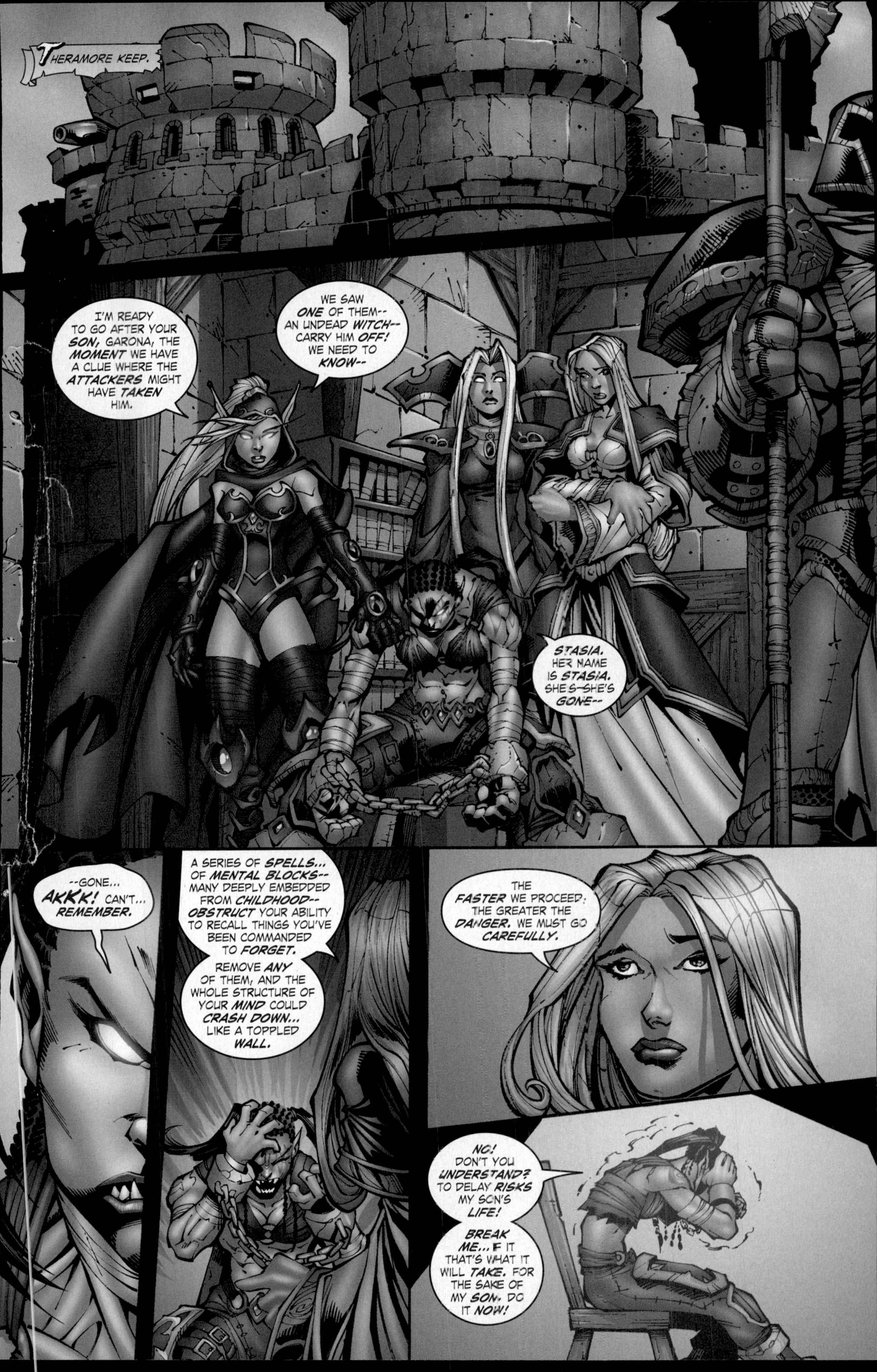
THERAMORE KEEP.
I'M READY TO GO AFTER YOUR SON, GARONA, THE MOMENT WE HAVE A CLUE WHERE THE ATTACKERS MIGHT HAVE TAKEN HIM.
WE SAW ONE OF THEM-- AN UNDEAD WITCH-- CARRY HIM OFF! WE NEED TO KNOW--
STASIA. HER NAME IS STASIA. SHE'S--SHE'S GONE--
--GONE... AKKK! CAN'T... REMEMBER.
A SERIES OF SPELLS... OF MENTAL BLOCKS-- MANY DEEPLY EMBEDDED FROM CHILDHOOD-- OBSTRUCT YOUR ABILITY TO RECALL THINGS YOU'VE BEEN COMMANDED TO FORGET.
REMOVE ANY OF THEM, AND THE WHOLE STRUCTURE OF YOUR MIND COULD CRASH DOWN... LIKE A TOPPLED WALL.
THE FASTER WE PROCEED, THE GREATER THE DANGER. WE MUST GO CAREFULLY.
NO! DON'T YOU UNDERSTAND? TO DELAY RISKS MY SON'S LIFE!
BREAK ME... IF THAT'S WHAT IT WILL TAKE. FOR THE SAKE OF MY SON, DO IT NOW!

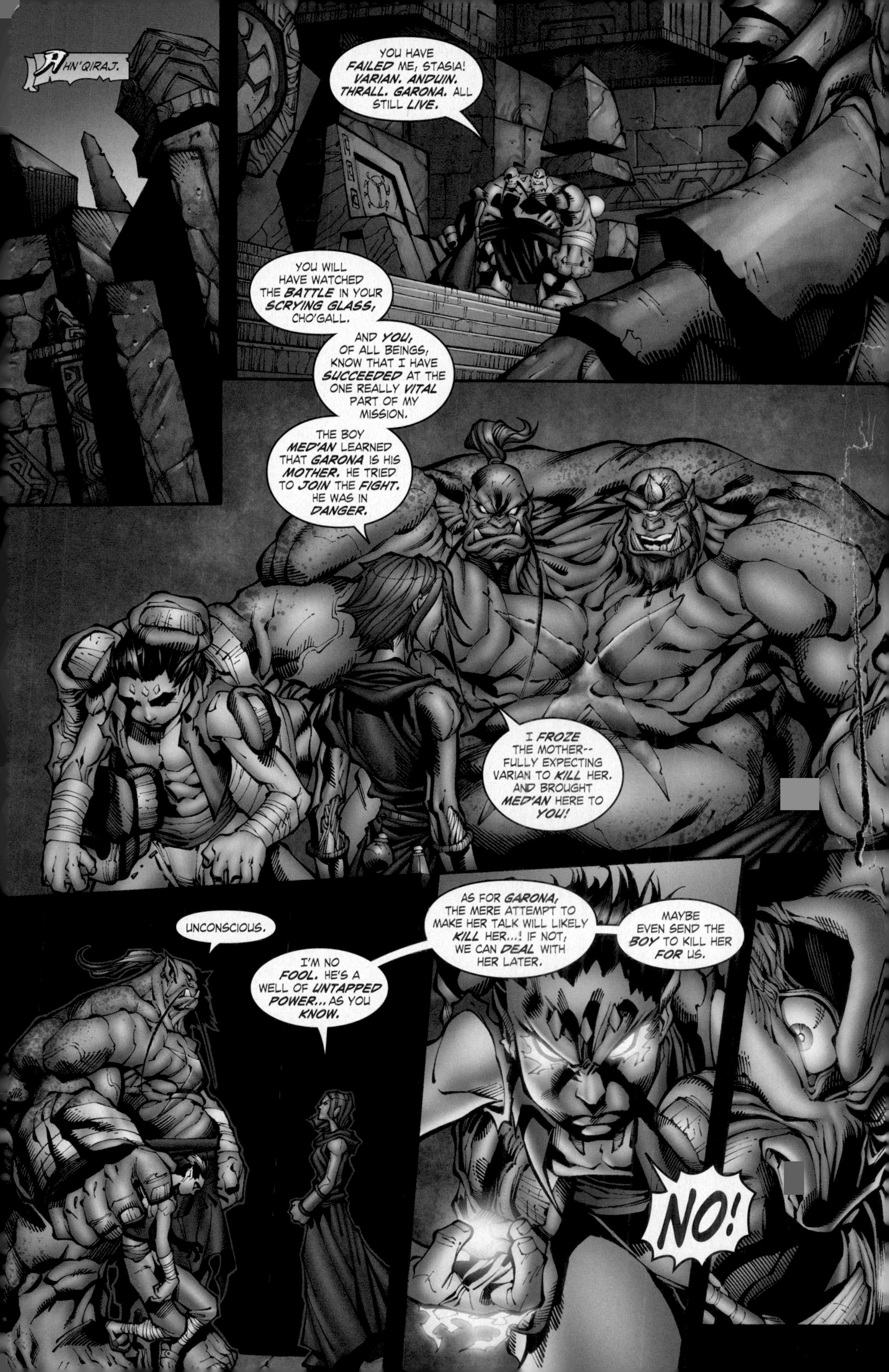
AHN'QIRAJ.
YOU HAVE FAILED ME, STASIA! VARIAN. ANDUIN. THRALL. GARONA. ALL STILL LIVE.
YOU WILL HAVE WATCHED THE BATTLE IN YOUR SCRYING GLASS, CHO'GALL.
AND YOU, OF ALL BEINGS, KNOW THAT I HAVE SUCCEEDED AT THE ONE REALLY VITAL PART OF MY MISSION.
THE BOY MED'AN LEARNED THAT GARONA IS HIS MOTHER. HE TRIED TO JOIN THE FIGHT. HE WAS IN DANGER.
I FROZE THE MOTHER-- FULLY EXPECTING VARIAN TO KILL HER. AND BROUGHT MED'AN HERE TO YOU!
UNCONSCIOUS.
I'M NO FOOL. HE'S A WELL OF UNTAPPED POWER... AS YOU KNOW.
AS FOR GARONA, THE MERE ATTEMPT TO MAKE HER TALK WILL LIKELY KILL HER...! IF NOT, WE CAN DEAL WITH HER LATER.
MAYBE EVEN SEND THE BOY TO KILL HER FOR US.
NO!

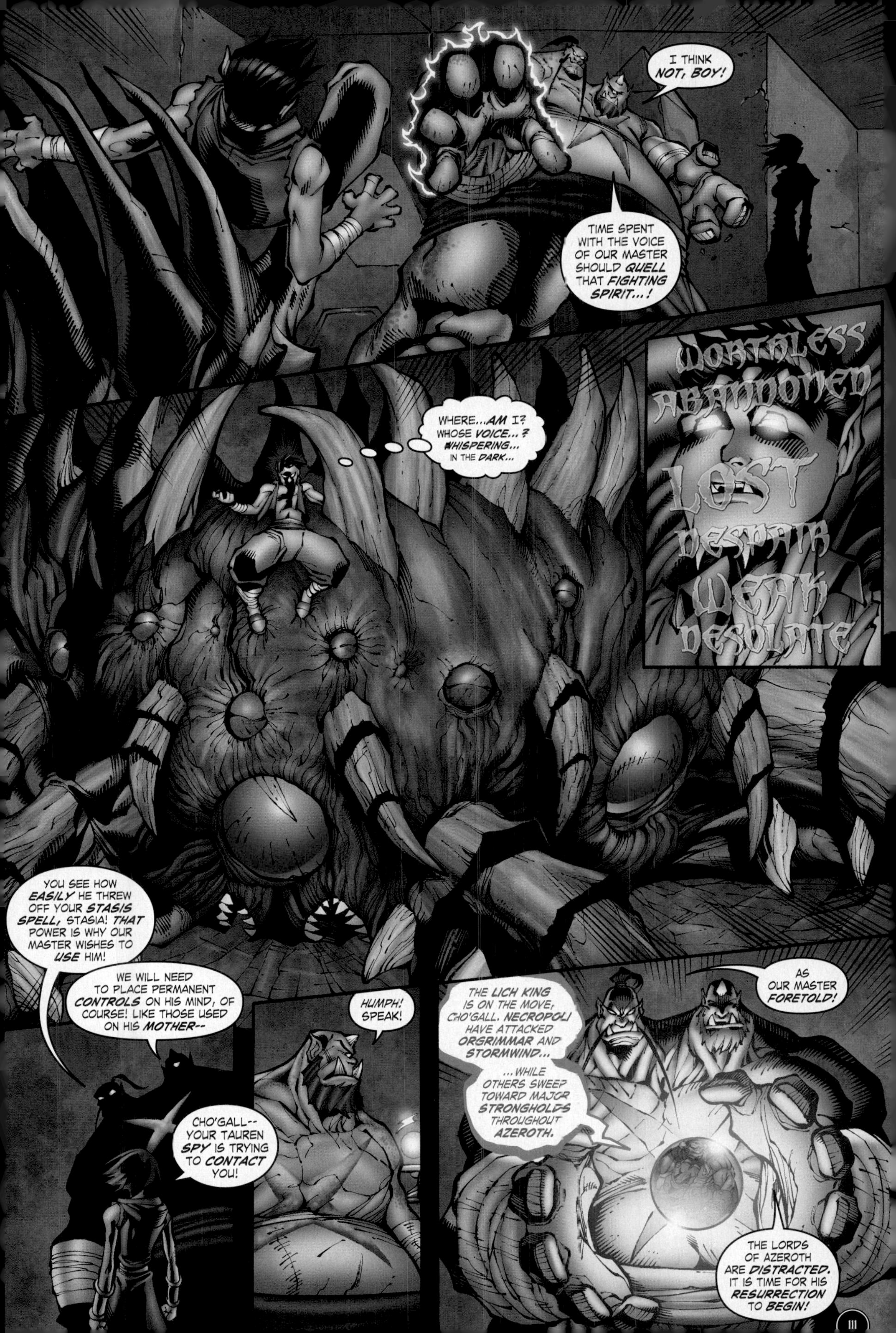
I THINK NOT, BOY!
TIME SPENT WITH THE VOICE OF OUR MASTER SHOULD QUELL THAT FIGHTING SPIRIT...!
WHERE...AM I? WHOSE VOICE...? WHISPERING... IN THE DARK...
WORTHLESS
ABANDONED
LOST
DESPAIR
WEAK
DESOLATE
YOU SEE HOW EASILY HE THREW OFF YOUR STASIS SPELL, STASIA! THAT POWER IS WHY OUR MASTER WISHES TO USE HIM!
WE WILL NEED TO PLACE PERMANENT CONTROLS ON HIS MIND, OF COURSE! LIKE THOSE USED ON HIS MOTHER--
CHO'GALL-- YOUR TAUREN SPY IS TRYING TO CONTACT YOU!
HUMPH! SPEAK!
THE LICH KING IS ON THE MOVE, CHO'GALL. NECROPOLI HAVE ATTACKED ORGRIMMAR AND STORMWIND...
...WHILE OTHERS SWEEP TOWARD MAJOR STRONGHOLDS THROUGHOUT AZEROTH.
AS OUR MASTER FORETOLD!
THE LORDS OF AZEROTH ARE DISTRACTED. IT IS TIME FOR HIS RESURRECTION TO BEGIN!

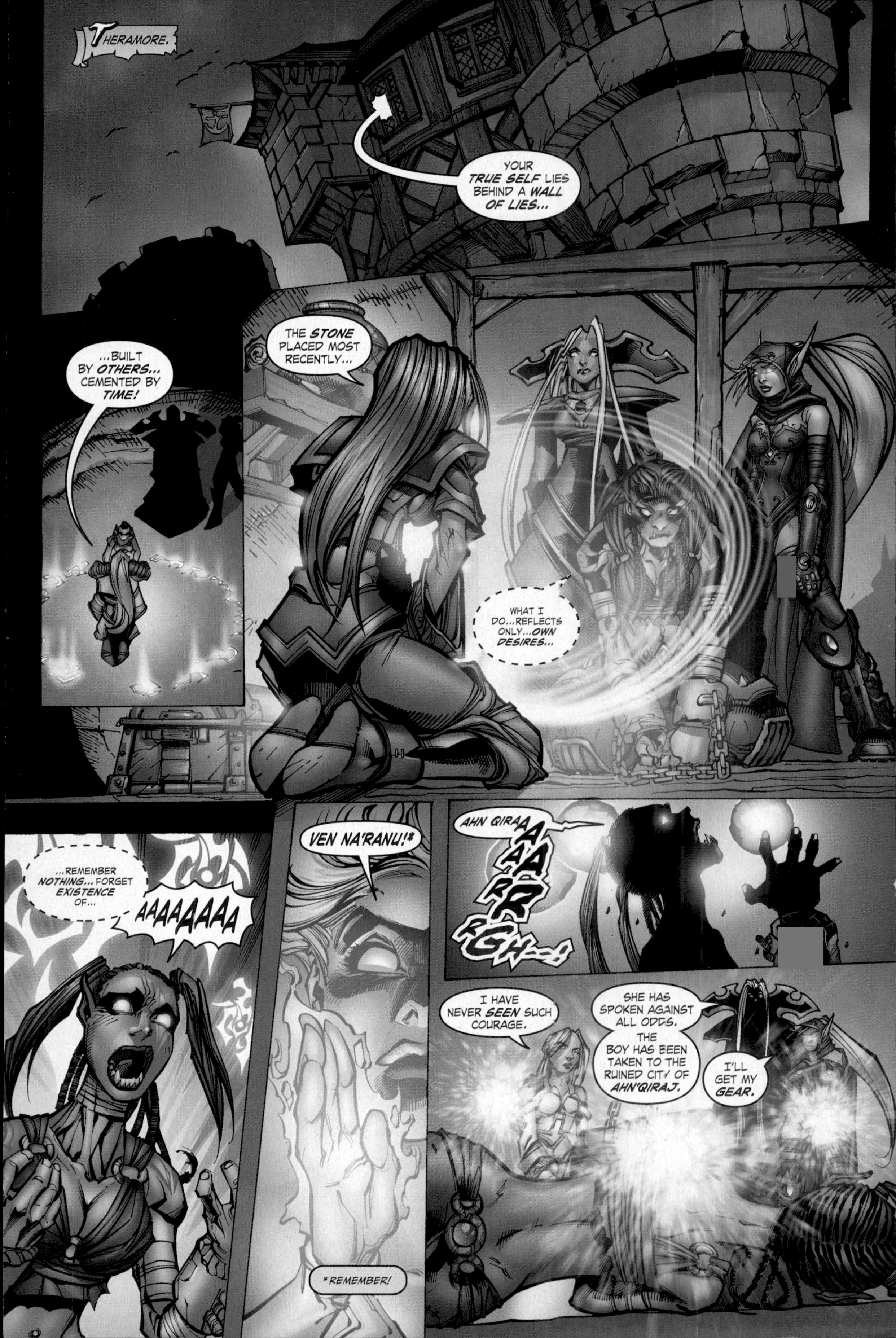
THERAMORE.
YOUR TRUE SELF LIES BEHIND A WALL OF LIES...
...BUILT BY OTHERS... CEMENTED BY TIME!
THE STONE PLACED MOST RECENTLY...
WHAT I DO...REFLECTS ONLY...OWN DESIRES...
...REMEMBER NOTHING...FORGET EXISTENCE OF...
AAAAAAAA
VEN NA'RANU!*
AHN QIRAAAAARRRGH--!
I HAVE NEVER SEEN SUCH COURAGE.
SHE HAS SPOKEN AGAINST ALL ODDS.
THE BOY HAS BEEN TAKEN TO THE RUINED CITY OF AHN'QIRAJ.
I'LL GET MY GEAR.
*REMEMBER!

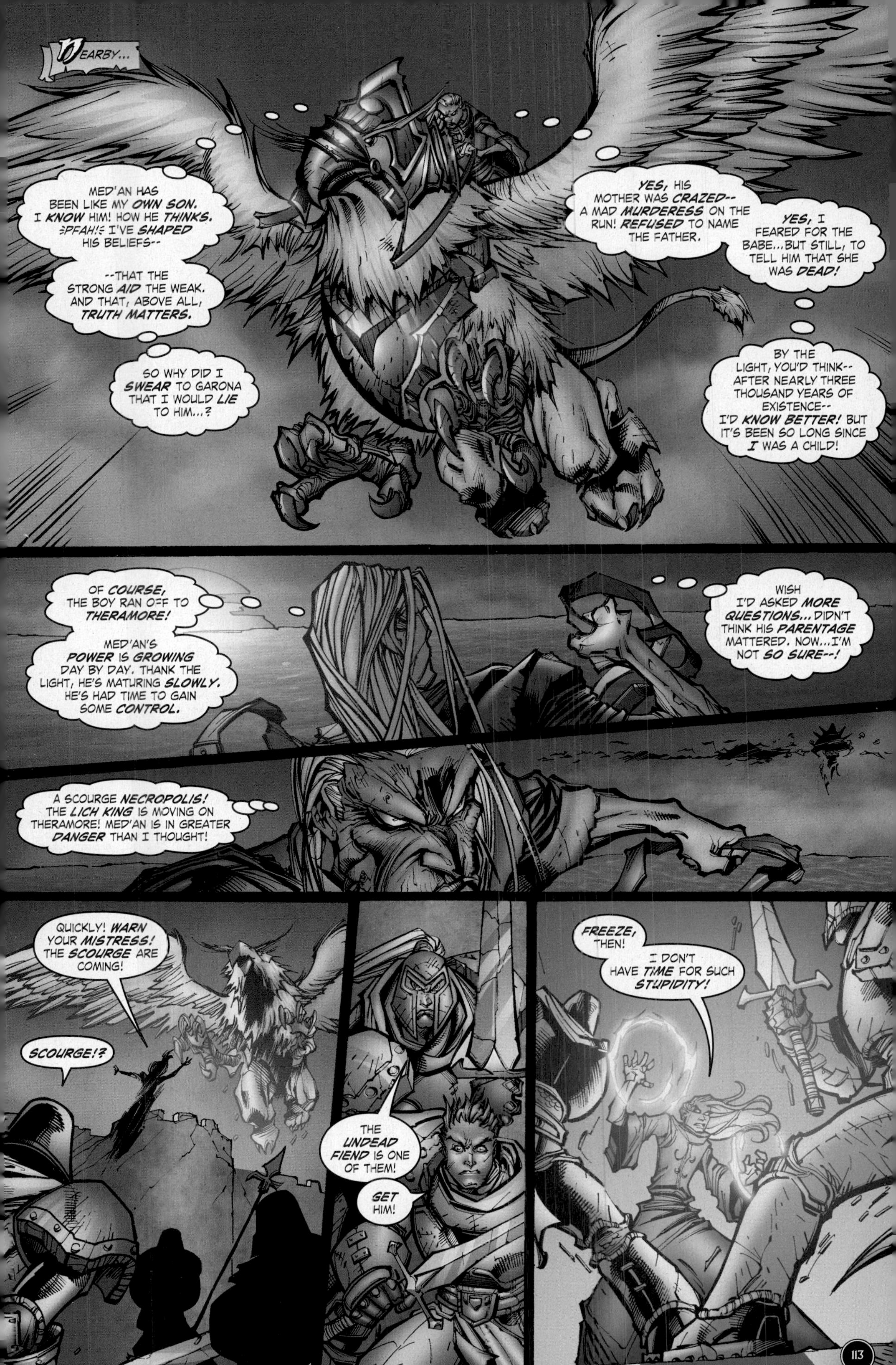
NEARBY...
MED'AN HAS BEEN LIKE MY OWN SON. I KNOW HIM! HOW HE THINKS. PFAH!! I'VE SHAPED HIS BELIEFS--
--THAT THE STRONG AID THE WEAK. AND THAT, ABOVE ALL, TRUTH MATTERS.
SO WHY DID I SWEAR TO GARONA THAT I WOULD LIE TO HIM...?
YES, HIS MOTHER WAS CRAZED-- A MAD MURDERESS ON THE RUN! REFUSED TO NAME THE FATHER.
YES, I FEARED FOR THE BABE...BUT STILL, TO TELL HIM THAT SHE WAS DEAD!
BY THE LIGHT, YOU'D THINK-- AFTER NEARLY THREE THOUSAND YEARS OF EXISTENCE-- I'D KNOW BETTER! BUT IT'S BEEN SO LONG SINCE I WAS A CHILD!
OF COURSE, THE BOY RAN OFF TO THERAMORE!
MED'AN'S POWER IS GROWING DAY BY DAY. THANK THE LIGHT, HE'S MATURING SLOWLY. HE'S HAD TIME TO GAIN SOME CONTROL.
WISH I'D ASKED MORE QUESTIONS...DIDN'T THINK HIS PARENTAGE MATTERED. NOW...I'M NOT SO SURE--!
A SCOURGE NECROPOLIS! THE LICH KING IS MOVING ON THERAMORE! MED'AN IS IN GREATER DANGER THAN I THOUGHT!
QUICKLY! WARN YOUR MISTRESS! THE SCOURGE ARE COMING!
SCOURGE!?
THE UNDEAD FIEND IS ONE OF THEM!
GET HIM!
FREEZE, THEN!
I DON'T HAVE TIME FOR SUCH STUPIDITY!

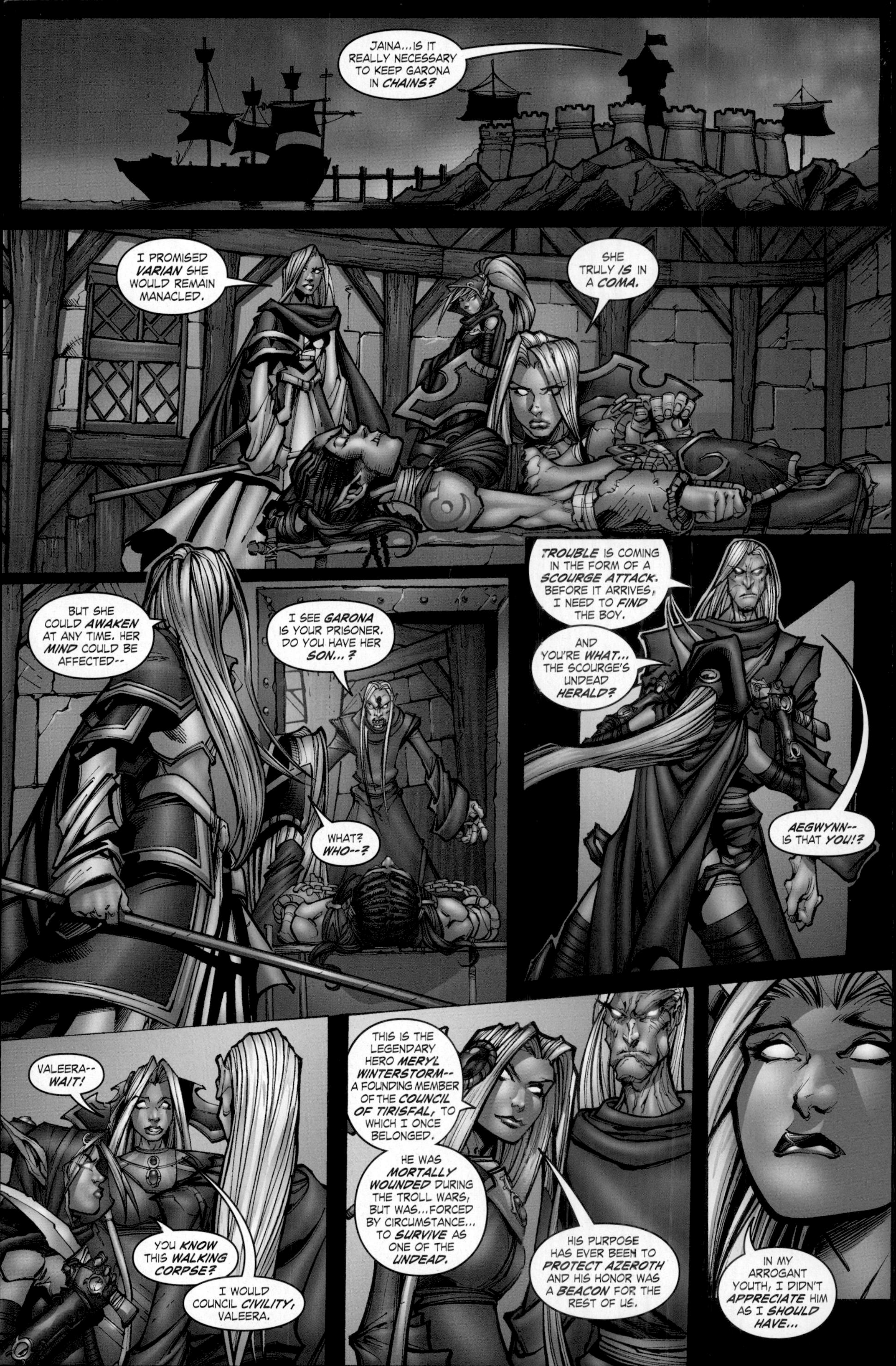
JAINA...IS IT REALLY NECESSARY TO KEEP GARONA IN CHAINS?
I PROMISED VARIAN SHE WOULD REMAIN MANACLED.
SHE TRULY IS IN A COMA.
BUT SHE COULD AWAKEN AT ANY TIME. HER MIND COULD BE AFFECTED--
I SEE GARONA IS YOUR PRISONER. DO YOU HAVE HER SON...?
WHAT? WHO--?
TROUBLE IS COMING IN THE FORM OF A SCOURGE ATTACK. BEFORE IT ARRIVES, I NEED TO FIND THE BOY.
AND YOU'RE WHAT... THE SCOURGE'S UNDEAD HERALD?
AEGWYNN-- IS THAT YOU!?
VALEERA-- WAIT!
YOU KNOW THIS WALKING CORPSE?
I WOULD COUNCIL CIVILITY, VALEERA.
THIS IS THE LEGENDARY HERO MERYL WINTERSTORM-- A FOUNDING MEMBER OF THE COUNCIL OF TIRISFAL, TO WHICH I ONCE BELONGED.
HE WAS MORTALLY WOUNDED DURING THE TROLL WARS, BUT WAS...FORCED BY CIRCUMSTANCE... TO SURVIVE AS ONE OF THE UNDEAD.
HIS PURPOSE HAS EVER BEEN TO PROTECT AZEROTH AND HIS HONOR WAS A BEACON FOR THE REST OF US.
IN MY ARROGANT YOUTH, I DIDN'T APPRECIATE HIM AS I SHOULD HAVE...

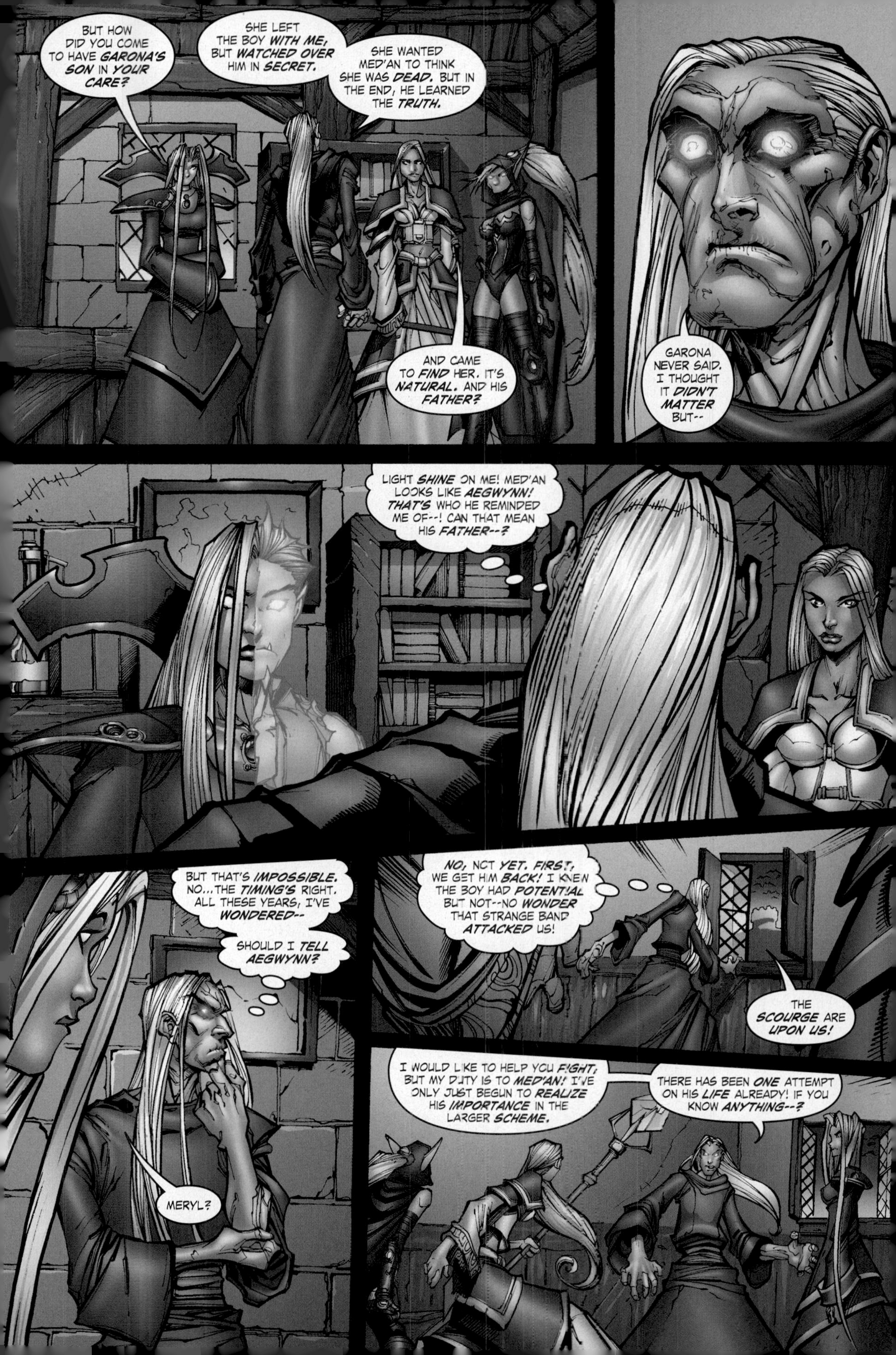
BUT HOW DID YOU COME TO HAVE GARONA'S SON IN YOUR CARE?
SHE LEFT THE BOY WITH ME, BUT WATCHED OVER HIM IN SECRET.
SHE WANTED MED'AN TO THINK SHE WAS DEAD. BUT IN THE END, HE LEARNED THE TRUTH.
AND CAME TO FIND HER. IT'S NATURAL. AND HIS FATHER?
GARONA NEVER SAID. I THOUGHT IT DIDN'T MATTER BUT--
LIGHT SHINE ON ME! MED'AN LOOKS LIKE AEGWYNN! THAT'S WHO HE REMINDED ME OF--! CAN THAT MEAN HIS FATHER--?
BUT THAT'S IMPOSSIBLE. NO...THE TIMING'S RIGHT. ALL THESE YEARS, I'VE WONDERED--
SHOULD I TELL AEGWYNN?
MERYL?
NO, NOT YET. FIRST, WE GET HIM BACK! I KNEW THE BOY HAD POTENTIAL BUT NOT--NO WONDER THAT STRANGE BAND ATTACKED US!
THE SCOURGE ARE UPON US!
I WOULD LIKE TO HELP YOU FIGHT, BUT MY DUTY IS TO MED'AN! I'VE ONLY JUST BEGUN TO REALIZE HIS IMPORTANCE IN THE LARGER SCHEME.
THERE HAS BEEN ONE ATTEMPT ON HIS LIFE ALREADY! IF YOU KNOW ANYTHING--?

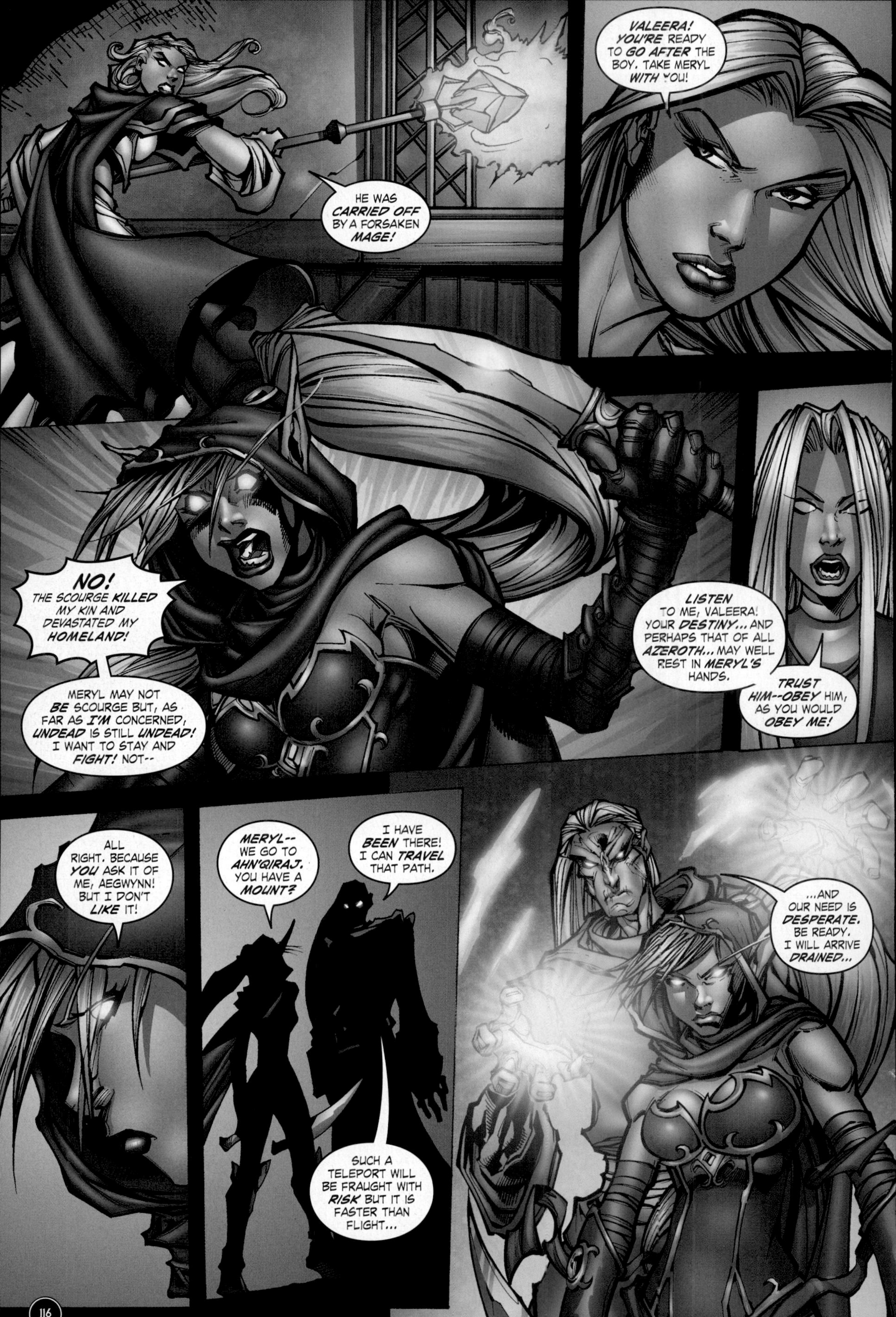

HE WAS CARRIED OFF BY A FORSAKEN MAGE!
VALEERA! YOU'RE READY TO GO AFTER THE BOY. TAKE MERYL WITH YOU!
NO! THE SCOURGE KILLED MY KIN AND DEVASTATED MY HOMELAND!
MERYL MAY NOT BE SCOURGE BUT, AS FAR AS I'M CONCERNED, UNDEAD IS STILL UNDEAD! I WANT TO STAY AND FIGHT! NOT--
LISTEN TO ME, VALEERA! YOUR DESTINY... AND PERHAPS THAT OF ALL AZEROTH... MAY WELL REST IN MERYL'S HANDS.
TRUST HIM--OBEY HIM, AS YOU WOULD OBEY ME!
ALL RIGHT. BECAUSE YOU ASK IT OF ME, AEGWYNN! BUT I DON'T LIKE IT!
MERYL-- WE GO TO AHN'QIRAJ. YOU HAVE A MOUNT?
I HAVE BEEN THERE! I CAN TRAVEL THAT PATH.
SUCH A TELEPORT WILL BE FRAUGHT WITH RISK BUT IT IS FASTER THAN FLIGHT...
...AND OUR NEED IS DESPERATE. BE READY. I WILL ARRIVE DRAINED...

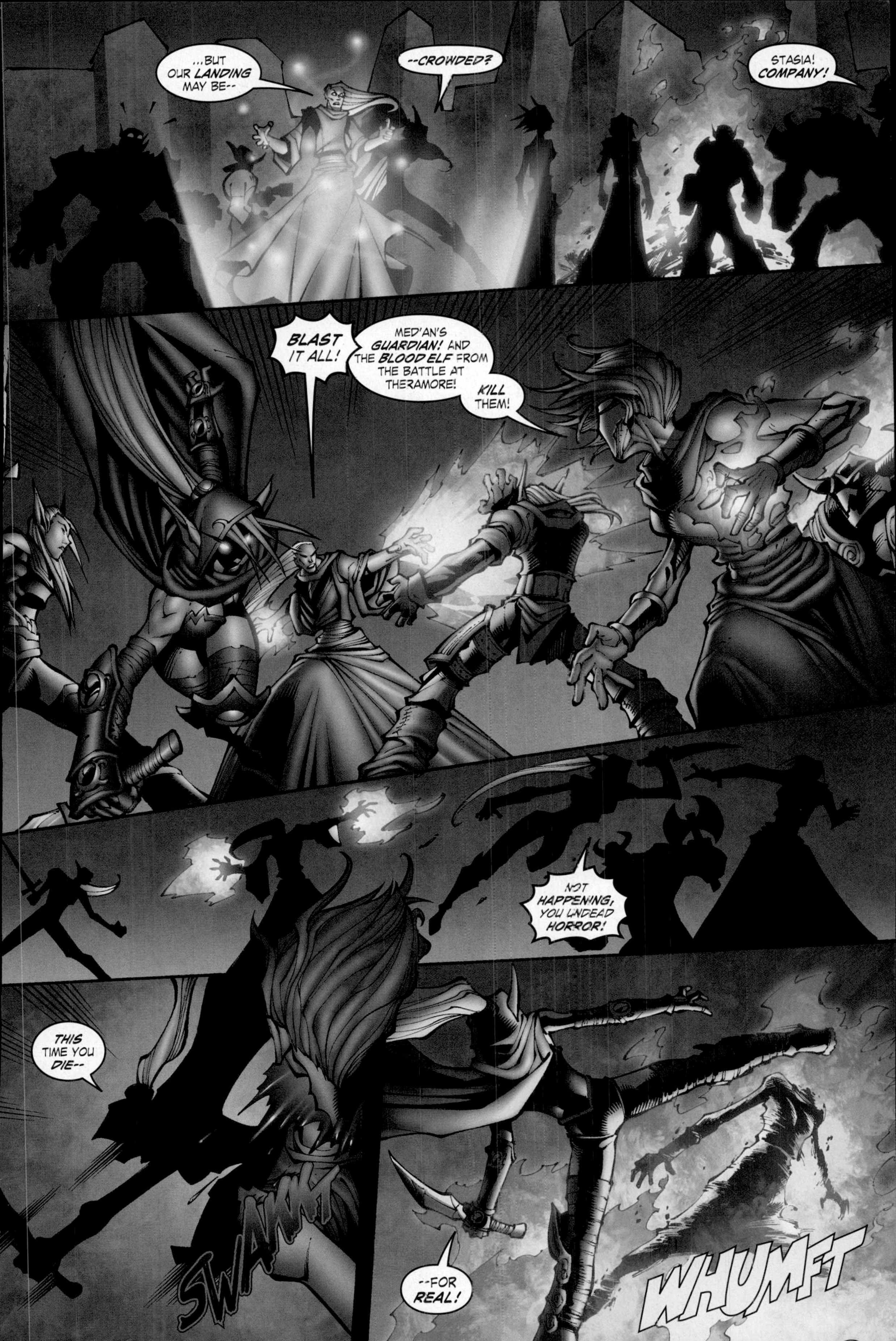

...BUT OUR LANDING MAY BE--
--CROWDED?
STASIA! COMPANY!
BLAST IT ALL!
MED'AN'S GUARDIAN! AND THE BLOOD ELF FROM THE BATTLE AT THERAMORE!
KILL THEM!
NOT HAPPENING, YOU UNDEAD HORROR!
THIS TIME YOU DIE--
--FOR REAL!
WHUMFT

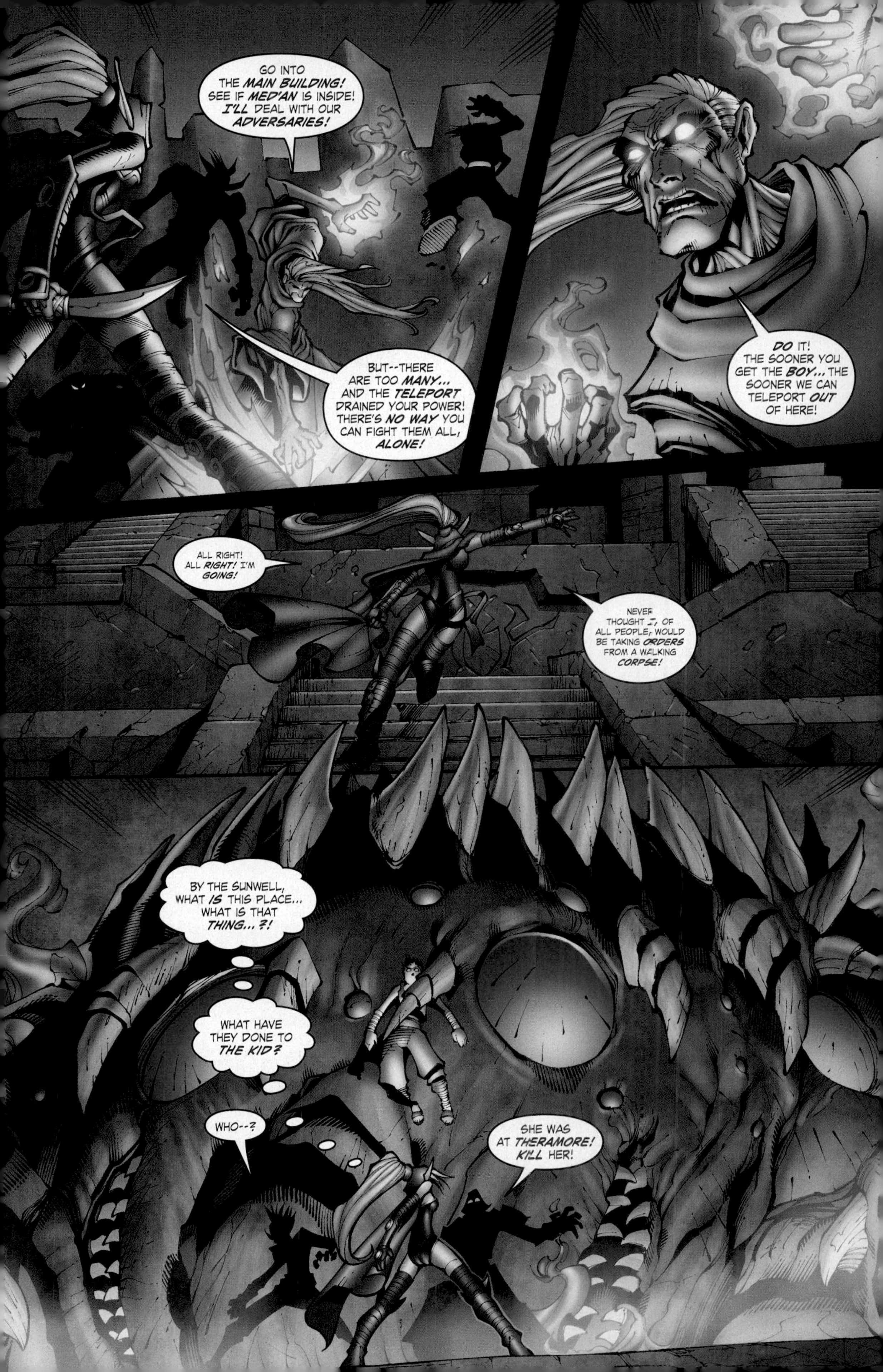
GO INTO THE MAIN BUILDING! SEE IF MED'AN IS INSIDE! I'LL DEAL WITH OUR ADVERSARIES!
BUT--THERE ARE TOO MANY... AND THE TELEPORT DRAINED YOUR POWER! THERE'S NO WAY YOU CAN FIGHT THEM ALL, ALONE!
DO IT! THE SOONER YOU GET THE BOY... THE SOONER WE CAN TELEPORT OUT OF HERE!
ALL RIGHT! ALL RIGHT! I'M GOING!
NEVER THOUGHT I, OF ALL PEOPLE, WOULD BE TAKING ORDERS FROM A WALKING CORPSE!
BY THE SUNWELL, WHAT IS THIS PLACE... WHAT IS THAT THING...?!
WHAT HAVE THEY DONE TO THE KID?
WHO--?
SHE WAS AT THERAMORE! KILL HER!

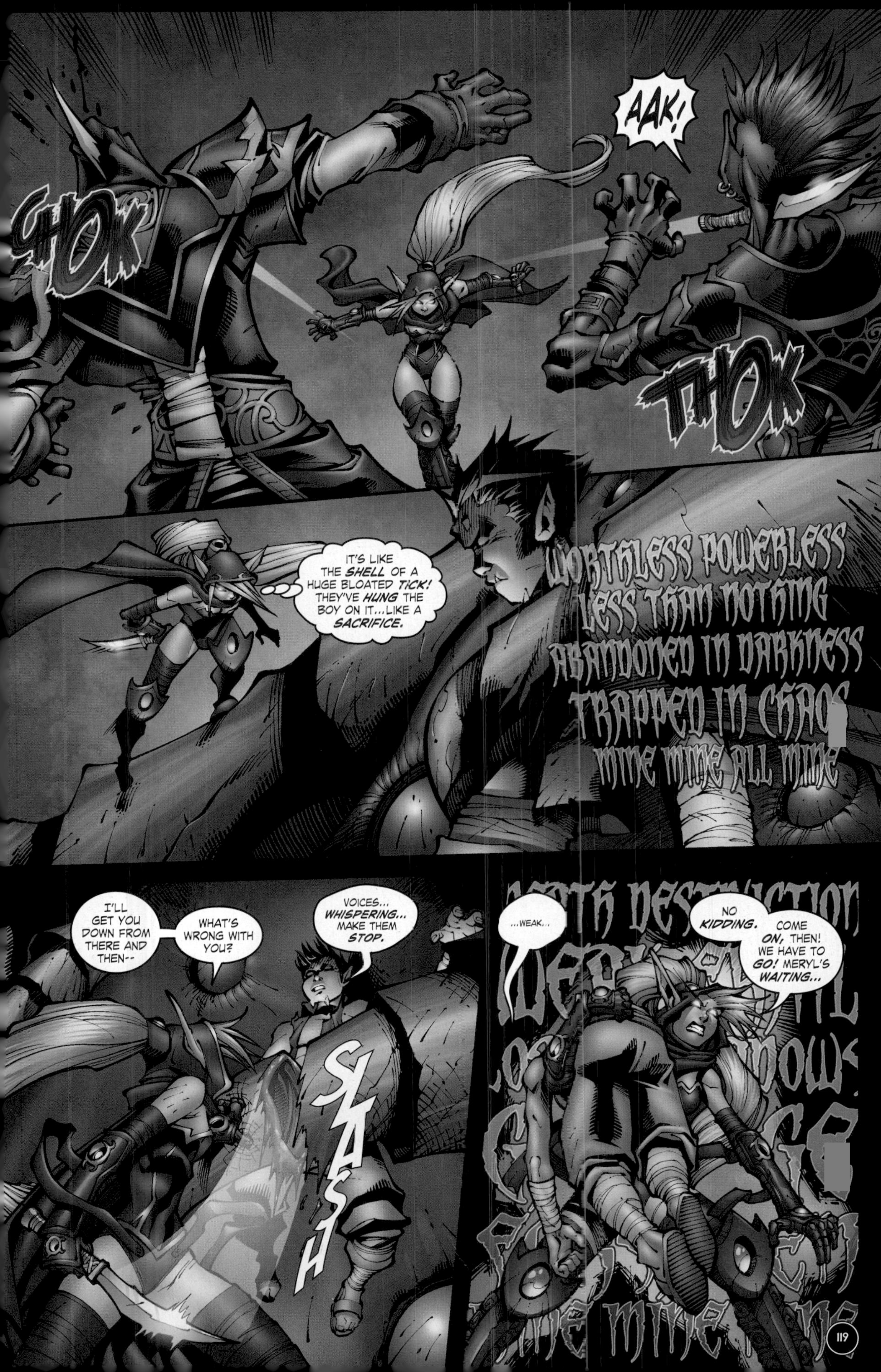

THOK
AAK!
THOK
IT'S LIKE THE SHELL OF A HUGE BLOATED TICK! THEY'VE HUNG THE BOY ON IT...LIKE A SACRIFICE.
WORTHLESS POWERLESS
LESS THAN NOTHING
ABANDONED IN DARKNESS
TRAPPED IN CHAO
MINE MINE ALL MINE
I'LL GET YOU DOWN FROM THERE AND THEN--
WHAT'S WRONG WITH YOU?
VOICES... WHISPERING... MAKE THEM STOP.
SLASH
...WEAK...
NO KIDDING.
COME ON, THEN! WE HAVE TO GO! MERYL'S WAITING...

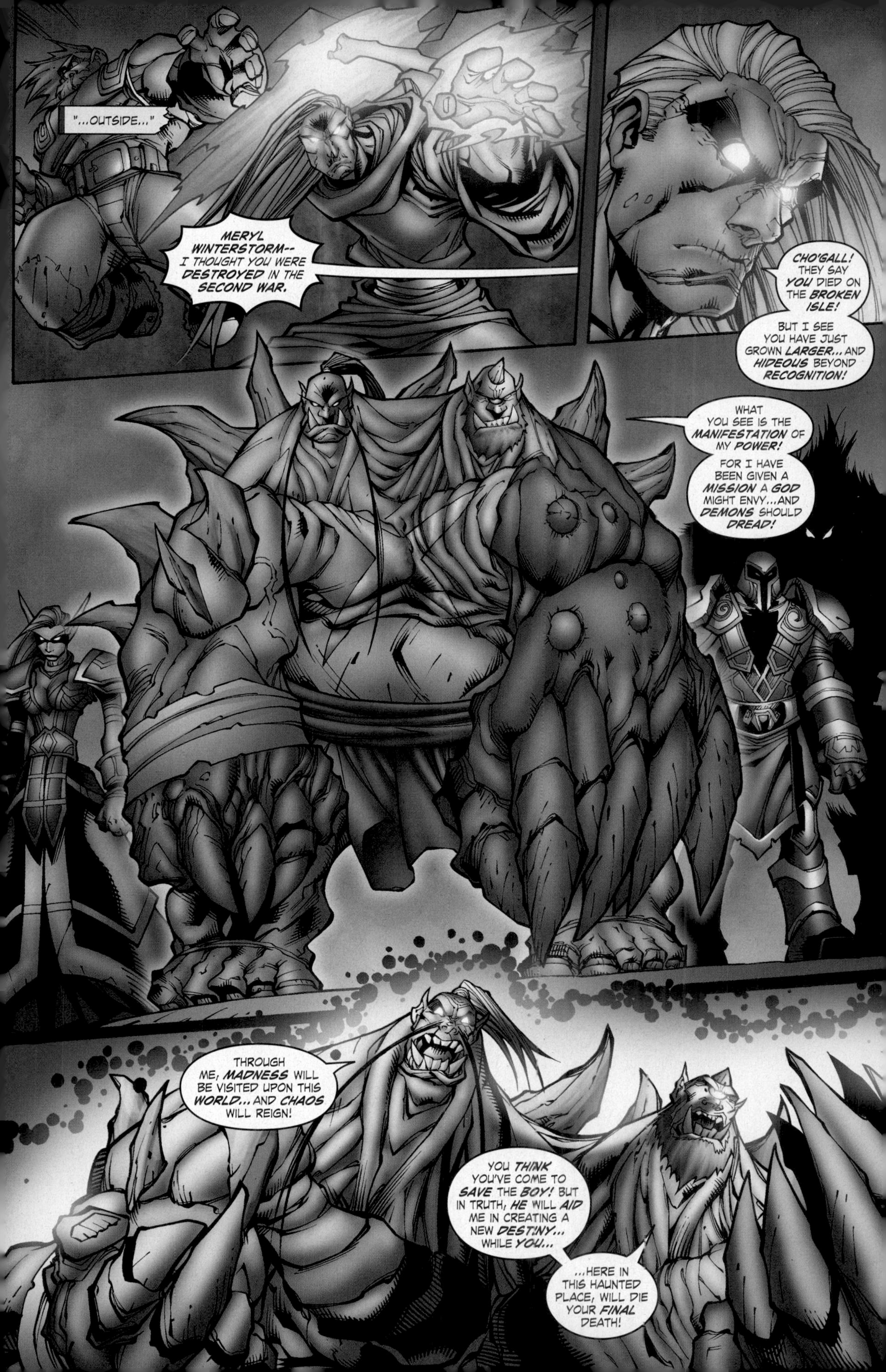
"...OUTSIDE..."
MERYL WINTERSTORM-- I THOUGHT YOU WERE DESTROYED IN THE SECOND WAR.
CHO'GALL! THEY SAY YOU DIED ON THE BROKEN ISLE!
BUT I SEE YOU HAVE JUST GROWN LARGER... AND HIDEOUS BEYOND RECOGNITION!
WHAT YOU SEE IS THE MANIFESTATION OF MY POWER!
FOR I HAVE BEEN GIVEN A MISSION A GOD MIGHT ENVY... AND DEMONS SHOULD DREAD!
THROUGH ME, MADNESS WILL BE VISITED UPON THIS WORLD... AND CHAOS WILL REIGN!
YOU THINK YOU'VE COME TO SAVE THE BOY! BUT IN TRUTH, HE WILL AID ME IN CREATING A NEW DESTINY... WHILE YOU...
...HERE IN THIS HAUNTED PLACE, WILL DIE YOUR FINAL DEATH!

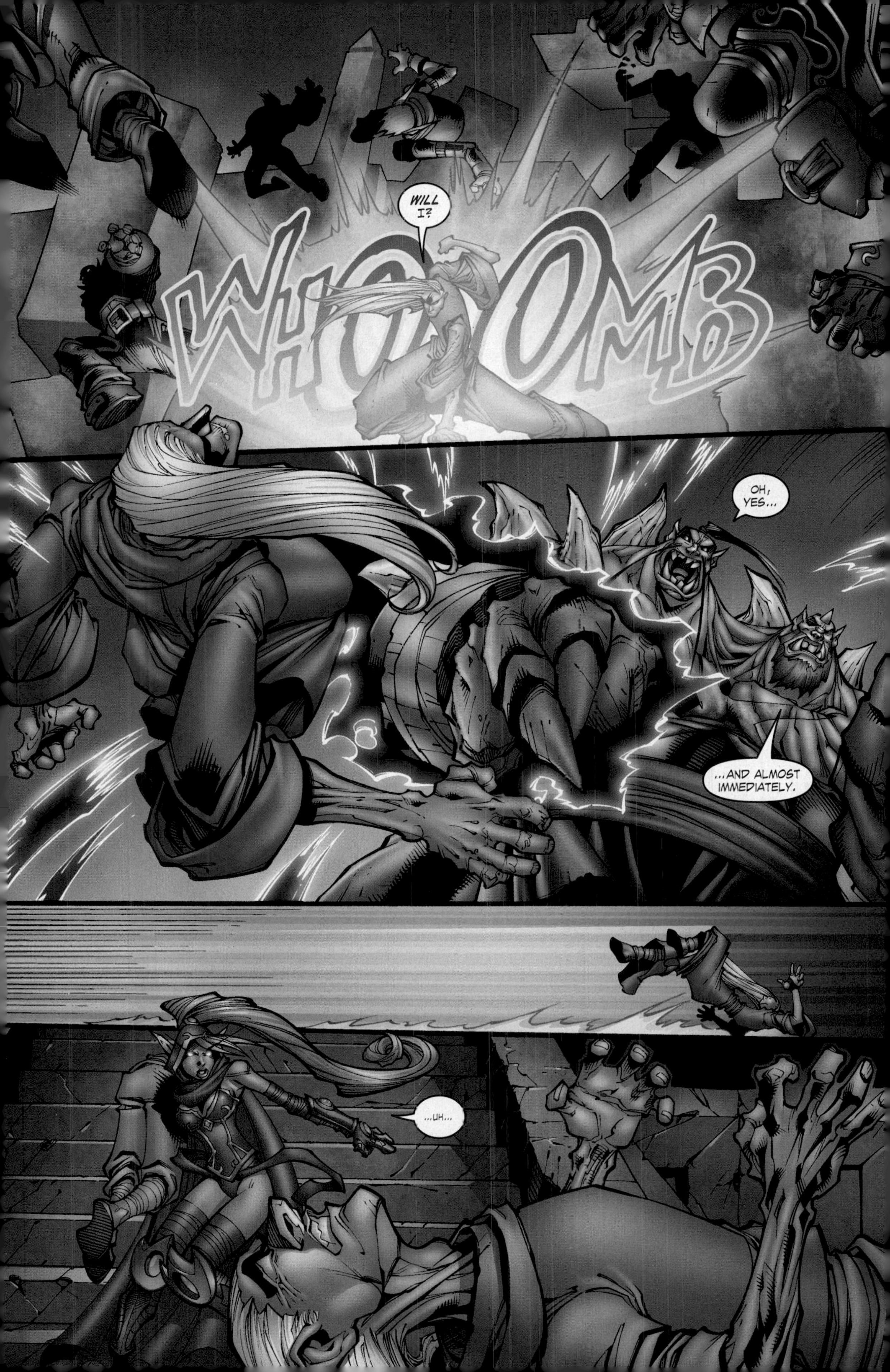
WILL I?
WHOOMB
OH, YES...
...AND ALMOST IMMEDIATELY.
...UH...

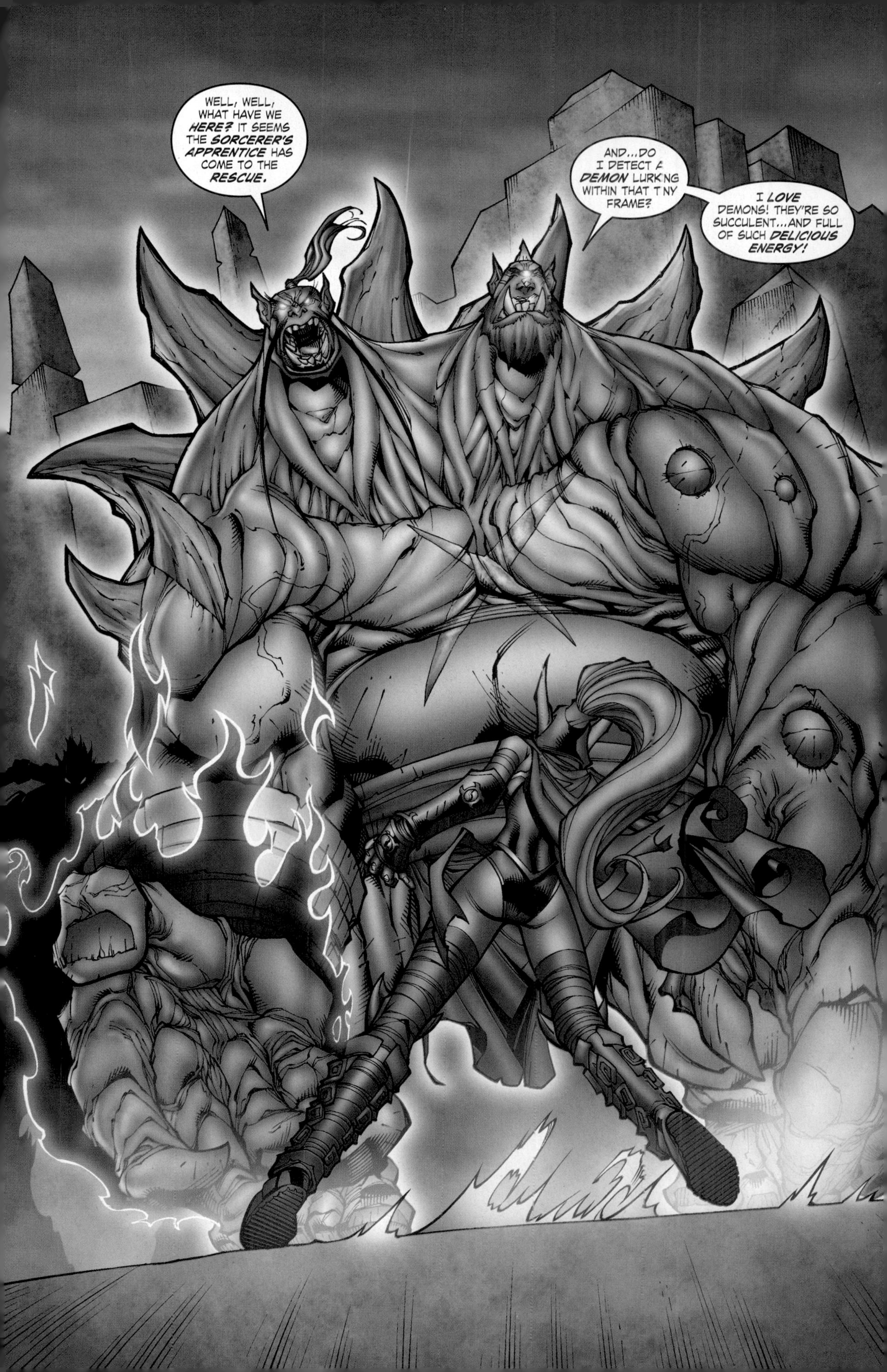
WELL, WELL, WHAT HAVE WE HERE? IT SEEMS THE SORCERER'S APPRENTICE HAS COME TO THE RESCUE.
AND...DO I DETECT A DEMON LURKING WITHIN THAT TINY FRAME?
I LOVE DEMONS! THEY'RE SO SUCCULENT...AND FULL OF SUCH DELICIOUS ENERGY!

CHAPTER 6

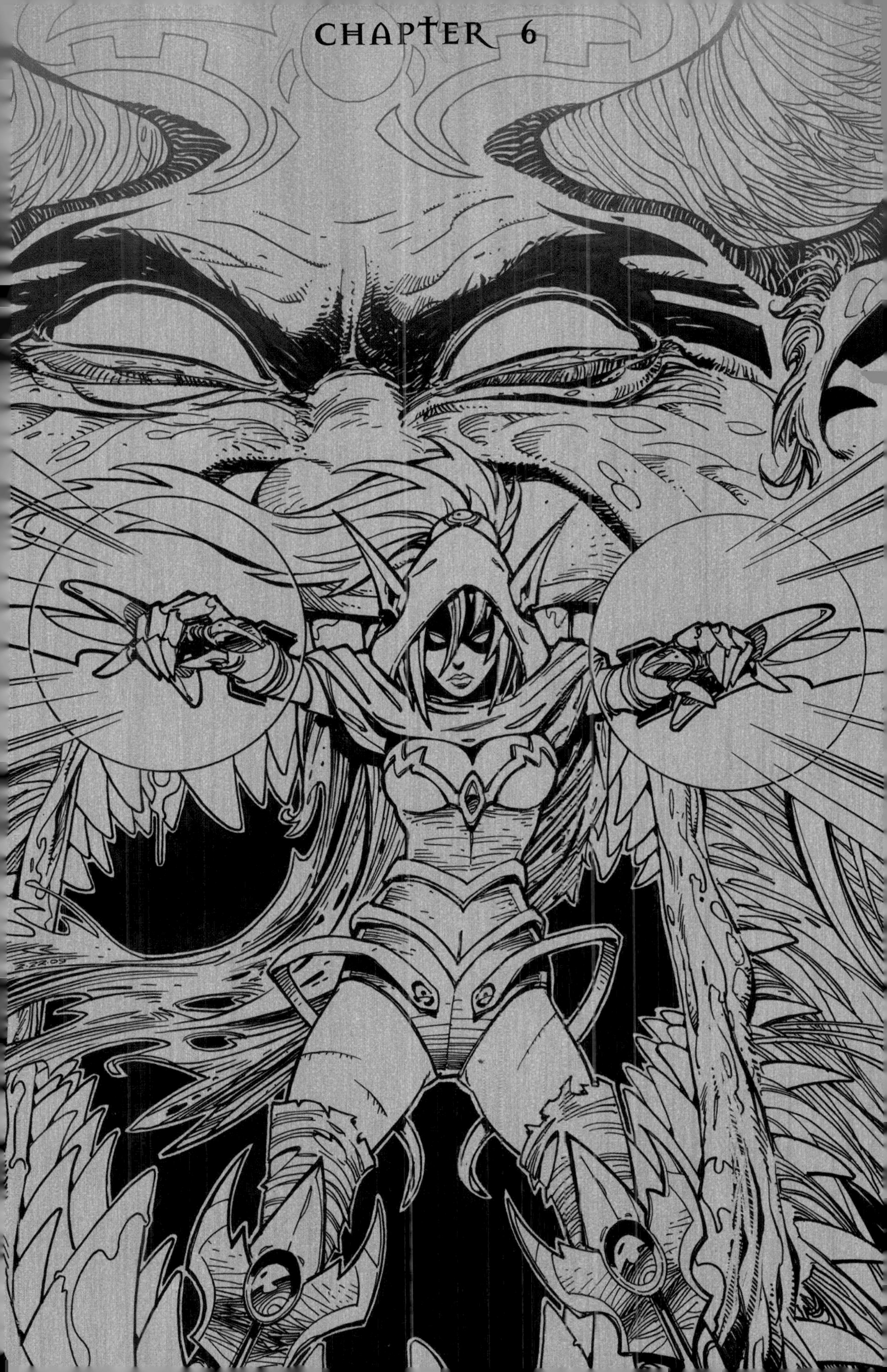

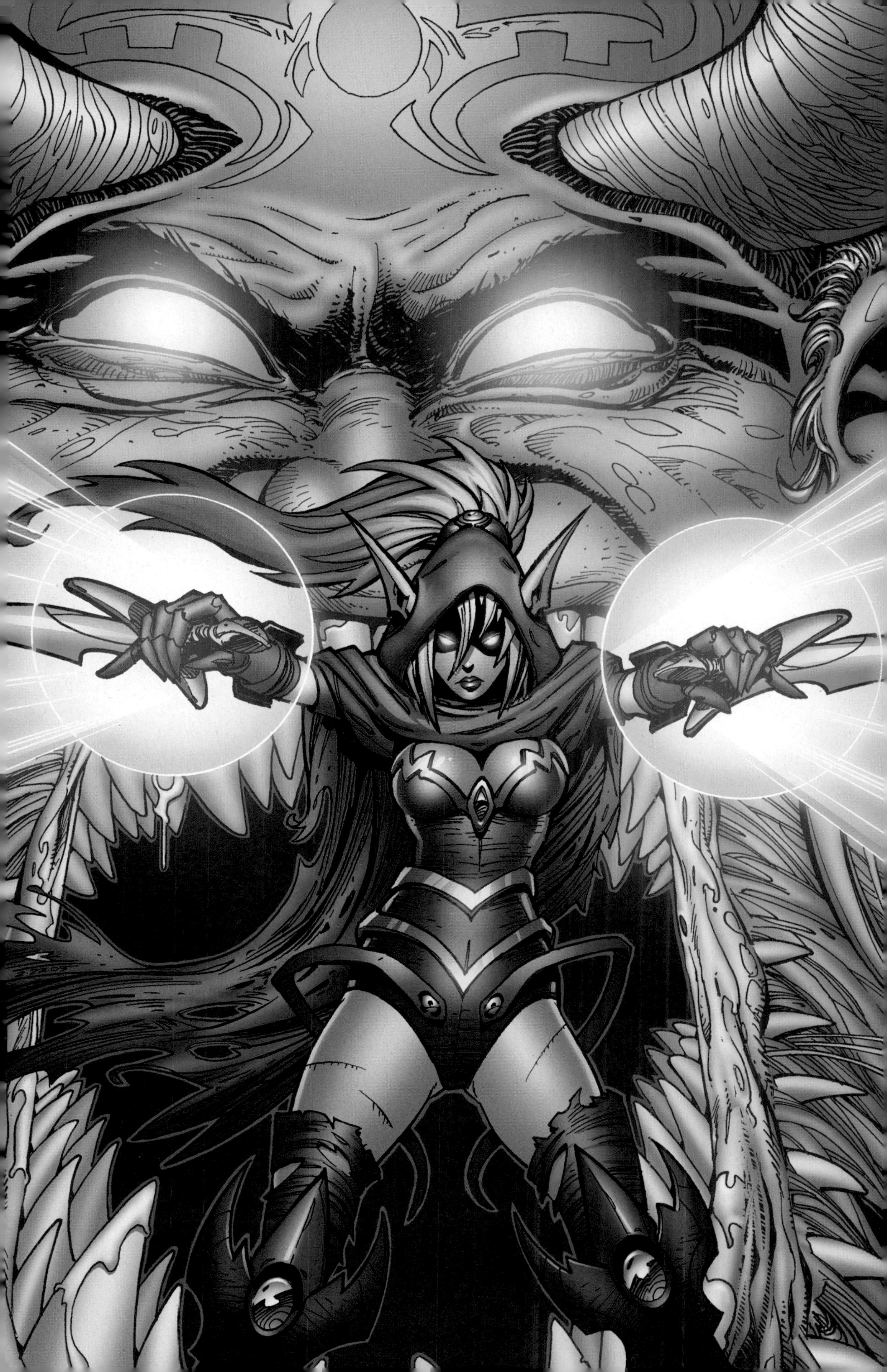

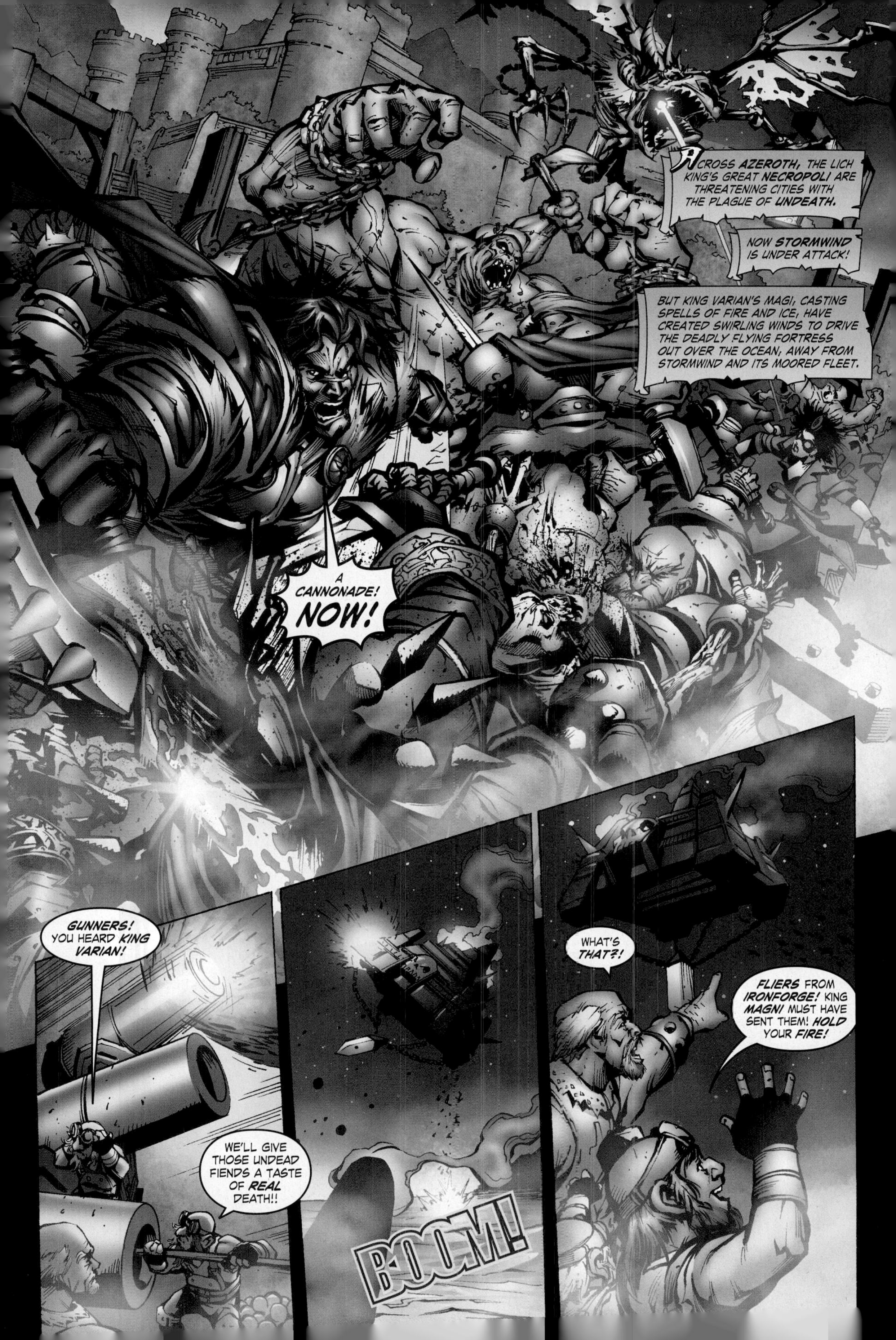
ACROSS AZEROTH, THE LICH KING'S GREAT NECROPOLI ARE THREATENING CITIES WITH THE PLAGUE OF UNDEATH.
NOW STORMWIND IS UNDER ATTACK!
BUT KING VARIAN'S MAGI, CASTING SPELLS OF FIRE AND ICE, HAVE CREATED SWIRLING WINDS TO DRIVE THE DEADLY FLYING FORTRESS OUT OVER THE OCEAN, AWAY FROM STORMWIND AND ITS MOORED FLEET.
A CANNONADE! NOW!
GUNNERS! YOU HEARD KING VARIAN!
WE'LL GIVE THOSE UNDEAD FIENDS A TASTE OF REAL DEATH!!
BOOM!
WHAT'S THAT?!
FLIERS FROM IRONFORGE! KING MAGNI MUST HAVE SENT THEM! HOLD YOUR FIRE!

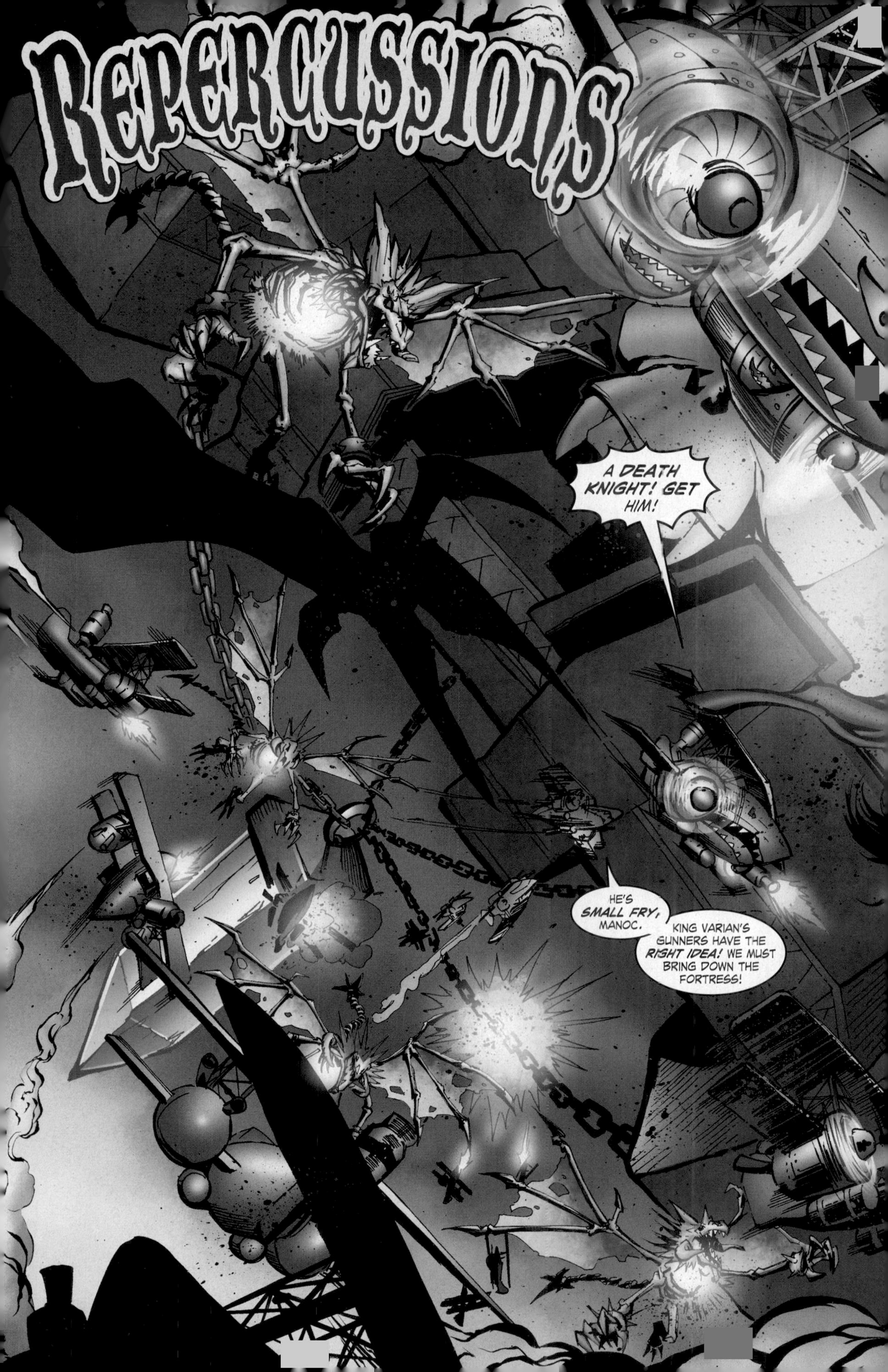
REPERCUSSIONS
A DEATH KNIGHT! GET HIM!
HE'S SMALL FRY, MANOC.
KING VARIAN'S GUNNERS HAVE THE RIGHT IDEA! WE MUST BRING DOWN THE FORTRESS!

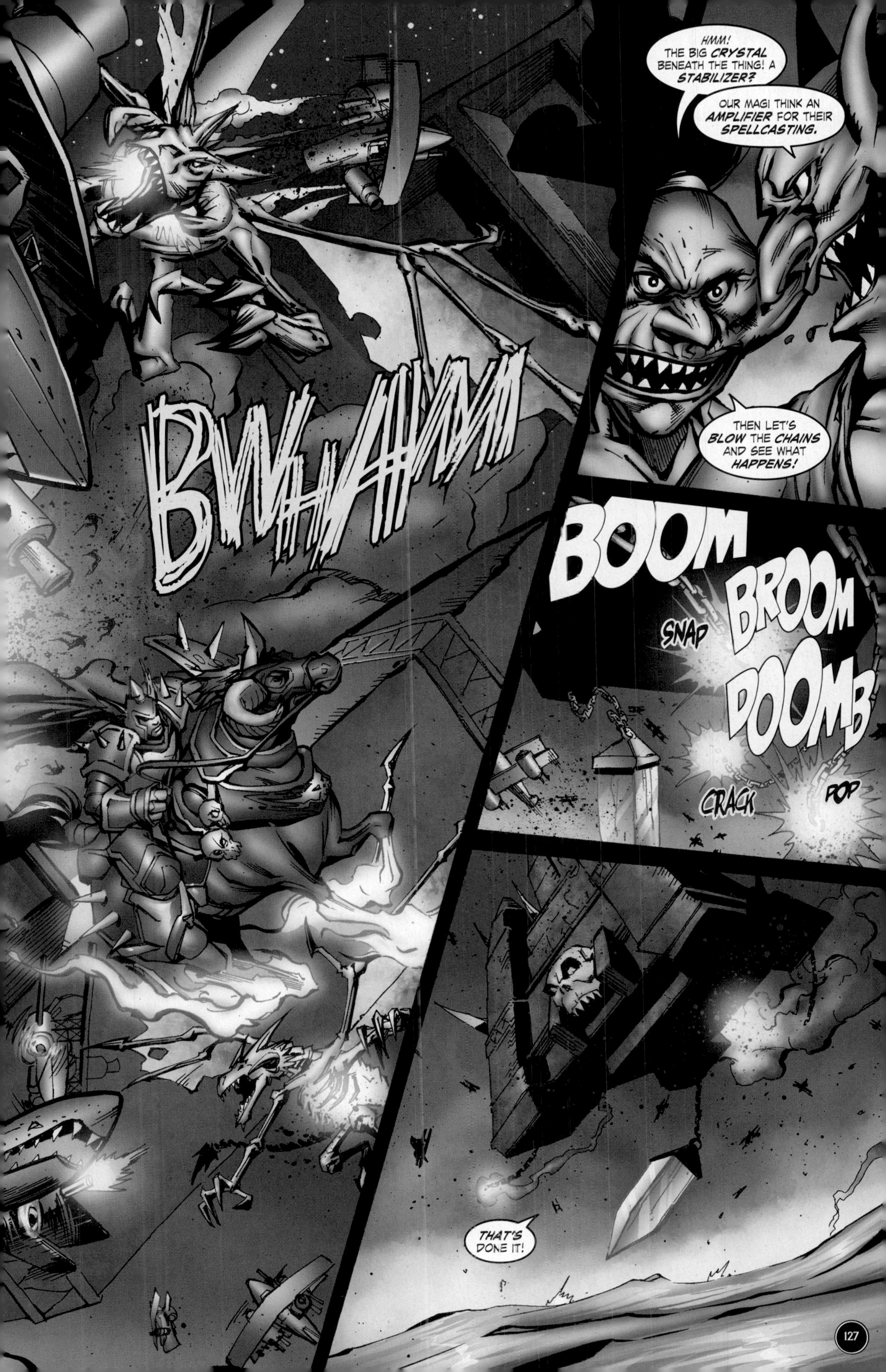
BWHAMM
HMM! THE BIG CRYSTAL BENEATH THE THING! A STABILIZER?
OUR MAGI THINK AN AMPLIFIER FOR THEIR SPELLCASTING.
THEN LET'S BLOW THE CHAINS AND SEE WHAT HAPPENS!
BOOM
BROOM
SNAP
DOOMB
CRACK
POP
THAT'S DONE IT!

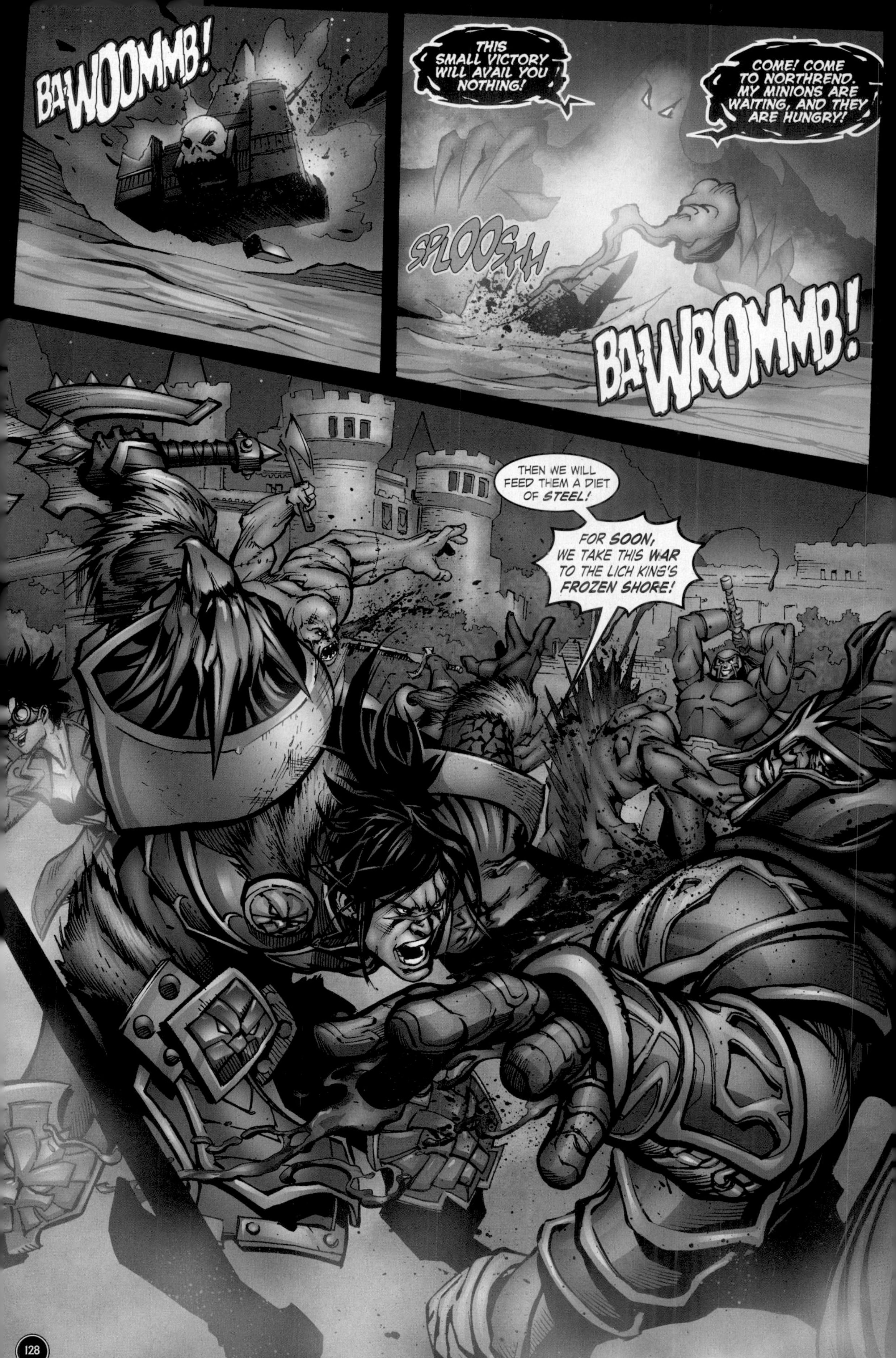
BA-WOOMMB!
THIS SMALL VICTORY WILL AVAIL YOU NOTHING!
COME! COME TO NORTHREND. MY MINIONS ARE WAITING, AND THEY ARE HUNGRY!
SPLOOSHH
BA-WROMMB!
THEN WE WILL FEED THEM A DIET OF STEEL!
FOR SOON, WE TAKE THIS WAR TO THE LICH KING'S FROZEN SHORE!

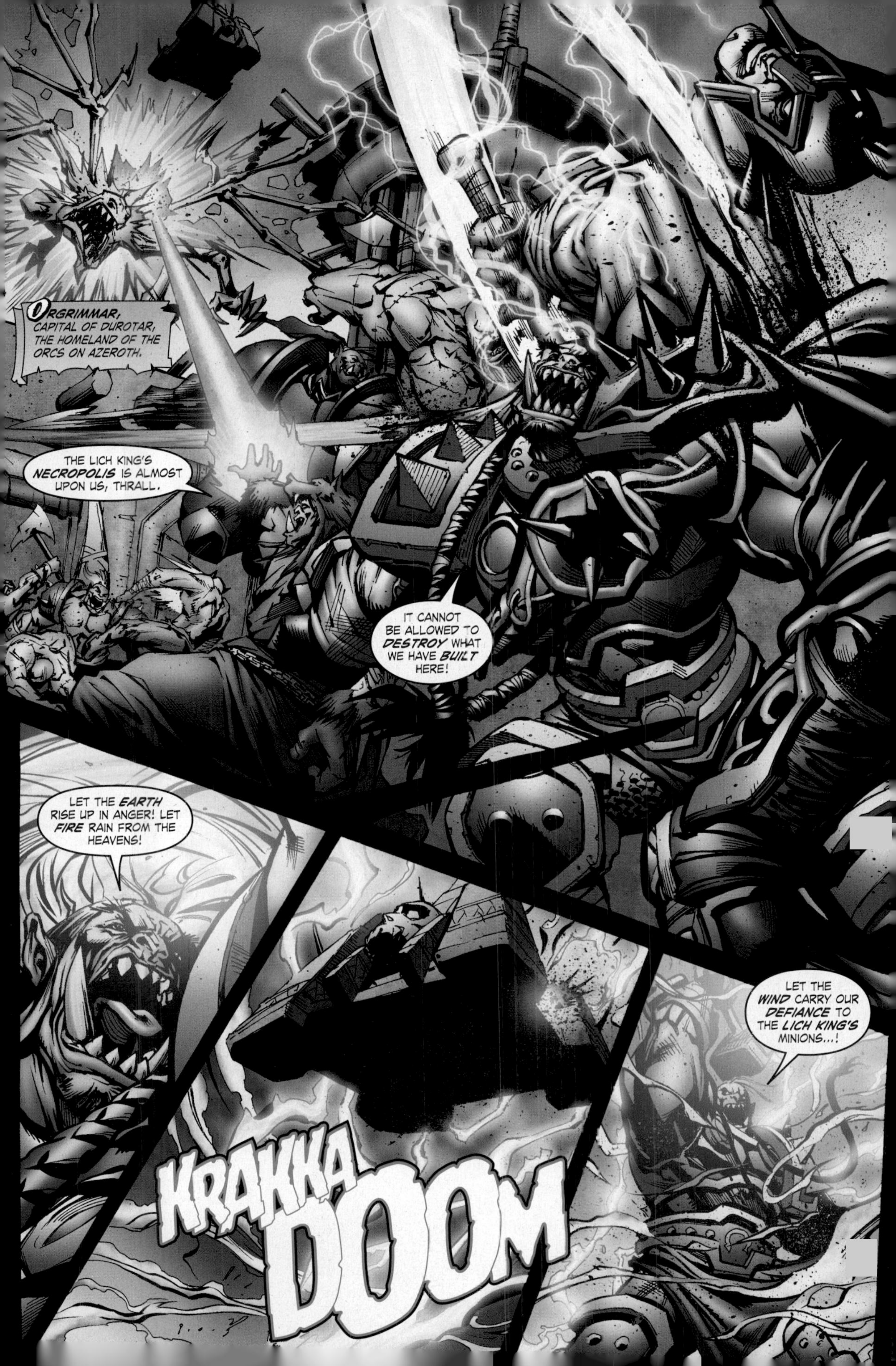
ORGRIMMAR, CAPITAL OF DUROTAR, THE HOMELAND OF THE ORCS ON AZEROTH.
THE LICH KING'S NECROPOLIS IS ALMOST UPON US, THRALL.
IT CANNOT BE ALLOWED TO DESTROY WHAT WE HAVE BUILT HERE!
LET THE EARTH RISE UP IN ANGER! LET FIRE RAIN FROM THE HEAVENS!
KRAKKA DOOM
LET THE WIND CARRY OUR DEFIANCE TO THE LICH KING'S MINIONS...!

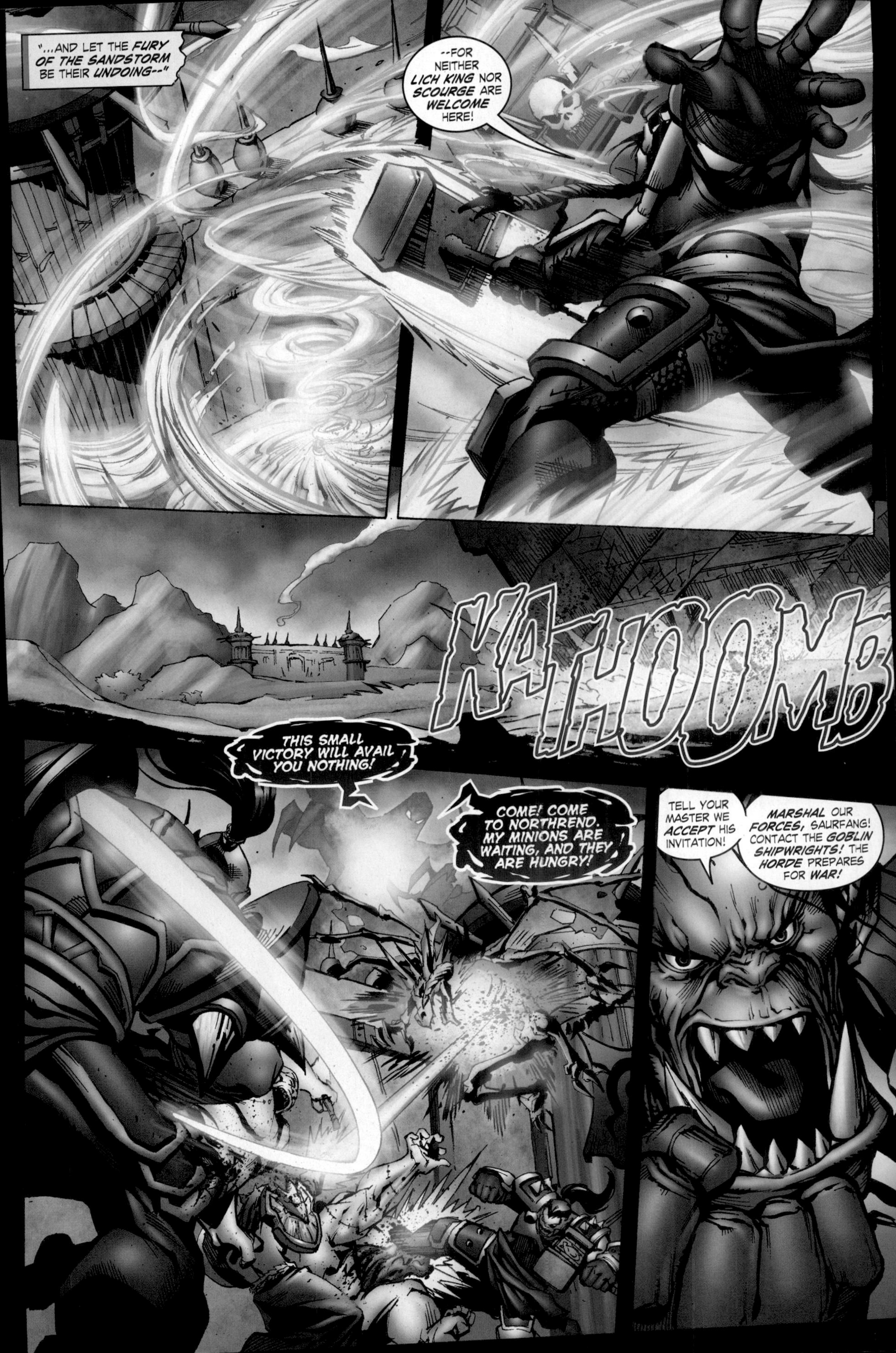
"...AND LET THE FURY OF THE SANDSTORM BE THEIR UNDOING--"
--FOR NEITHER LICH KING NOR SCOURGE ARE WELCOME HERE!
KATHOOMB
THIS SMALL VICTORY WILL AVAIL YOU NOTHING!
COME! COME TO NORTHREND. MY MINIONS ARE WAITING, AND THEY ARE HUNGRY!
TELL YOUR MASTER WE ACCEPT HIS INVITATION!
MARSHAL OUR FORCES, SAURFANG! CONTACT THE GOBLIN SHIPWRIGHTS! THE HORDE PREPARES FOR WAR!

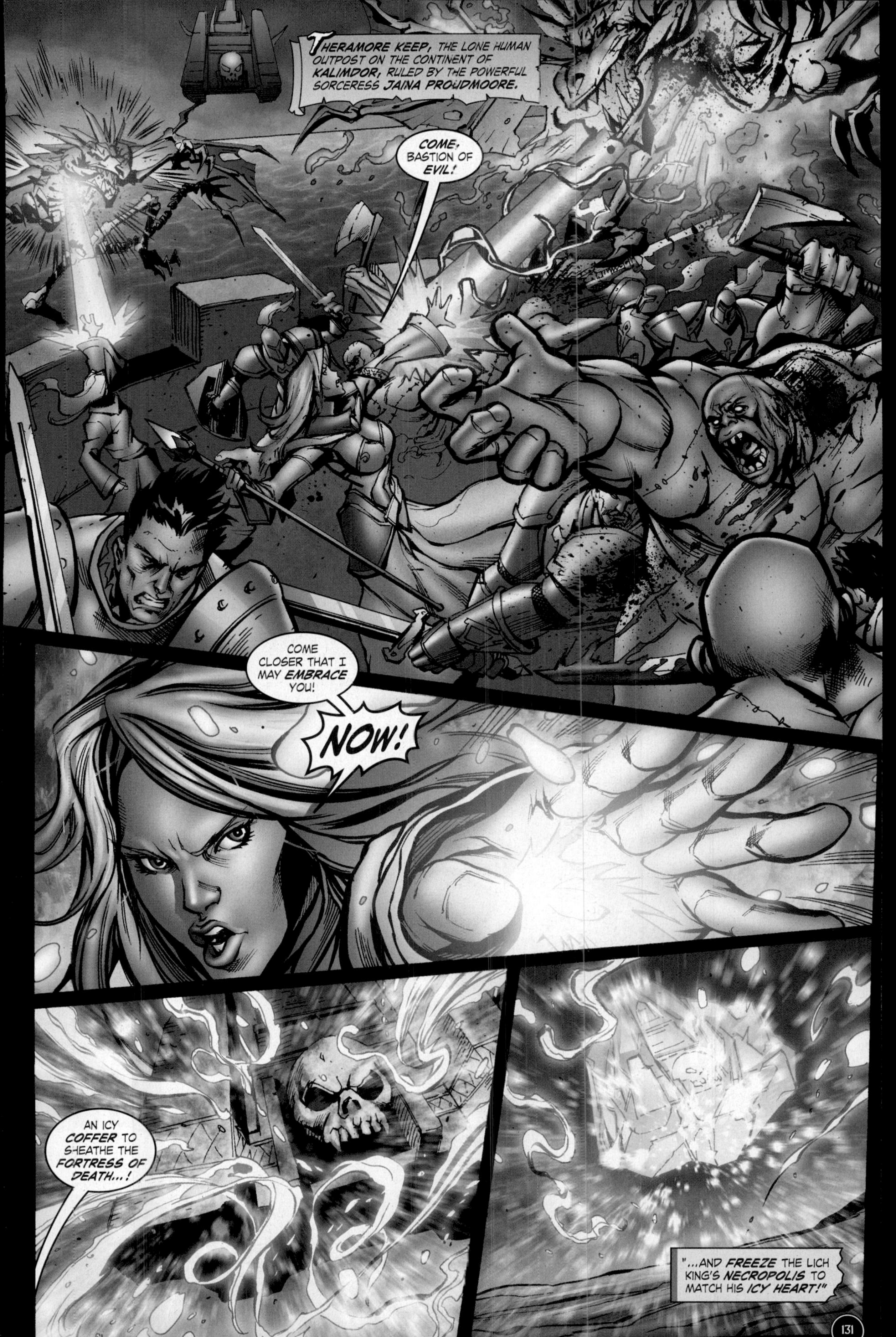
THERAMORE KEEP, THE LONE HUMAN OUTPOST ON THE CONTINENT OF KALIMDOR, RULED BY THE POWERFUL SORCERESS JAINA PROUDMOORE.
COME, BASTION OF EVIL!
COME CLOSER THAT I MAY EMBRACE YOU!
NOW!
AN ICY COFFER TO SHEATHE THE FORTRESS OF DEATH...!
"...AND FREEZE THE LICH KING'S NECROPOLIS TO MATCH HIS ICY HEART!"

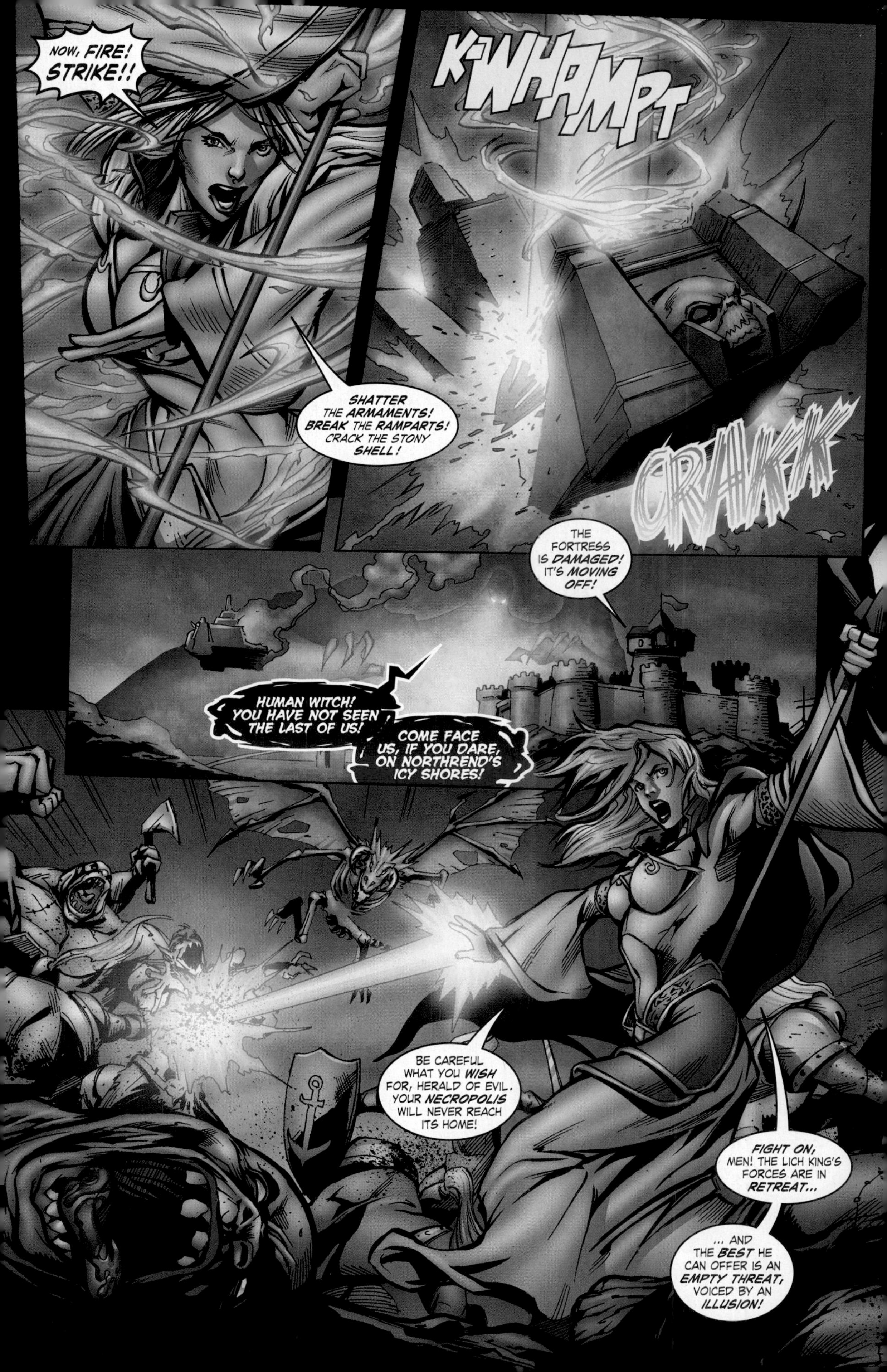
NOW, FIRE! STRIKE!!
SHATTER THE ARMAMENTS! BREAK THE RAMPARTS! CRACK THE STONY SHELL!
K-WHAMPT
CRAKK
THE FORTRESS IS DAMAGED! IT'S MOVING OFF!
HUMAN WITCH! YOU HAVE NOT SEEN THE LAST OF US!
COME FACE US, IF YOU DARE, ON NORTHREND'S ICY SHORES!
BE CAREFUL WHAT YOU WISH FOR, HERALD OF EVIL. YOUR NECROPOLIS WILL NEVER REACH ITS HOME!
FIGHT ON, MEN! THE LICH KING'S FORCES ARE IN RETREAT...
... AND THE BEST HE CAN OFFER IS AN EMPTY THREAT, VOICED BY AN ILLUSION!

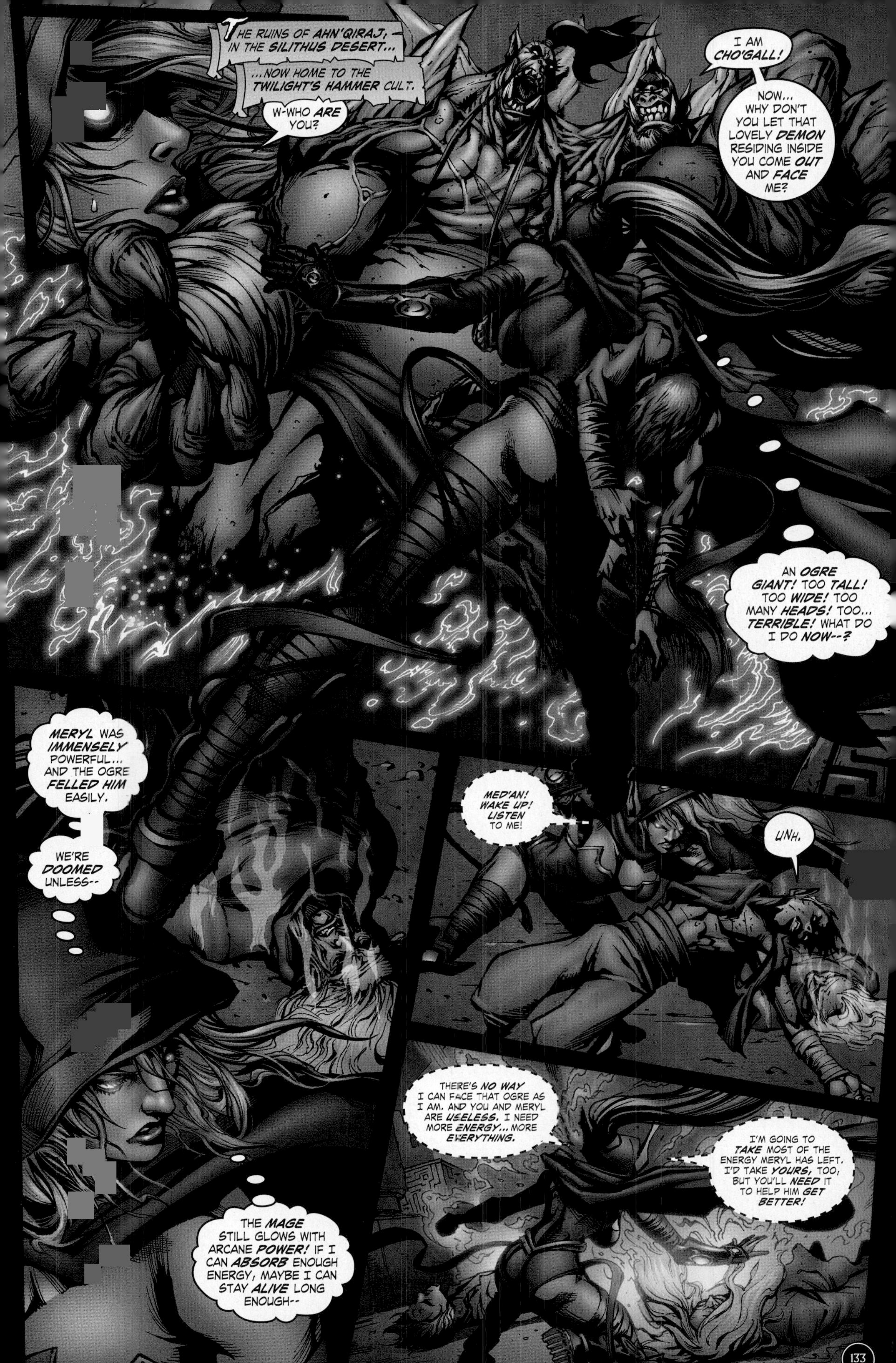

THE RUINS OF AHN'QIRAJ, IN THE SILITHUS DESERT...
...NOW HOME TO THE TWILIGHT'S HAMMER CULT.
W-WHO ARE YOU?
I AM CHO'GALL!
NOW... WHY DON'T YOU LET THAT LOVELY DEMON RESIDING INSIDE YOU COME OUT AND FACE ME?
AN OGRE GIANT! TOO TALL! TOO WIDE! TOO MANY HEADS! TOO... TERRIBLE! WHAT DO I DO NOW--?
MERYL WAS IMMENSELY POWERFUL... AND THE OGRE FELLED HIM EASILY.
WE'RE DOOMED UNLESS--
MED'AN! WAKE UP! LISTEN TO ME!
UNH.
THE MAGE STILL GLOWS WITH ARCANE POWER! IF I CAN ABSORB ENOUGH ENERGY, MAYBE I CAN STAY ALIVE LONG ENOUGH--
THERE'S NO WAY I CAN FACE THAT OGRE AS I AM. AND YOU AND MERYL ARE USELESS. I NEED MORE ENERGY... MORE EVERYTHING.
I'M GOING TO TAKE MOST OF THE ENERGY MERYL HAS LEFT. I'D TAKE YOURS, TOO, BUT YOU'LL NEED IT TO HELP HIM GET BETTER!

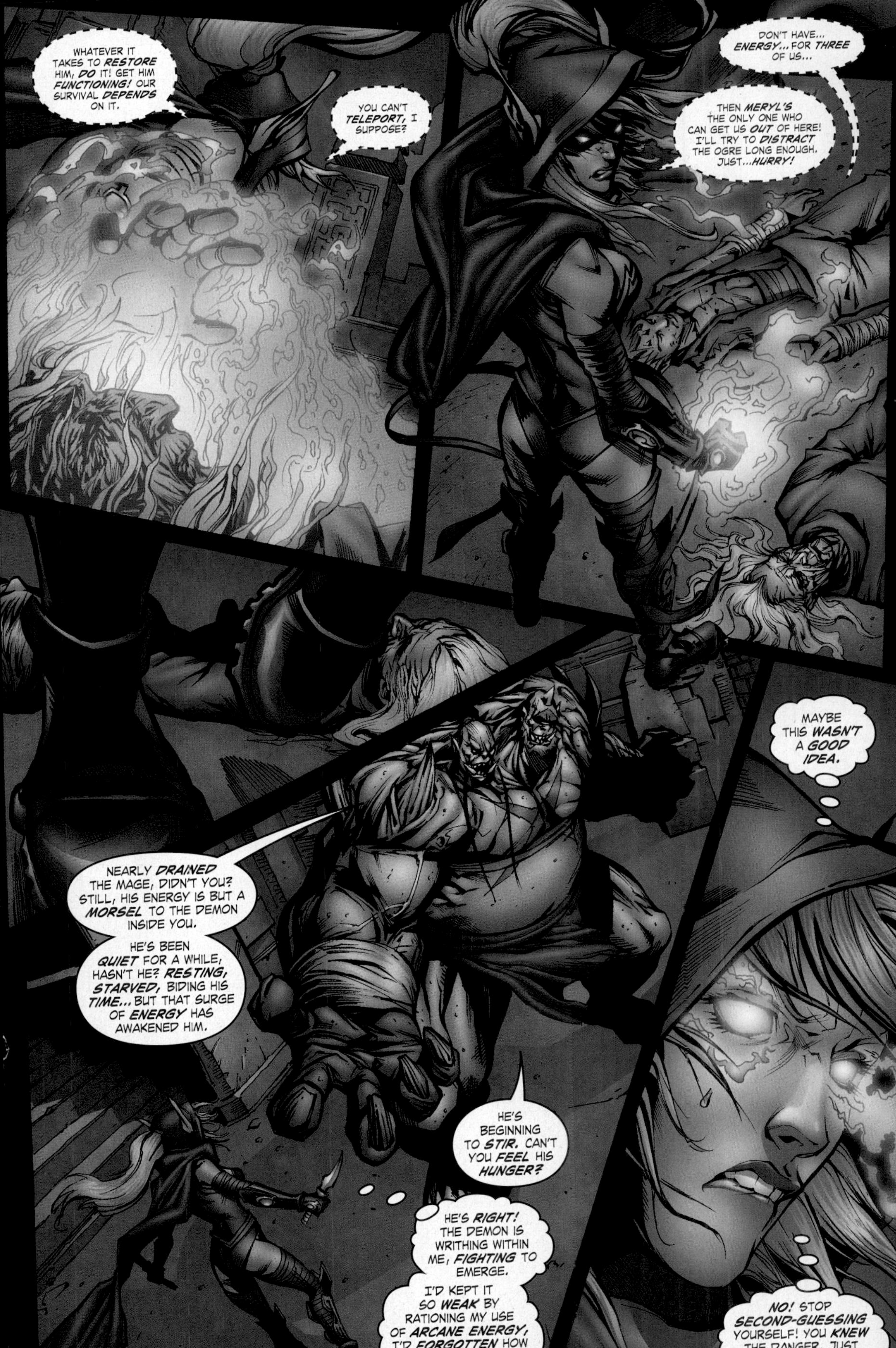
WHATEVER IT TAKES TO RESTORE HIM, DO IT! GET HIM FUNCTIONING! OUR SURVIVAL DEPENDS ON IT.
YOU CAN'T TELEPORT, I SUPPOSE?
DON'T HAVE... ENERGY... FOR THREE OF US...
THEN MERYL'S THE ONLY ONE WHO CAN GET US OUT OF HERE! I'LL TRY TO DISTRACT THE OGRE LONG ENOUGH. JUST...HURRY!
NEARLY DRAINED THE MAGE, DIDN'T YOU? STILL, HIS ENERGY IS BUT A MORSEL TO THE DEMON INSIDE YOU.
HE'S BEEN QUIET FOR A WHILE, HASN'T HE? RESTING, STARVED, BIDING HIS TIME... BUT THAT SURGE OF ENERGY HAS AWAKENED HIM.
HE'S BEGINNING TO STIR. CAN'T YOU FEEL HIS HUNGER?
HE'S RIGHT! THE DEMON IS WRITHING WITHIN ME, FIGHTING TO EMERGE.
I'D KEPT IT SO WEAK BY RATIONING MY USE OF ARCANE ENERGY, I'D FORGOTTEN HOW MUCH STRONGER IT COULD BECOME.
MAYBE THIS WASN'T A GOOD IDEA.
NO! STOP SECOND-GUESSING YOURSELF! YOU KNEW THE DANGER. JUST PLAY THE HAND YOU'VE DRAWN!

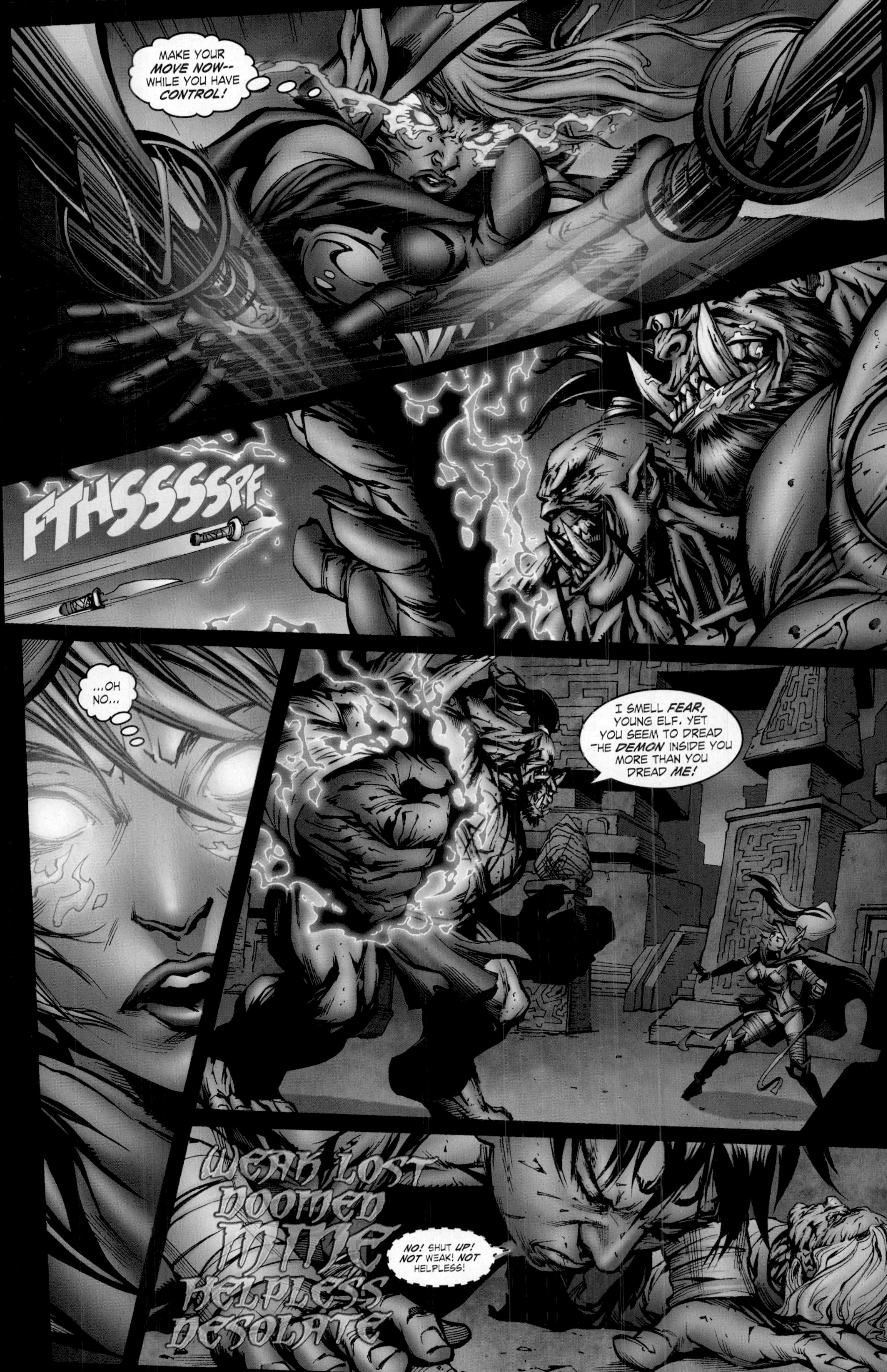
MAKE YOUR MOVE NOW-- WHILE YOU HAVE CONTROL!
FTHSSSSPF
...OH NO...
I SMELL FEAR, YOUNG ELF. YET YOU SEEM TO DREAD THE DEMON INSIDE YOU MORE THAN YOU DREAD ME!
WEAK LOST DOOMED MINE HELPLESS DESOLATE
NO! SHUT UP! NOT WEAK! NOT HELPLESS!

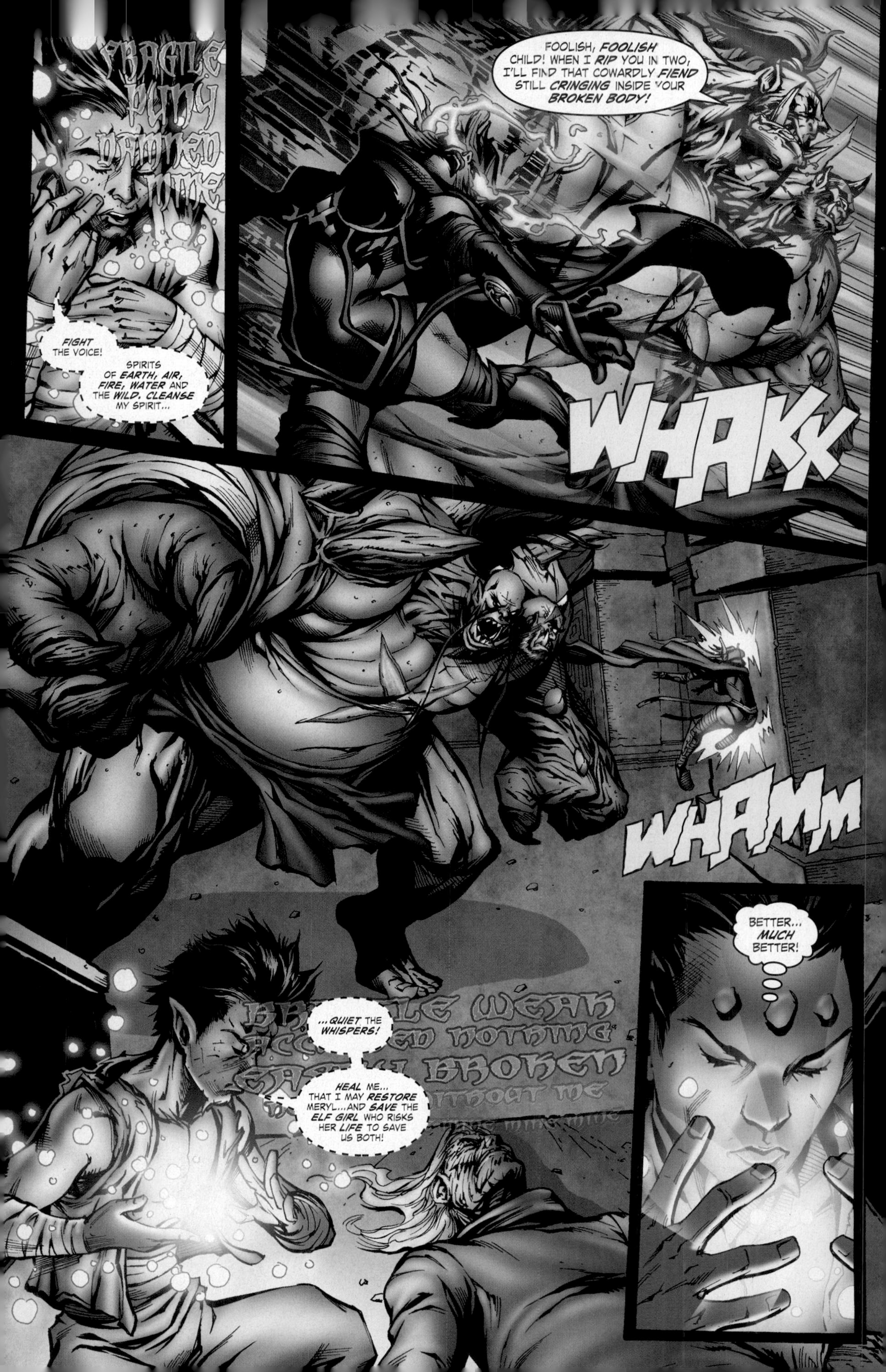
FRAGILE
PUNY
DAMNED
FIGHT THE VOICE!
SPIRITS OF EARTH, AIR, FIRE, WATER AND THE WILD. CLEANSE MY SPIRIT...
FOOLISH, FOOLISH CHILD! WHEN I RIP YOU IN TWO, I'LL FIND THAT COWARDLY FIEND STILL CRINGING INSIDE YOUR BROKEN BODY!
WHAKK
WHAMM
WEAK
NOTHING
BROKEN
...QUIET THE WHISPERS!
HEAL ME... THAT I MAY RESTORE MERYL...AND SAVE THE ELF GIRL WHO RISKS HER LIFE TO SAVE US BOTH!
BETTER... MUCH BETTER!

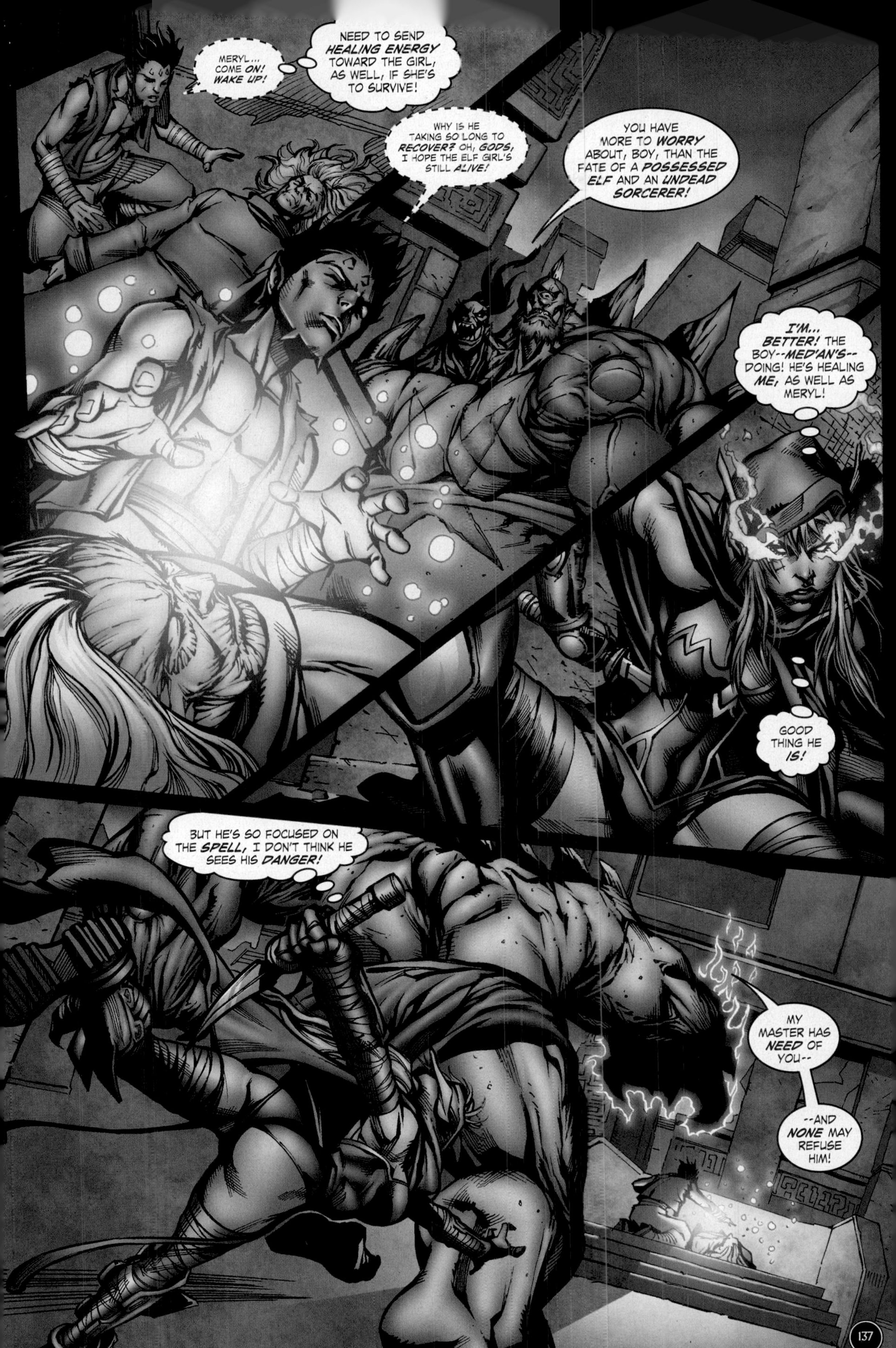
MERYL... COME ON! WAKE UP!
NEED TO SEND HEALING ENERGY TOWARD THE GIRL, AS WELL, IF SHE'S TO SURVIVE!
WHY IS HE TAKING SO LONG TO RECOVER? OH, GODS, I HOPE THE ELF GIRL'S STILL ALIVE!
YOU HAVE MORE TO WORRY ABOUT, BOY, THAN THE FATE OF A POSSESSED ELF AND AN UNDEAD SORCERER!
I'M... BETTER! THE BOY--MED'AN'S--DOING! HE'S HEALING ME, AS WELL AS MERYL!
GOOD THING HE IS!
BUT HE'S SO FOCUSED ON THE SPELL, I DON'T THINK HE SEES HIS DANGER!
MY MASTER HAS NEED OF YOU--
--AND NONE MAY REFUSE HIM!

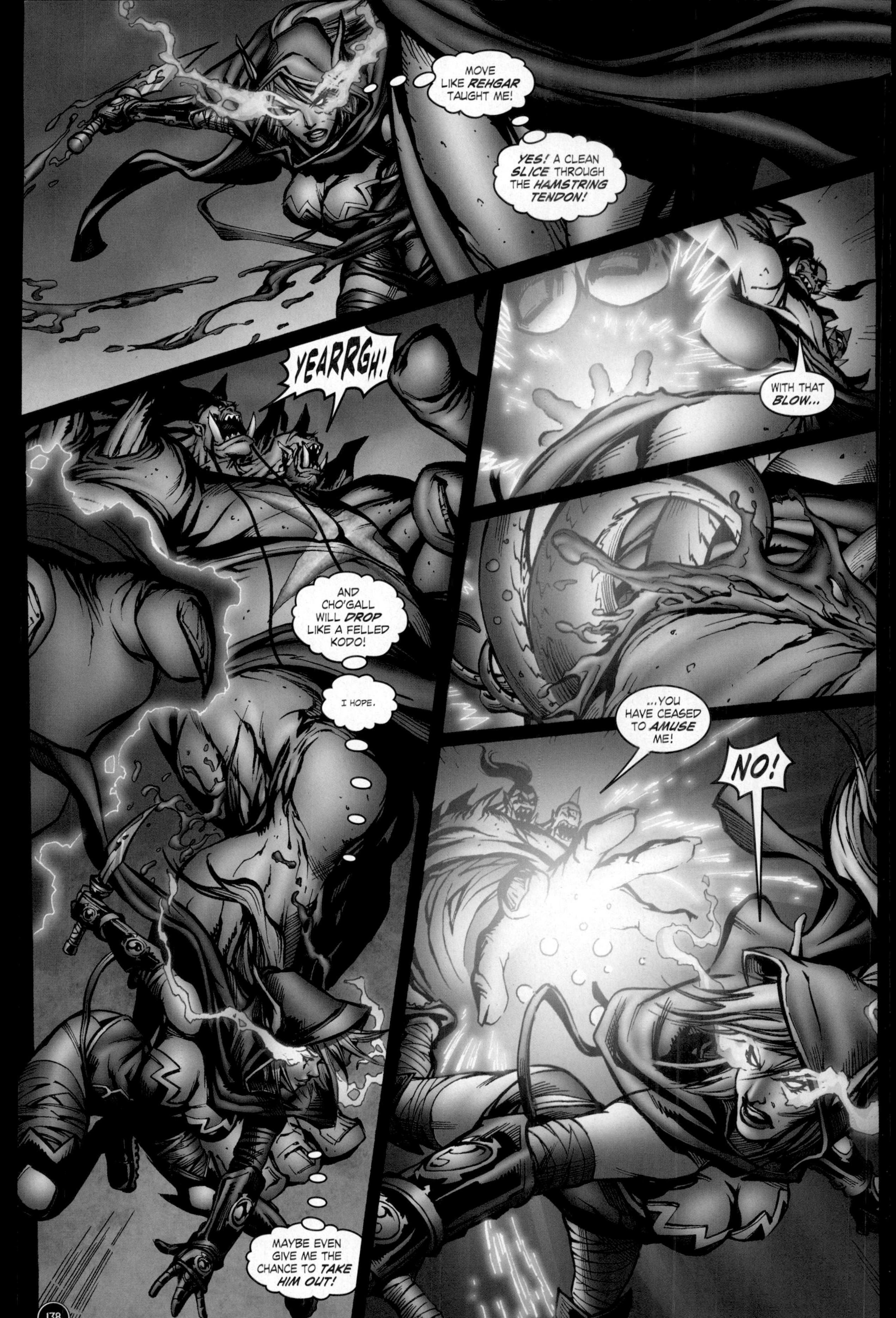
MOVE LIKE REHGAR TAUGHT ME!
YES! A CLEAN SLICE THROUGH THE HAMSTRING TENDON!
YEARRGH!
WITH THAT BLOW...
AND CHO'GALL WILL DROP LIKE A FELLED KODO!
I HOPE.
MAYBE EVEN GIVE ME THE CHANCE TO TAKE HIM OUT!
...YOU HAVE CEASED TO AMUSE ME!
NO!

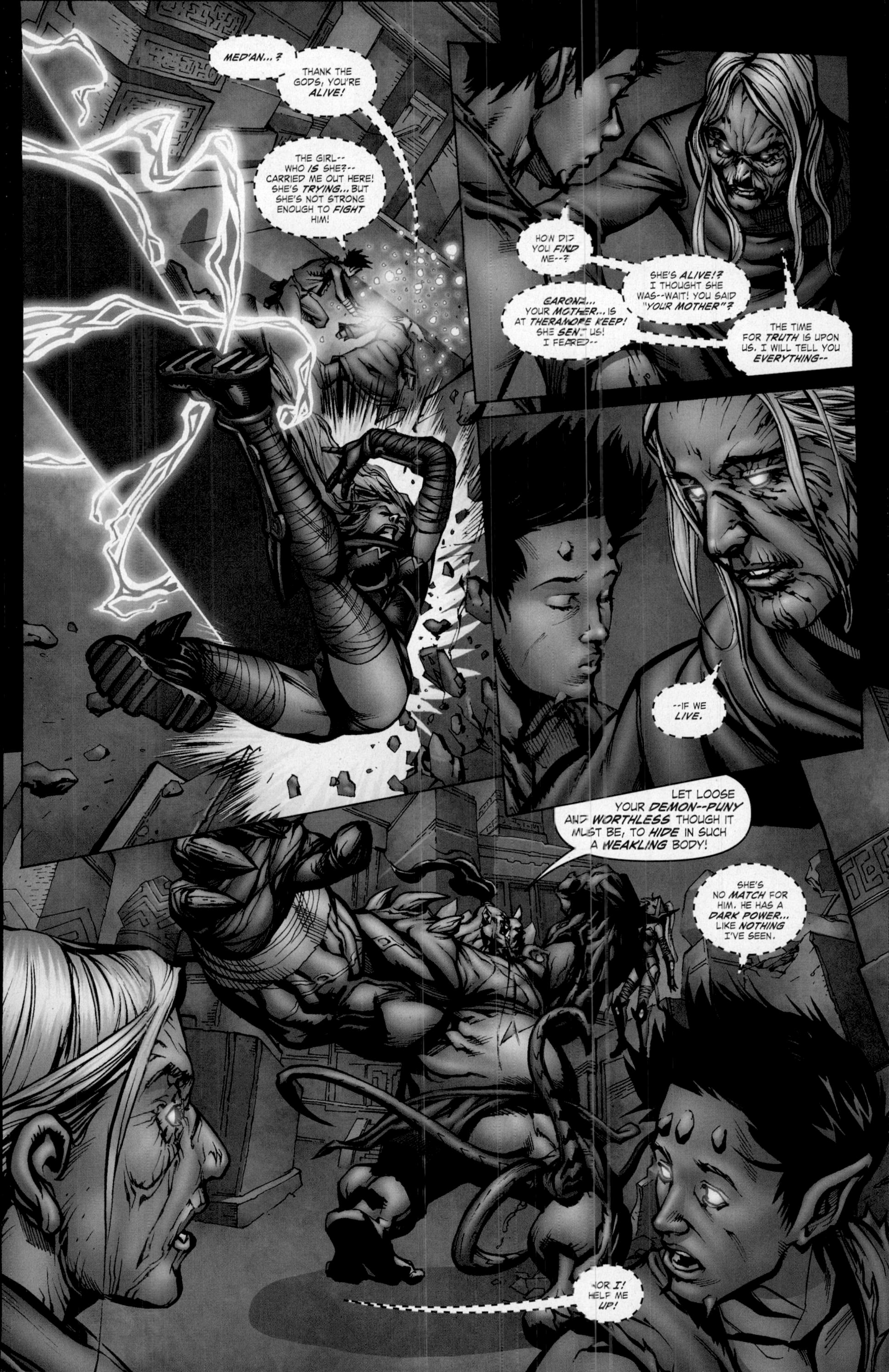
MED'AN...?
THANK THE GODS, YOU'RE ALIVE!
THE GIRL--WHO IS SHE?--CARRIED ME OUT HERE! SHE'S TRYING... BUT SHE'S NOT STRONG ENOUGH TO FIGHT HIM!
HOW DID YOU FIND ME--?
GARONA... YOUR MOTHER... IS AT THERAMORE KEEP! SHE SENT US! I FEARED--
SHE'S ALIVE!? I THOUGHT SHE WAS--WAIT! YOU SAID "YOUR MOTHER"?
THE TIME FOR TRUTH IS UPON US. I WILL TELL YOU EVERYTHING--
--IF WE LIVE.
LET LOOSE YOUR DEMON--PUNY AND WORTHLESS THOUGH IT MUST BE, TO HIDE IN SUCH A WEAKLING BODY!
SHE'S NO MATCH FOR HIM. HE HAS A DARK POWER... LIKE NOTHING I'VE SEEN.
NOR I! HELP ME UP!

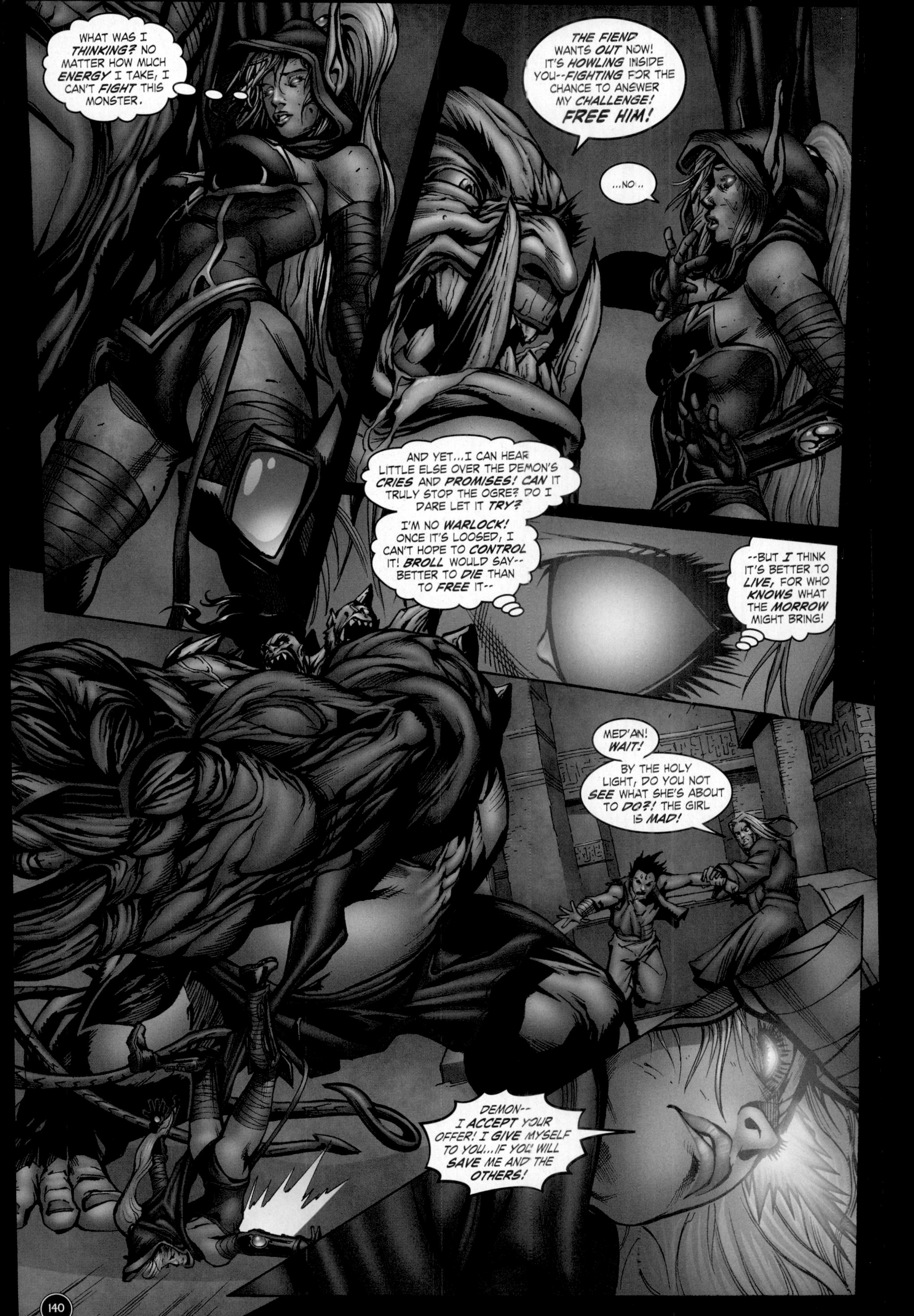

WHAT WAS I THINKING? NO MATTER HOW MUCH ENERGY I TAKE, I CAN'T FIGHT THIS MONSTER.
THE FIEND WANTS OUT NOW! IT'S HOWLING INSIDE YOU--FIGHTING FOR THE CHANCE TO ANSWER MY CHALLENGE! FREE HIM!
...NO...
AND YET...I CAN HEAR LITTLE ELSE OVER THE DEMON'S CRIES AND PROMISES! CAN IT TRULY STOP THE OGRE? DO I DARE LET IT TRY?
I'M NO WARLOCK! ONCE IT'S LOOSED, I CAN'T HOPE TO CONTROL IT! BROLL WOULD SAY-- BETTER TO DIE THAN TO FREE IT--
--BUT I THINK IT'S BETTER TO LIVE, FOR WHO KNOWS WHAT THE MORROW MIGHT BRING!
MED'AN! WAIT!
BY THE HOLY LIGHT, DO YOU NOT SEE WHAT SHE'S ABOUT TO DO?! THE GIRL IS MAD!
DEMON-- I ACCEPT YOUR OFFER! I GIVE MYSELF TO YOU...IF YOU WILL SAVE ME AND THE OTHERS!

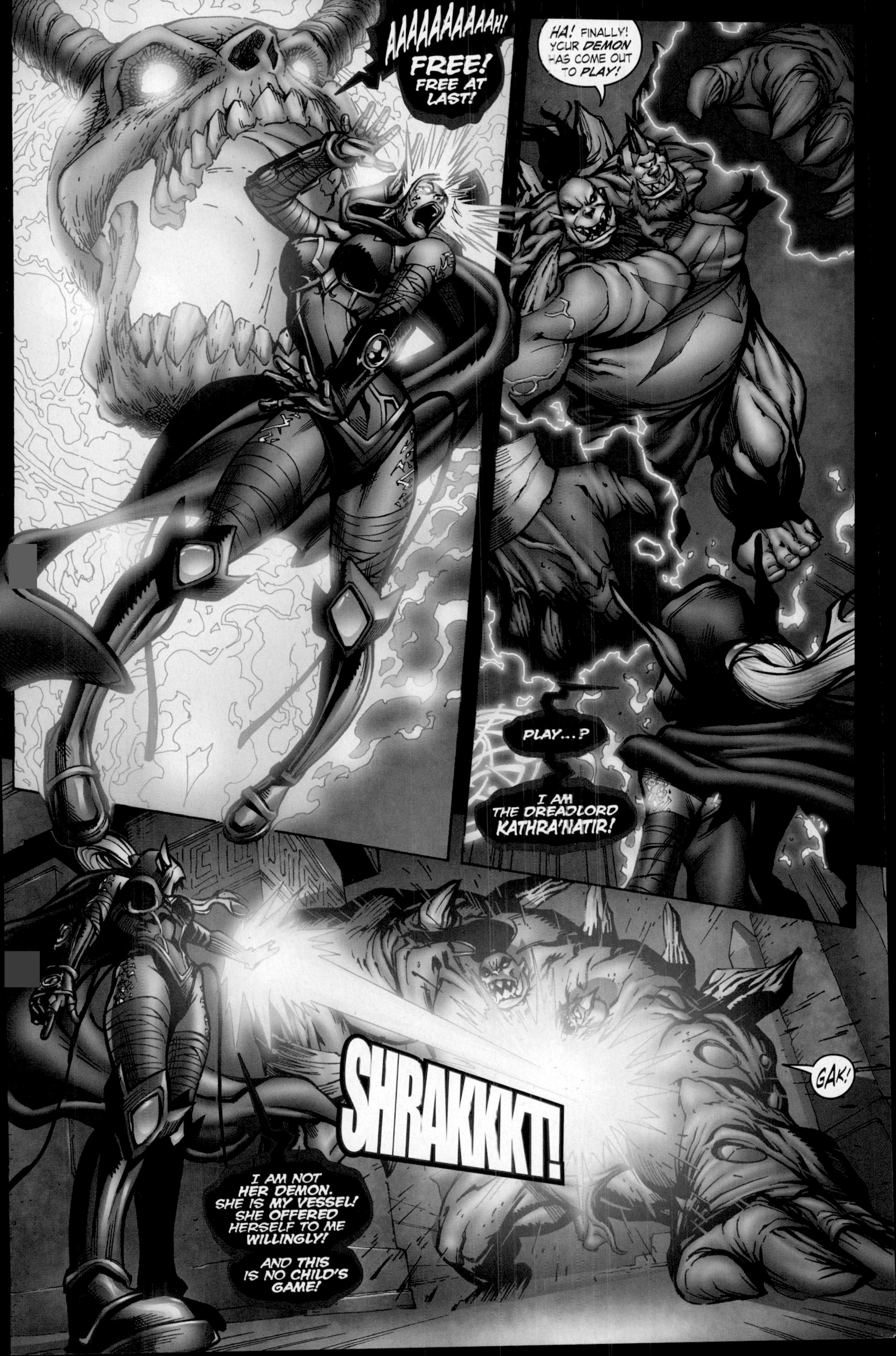

AAAAAAAAAH!
FREE! FREE AT LAST!
HA! FINALLY! YOUR DEMON HAS COME OUT TO PLAY!
PLAY...?
I AM THE DREADLORD KATHRA'NATIR!
SHRAKKKT!
GAK!
I AM NOT HER DEMON. SHE IS MY VESSEL! SHE OFFERED HERSELF TO ME WILLINGLY!
AND THIS IS NO CHILD'S GAME!

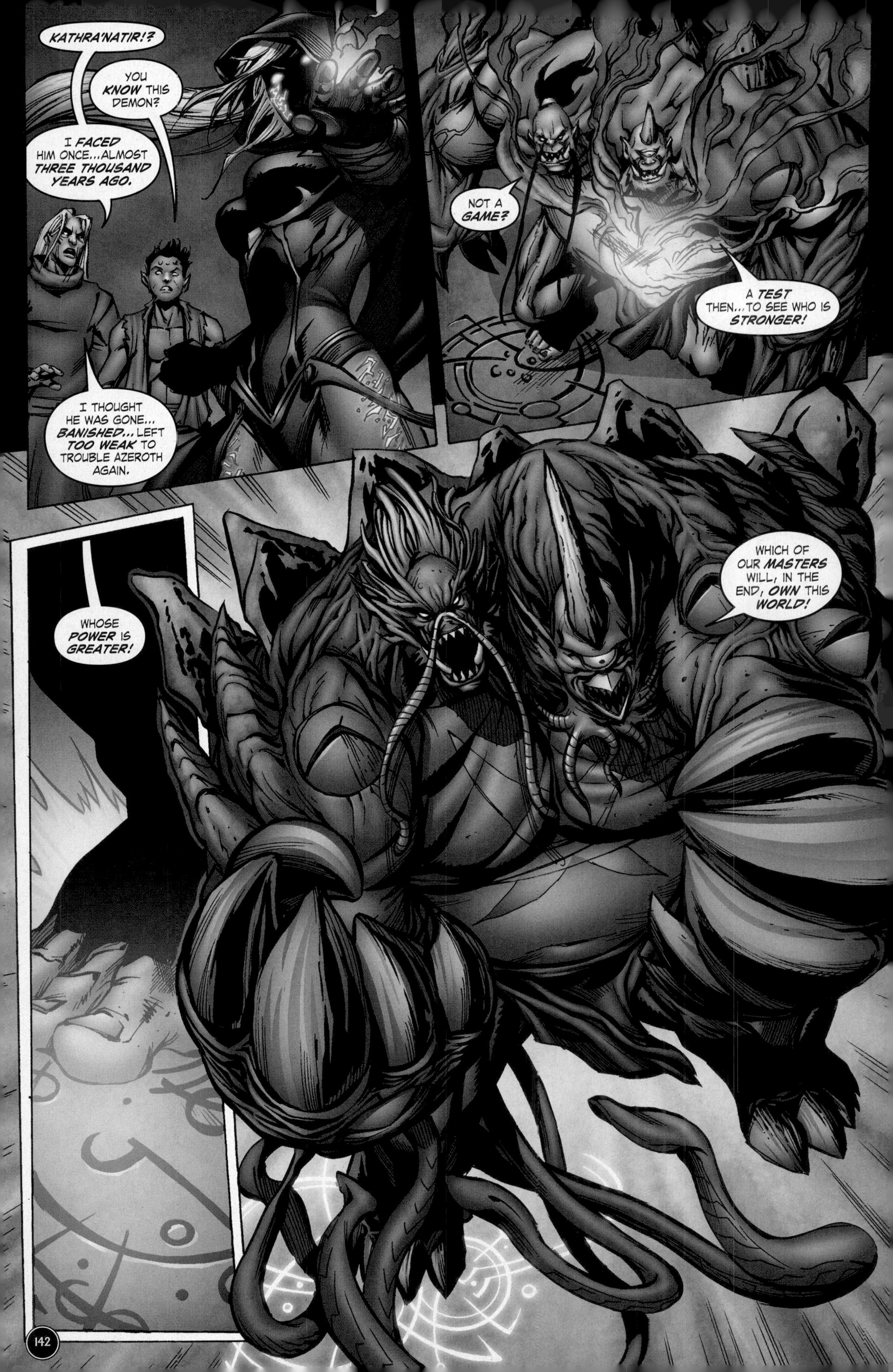
KATHRA'NATIR!?
YOU KNOW THIS DEMON?
I FACED HIM ONCE...ALMOST THREE THOUSAND YEARS AGO.
I THOUGHT HE WAS GONE... BANISHED... LEFT TOO WEAK TO TROUBLE AZEROTH AGAIN.
NOT A GAME?
A TEST THEN...TO SEE WHO IS STRONGER!
WHOSE POWER IS GREATER!
WHICH OF OUR MASTERS WILL, IN THE END, OWN THIS WORLD!

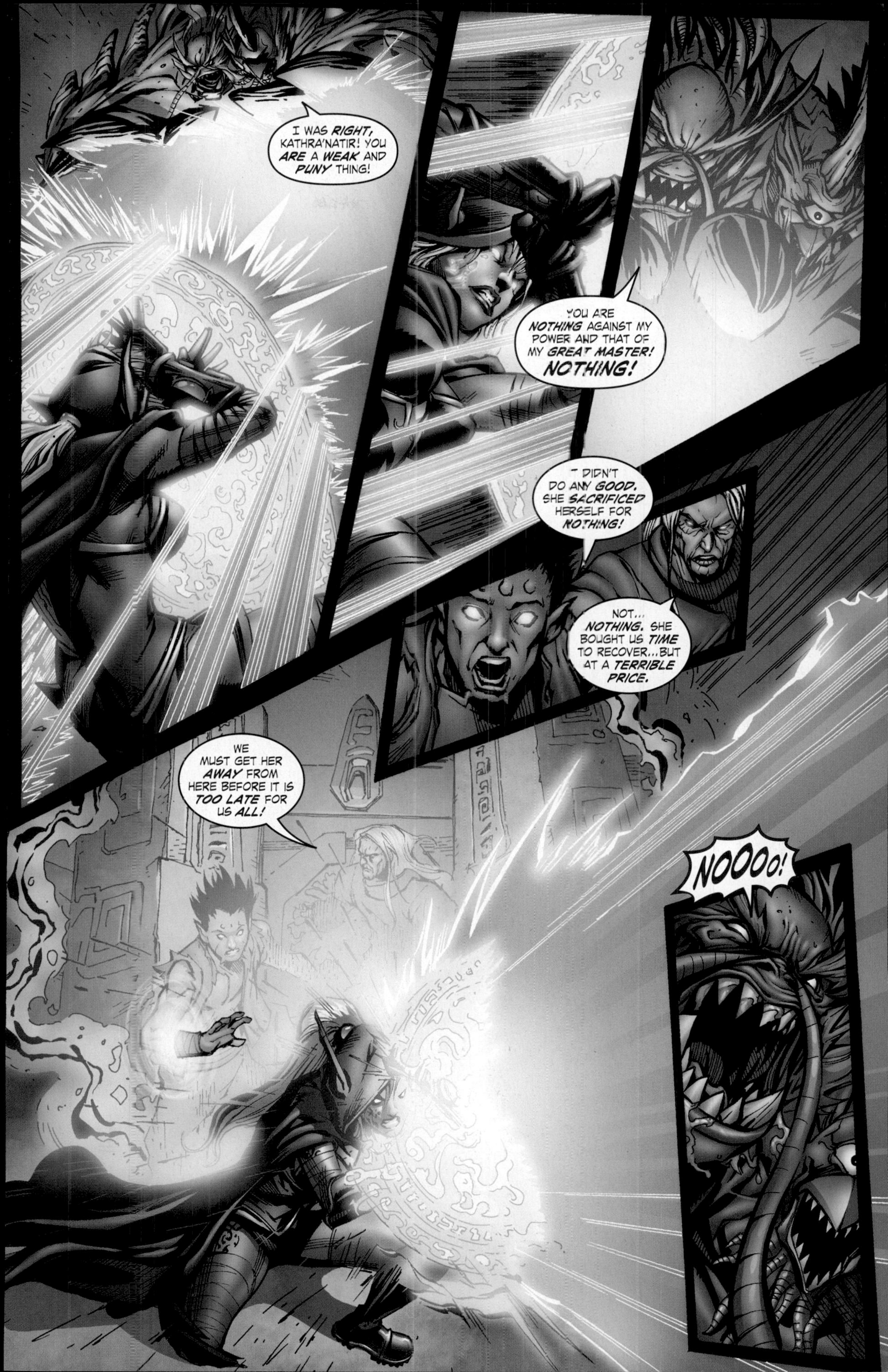
I WAS RIGHT, KATHRA'NATIR! YOU ARE A WEAK AND PUNY THING!
YOU ARE NOTHING AGAINST MY POWER AND THAT OF MY GREAT MASTER! NOTHING!
I DIDN'T DO ANY GOOD. SHE SACRIFICED HERSELF FOR NOTHING!
NOT... NOTHING. SHE BOUGHT US TIME TO RECOVER...BUT AT A TERRIBLE PRICE.
WE MUST GET HER AWAY FROM HERE BEFORE IT IS TOO LATE FOR US ALL!
NOOOo!

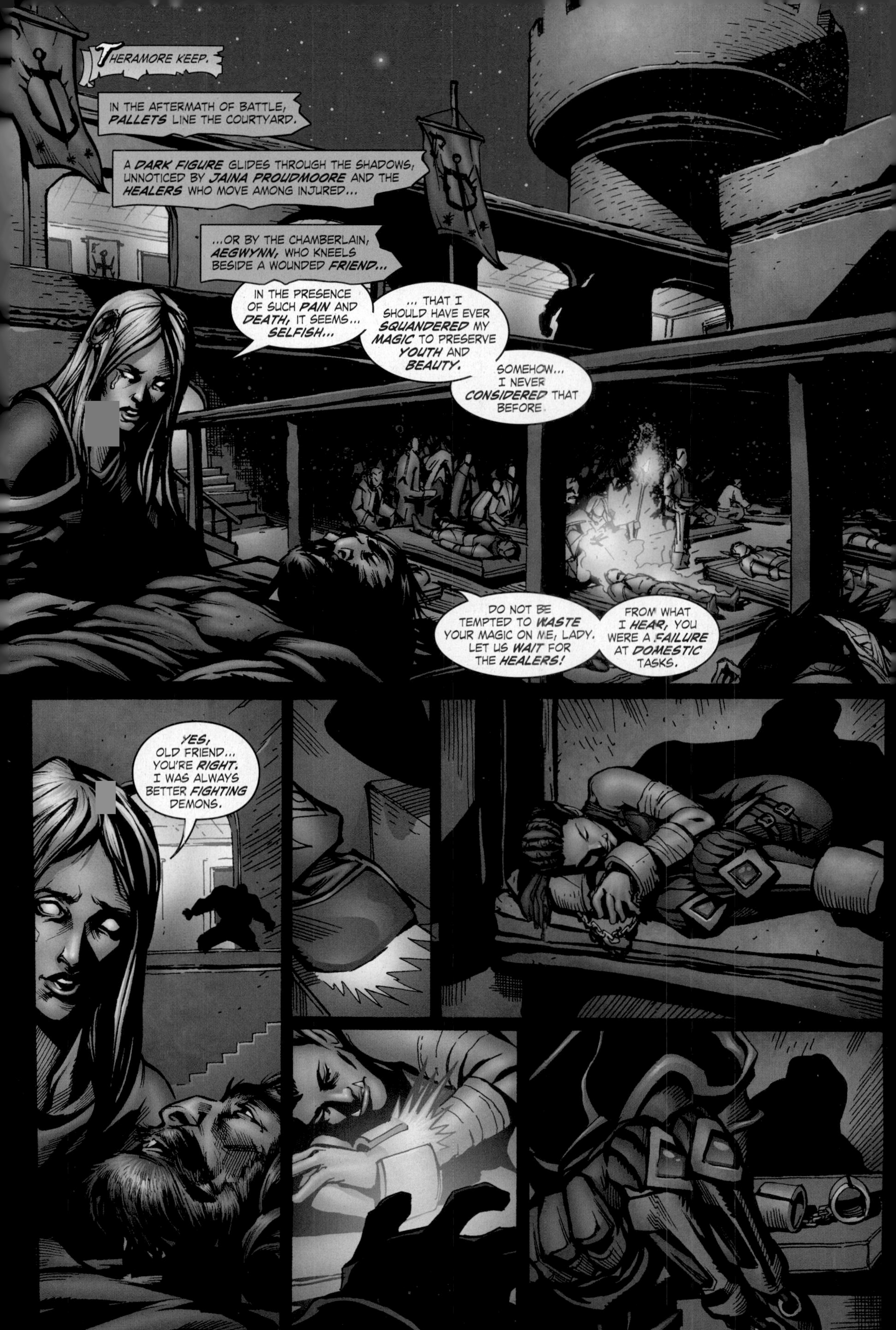
THERAMORE KEEP.
IN THE AFTERMATH OF BATTLE, PALLETS LINE THE COURTYARD.
A DARK FIGURE GLIDES THROUGH THE SHADOWS, UNNOTICED BY JAINA PROUDMOORE AND THE HEALERS WHO MOVE AMONG INJURED...
...OR BY THE CHAMBERLAIN, AEGWYNN, WHO KNEELS BESIDE A WOUNDED FRIEND...
IN THE PRESENCE OF SUCH PAIN AND DEATH, IT SEEMS... SELFISH...
... THAT I SHOULD HAVE EVER SQUANDERED MY MAGIC TO PRESERVE YOUTH AND BEAUTY.
SOMEHOW... I NEVER CONSIDERED THAT BEFORE.
DO NOT BE TEMPTED TO WASTE YOUR MAGIC ON ME, LADY. LET US WAIT FOR THE HEALERS!
FROM WHAT I HEAR, YOU WERE A FAILURE AT DOMESTIC TASKS.
YES, OLD FRIEND... YOU'RE RIGHT. I WAS ALWAYS BETTER FIGHTING DEMONS.

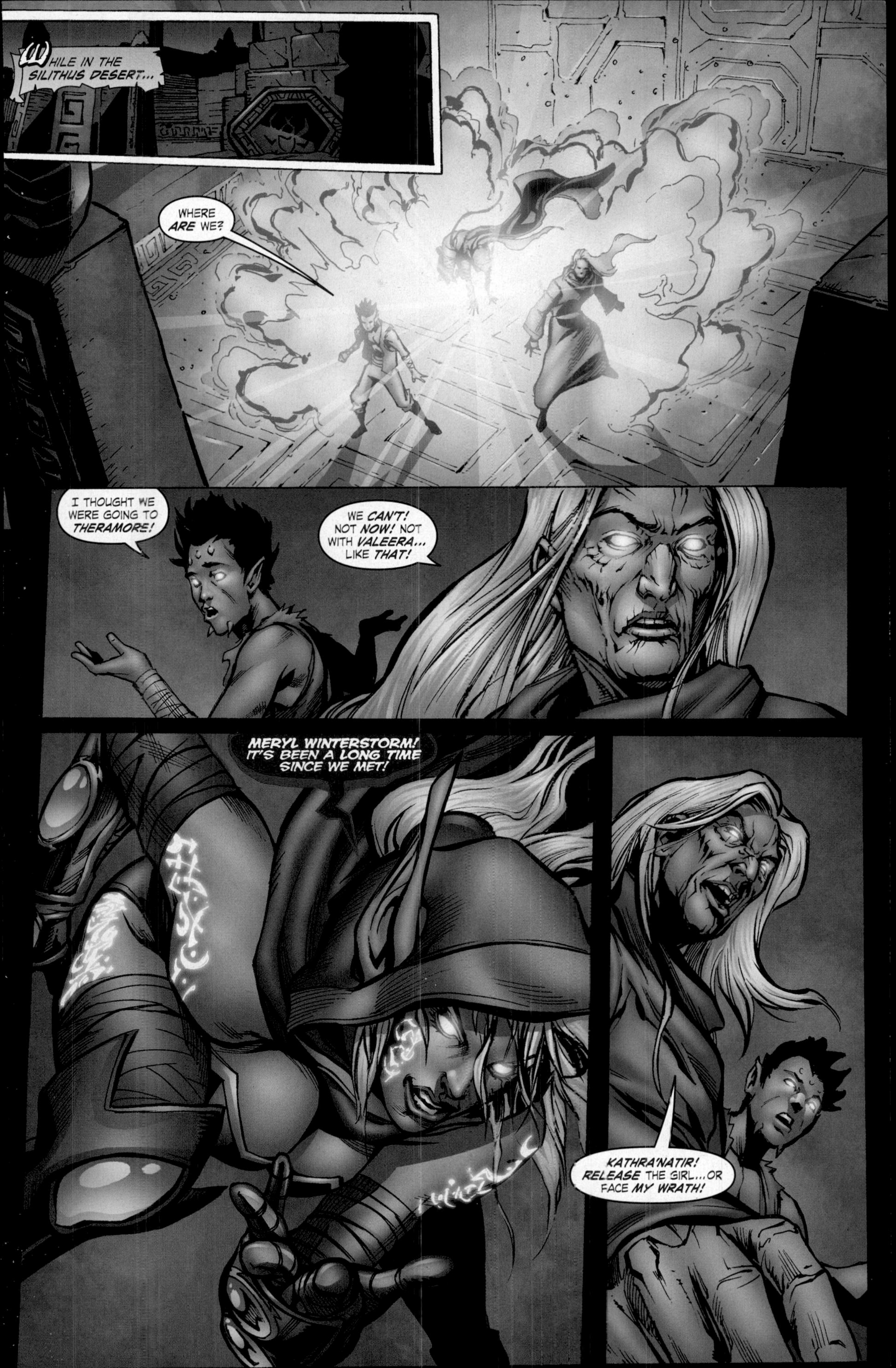
WHILE IN THE SILITHUS DESERT...
WHERE ARE WE?
I THOUGHT WE WERE GOING TO THERAMORE!
WE CAN'T! NOT NOW! NOT WITH VALEERA... LIKE THAT!
MERYL WINTERSTORM! IT'S BEEN A LONG TIME SINCE WE MET!
KATHRA'NATIR! RELEASE THE GIRL...OR FACE MY WRATH!

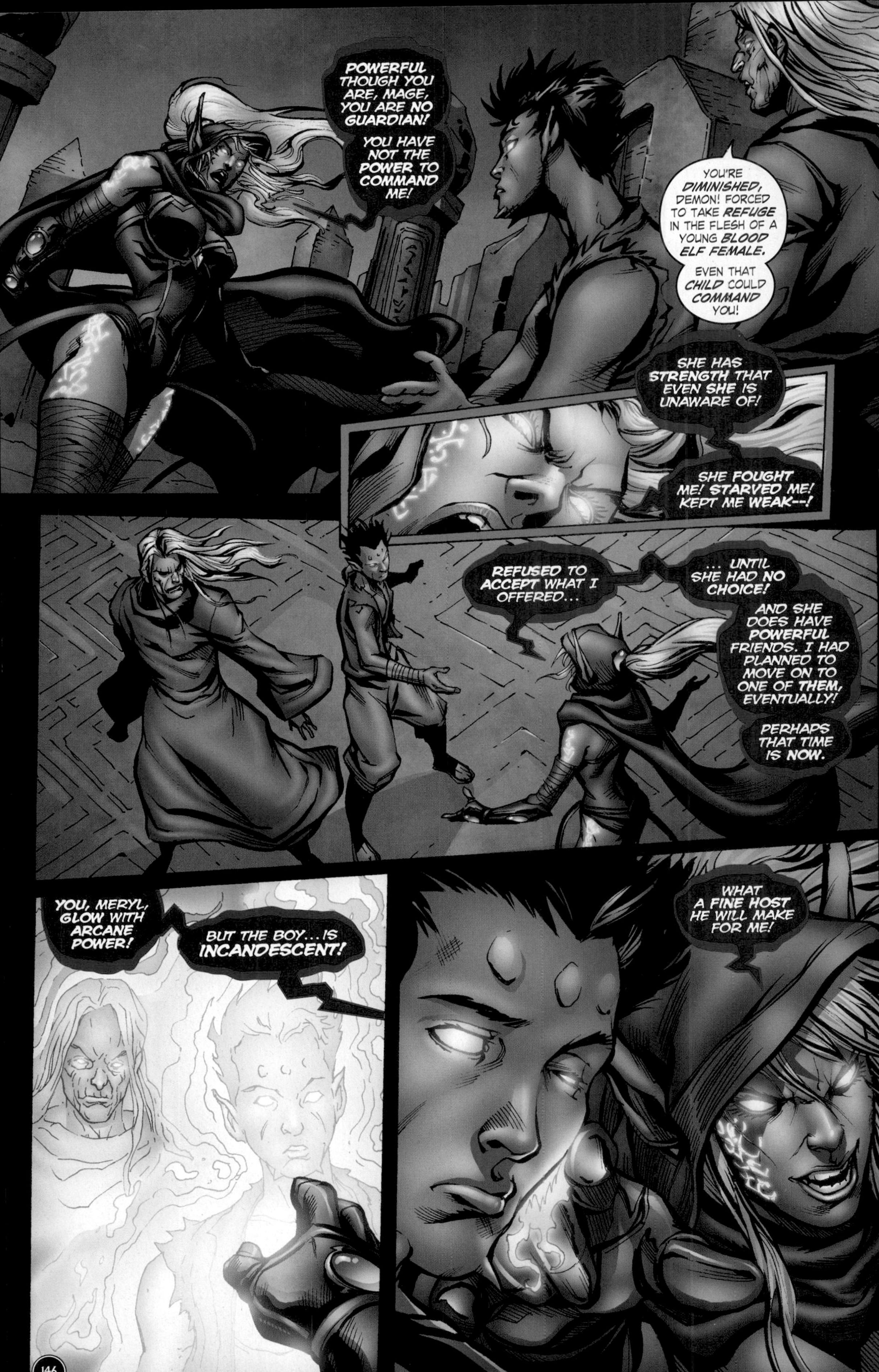

POWERFUL THOUGH YOU ARE, MAGE, YOU ARE NO GUARDIAN!
YOU HAVE NOT THE POWER TO COMMAND ME!
YOU'RE DIMINISHED, DEMON! FORCED TO TAKE REFUGE IN THE FLESH OF A YOUNG BLOOD ELF FEMALE.
EVEN THAT CHILD COULD COMMAND YOU!
SHE HAS STRENGTH THAT EVEN SHE IS UNAWARE OF!
SHE FOUGHT ME! STARVED ME! KEPT ME WEAK--!
REFUSED TO ACCEPT WHAT I OFFERED...
... UNTIL SHE HAD NO CHOICE!
AND SHE DOES HAVE POWERFUL FRIENDS. I HAD PLANNED TO MOVE ON TO ONE OF THEM, EVENTUALLY!
PERHAPS THAT TIME IS NOW.
YOU, MERYL, GLOW WITH ARCANE POWER!
BUT THE BOY... IS INCANDESCENT!
WHAT A FINE HOST HE WILL MAKE FOR ME!

CHAPTER 7

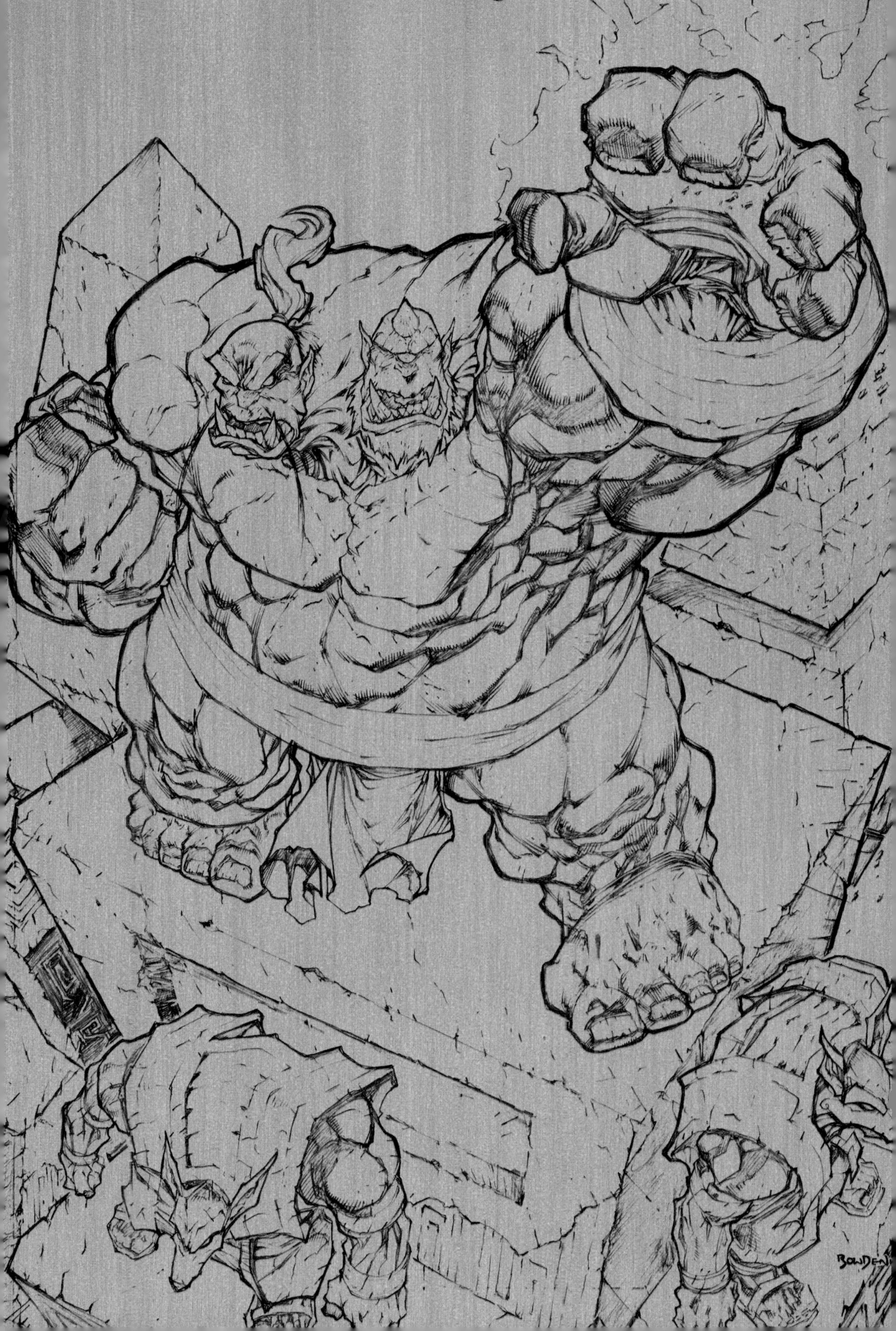
BOWDEN

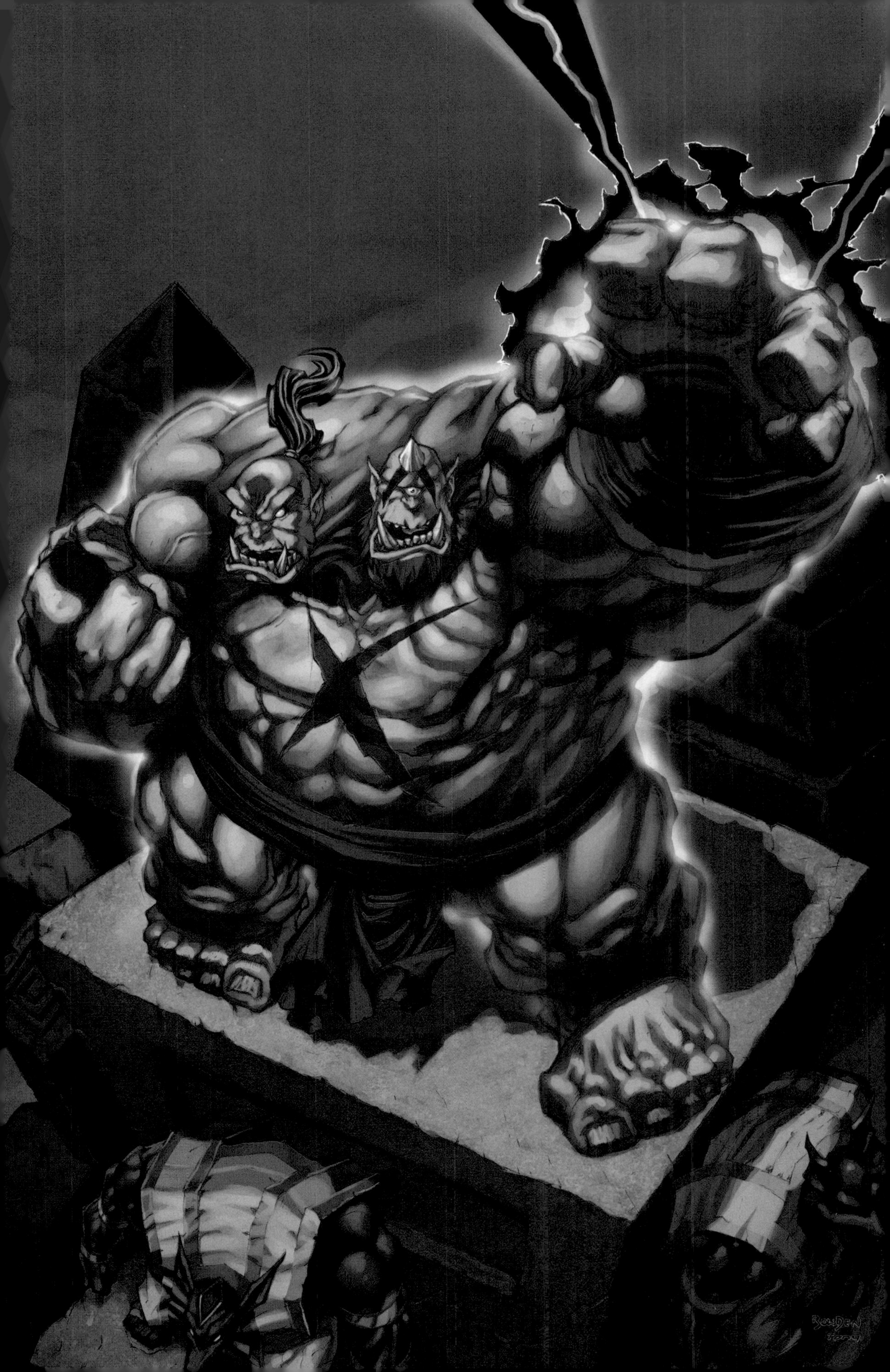

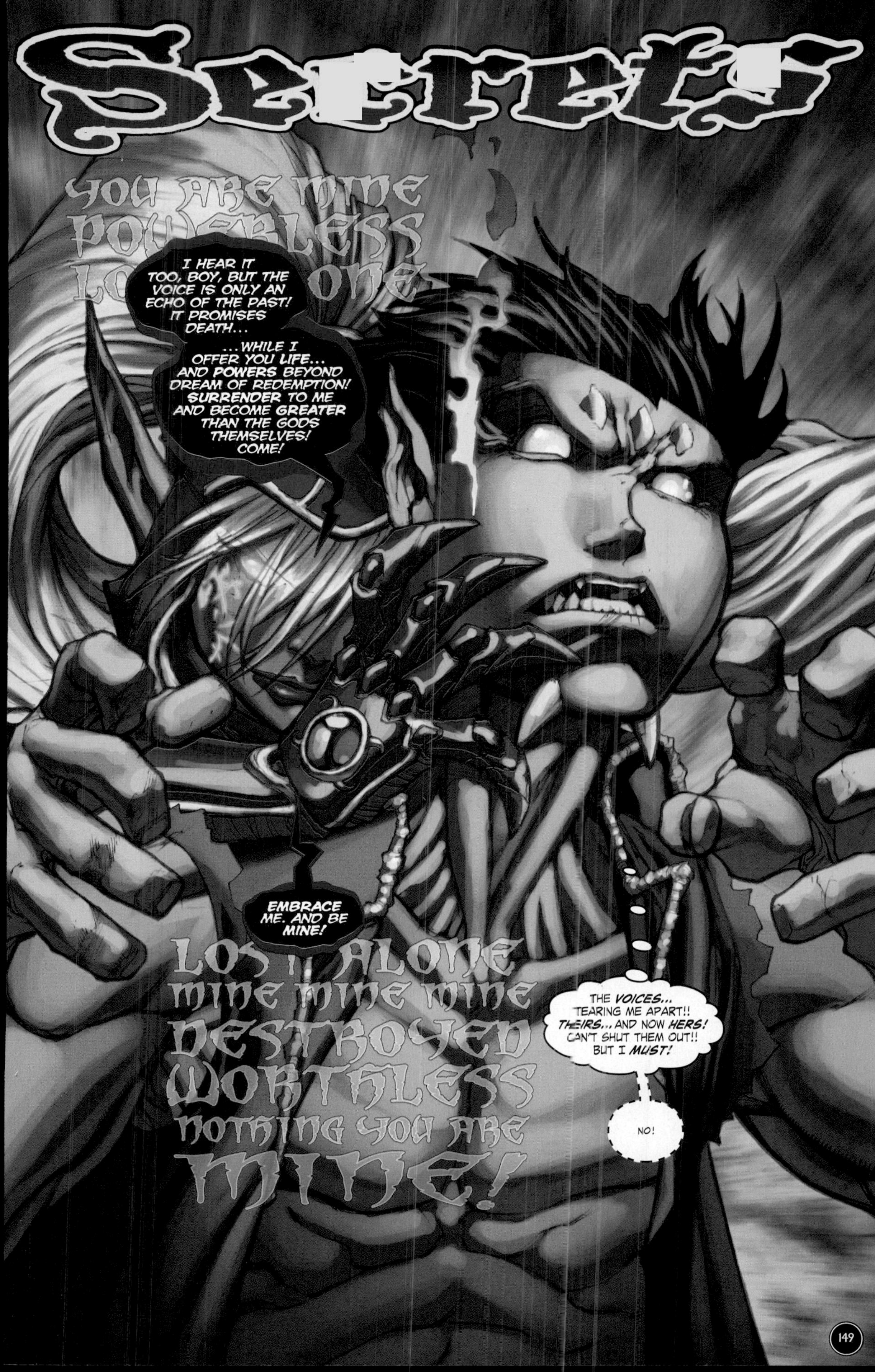

YOU ARE MINE
POWERLESS
I HEAR IT TOO, BOY, BUT THE VOICE IS ONLY AN ECHO OF THE PAST! IT PROMISES DEATH...
...WHILE I OFFER YOU LIFE... AND POWERS BEYOND DREAM OF REDEMPTION! SURRENDER TO ME AND BECOME GREATER THAN THE GODS THEMSELVES! COME!
EMBRACE ME. AND BE MINE!
MINE MINE MINE
DESTROYED
WORTHLESS
NOTHING YOU ARE
MINE!
THE VOICES... TEARING ME APART!! THEIRS... AND NOW HERS! CAN'T SHUT THEM OUT!! BUT I MUST!
NO!

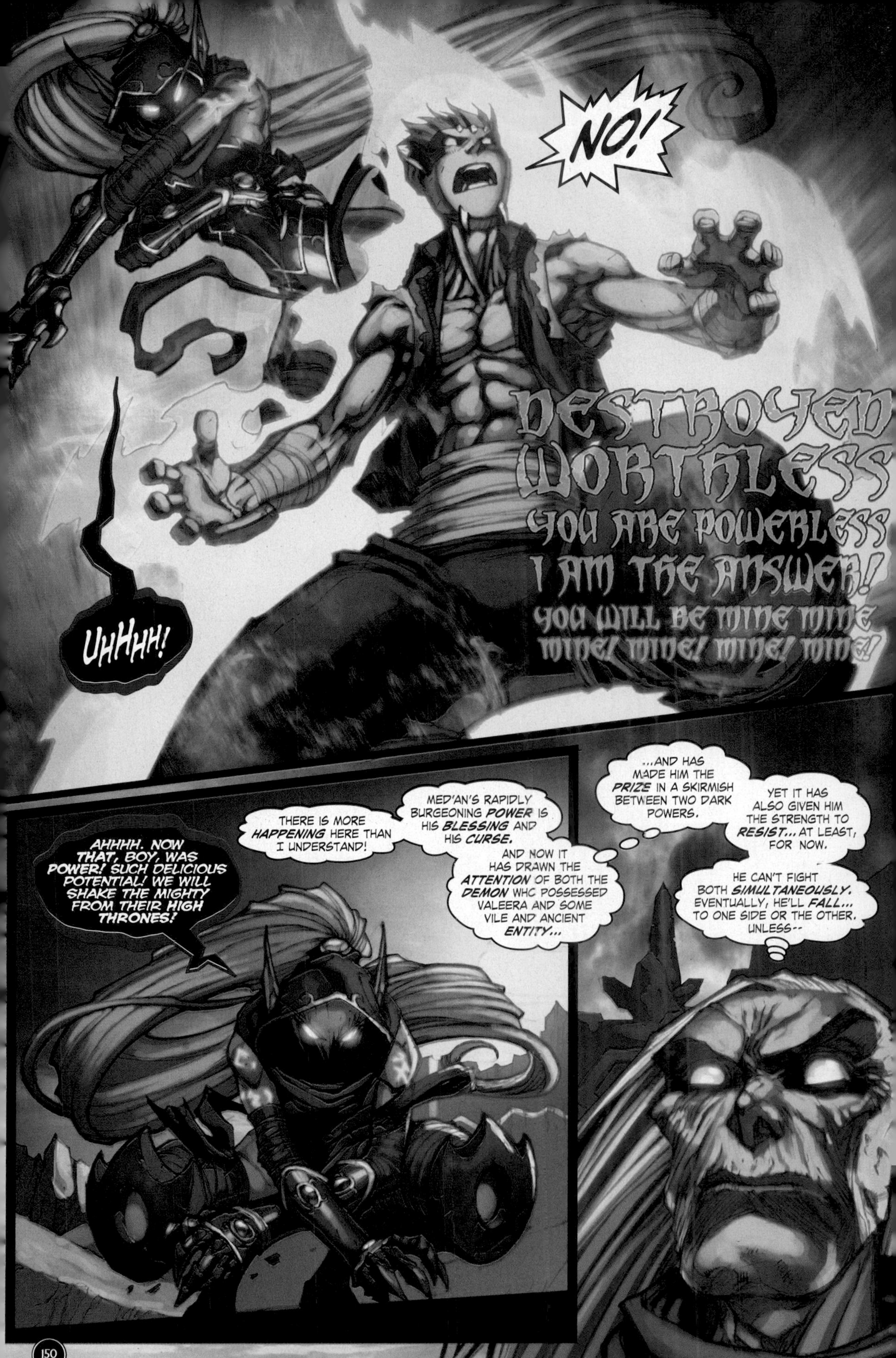
NO!
DESTROYED
WORTHLESS
YOU ARE POWERLESS
I AM THE ANSWER!
YOU WILL BE MINE MINE
MINE! MINE! MINE! MINE!
UHHHH!
AHHHH. NOW THAT, BOY, WAS POWER! SUCH DELICIOUS POTENTIAL! WE WILL SHAKE THE MIGHTY FROM THEIR HIGH THRONES!
THERE IS MORE HAPPENING HERE THAN I UNDERSTAND!
MED'AN'S RAPIDLY BURGEONING POWER IS HIS BLESSING AND HIS CURSE.
AND NOW IT HAS DRAWN THE ATTENTION OF BOTH THE DEMON WHO POSSESSED VALEERA AND SOME VILE AND ANCIENT ENTITY...
...AND HAS MADE HIM THE PRIZE IN A SKIRMISH BETWEEN TWO DARK POWERS.
YET IT HAS ALSO GIVEN HIM THE STRENGTH TO RESIST... AT LEAST, FOR NOW.
HE CAN'T FIGHT BOTH SIMULTANEOUSLY. EVENTUALLY, HE'LL FALL... TO ONE SIDE OR THE OTHER. UNLESS--

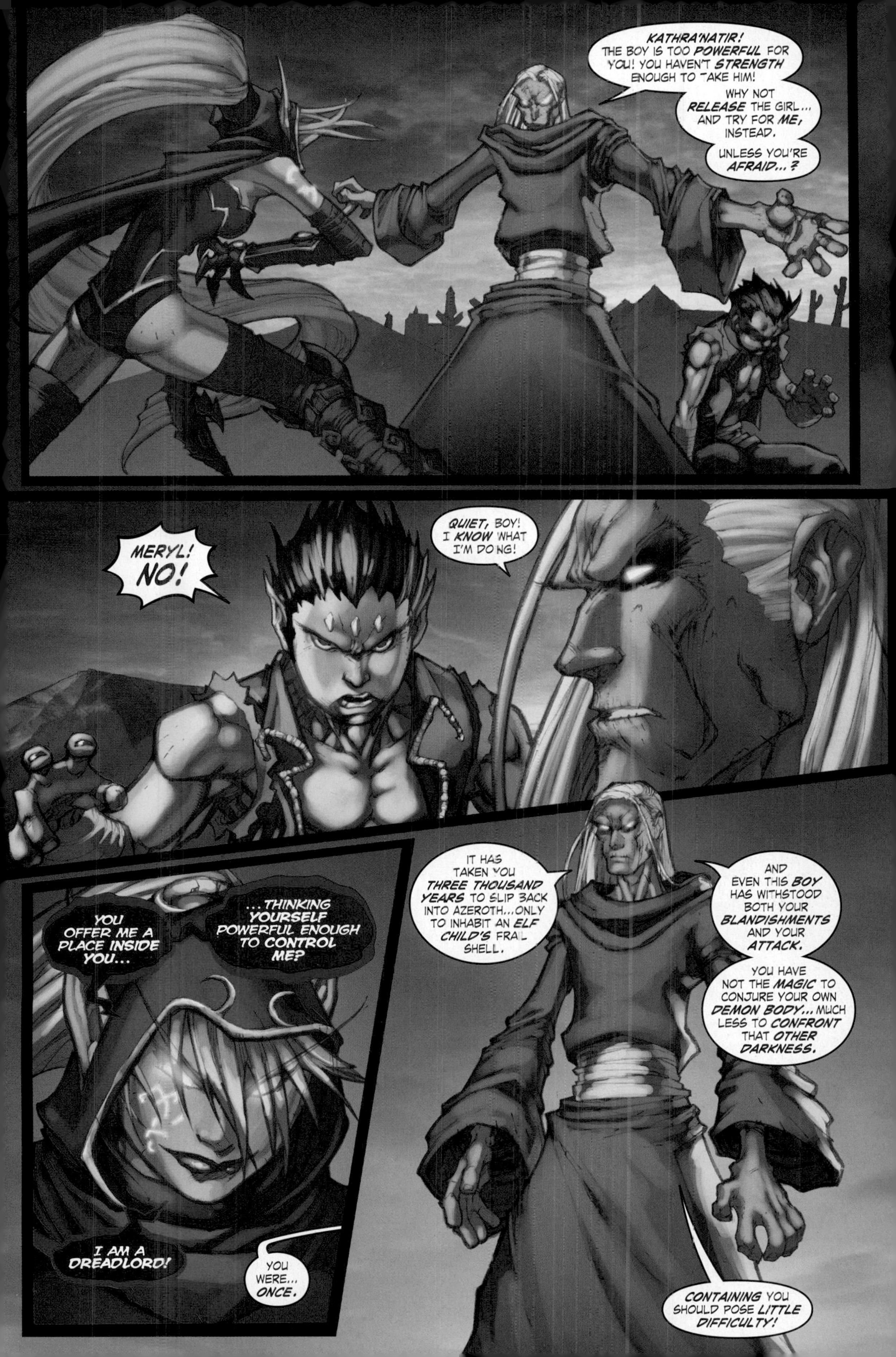
KATHRA'NATIR! THE BOY IS TOO POWERFUL FOR YOU! YOU HAVEN'T STRENGTH ENOUGH TO TAKE HIM!
WHY NOT RELEASE THE GIRL... AND TRY FOR ME, INSTEAD.
UNLESS YOU'RE AFRAID...?
MERYL! NO!
QUIET, BOY! I KNOW WHAT I'M DOING!
YOU OFFER ME A PLACE INSIDE YOU...
...THINKING YOURSELF POWERFUL ENOUGH TO CONTROL ME?
I AM A DREADLORD!
YOU WERE... ONCE.
IT HAS TAKEN YOU THREE THOUSAND YEARS TO SLIP BACK INTO AZEROTH...ONLY TO INHABIT AN ELF CHILD'S FRAIL SHELL.
AND EVEN THIS BOY HAS WITHSTOOD BOTH YOUR BLANDISHMENTS AND YOUR ATTACK.
YOU HAVE NOT THE MAGIC TO CONJURE YOUR OWN DEMON BODY... MUCH LESS TO CONFRONT THAT OTHER DARKNESS.
CONTAINING YOU SHOULD POSE LITTLE DIFFICULTY!

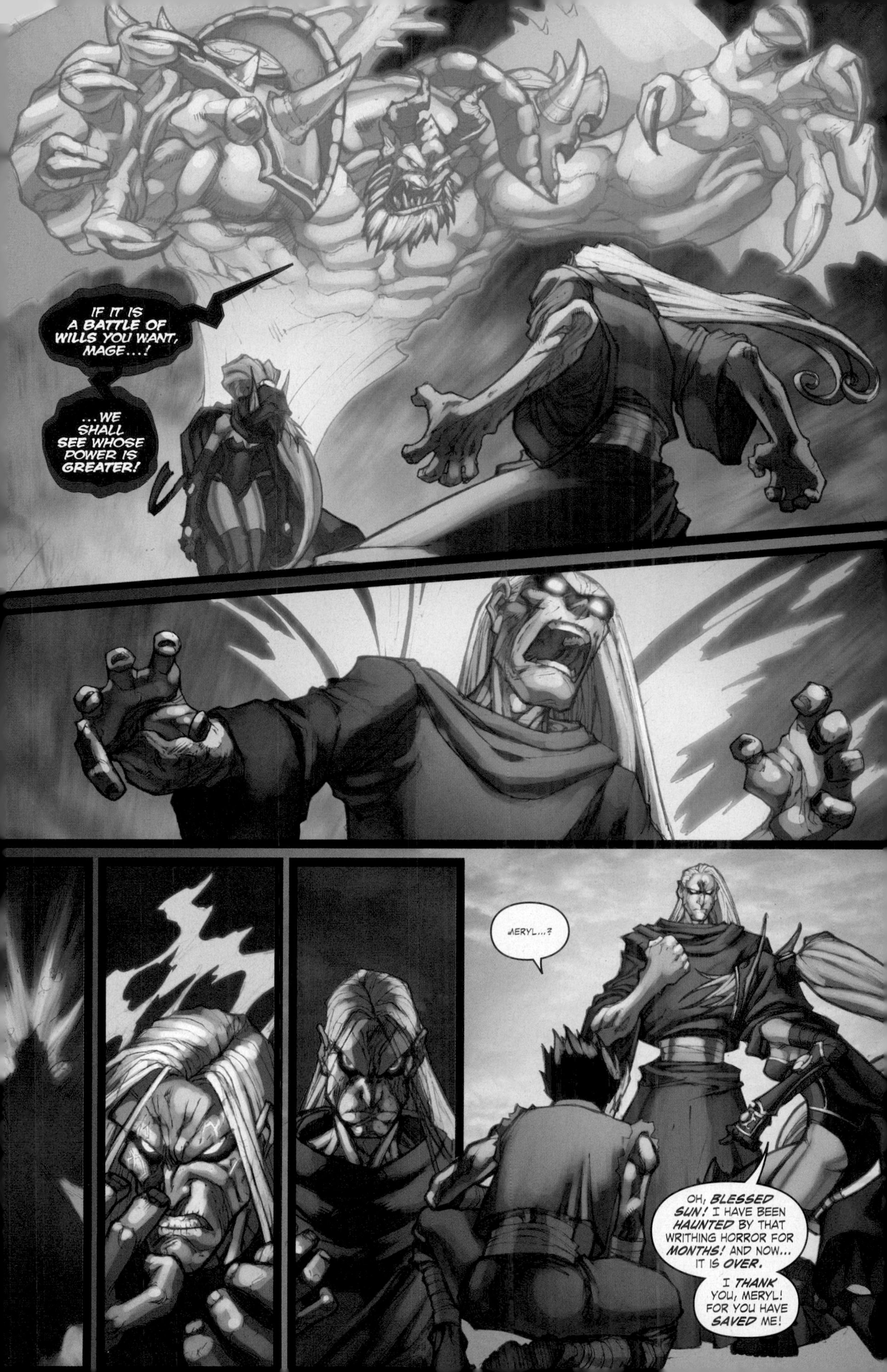
IF IT IS A BATTLE OF WILLS YOU WANT, MAGE...!
...WE SHALL SEE WHOSE POWER IS GREATER!
MERYL...?
OH, BLESSED SUN! I HAVE BEEN HAUNTED BY THAT WRITHING HORROR FOR MONTHS! AND NOW... IT IS OVER.
I THANK YOU, MERYL! FOR YOU HAVE SAVED ME!

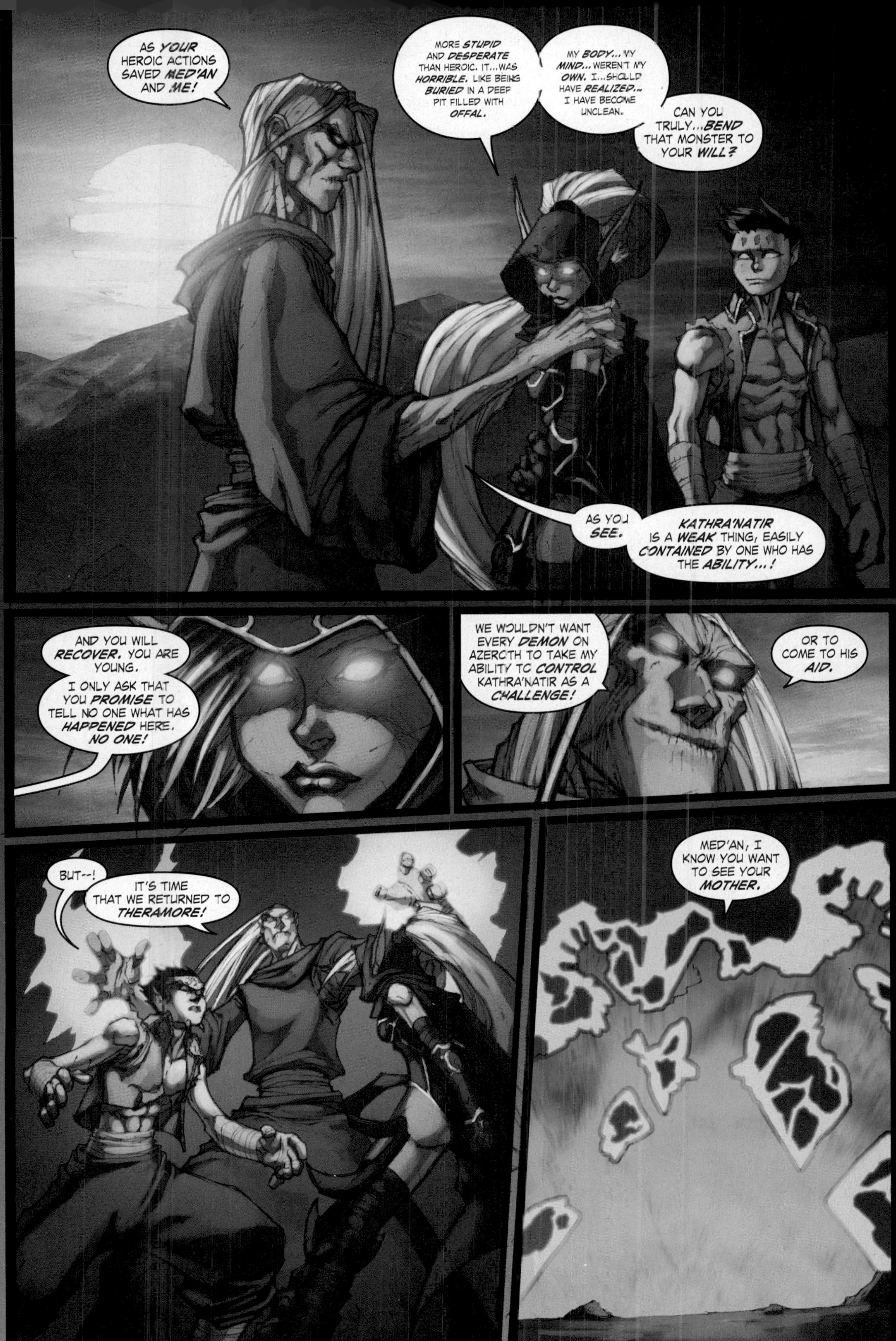
AS YOUR HEROIC ACTIONS SAVED MED'AN AND ME!
MORE STUPID AND DESPERATE THAN HEROIC. IT...WAS HORRIBLE. LIKE BEING BURIED IN A DEEP PIT FILLED WITH OFFAL.
MY BODY... MY MIND... WEREN'T MY OWN. I...SHOULD HAVE REALIZED... I HAVE BECOME UNCLEAN.
CAN YOU TRULY...BEND THAT MONSTER TO YOUR WILL?
AS YOU SEE.
KATHRA'NATIR IS A WEAK THING, EASILY CONTAINED BY ONE WHO HAS THE ABILITY...!
AND YOU WILL RECOVER. YOU ARE YOUNG.
I ONLY ASK THAT YOU PROMISE TO TELL NO ONE WHAT HAS HAPPENED HERE. NO ONE!
WE WOULDN'T WANT EVERY DEMON ON AZEROTH TO TAKE MY ABILITY TO CONTROL KATHRA'NATIR AS A CHALLENGE!
OR TO COME TO HIS AID.
BUT--!
IT'S TIME THAT WE RETURNED TO THERAMORE!
MED'AN, I KNOW YOU WANT TO SEE YOUR MOTHER.

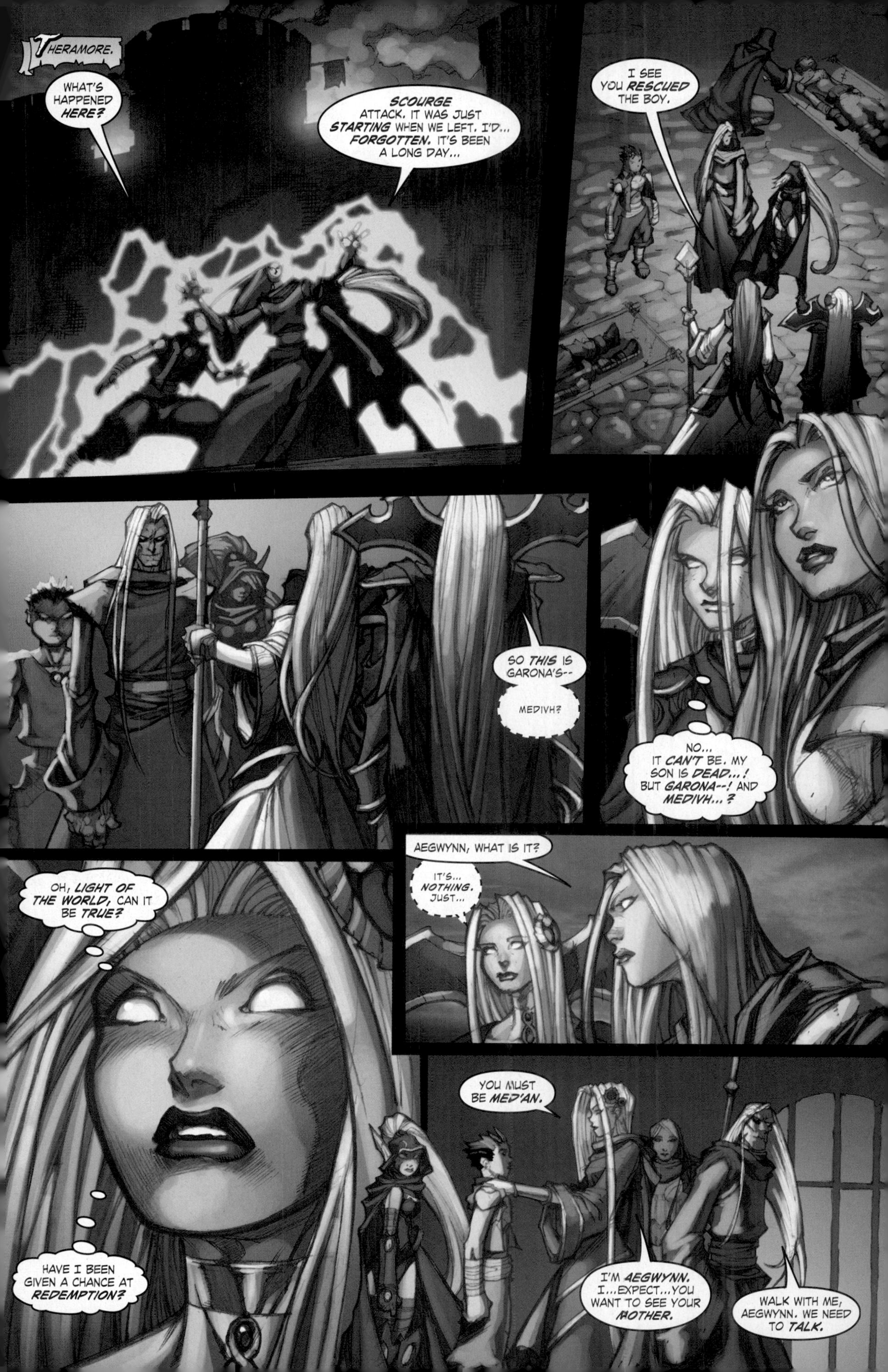
THERAMORE.
WHAT'S HAPPENED HERE?
SCOURGE ATTACK. IT WAS JUST STARTING WHEN WE LEFT. I'D... FORGOTTEN. IT'S BEEN A LONG DAY...
I SEE YOU RESCUED THE BOY.
SO THIS IS GARONA'S--
MEDIVH?
NO... IT CAN'T BE. MY SON IS DEAD...! BUT GARONA--! AND MEDIVH...?
OH, LIGHT OF THE WORLD, CAN IT BE TRUE?
HAVE I BEEN GIVEN A CHANCE AT REDEMPTION?
AEGWYNN, WHAT IS IT?
IT'S... NOTHING. JUST...
YOU MUST BE MED'AN.
I'M AEGWYNN. I...EXPECT...YOU WANT TO SEE YOUR MOTHER.
WALK WITH ME, AEGWYNN. WE NEED TO TALK.

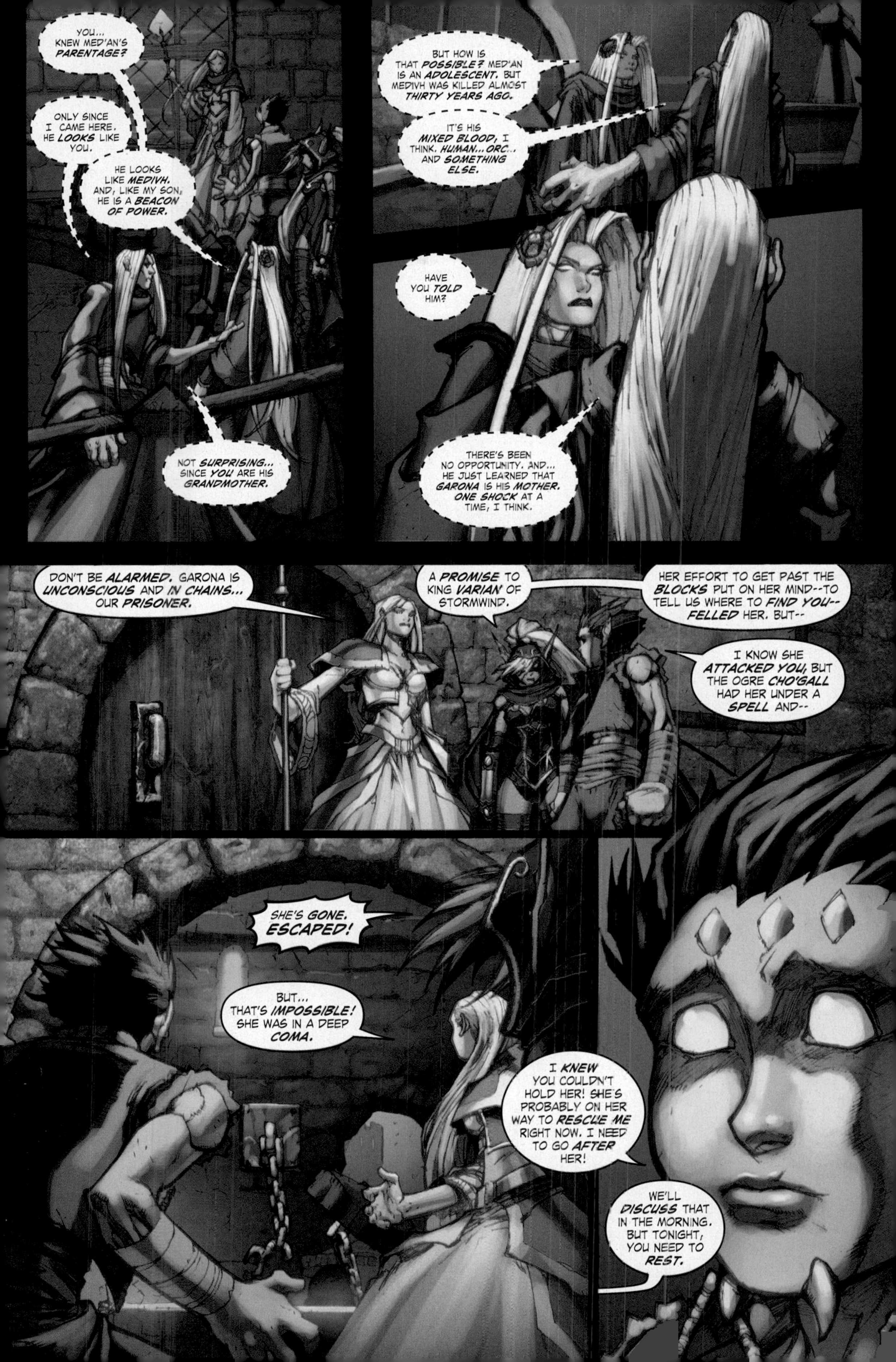
YOU... KNEW MED'AN'S PARENTAGE?
ONLY SINCE I CAME HERE. HE LOOKS LIKE YOU.
HE LOOKS LIKE MEDIVH. AND, LIKE MY SON, HE IS A BEACON OF POWER.
NOT SURPRISING... SINCE YOU ARE HIS GRANDMOTHER.
BUT HOW IS THAT POSSIBLE? MED'AN IS AN ADOLESCENT. BUT MEDIVH WAS KILLED ALMOST THIRTY YEARS AGO.
IT'S HIS MIXED BLOOD, I THINK. HUMAN...ORC... AND SOMETHING ELSE.
HAVE YOU TOLD HIM?
THERE'S BEEN NO OPPORTUNITY. AND... HE JUST LEARNED THAT GARONA IS HIS MOTHER. ONE SHOCK AT A TIME, I THINK.
DON'T BE ALARMED. GARONA IS UNCONSCIOUS AND IN CHAINS... OUR PRISONER.
A PROMISE TO KING VARIAN OF STORMWIND.
HER EFFORT TO GET PAST THE BLOCKS PUT ON HER MIND--TO TELL US WHERE TO FIND YOU--FELLED HER. BUT--
I KNOW SHE ATTACKED YOU, BUT THE OGRE CHO'GALL HAD HER UNDER A SPELL AND--
SHE'S GONE. ESCAPED!
BUT... THAT'S IMPOSSIBLE! SHE WAS IN A DEEP COMA.
I KNEW YOU COULDN'T HOLD HER! SHE'S PROBABLY ON HER WAY TO RESCUE ME RIGHT NOW. I NEED TO GO AFTER HER!
WE'LL DISCUSS THAT IN THE MORNING. BUT TONIGHT, YOU NEED TO REST.

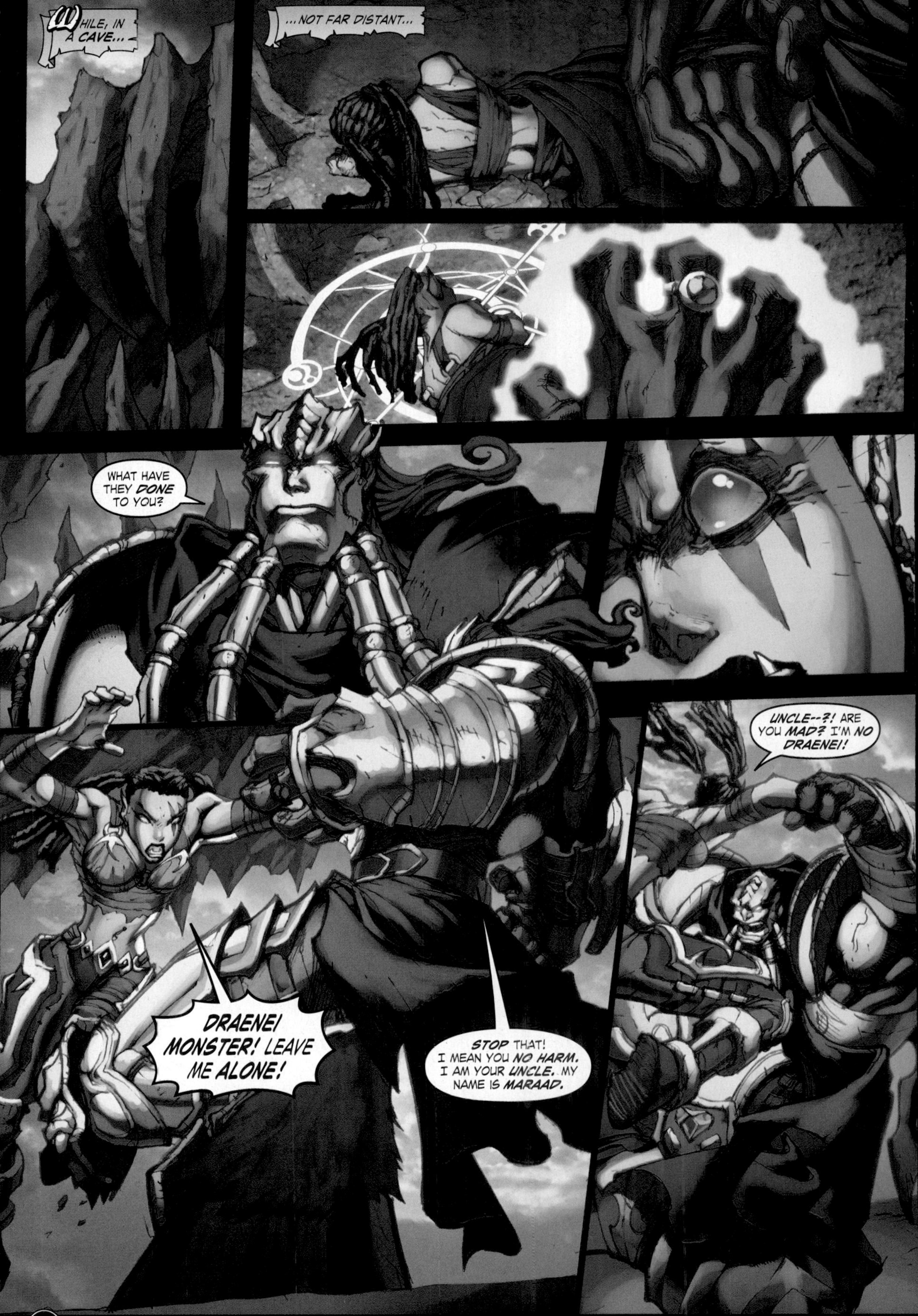
WHILE, IN A CAVE...
...NOT FAR DISTANT...
WHAT HAVE THEY DONE TO YOU?
DRAENEI MONSTER! LEAVE ME ALONE!
STOP THAT! I MEAN YOU NO HARM. I AM YOUR UNCLE. MY NAME IS MARAAD.
UNCLE--?! ARE YOU MAD? I'M NO DRAENEI!

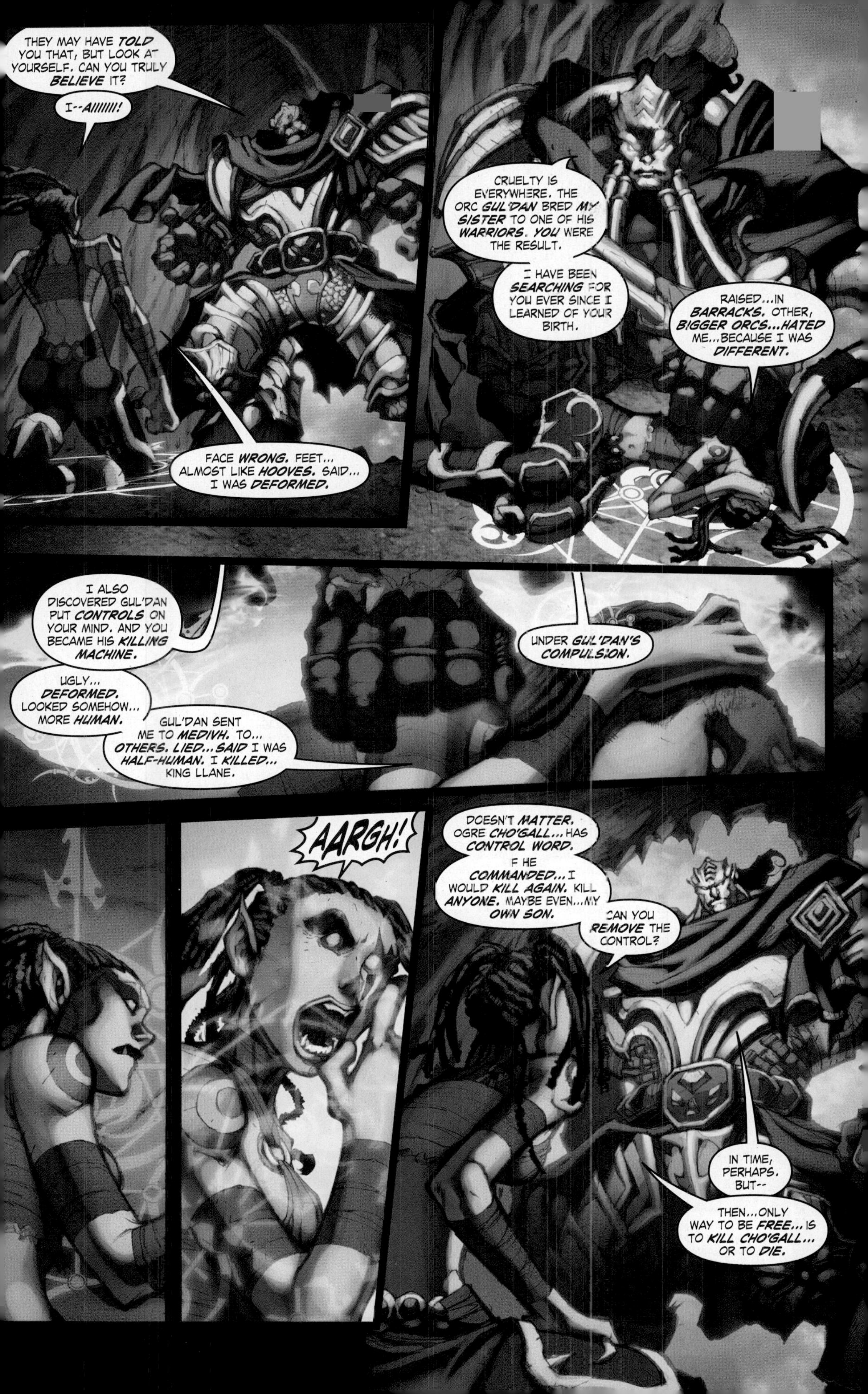
THEY MAY HAVE TOLD YOU THAT, BUT LOOK AT YOURSELF. CAN YOU TRULY BELIEVE IT?
I--AIIIIIII!
FACE WRONG. FEET... ALMOST LIKE HOOVES. SAID... I WAS DEFORMED.
CRUELTY IS EVERYWHERE. THE ORC GUL'DAN BRED MY SISTER TO ONE OF HIS WARRIORS. YOU WERE THE RESULT.
I HAVE BEEN SEARCHING FOR YOU EVER SINCE I LEARNED OF YOUR BIRTH.
RAISED...IN BARRACKS. OTHER, BIGGER ORCS...HATED ME...BECAUSE I WAS DIFFERENT.
I ALSO DISCOVERED GUL'DAN PUT CONTROLS ON YOUR MIND. AND YOU BECAME HIS KILLING MACHINE.
UGLY... DEFORMED. LOOKED SOMEHOW... MORE HUMAN.
GUL'DAN SENT ME TO MEDIVH. TO... OTHERS. LIED...SAID I WAS HALF-HUMAN. I KILLED... KING LLANE.
UNDER GUL'DAN'S COMPULSION.
AARGH!
DOESN'T MATTER. OGRE CHO'GALL...HAS CONTROL WORD.
IF HE COMMANDED...I WOULD KILL AGAIN. KILL ANYONE. MAYBE EVEN...MY OWN SON.
CAN YOU REMOVE THE CONTROL?
IN TIME, PERHAPS. BUT--
THEN...ONLY WAY TO BE FREE...IS TO KILL CHO'GALL... OR TO DIE.

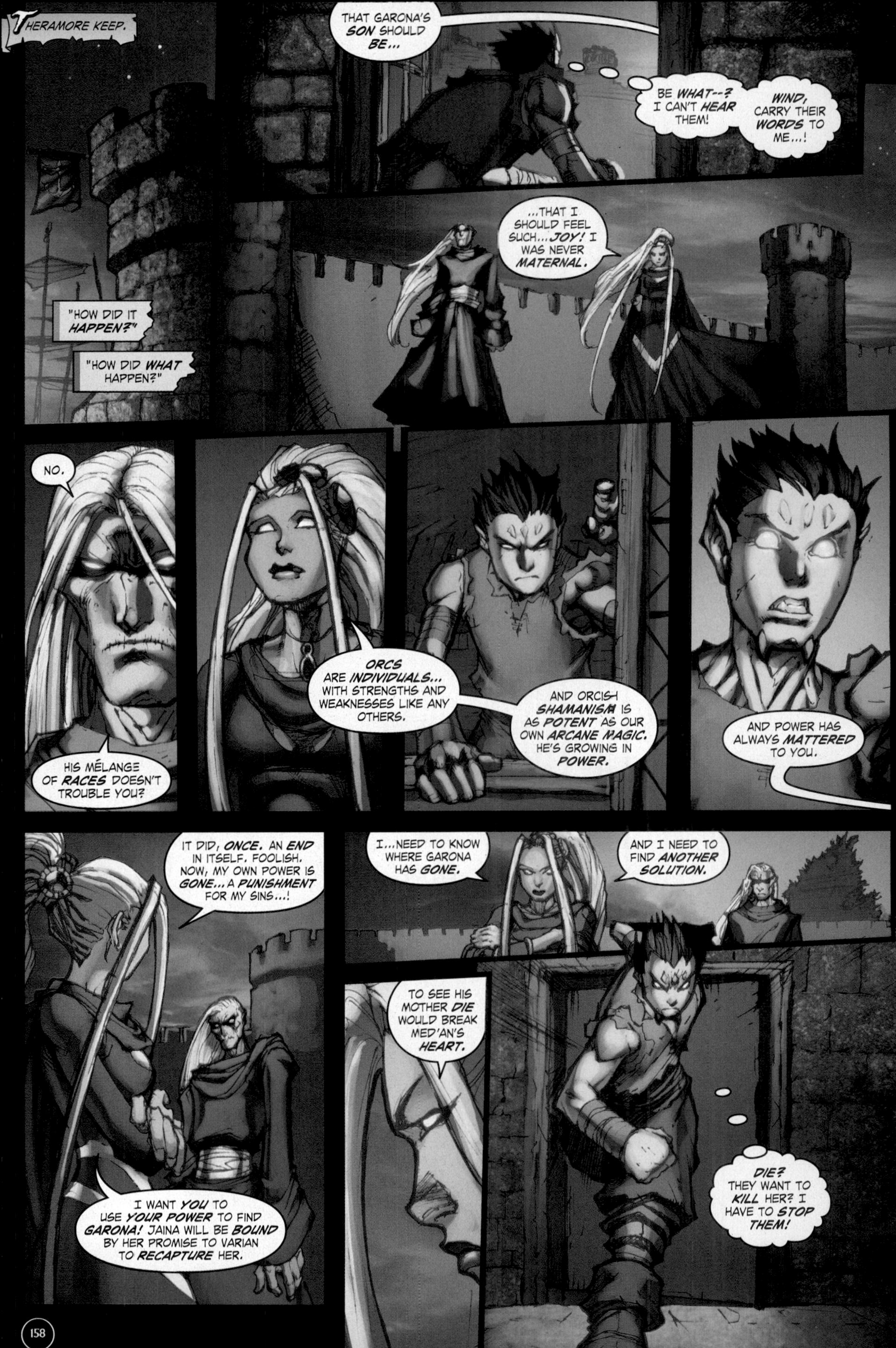
THERAMORE KEEP.
THAT GARONA'S SON SHOULD BE...
BE WHAT--? I CAN'T HEAR THEM!
WIND, CARRY THEIR WORDS TO ME...!
...THAT I SHOULD FEEL SUCH... JOY! I WAS NEVER MATERNAL.
"HOW DID IT HAPPEN?"
"HOW DID WHAT HAPPEN?"
NO.
HIS MÉLANGE OF RACES DOESN'T TROUBLE YOU?
ORCS ARE INDIVIDUALS... WITH STRENGTHS AND WEAKNESSES LIKE ANY OTHERS.
AND ORCISH SHAMANISM IS AS POTENT AS OUR OWN ARCANE MAGIC. HE'S GROWING IN POWER.
AND POWER HAS ALWAYS MATTERED TO YOU.
IT DID, ONCE. AN END IN ITSELF. FOOLISH. NOW, MY OWN POWER IS GONE... A PUNISHMENT FOR MY SINS...!
I WANT YOU TO USE YOUR POWER TO FIND GARONA! JAINA WILL BE BOUND BY HER PROMISE TO VARIAN TO RECAPTURE HER.
I...NEED TO KNOW WHERE GARONA HAS GONE.
AND I NEED TO FIND ANOTHER SOLUTION.
TO SEE HIS MOTHER DIE WOULD BREAK MED'AN'S HEART.
DIE? THEY WANT TO KILL HER? I HAVE TO STOP THEM!

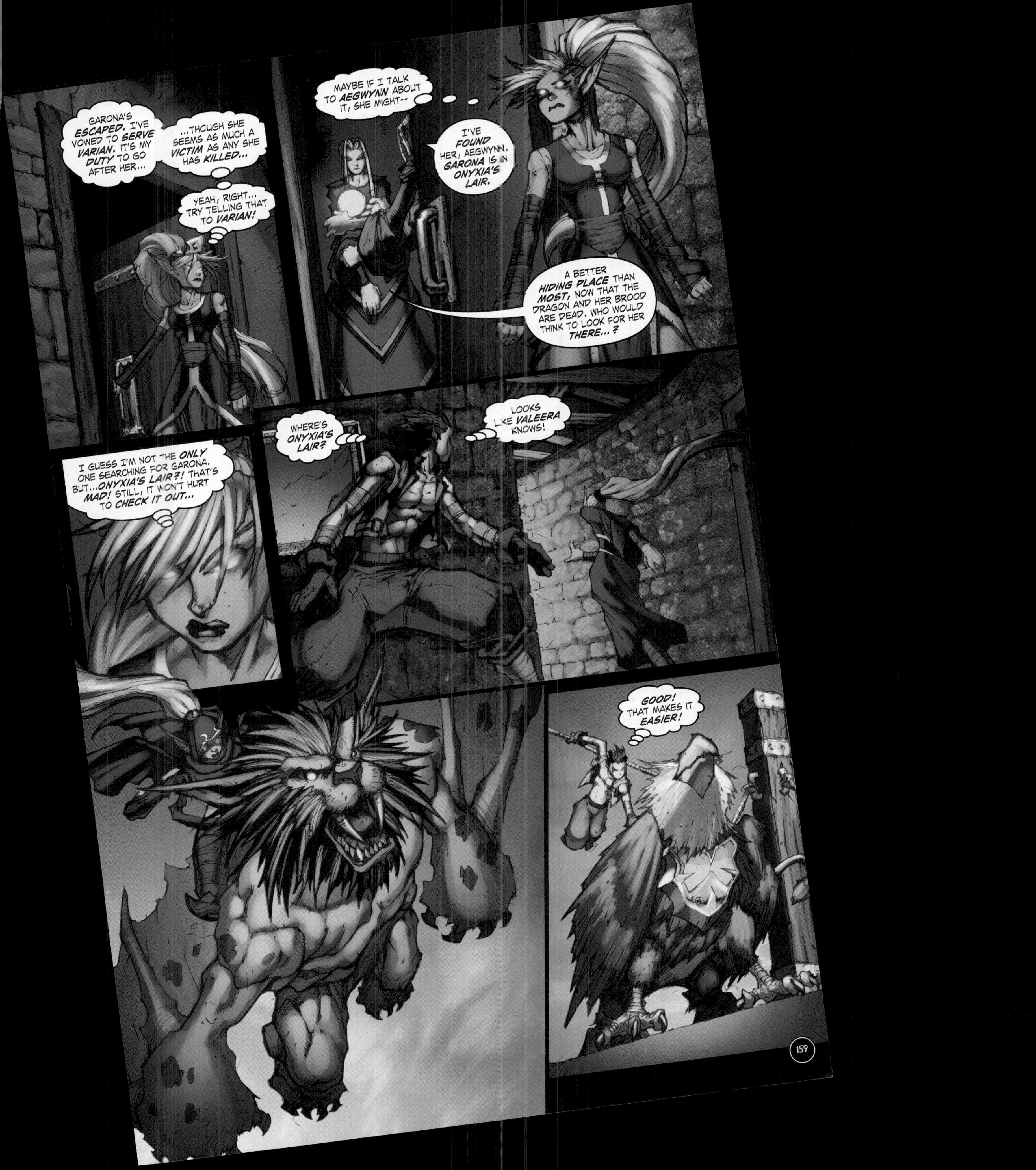
GARONA'S ESCAPED. I'VE VOWED TO SERVE VARIAN. IT'S MY DUTY TO GO AFTER HER...
...THOUGH SHE SEEMS AS MUCH A VICTIM AS ANY SHE HAS KILLED...
YEAH, RIGHT... TRY TELLING THAT TO VARIAN!
MAYBE IF I TALK TO AEGWYNN ABOUT IT, SHE MIGHT--
I'VE FOUND HER, AEGWYNN. GARONA IS IN ONYXIA'S LAIR.
A BETTER HIDING PLACE THAN MOST, NOW THAT THE DRAGON AND HER BROOD ARE DEAD. WHO WOULD THINK TO LOOK FOR HER THERE...?
I GUESS I'M NOT THE ONLY ONE SEARCHING FOR GARONA. BUT...ONYXIA'S LAIR?! THAT'S MAD! STILL, IT WON'T HURT TO CHECK IT OUT...
WHERE'S ONYXIA'S LAIR?
LOOKS LIKE VALEERA KNOWS!
GOOD! THAT MAKES IT EASIER!

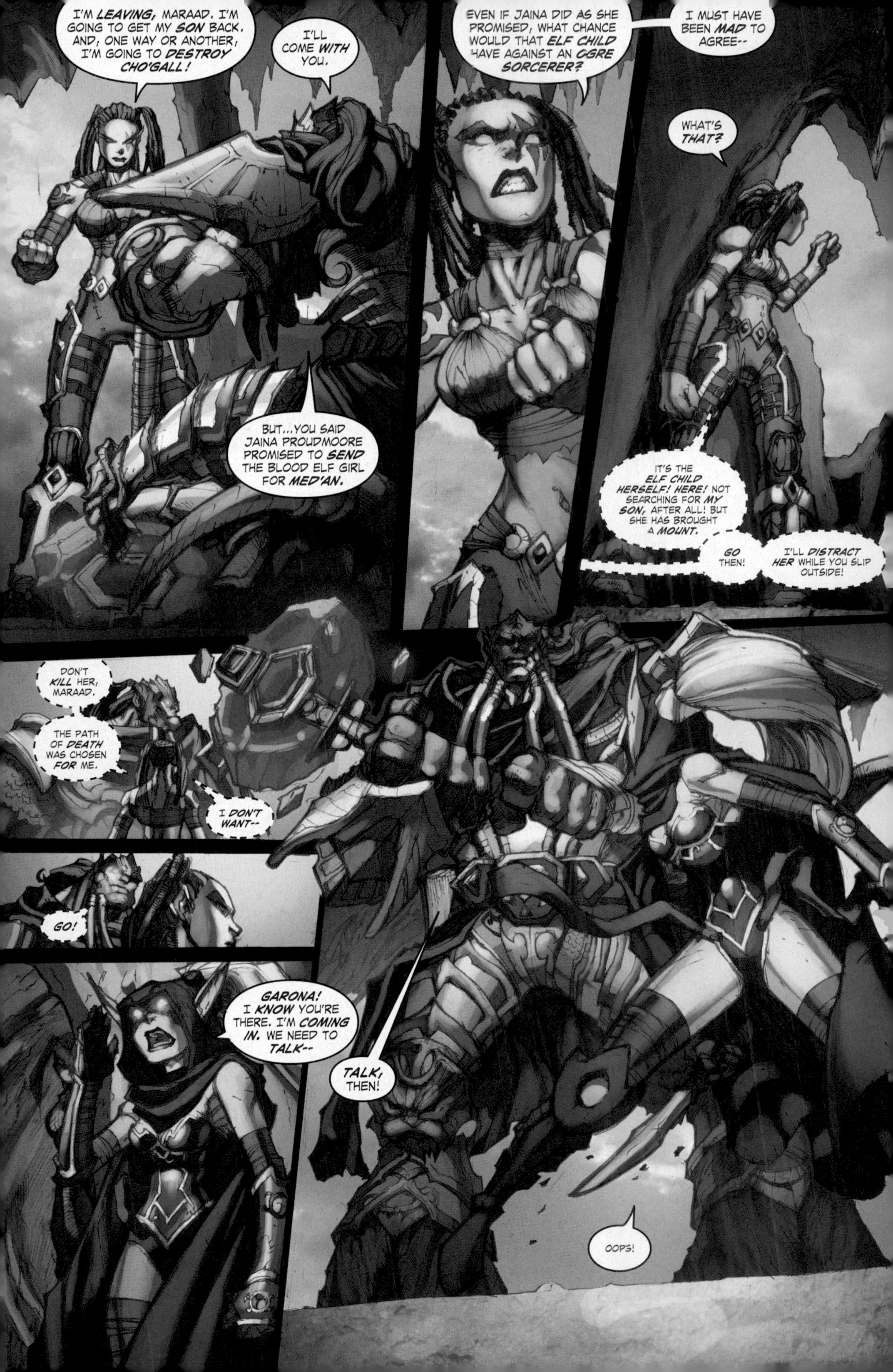
I'M LEAVING, MARAAD. I'M GOING TO GET MY SON BACK. AND, ONE WAY OR ANOTHER, I'M GOING TO DESTROY CHO'GALL!
I'LL COME WITH YOU.
BUT...YOU SAID JAINA PROUDMOORE PROMISED TO SEND THE BLOOD ELF GIRL FOR MED'AN.
EVEN IF JAINA DID AS SHE PROMISED, WHAT CHANCE WOULD THAT ELF CHILD HAVE AGAINST AN OGRE SORCERER?
I MUST HAVE BEEN MAD TO AGREE--
WHAT'S THAT?
IT'S THE ELF CHILD HERSELF! HERE! NOT SEARCHING FOR MY SON, AFTER ALL! BUT SHE HAS BROUGHT A MOUNT.
GO THEN!
I'LL DISTRACT HER WHILE YOU SLIP OUTSIDE!
DON'T KILL HER, MARAAD.
THE PATH OF DEATH WAS CHOSEN FOR ME.
I DON'T WANT--
GO!
GARONA! I KNOW YOU'RE THERE. I'M COMING IN. WE NEED TO TALK--
TALK, THEN!
OOPS!

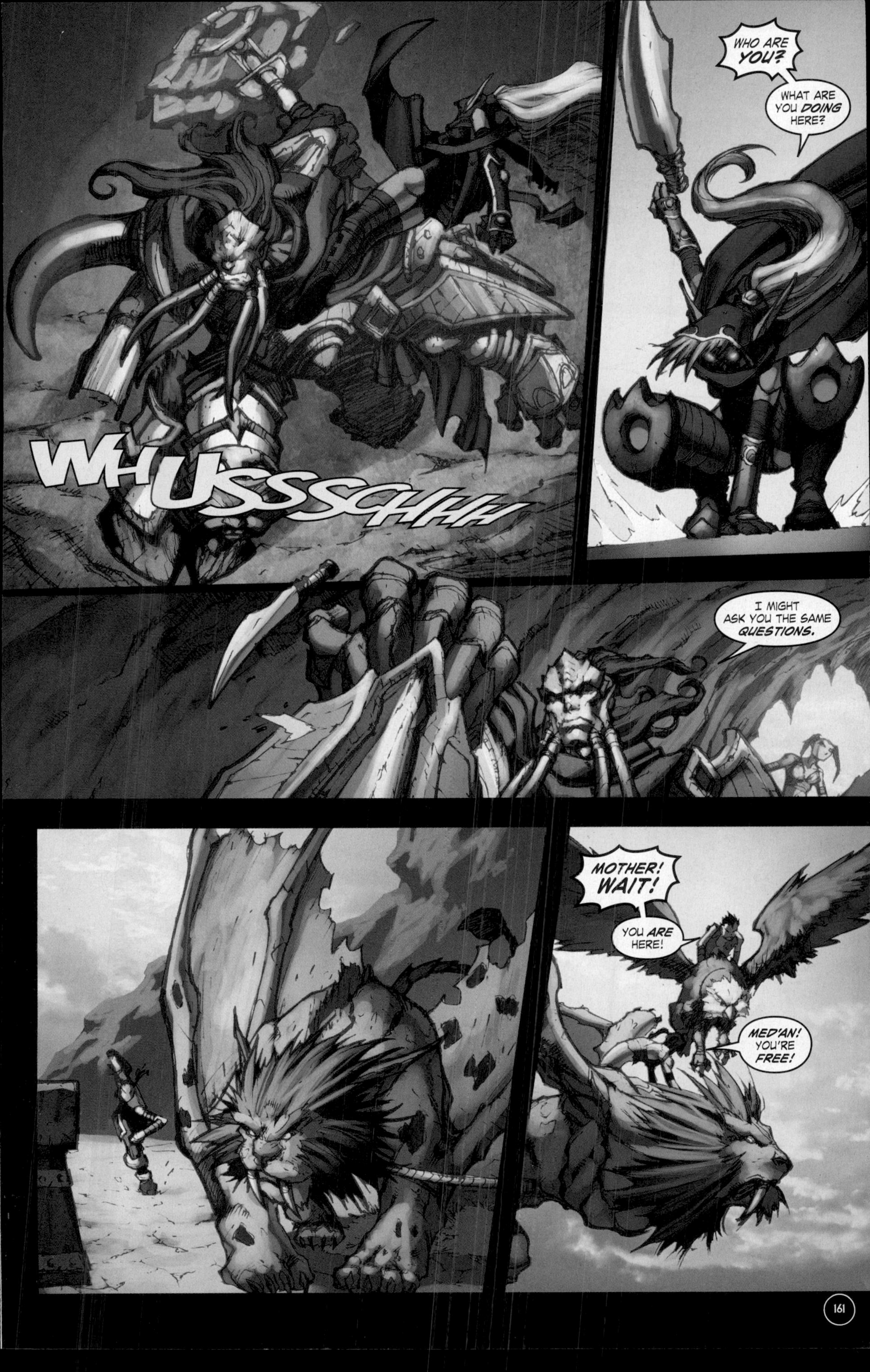
WHUSSSCHHH
WHO ARE YOU?
WHAT ARE YOU DOING HERE?
I MIGHT ASK YOU THE SAME QUESTIONS.
MOTHER! WAIT!
YOU ARE HERE!
MED'AN! YOU'RE FREE!

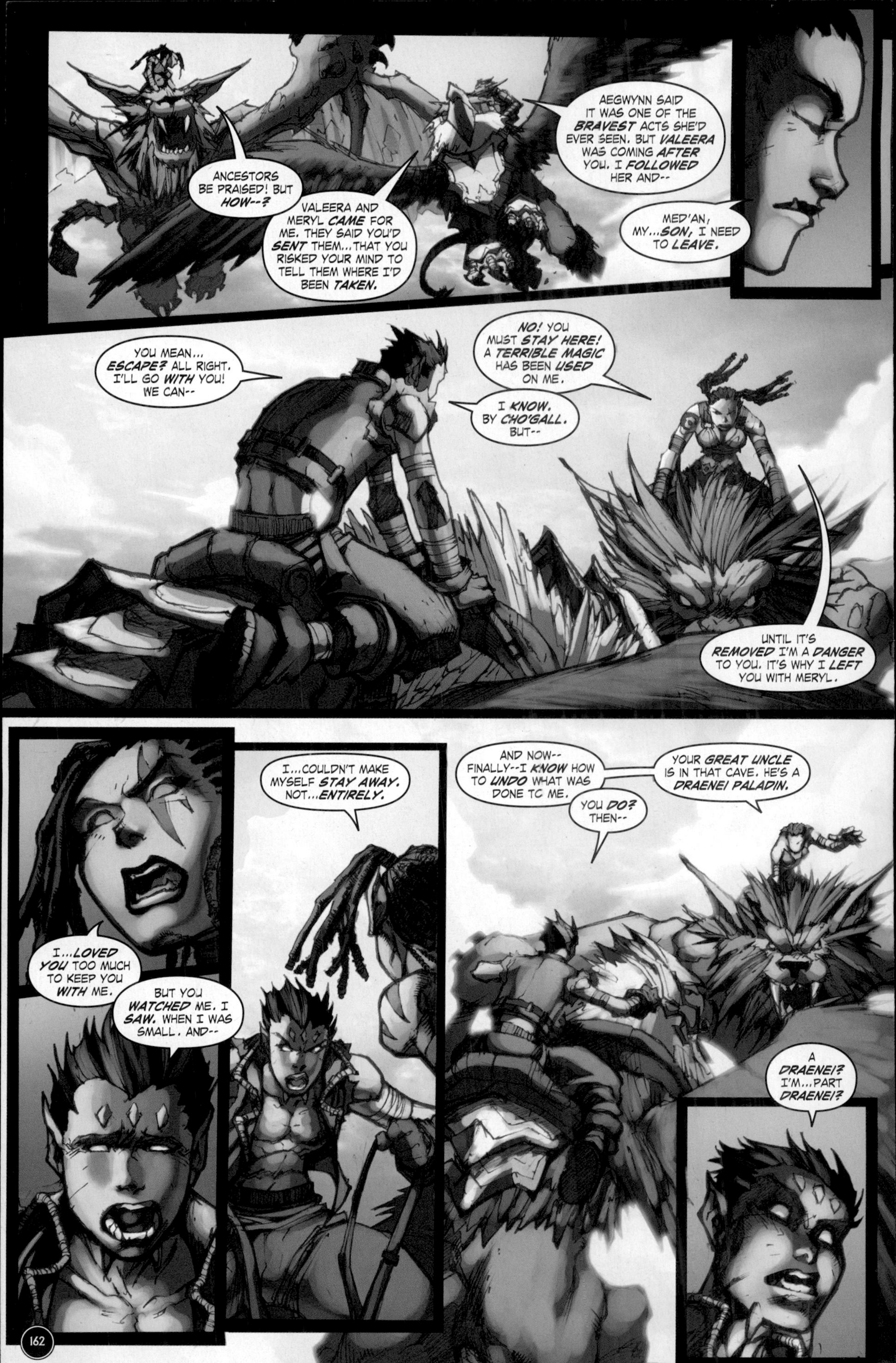
ANCESTORS BE PRAISED! BUT HOW--?
VALEERA AND MERYL CAME FOR ME. THEY SAID YOU'D SENT THEM...THAT YOU RISKED YOUR MIND TO TELL THEM WHERE I'D BEEN TAKEN.
AEGWYNN SAID IT WAS ONE OF THE BRAVEST ACTS SHE'D EVER SEEN. BUT VALEERA WAS COMING AFTER YOU. I FOLLOWED HER AND--
MED'AN, MY...SON, I NEED TO LEAVE.
YOU MEAN... ESCAPE? ALL RIGHT. I'LL GO WITH YOU! WE CAN--
NO! YOU MUST STAY HERE! A TERRIBLE MAGIC HAS BEEN USED ON ME.
I KNOW. BY CHO'GALL. BUT--
UNTIL IT'S REMOVED I'M A DANGER TO YOU. IT'S WHY I LEFT YOU WITH MERYL.
I...COULDN'T MAKE MYSELF STAY AWAY. NOT...ENTIRELY.
I...LOVED YOU TOO MUCH TO KEEP YOU WITH ME.
BUT YOU WATCHED ME. I SAW. WHEN I WAS SMALL. AND--
AND NOW-- FINALLY--I KNOW HOW TO UNDO WHAT WAS DONE TO ME.
YOU DO? THEN--
YOUR GREAT UNCLE IS IN THAT CAVE. HE'S A DRAENEI PALADIN.
A DRAENEI? I'M...PART DRAENEI?

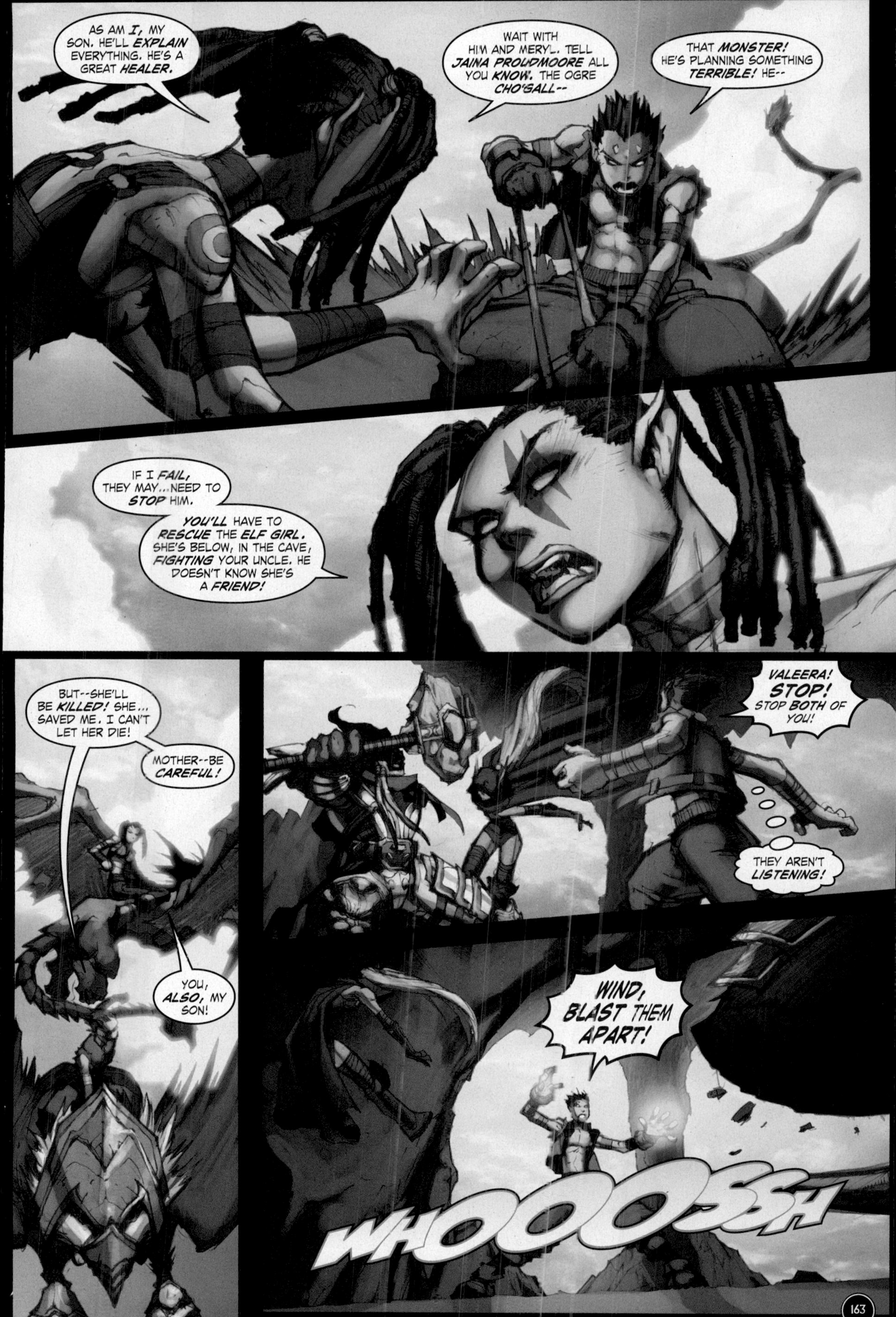
AS AM I, MY SON. HE'LL EXPLAIN EVERYTHING. HE'S A GREAT HEALER.
WAIT WITH HIM AND MERYL. TELL JAINA PROUDMOORE ALL YOU KNOW. THE OGRE CHO'GALL--
THAT MONSTER! HE'S PLANNING SOMETHING TERRIBLE! HE--
IF I FAIL, THEY MAY...NEED TO STOP HIM.
YOU'LL HAVE TO RESCUE THE ELF GIRL. SHE'S BELOW, IN THE CAVE, FIGHTING YOUR UNCLE. HE DOESN'T KNOW SHE'S A FRIEND!
BUT--SHE'LL BE KILLED! SHE... SAVED ME. I CAN'T LET HER DIE!
MOTHER--BE CAREFUL!
YOU, ALSO, MY SON!
VALEERA! STOP! STOP BOTH OF YOU!
THEY AREN'T LISTENING!
WIND, BLAST THEM APART!
WHOOOOSSH

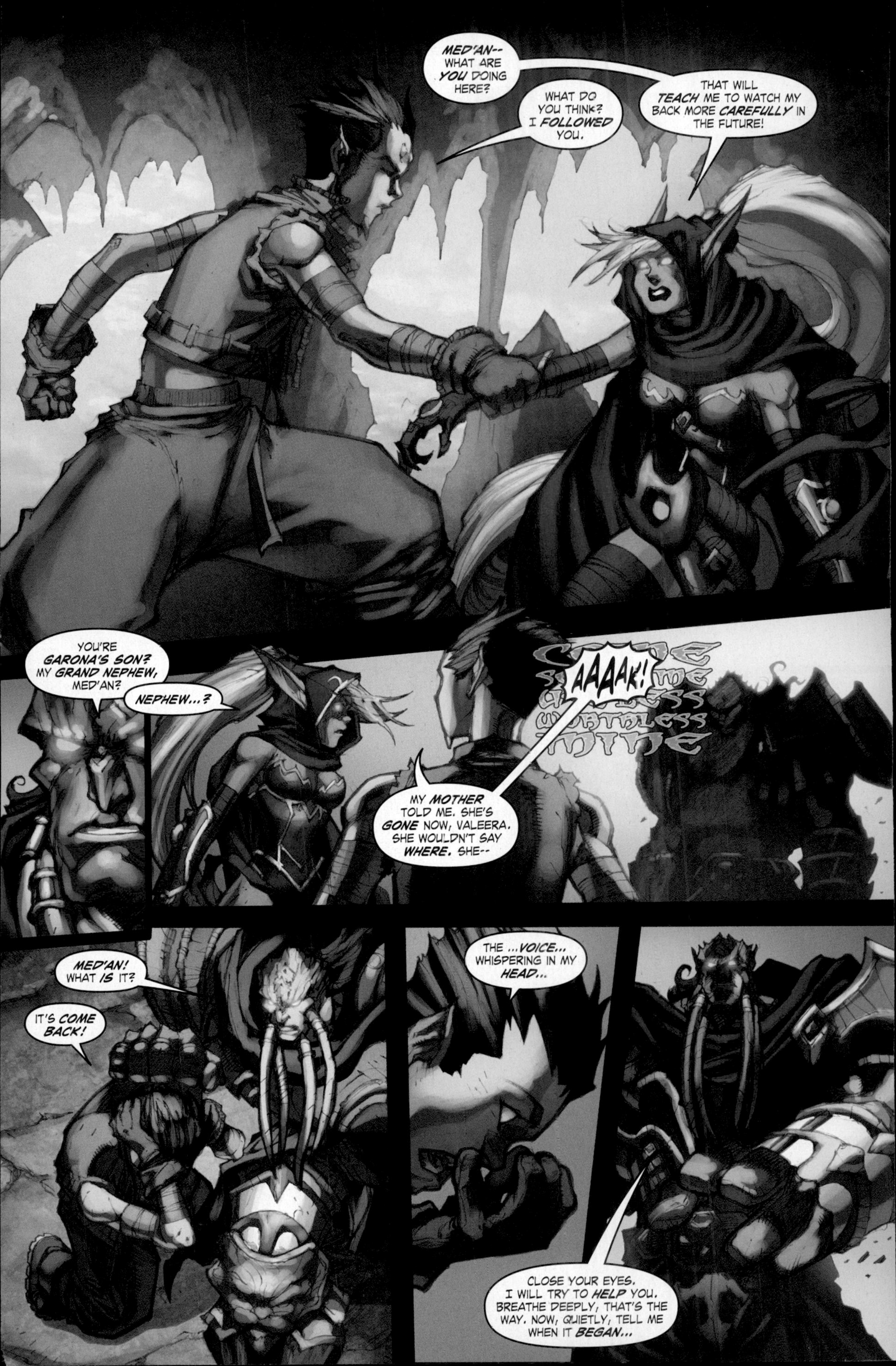
MED'AN-- WHAT ARE YOU DOING HERE?
WHAT DO YOU THINK? I FOLLOWED YOU.
THAT WILL TEACH ME TO WATCH MY BACK MORE CAREFULLY IN THE FUTURE!
YOU'RE GARONA'S SON? MY GRAND NEPHEW, MED'AN?
NEPHEW...?
MY MOTHER TOLD ME. SHE'S GONE NOW, VALEERA. SHE WOULDN'T SAY WHERE. SHE--
AAAAK!
MED'AN! WHAT IS IT?
IT'S COME BACK!
THE ...VOICE... WHISPERING IN MY HEAD...
CLOSE YOUR EYES. I WILL TRY TO HELP YOU. BREATHE DEEPLY, THAT'S THE WAY. NOW, QUIETLY, TELL ME WHEN IT BEGAN...

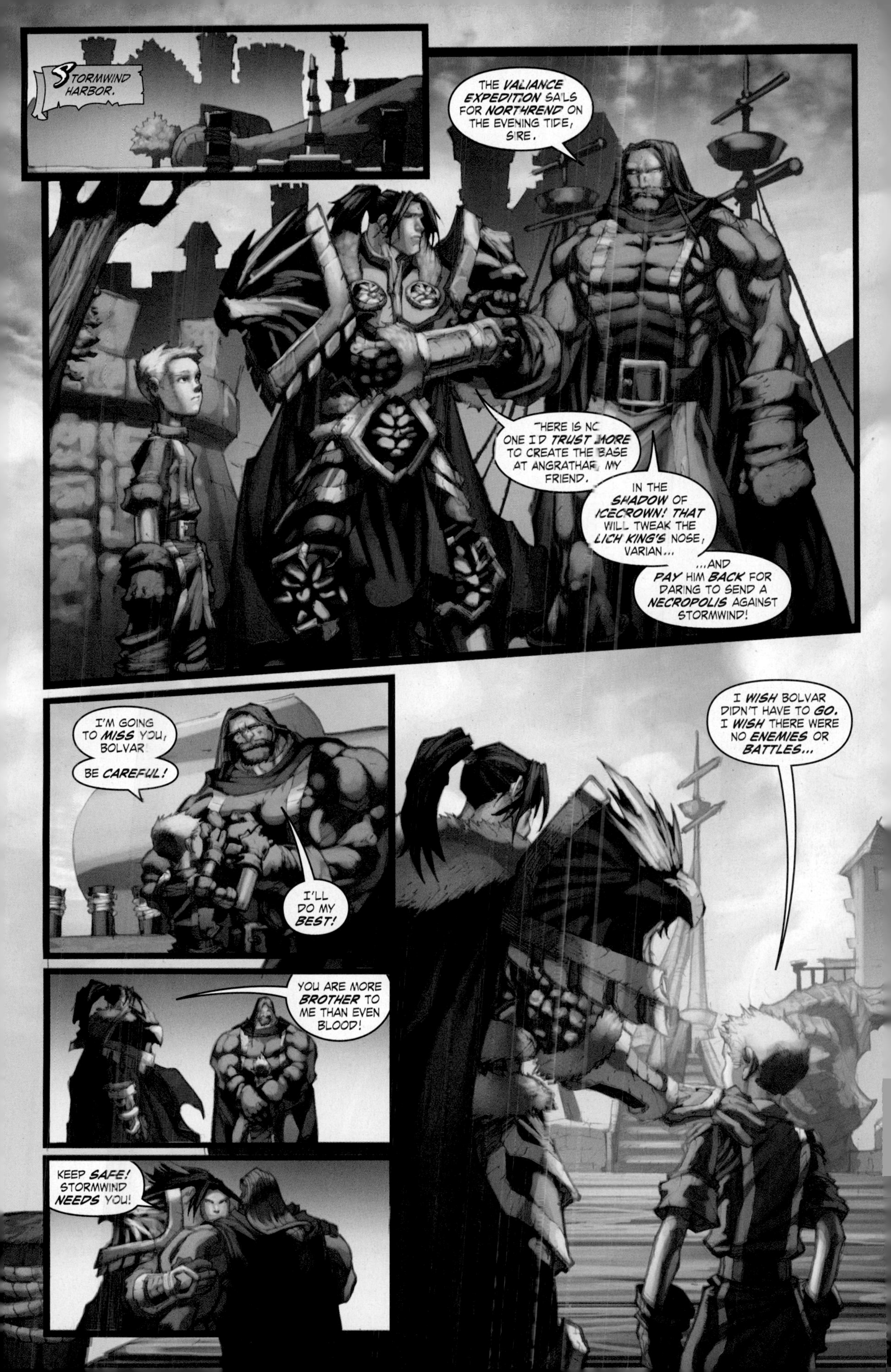
STORMWIND HARBOR.
THE VALIANCE EXPEDITION SAILS FOR NORTHREND ON THE EVENING TIDE, SIRE.
THERE IS NO ONE I'D TRUST MORE TO CREATE THE BASE AT ANGRATHAR, MY FRIEND.
IN THE SHADOW OF ICECROWN! THAT WILL TWEAK THE LICH KING'S NOSE, VARIAN...
...AND PAY HIM BACK FOR DARING TO SEND A NECROPOLIS AGAINST STORMWIND!
I'M GOING TO MISS YOU, BOLVAR.
BE CAREFUL!
I'LL DO MY BEST!
I WISH BOLVAR DIDN'T HAVE TO GO. I WISH THERE WERE NO ENEMIES OR BATTLES...
YOU ARE MORE BROTHER TO ME THAN EVEN BLOOD!
KEEP SAFE! STORMWIND NEEDS YOU!

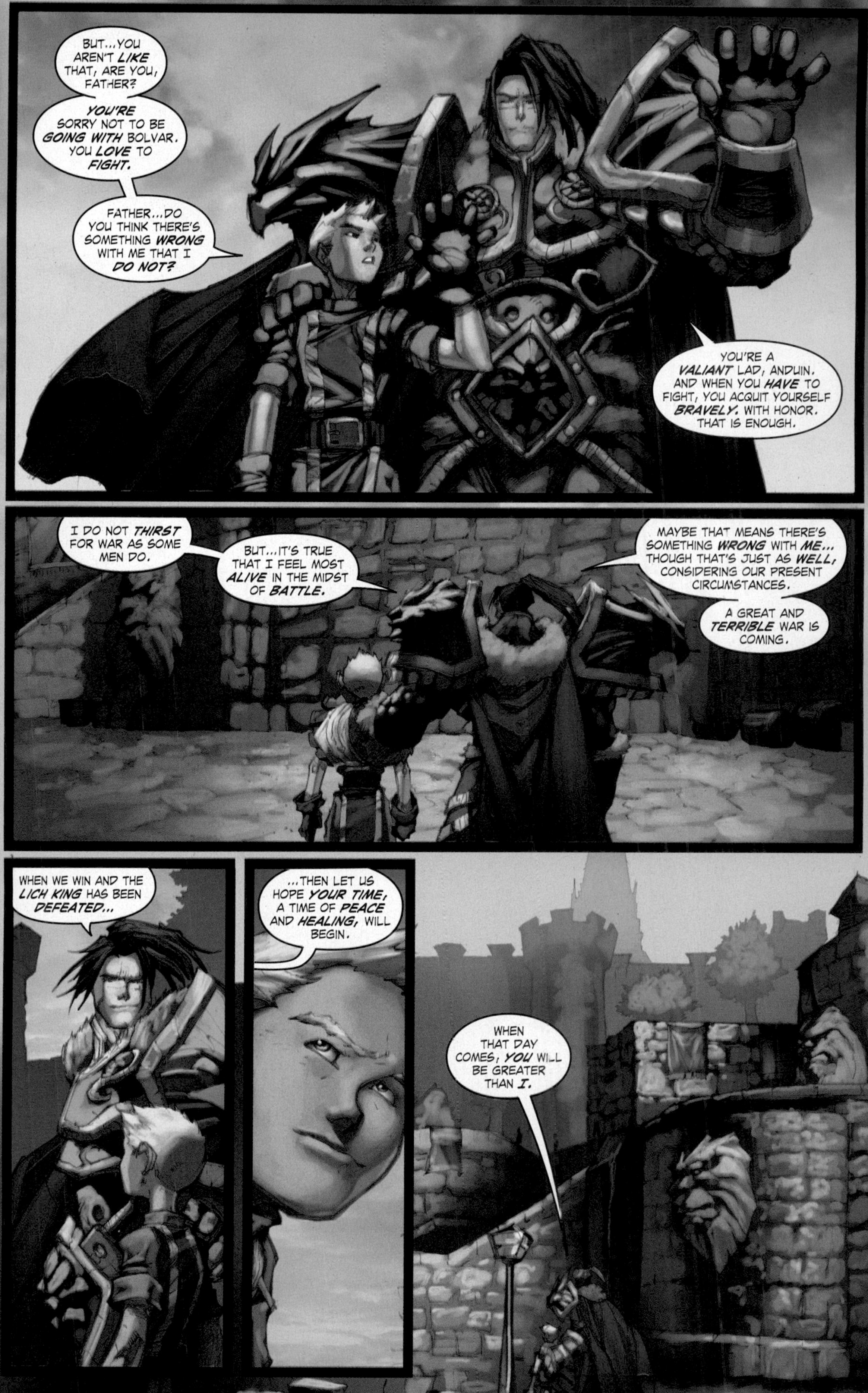
BUT...YOU AREN'T LIKE THAT, ARE YOU, FATHER?
YOU'RE SORRY NOT TO BE GOING WITH BOLVAR. YOU LOVE TO FIGHT.
FATHER...DO YOU THINK THERE'S SOMETHING WRONG WITH ME THAT I DO NOT?
YOU'RE A VALIANT LAD, ANDUIN. AND WHEN YOU HAVE TO FIGHT, YOU ACQUIT YOURSELF BRAVELY. WITH HONOR. THAT IS ENOUGH.
I DO NOT THIRST FOR WAR AS SOME MEN DO.
BUT...IT'S TRUE THAT I FEEL MOST ALIVE IN THE MIDST OF BATTLE.
MAYBE THAT MEANS THERE'S SOMETHING WRONG WITH ME...THOUGH THAT'S JUST AS WELL, CONSIDERING OUR PRESENT CIRCUMSTANCES.
A GREAT AND TERRIBLE WAR IS COMING.
WHEN WE WIN AND THE LICH KING HAS BEEN DEFEATED...
...THEN LET US HOPE YOUR TIME, A TIME OF PEACE AND HEALING, WILL BEGIN.
WHEN THAT DAY COMES, YOU WILL BE GREATER THAN I.

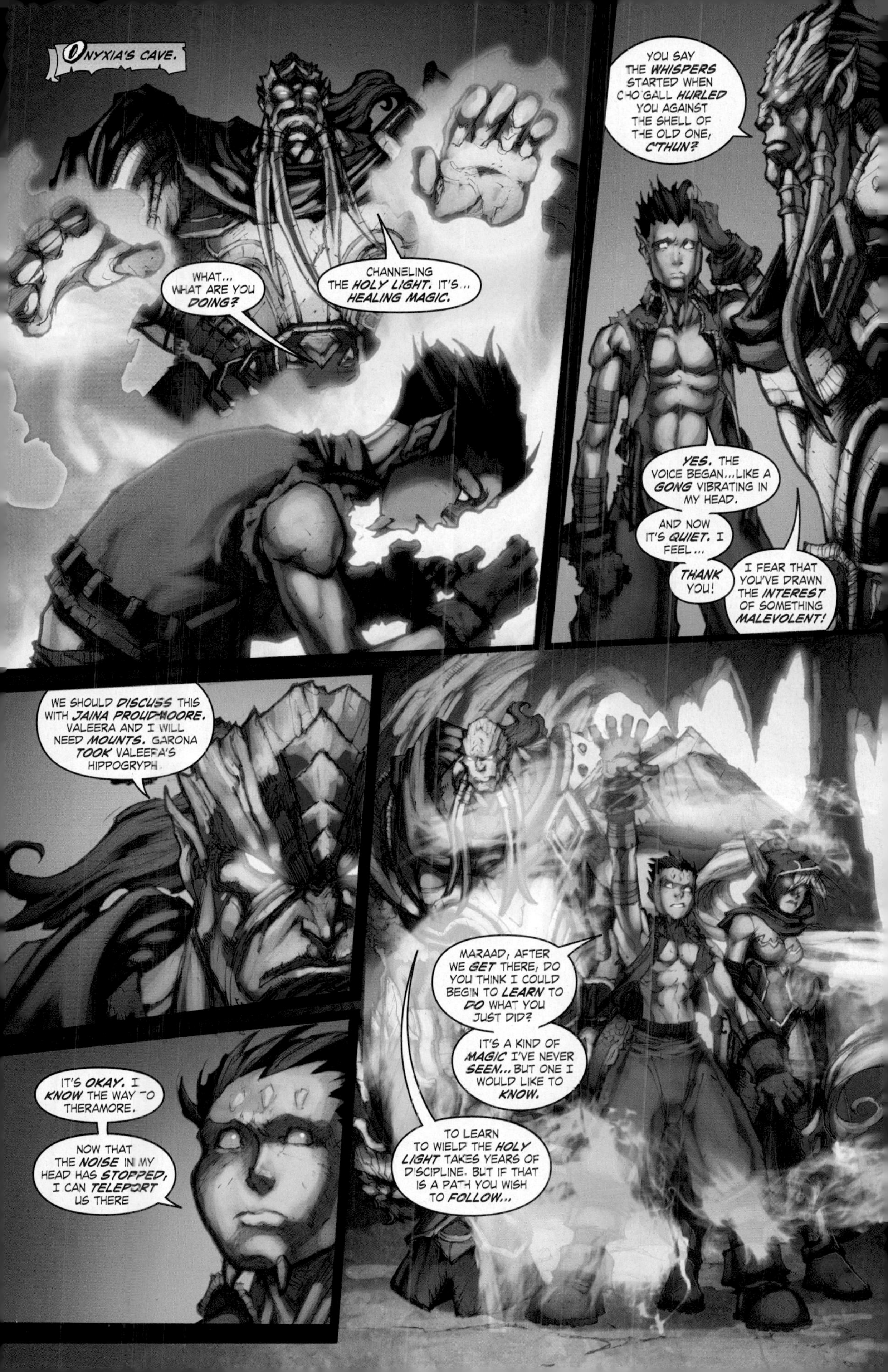
ONYXIA'S CAVE.
WHAT... WHAT ARE YOU DOING?
CHANNELING THE HOLY LIGHT. IT'S... HEALING MAGIC.
YOU SAY THE WHISPERS STARTED WHEN CHO'GALL HURLED YOU AGAINST THE SHELL OF THE OLD ONE, C'THUN?
YES. THE VOICE BEGAN...LIKE A GONG VIBRATING IN MY HEAD.
AND NOW IT'S QUIET. I FEEL...
THANK YOU!
I FEAR THAT YOU'VE DRAWN THE INTEREST OF SOMETHING MALEVOLENT!
WE SHOULD DISCUSS THIS WITH JAINA PROUDMOORE. VALEERA AND I WILL NEED MOUNTS. GARONA TOOK VALEERA'S HIPPOGRYPH.
IT'S OKAY. I KNOW THE WAY TO THERAMORE.
NOW THAT THE NOISE IN MY HEAD HAS STOPPED, I CAN TELEPORT US THERE.
MARAAD, AFTER WE GET THERE, DO YOU THINK I COULD BEGIN TO LEARN TO DO WHAT YOU JUST DID?
IT'S A KIND OF MAGIC I'VE NEVER SEEN...BUT ONE I WOULD LIKE TO KNOW.
TO LEARN TO WIELD THE HOLY LIGHT TAKES YEARS OF DISCIPLINE. BUT IF THAT IS A PATH YOU WISH TO FOLLOW...

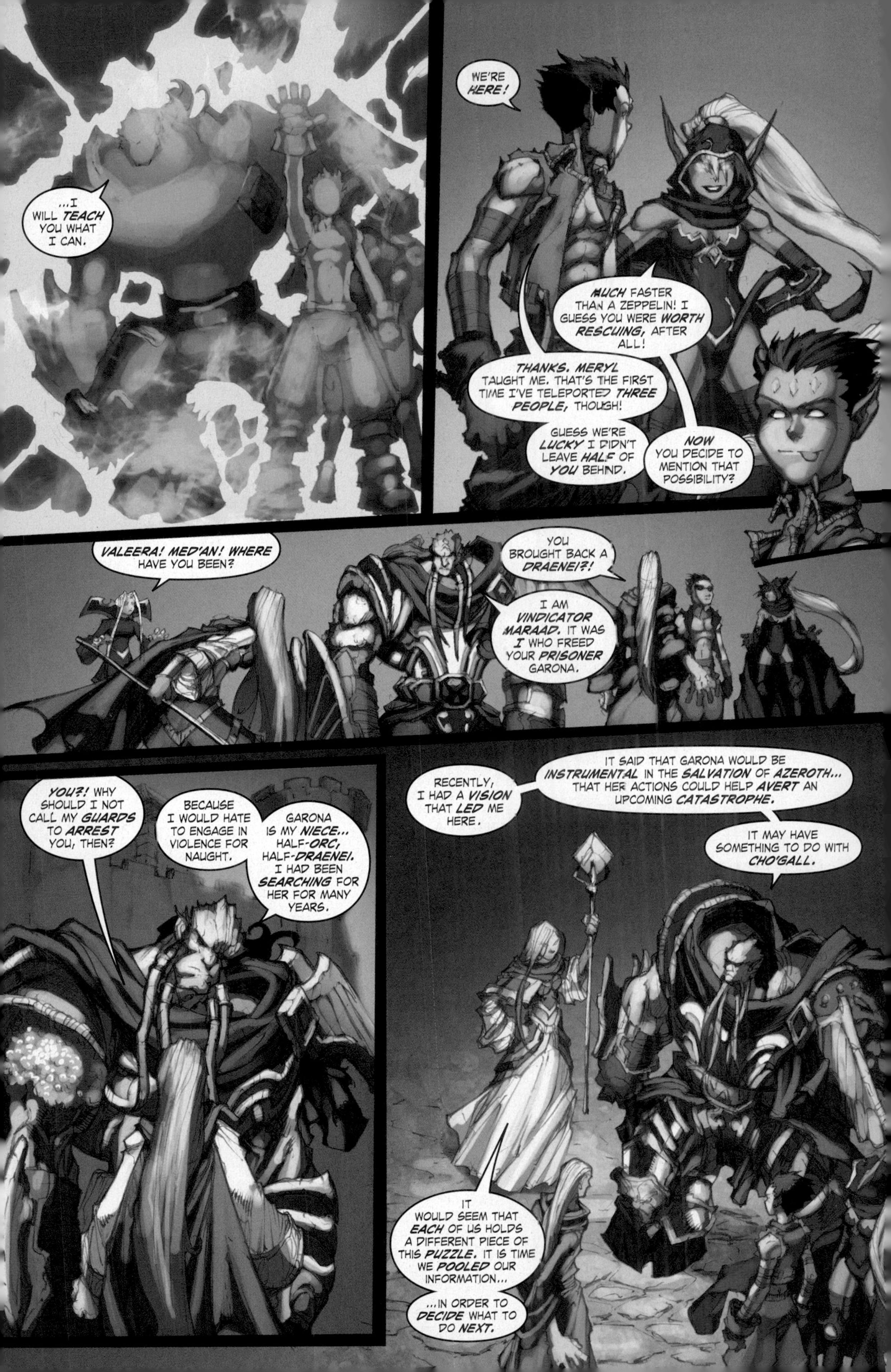
...I WILL TEACH YOU WHAT I CAN.
WE'RE HERE!
MUCH FASTER THAN A ZEPPELIN! I GUESS YOU WERE WORTH RESCUING, AFTER ALL!
THANKS. MERYL TAUGHT ME. THAT'S THE FIRST TIME I'VE TELEPORTED THREE PEOPLE, THOUGH!
GUESS WE'RE LUCKY I DIDN'T LEAVE HALF OF YOU BEHIND.
NOW YOU DECIDE TO MENTION THAT POSSIBILITY?
VALEERA! MED'AN! WHERE HAVE YOU BEEN?
YOU BROUGHT BACK A DRAENEI?!
I AM VINDICATOR MARAAD. IT WAS I WHO FREED YOUR PRISONER GARONA.
YOU?! WHY SHOULD I NOT CALL MY GUARDS TO ARREST YOU, THEN?
BECAUSE I WOULD HATE TO ENGAGE IN VIOLENCE FOR NAUGHT.
GARONA IS MY NIECE... HALF-ORC, HALF-DRAENEI. I HAD BEEN SEARCHING FOR HER FOR MANY YEARS.
RECENTLY, I HAD A VISION THAT LED ME HERE.
IT SAID THAT GARONA WOULD BE INSTRUMENTAL IN THE SALVATION OF AZEROTH... THAT HER ACTIONS COULD HELP AVERT AN UPCOMING CATASTROPHE.
IT MAY HAVE SOMETHING TO DO WITH CHO'GALL.
IT WOULD SEEM THAT EACH OF US HOLDS A DIFFERENT PIECE OF THIS PUZZLE. IT IS TIME WE POOLED OUR INFORMATION...
...IN ORDER TO DECIDE WHAT TO DO NEXT.

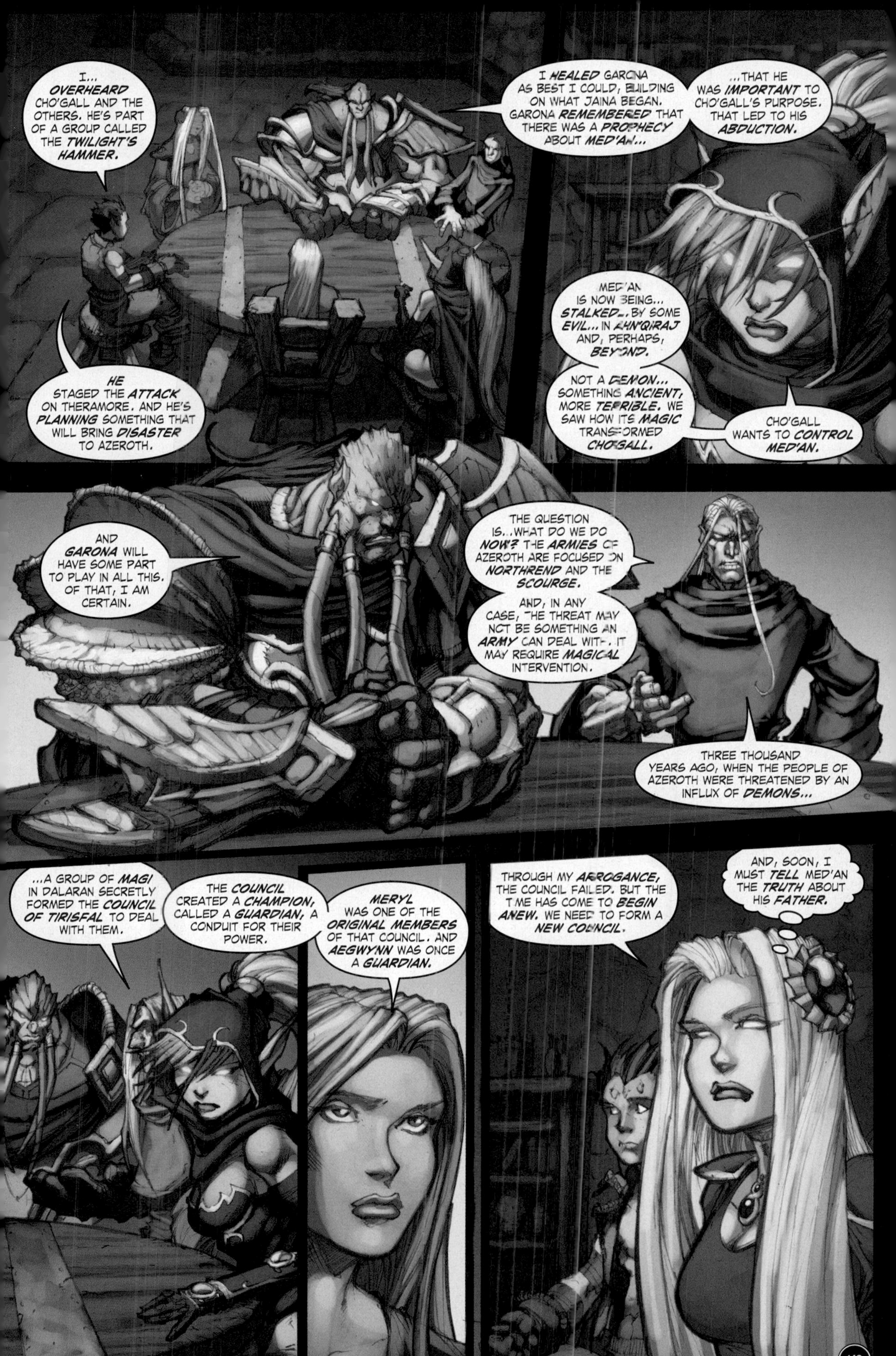
I... OVERHEARD CHO'GALL AND THE OTHERS. HE'S PART OF A GROUP CALLED THE TWILIGHT'S HAMMER.
HE STAGED THE ATTACK ON THERAMORE. AND HE'S PLANNING SOMETHING THAT WILL BRING DISASTER TO AZEROTH.
I HEALED GARONA AS BEST I COULD, BUILDING ON WHAT JAINA BEGAN. GARONA REMEMBERED THAT THERE WAS A PROPHECY ABOUT MED'AN...
...THAT HE WAS IMPORTANT TO CHO'GALL'S PURPOSE. THAT LED TO HIS ABDUCTION.
MED'AN IS NOW BEING... STALKED... BY SOME EVIL... IN AHN'QIRAJ AND, PERHAPS, BEYOND.
NOT A DEMON... SOMETHING ANCIENT, MORE TERRIBLE. WE SAW HOW ITS MAGIC TRANSFORMED CHO'GALL.
CHO'GALL WANTS TO CONTROL MED'AN.
AND GARONA WILL HAVE SOME PART TO PLAY IN ALL THIS. OF THAT, I AM CERTAIN.
THE QUESTION IS...WHAT DO WE DO NOW? THE ARMIES OF AZEROTH ARE FOCUSED ON NORTHREND AND THE SCOURGE.
AND, IN ANY CASE, THE THREAT MAY NOT BE SOMETHING AN ARMY CAN DEAL WITH. IT MAY REQUIRE MAGICAL INTERVENTION.
THREE THOUSAND YEARS AGO, WHEN THE PEOPLE OF AZEROTH WERE THREATENED BY AN INFLUX OF DEMONS...
...A GROUP OF MAGI IN DALARAN SECRETLY FORMED THE COUNCIL OF TIRISFAL TO DEAL WITH THEM.
THE COUNCIL CREATED A CHAMPION, CALLED A GUARDIAN, A CONDUIT FOR THEIR POWER.
MERYL WAS ONE OF THE ORIGINAL MEMBERS OF THAT COUNCIL. AND AEGWYNN WAS ONCE A GUARDIAN.
THROUGH MY ARROGANCE, THE COUNCIL FAILED. BUT THE TIME HAS COME TO BEGIN ANEW. WE NEED TO FORM A NEW COUNCIL.
AND, SOON, I MUST TELL MED'AN THE TRUTH ABOUT HIS FATHER.

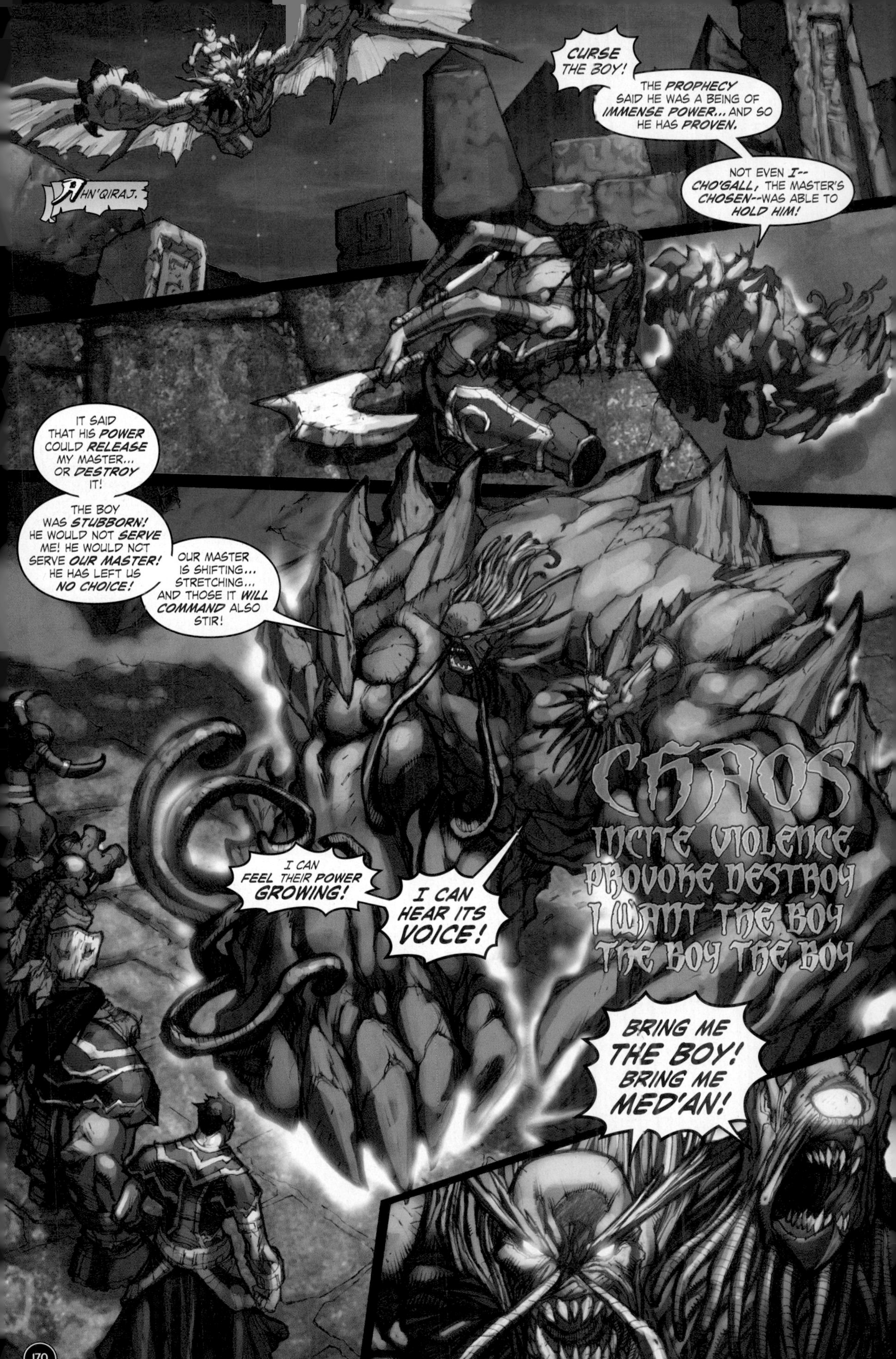

AHN'QIRAJ.
CURSE THE BOY!
THE PROPHECY SAID HE WAS A BEING OF IMMENSE POWER... AND SO HE HAS PROVEN.
NOT EVEN I--CHO'GALL, THE MASTER'S CHOSEN--WAS ABLE TO HOLD HIM!
IT SAID THAT HIS POWER COULD RELEASE MY MASTER... OR DESTROY IT!
THE BOY WAS STUBBORN! HE WOULD NOT SERVE ME! HE WOULD NOT SERVE OUR MASTER! HE HAS LEFT US NO CHOICE!
OUR MASTER IS SHIFTING... STRETCHING... AND THOSE IT WILL COMMAND ALSO STIR!
I CAN FEEL THEIR POWER GROWING!
I CAN HEAR ITS VOICE!
CHAOS
INCITE VIOLENCE
PROVOKE DESTROY
I WANT THE BOY
THE BOY THE BOY
BRING ME THE BOY! BRING ME MED'AN!

Creating a Cover

Covers usually start with sketches—the artist and editor discuss dynamic moments coming up in the story, pick a character or scene to focus on, then the artist distills those ideas into an image (or two, or three). For cover 21, the original focus was Maraad's charge at Cho'gall. Everyone involved selects a favorite cover, then we pick the image apart—and sometimes you discover none of the sketches fits quite right.

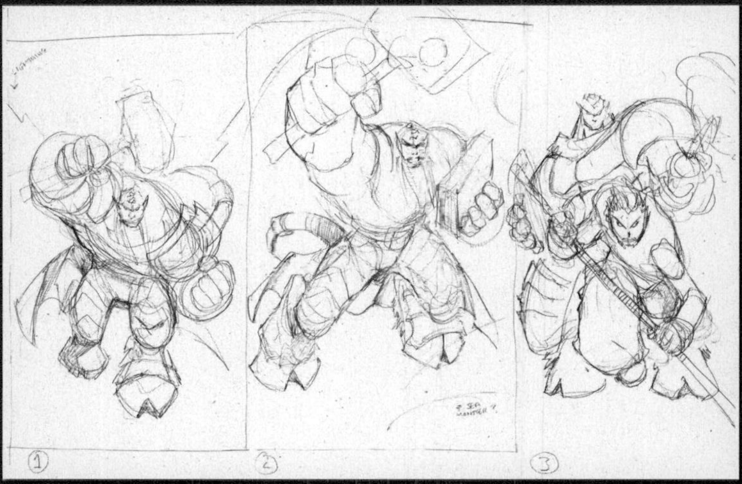
1
2
3

Mike went back to the drawing board, and came up with these layouts, to bring the focus back to Cho'gall. They were close, but not quite there.

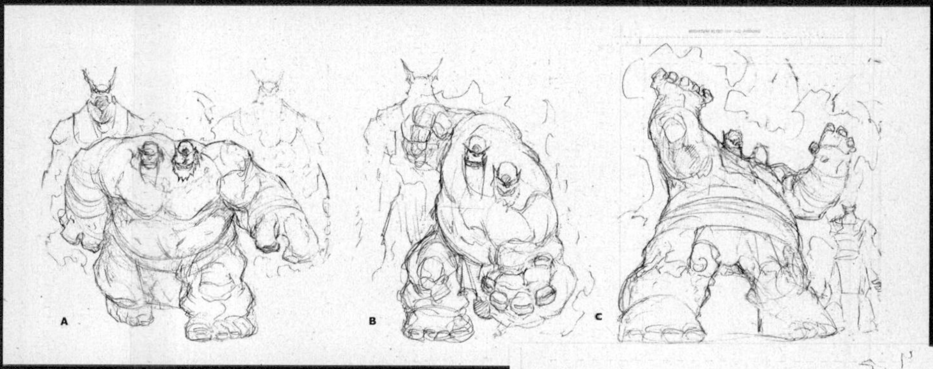
A
B
C

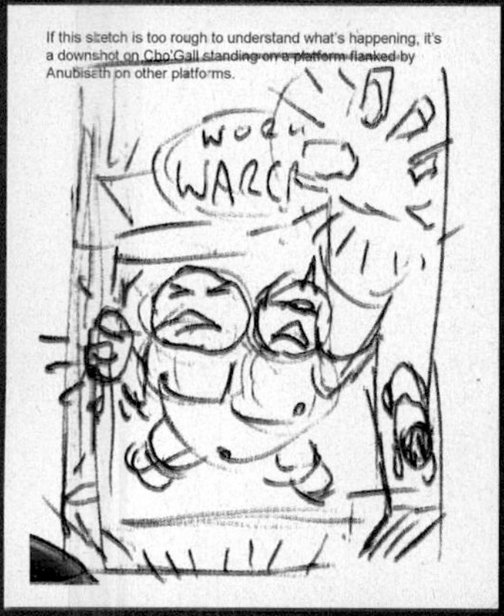
If this sketch is too rough to understand what's happening, it's a downshot on Cho'Gall standing on a platform flanked by Anubiseth on other platforms.

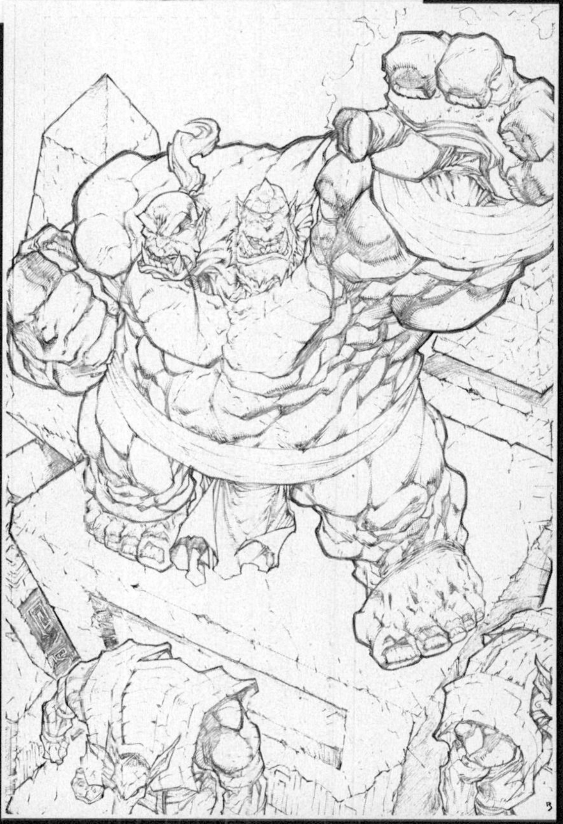

When the changes we wanted became a little hard to describe, an anonymous non-artist grabbed a pen to demonstrate!

Fortunately, Mike Bowden was able to take that pose, and make something awesome.

Once the final pencils for cover 21 were approved, we turned it over to Tony Washington for coloring. Here you can appreciate just a little of the time Tony spends.

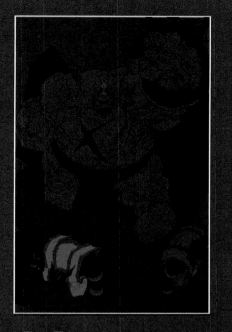

Stage 1: Flats. This is where the colorist blocks out the large areas of color, and starts to figure out important points—like where the folds of Cho'gall's loincloth end and where his toes begin!

Stage 2: Lighting. This step often gets blended into step 3, but here, Tony took a moment to show WildStorm and Blizzard how this scene would be lit. Now the top of the platform pops out, making it more three-dimensional, and the sky of Ahn'Qiraj is an eerie orange-red.

Stage 3: Rendering. This is where Tony's attention to detail starts to pay off. The anubisaths are first colored, then cast into shadow. The hair (on both heads) gets highlights, making it look more natural. Each of Cho'gall's many, many muscles are highlighted, playing off the shadow lines Mike established in the pencils.

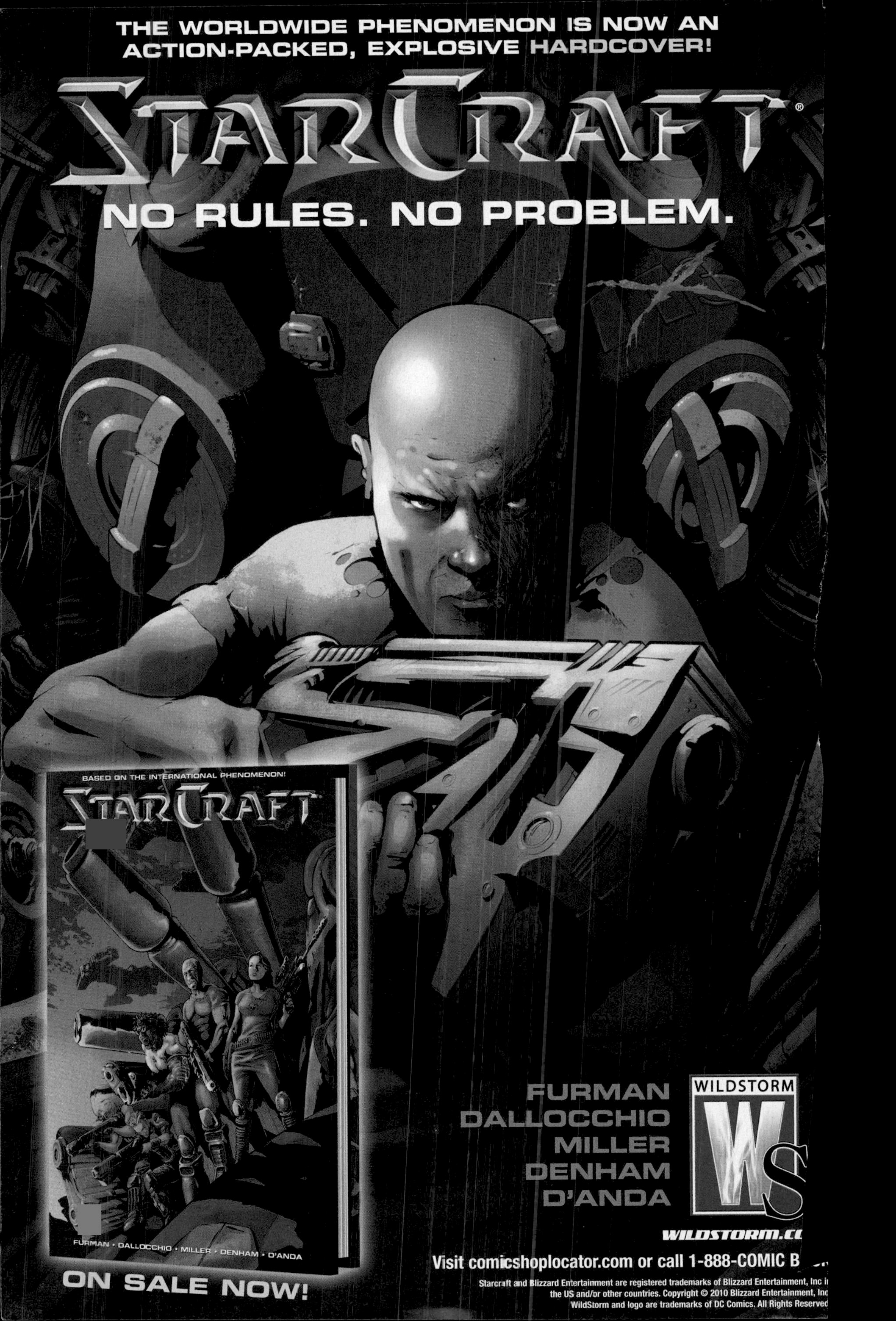
THE WORLDWIDE PHENOMENON IS NOW AN ACTION-PACKED, EXPLOSIVE HARDCOVER!
STARCRAFT®
NO RULES. NO PROBLEM.
BASED ON THE INTERNATIONAL PHENOMENON!
STARCRAFT
FURMAN • DALLOCCHIO • MILLER • DENHAM • D'ANDA
ON SALE NOW!
FURMAN
DALLOCCHIO
MILLER
DENHAM
D'ANDA
WILDSTORM
WS
WILDSTORM.C
Visit comicshoplocator.com or call 1-888-COMIC B
Starcraft and Blizzard Entertainment are registered trademarks of Blizzard Entertainment, Inc i
the US and/or other countries. Copyright © 2010 Blizzard Entertainment, Inc
WildStorm and logo are trademarks of DC Comics. All Rights Reserved

WORLD OF WARCRAFT®

AN AMNESIAC WASHES UP ON THE SHORES OF KALIMDOR, STARTING THE EPIC QUEST OF THE WARRIOR LO'GOSH, AND HIS UNLIKELY ALLIES BROLL BEARMANTLE AND VALEERA SANGUINAR. STRIKING UNEASY RELATIONSHIPS WITH OTHER RACES, AS WELL AS EACH OTHER, THEY MUST FIGHT BOTH THE ALLIANCE AND THE HORDE AS THEY STRUGGLE TO UNCOVER THE SECRETS OF LO'GOSH'S PAST! WRITTEN BY WALTER SIMONSON (**THE JUDAS COIN**, *THOR*) AND ILLUSTRATED BY LUDO LULLABI (*LANFEUST QUEST*) AND SANDRA HOPE (**JUSTICE LEAGUE OF AMERICA**), THIS IS THE LATEST SAGA SET IN THE *WORLD OF WARCRAFT*!

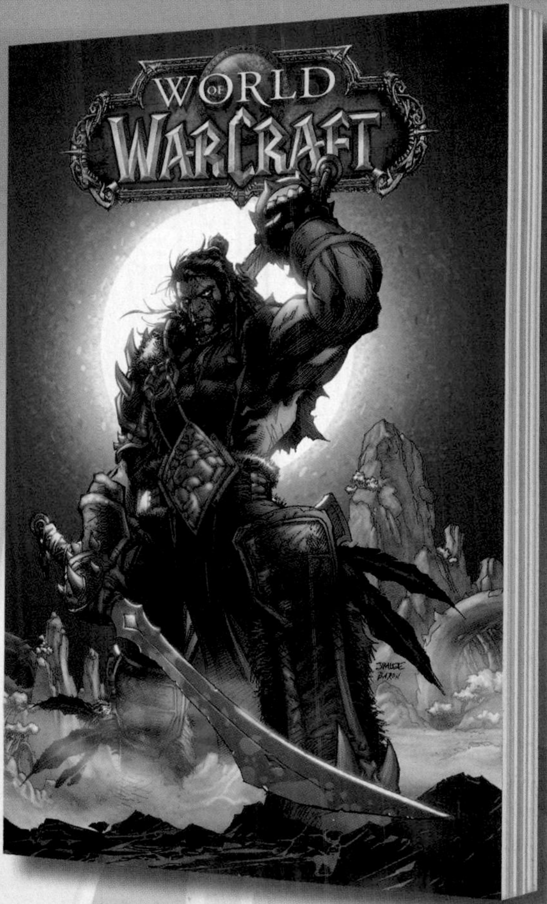
WORLD OF WARCRAFT

WORLD OF WARCRAFT BOOK TWO

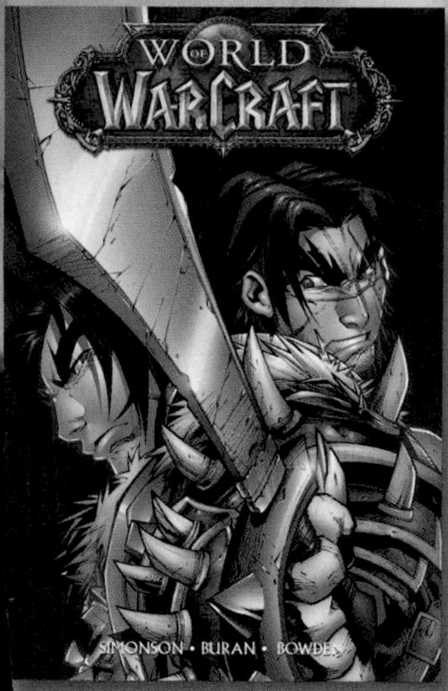
WORLD OF WARCRAFT
SIMONSON • BURAN • BOWDEN

Simonson
Buran • Bowden

WORLD OF WARCRAFT BOOK FOUR COMING FALL 2010

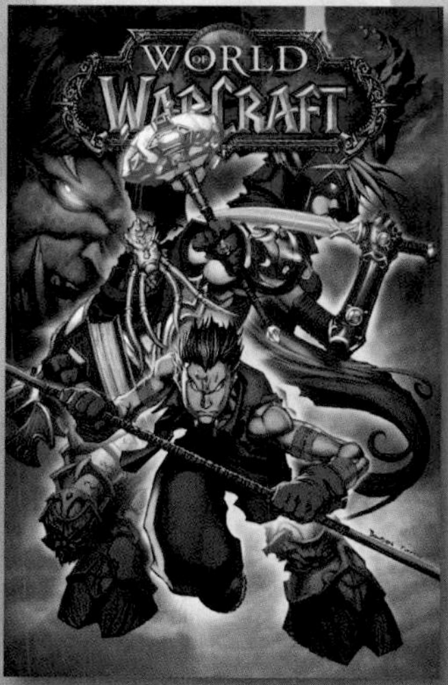
WORLD OF WARCRAFT

Simonson • Simonson
Bowden • Washington

WORLD OF WARCRAFT: ASHBRINGER

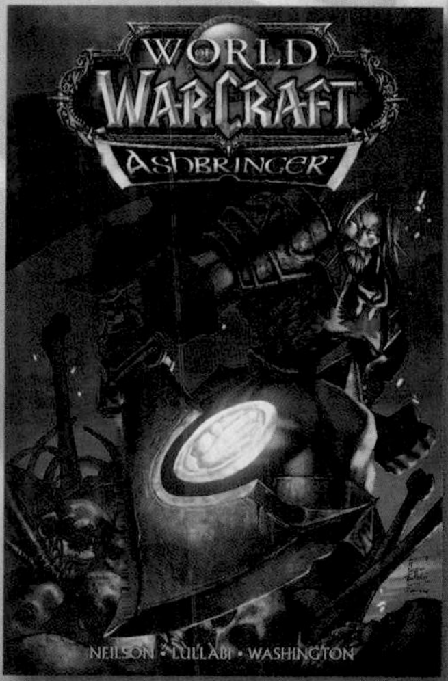
WORLD OF WARCRAFT
ASHBRINGER
NEILSON • LULLABI • WASHINGTON

Neilson
Lullabi • Washington

SEARCH THE **GRAPHIC NOVELS SECTION** OF
WILDSTORM.COM
FOR ART AND INFORMATION ON ALL OF OUR BOOKS!

Garona's failed to complete her mission...but she still must seek redemption. Her story continues in

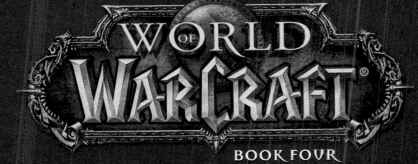

BOOK FOUR

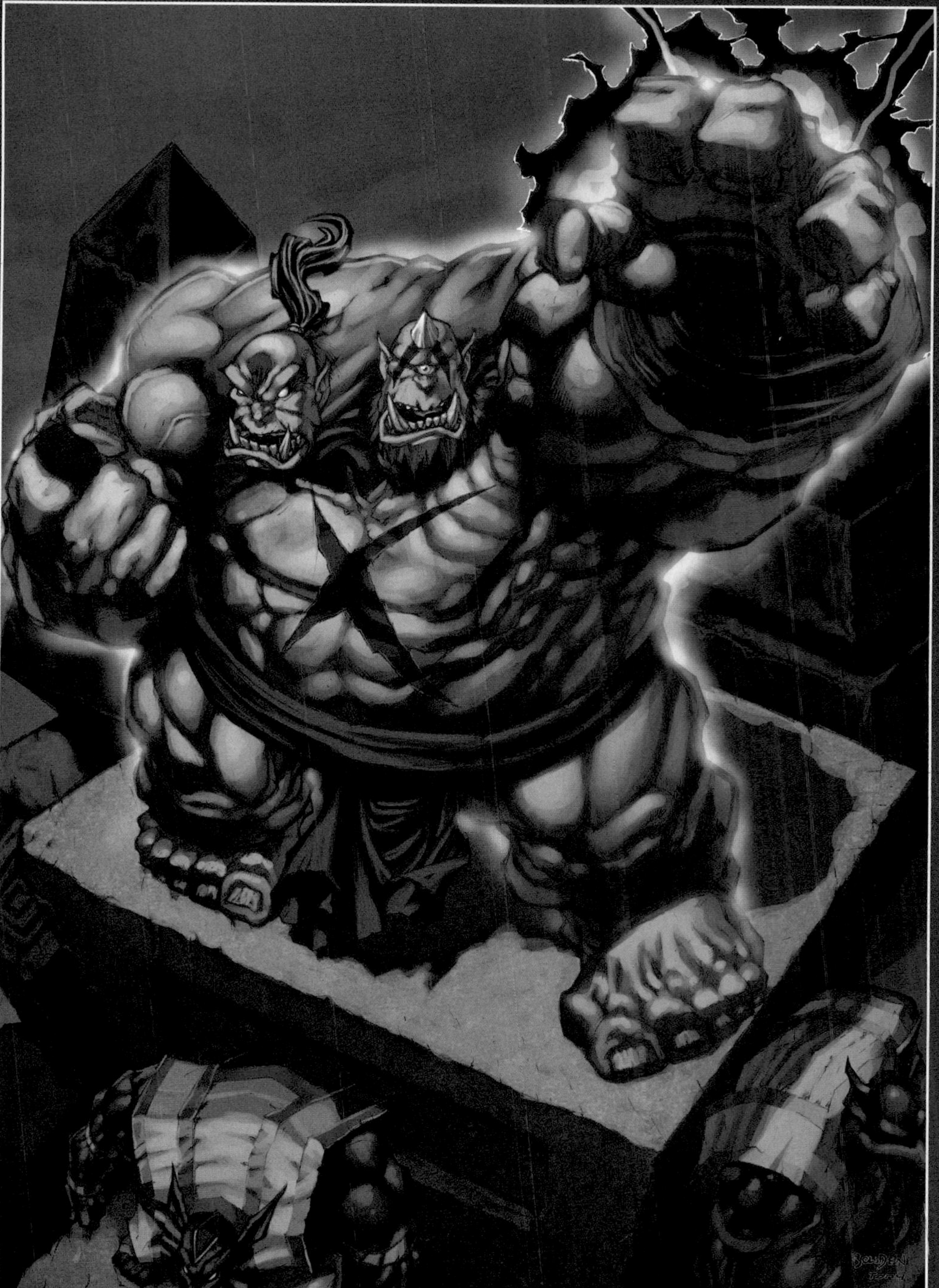

Stage 4: Effects. Not every book gets to have characters lit by their own magic, but WORLD OF WARCRAFT makes the best of every opportunity—not only does the entire body glow, so do the eyes!